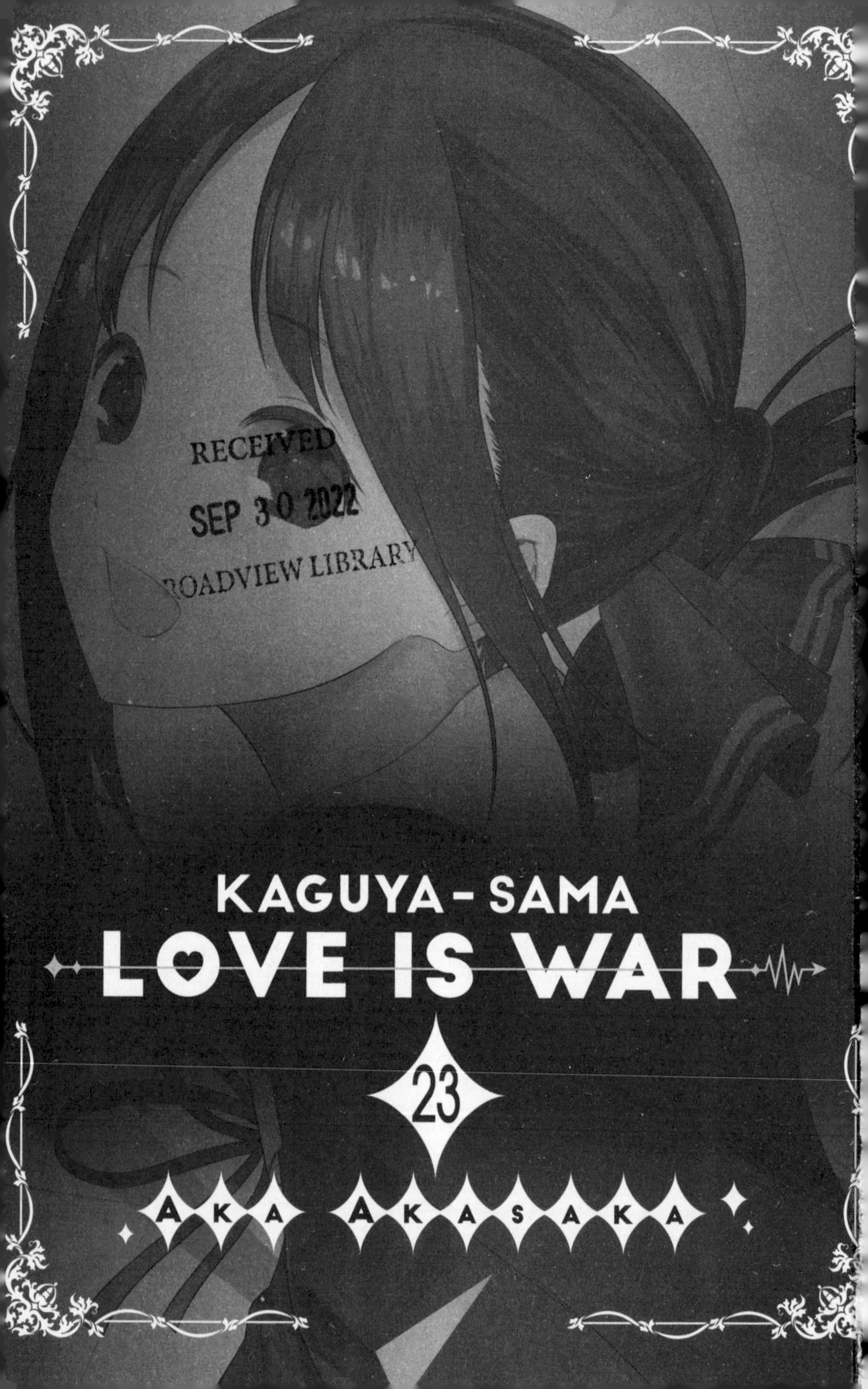
KAGUYA-SAMA
LOVE IS WAR
23
AKA AKASAKA

Meet the Characters!

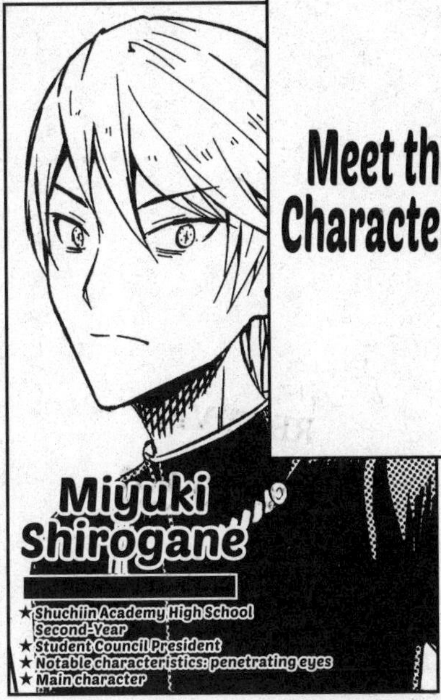
Miyuki Shirogane
★ Shuchiin Academy High School Second-Year
★ Student Council President
★ Notable characteristics: penetrating eyes
★ Main character

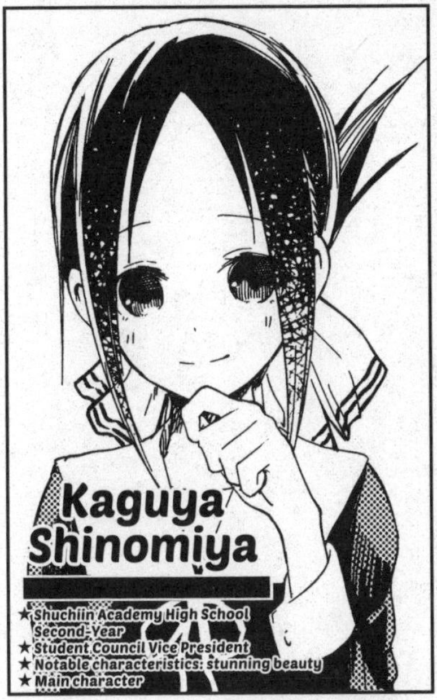
Kaguya Shinomiya
★ Shuchiin Academy High School Second-Year
★ Student Council Vice President
★ Notable characteristics: stunning beauty
★ Main character

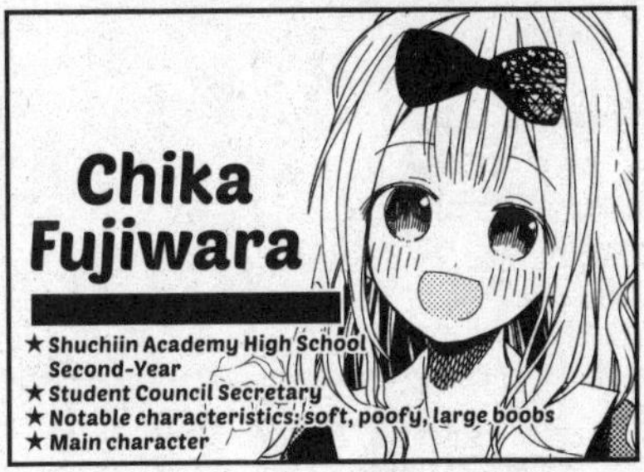
Chika Fujiwara
★ Shuchiin Academy High School Second-Year
★ Student Council Secretary
★ Notable characteristics: soft, poofy, large boobs
★ Main character

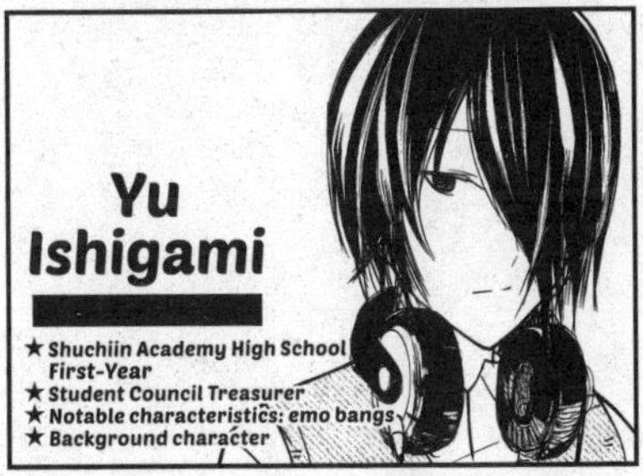
Yu Ishigami
★ Shuchiin Academy High School First-Year
★ Student Council Treasurer
★ Notable characteristics: emo bangs
★ Background character

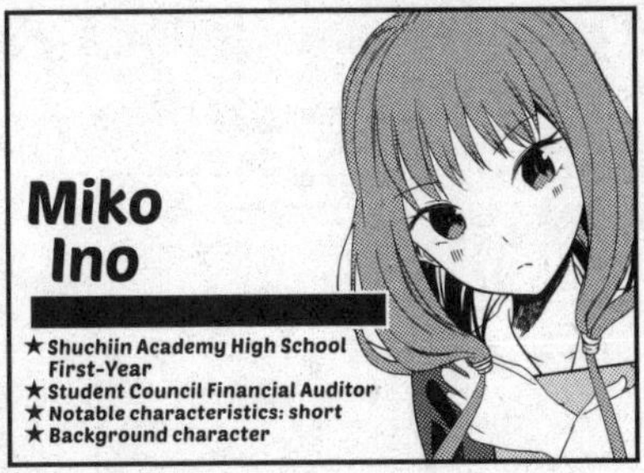
Miko Ino
★ Shuchiin Academy High School First-Year
★ Student Council Financial Auditor
★ Notable characteristics: short
★ Background character

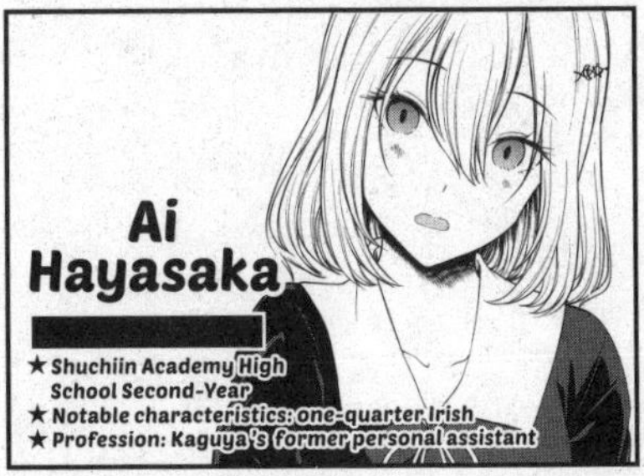
Ai Hayasaka
★ Shuchiin Academy High School Second-Year
★ Notable characteristics: one-quarter Irish
★ Profession: Kaguya's former personal assistant

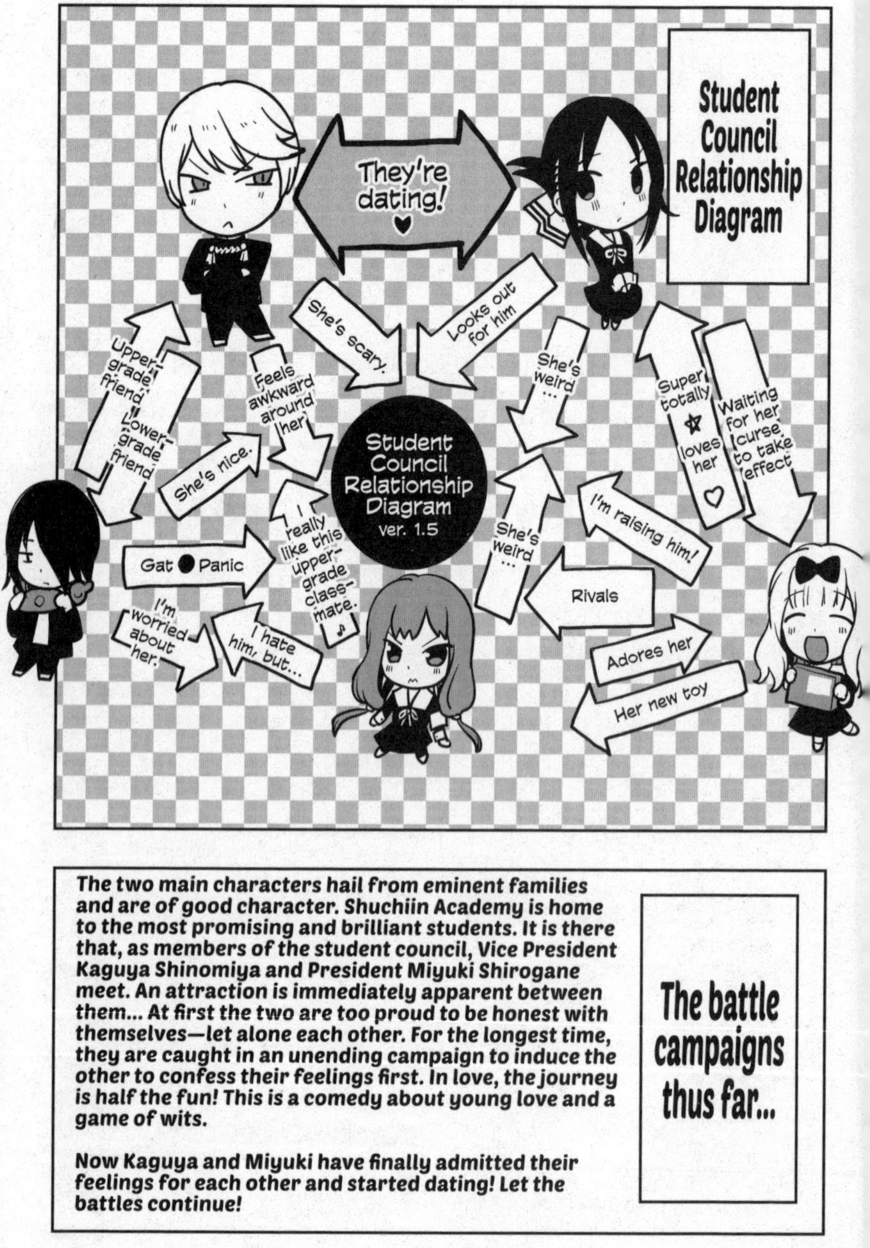
Student Council Relationship Diagram
They're dating!
She's scary.
Looks out for him
Upper-grade friend
Lower-grade friend
Feels awkward around her
She's nice.
Student Council Relationship Diagram ver. 1.5
She's weird...
Super totally ☆ loves her ♡
Waiting for her curse to take effect
I'm raising him!
She's weird...
Gat ● Panic
I really like this upper-grade class-mate. ♪
Rivals
I'm worried about her.
I hate him, but...
Adores her
Her new toy

The battle campaigns thus far...

The two main characters hail from eminent families and are of good character. Shuchiin Academy is home to the most promising and brilliant students. It is there that, as members of the student council, Vice President Kaguya Shinomiya and President Miyuki Shirogane meet. An attraction is immediately apparent between them... At first the two are too proud to be honest with themselves—let alone each other. For the longest time, they are caught in an unending campaign to induce the other to confess their feelings first. In love, the journey is half the fun! This is a comedy about young love and a game of wits.

Now Kaguya and Miyuki have finally admitted their feelings for each other and started dating! Let the battles continue!

KAGUYA-SAMA LOVE IS WAR

BATTLE CAMPAIGNS 23

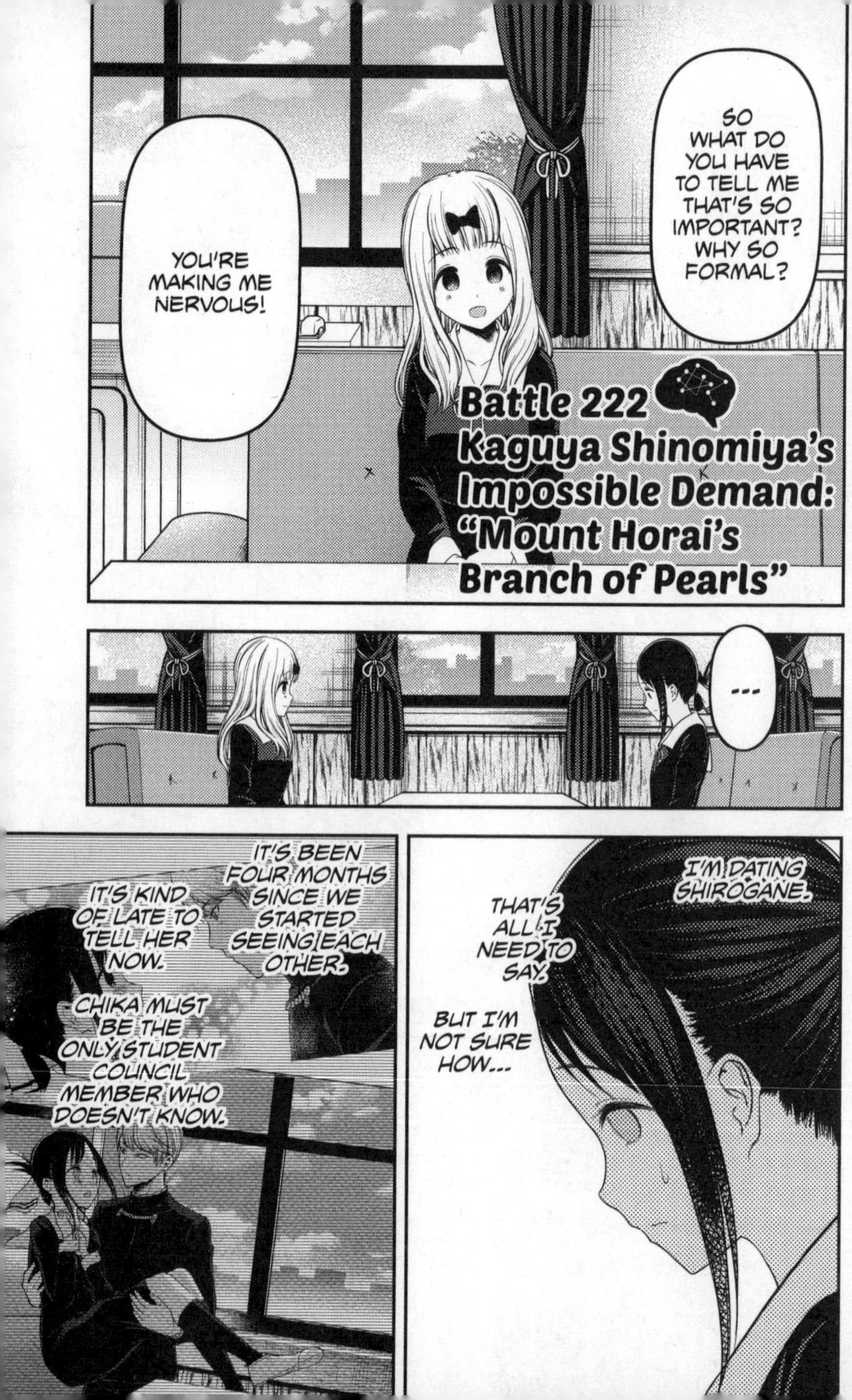
SO WHAT DO YOU HAVE TO TELL ME THAT'S SO IMPORTANT? WHY SO FORMAL?
YOU'RE MAKING ME NERVOUS!
Battle 222 Kaguya Shinomiya's Impossible Demand: "Mount Horai's Branch of Pearls"
...
I'M DATING SHIROGANE.
THAT'S ALL I NEED TO SAY.
BUT I'M NOT SURE HOW...
IT'S BEEN FOUR MONTHS SINCE WE STARTED SEEING EACH OTHER.
IT'S KIND OF LATE TO TELL HER NOW.
CHIKA MUST BE THE ONLY STUDENT COUNCIL MEMBER WHO DOESN'T KNOW.

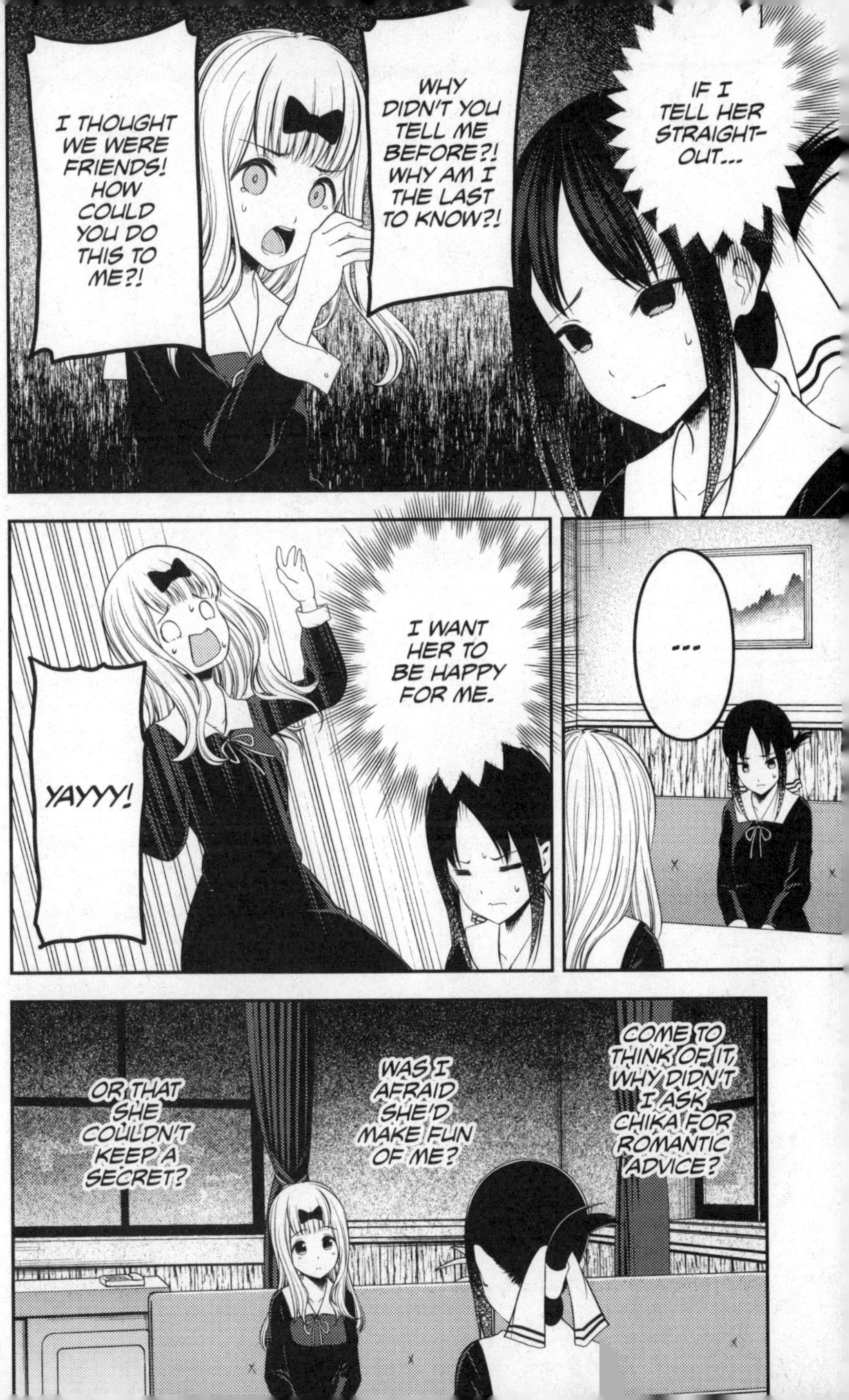
IF I TELL HER STRAIGHT-OUT...
WHY DIDN'T YOU TELL ME BEFORE?! WHY AM I THE LAST TO KNOW?!
I THOUGHT WE WERE FRIENDS! HOW COULD YOU DO THIS TO ME?!
...
I WANT HER TO BE HAPPY FOR ME.
YAYYY!
COME TO THINK OF IT, WHY DIDN'T I ASK CHIKA FOR ROMANTIC ADVICE?
WAS I AFRAID SHE'D MAKE FUN OF ME?
OR THAT SHE COULDN'T KEEP A SECRET?

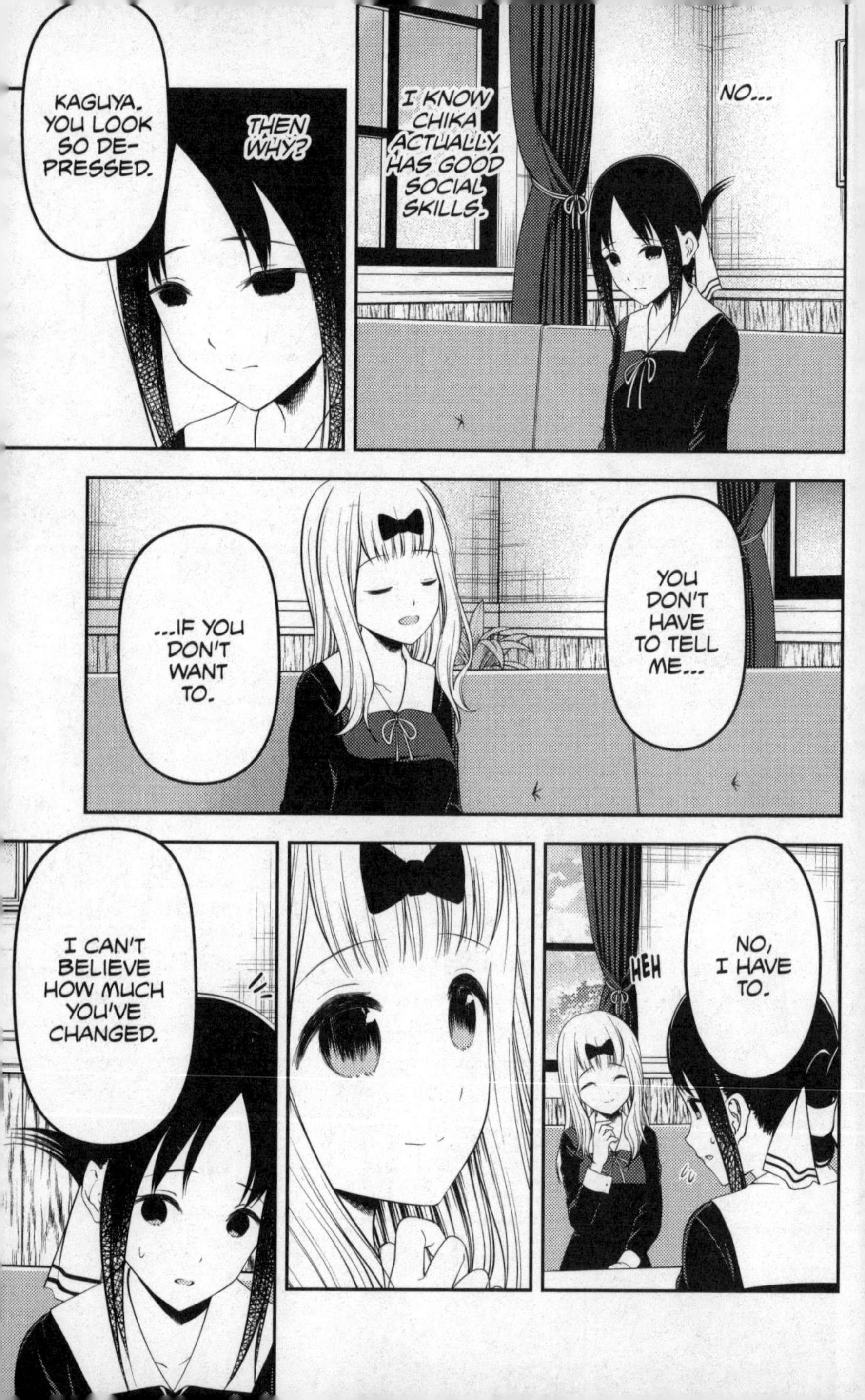
NO...
I KNOW CHIKA ACTUALLY HAS GOOD SOCIAL SKILLS.
THEN WHY?
KAGUYA. YOU LOOK SO DE-PRESSED.
YOU DON'T HAVE TO TELL ME...
...IF YOU DON'T WANT TO.
NO, I HAVE TO.
HEH
I CAN'T BELIEVE HOW MUCH YOU'VE CHANGED.

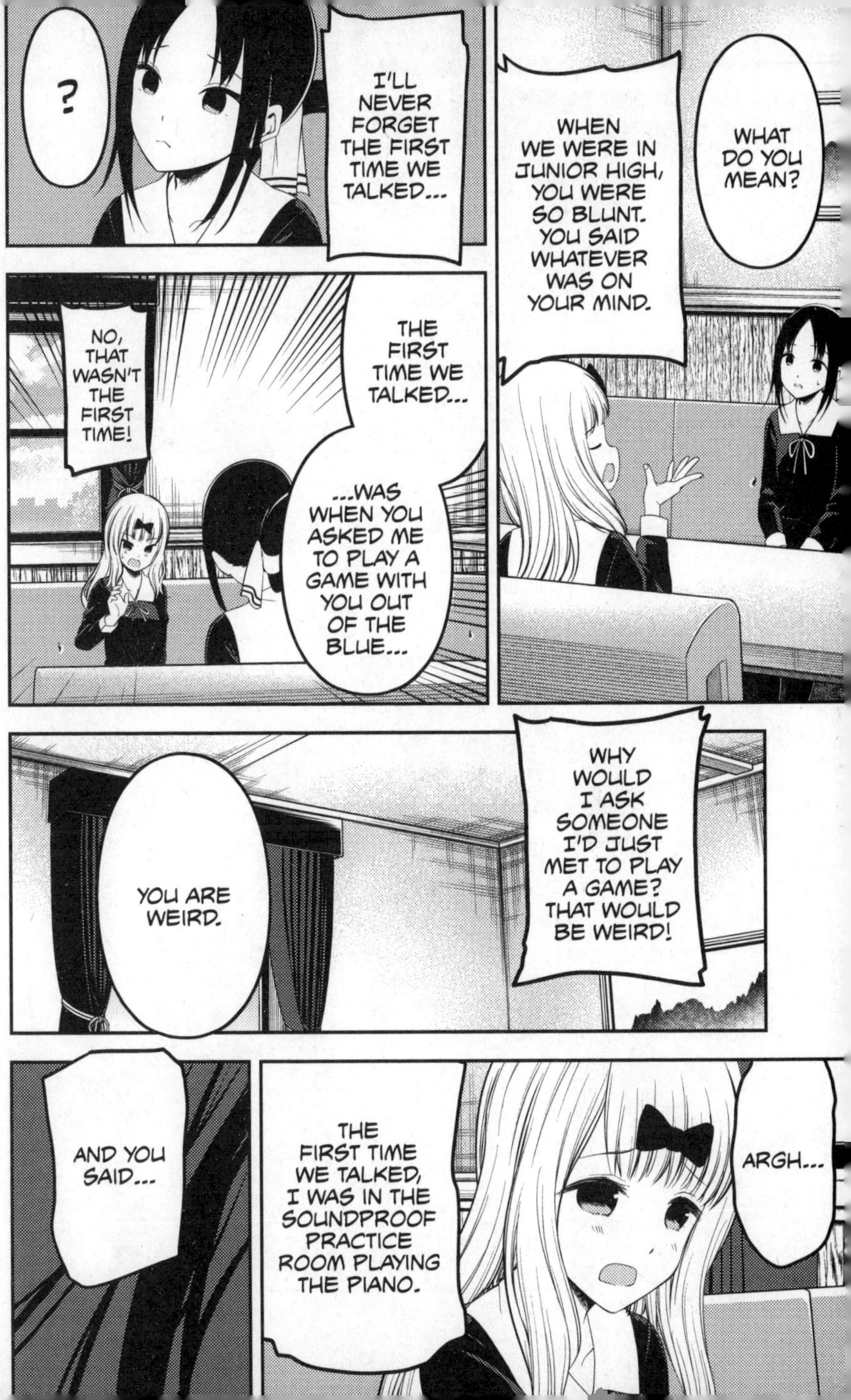
WHAT DO YOU MEAN?
WHEN WE WERE IN JUNIOR HIGH, YOU WERE SO BLUNT. YOU SAID WHATEVER WAS ON YOUR MIND.
I'LL NEVER FORGET THE FIRST TIME WE TALKED...
?
THE FIRST TIME WE TALKED...
...WAS WHEN YOU ASKED ME TO PLAY A GAME WITH YOU OUT OF THE BLUE...
NO, THAT WASN'T THE FIRST TIME!
WHY WOULD I ASK SOMEONE I'D JUST MET TO PLAY A GAME? THAT WOULD BE WEIRD!
YOU ARE WEIRD.
ARGH...
THE FIRST TIME WE TALKED, I WAS IN THE SOUNDPROOF PRACTICE ROOM PLAYING THE PIANO.
AND YOU SAID...

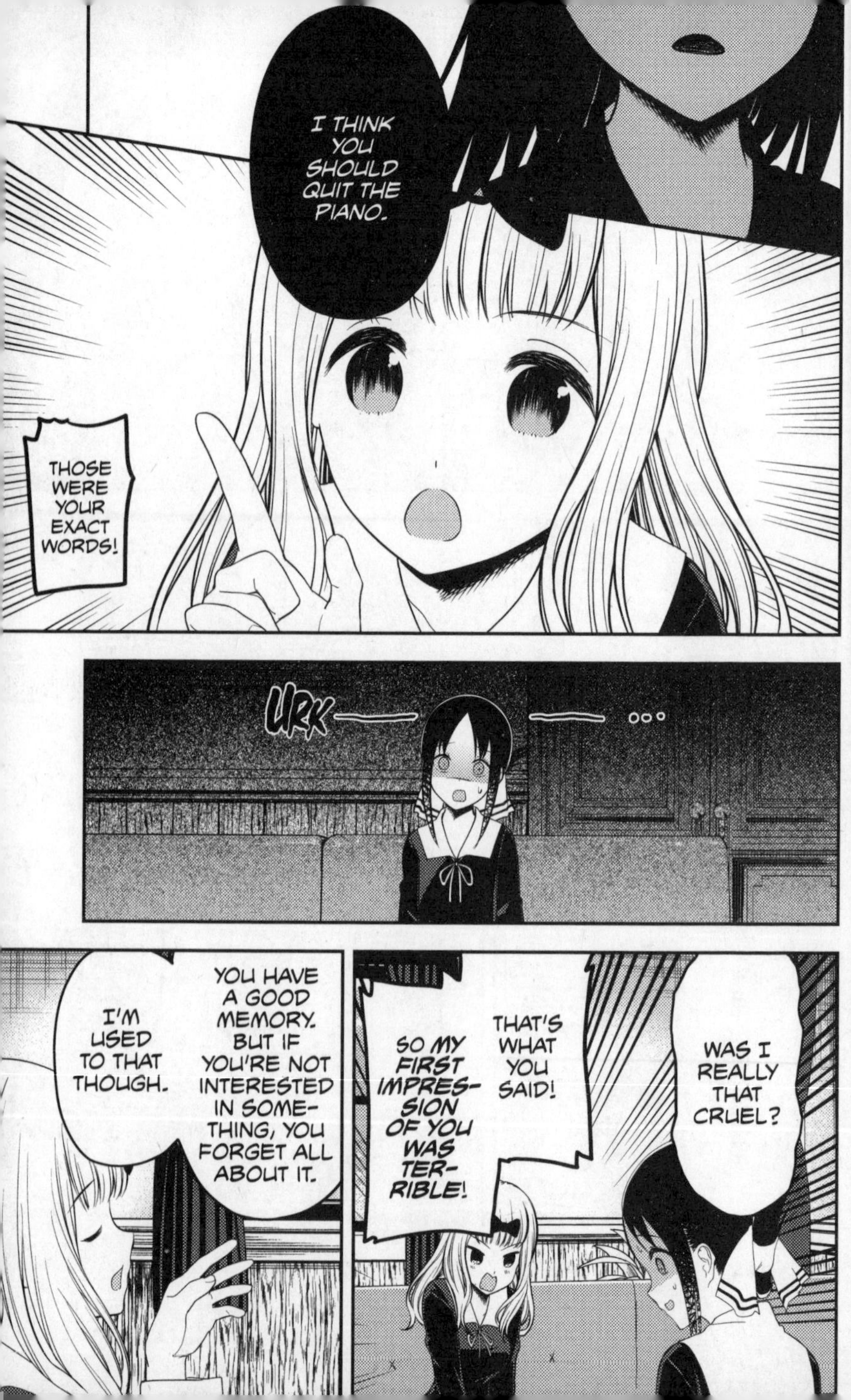
I THINK YOU SHOULD QUIT THE PIANO.
THOSE WERE YOUR EXACT WORDS!
URK———— ————...
WAS I REALLY THAT CRUEL?
THAT'S WHAT YOU SAID!
SO MY *FIRST IMPRESSION* OF YOU *WAS TERRIBLE!*
YOU HAVE A GOOD MEMORY. BUT IF YOU'RE NOT INTERESTED IN SOMETHING, YOU FORGET ALL ABOUT IT.
I'M USED TO THAT THOUGH.

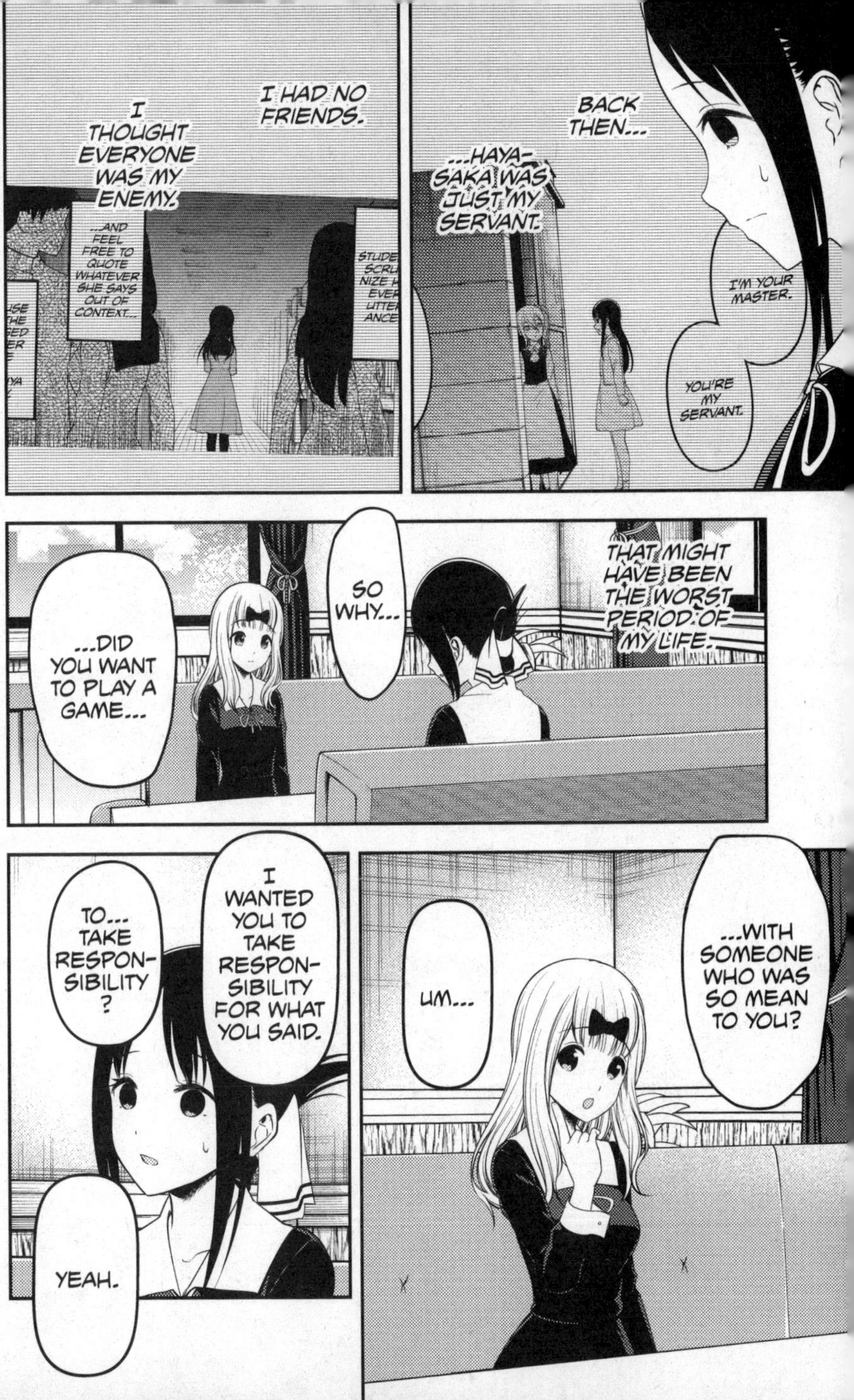
BACK THEN...
...HAYA-SAKA WAS JUST MY SERVANT.
I'M YOUR MASTER.
YOU'RE MY SERVANT.
I HAD NO FRIENDS.
I THOUGHT EVERYONE WAS MY ENEMY.
...AND FEEL FREE TO QUOTE WHATEVER SHE SAYS OUT OF CONTEXT...
THAT MIGHT HAVE BEEN THE WORST PERIOD OF MY LIFE.
SO WHY...
...DID YOU WANT TO PLAY A GAME...
...WITH SOMEONE WHO WAS SO MEAN TO YOU?
UM...
I WANTED YOU TO TAKE RESPON-SIBILITY FOR WHAT YOU SAID.
TO... TAKE RESPON-SIBILITY?
YEAH.

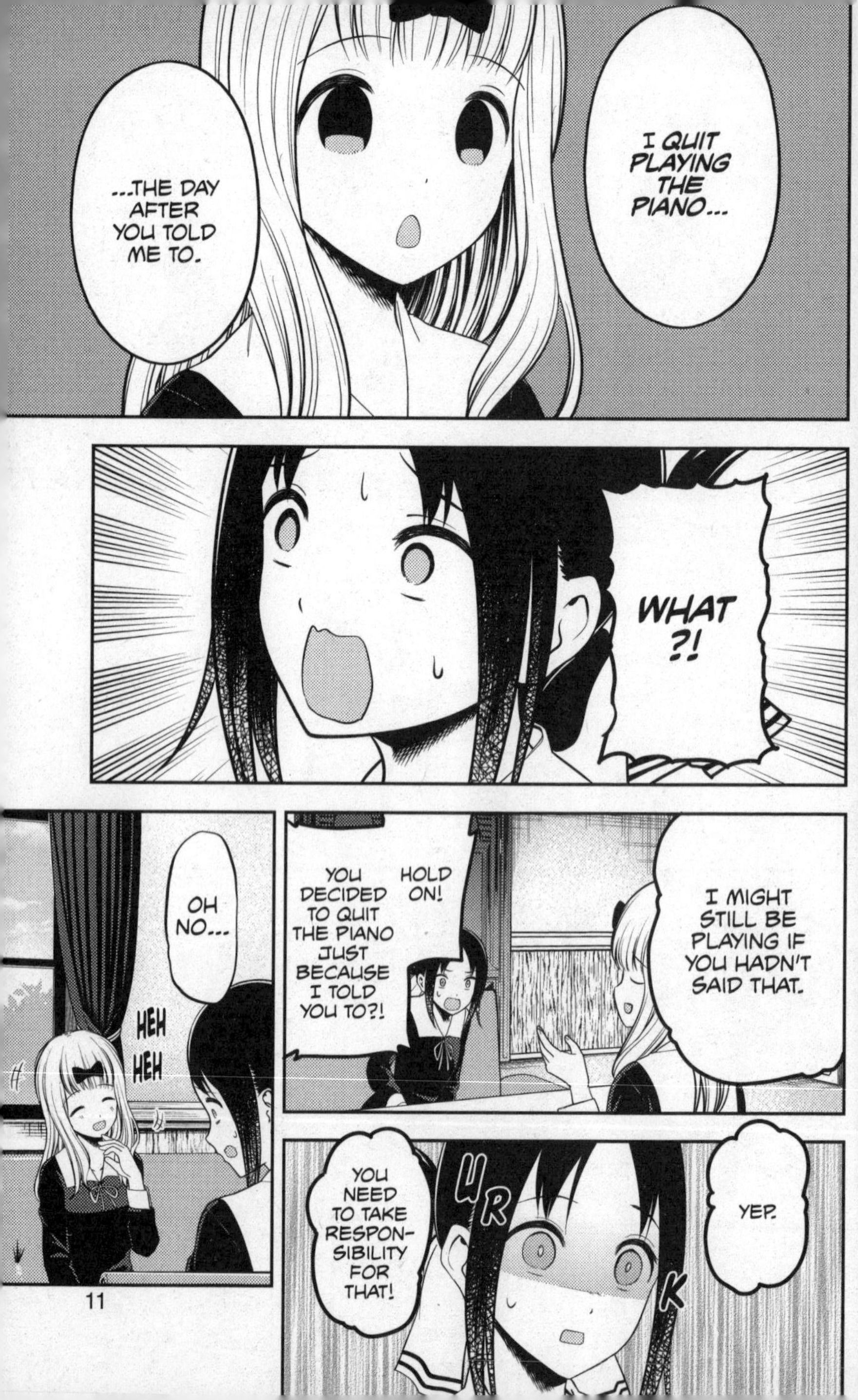
I QUIT PLAYING THE PIANO...
...THE DAY AFTER YOU TOLD ME TO.
WHAT?!
I MIGHT STILL BE PLAYING IF YOU HADN'T SAID THAT.
HOLD ON!
YOU DECIDED TO QUIT THE PIANO JUST BECAUSE I TOLD YOU TO?!
YEP.
URK
YOU NEED TO TAKE RESPONSIBILITY FOR THAT!
OH NO...
HEH HEH

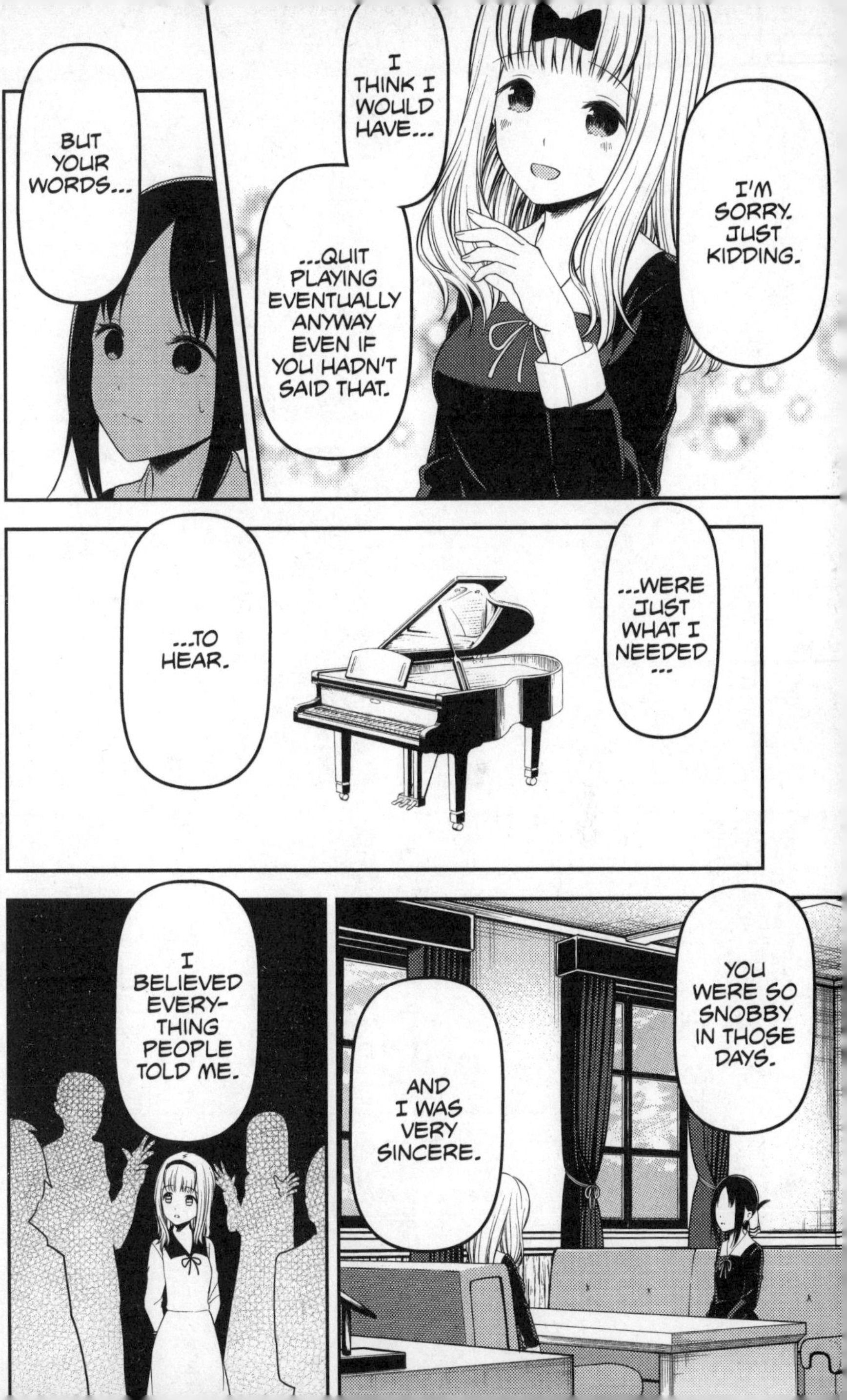
I'M SORRY. JUST KIDDING.
I THINK I WOULD HAVE...
...QUIT PLAYING EVENTUALLY ANYWAY EVEN IF YOU HADN'T SAID THAT.
BUT YOUR WORDS...
...WERE JUST WHAT I NEEDED ...
...TO HEAR.
YOU WERE SO SNOBBY IN THOSE DAYS.
AND I WAS VERY SINCERE.
I BELIEVED EVERY-THING PEOPLE TOLD ME.

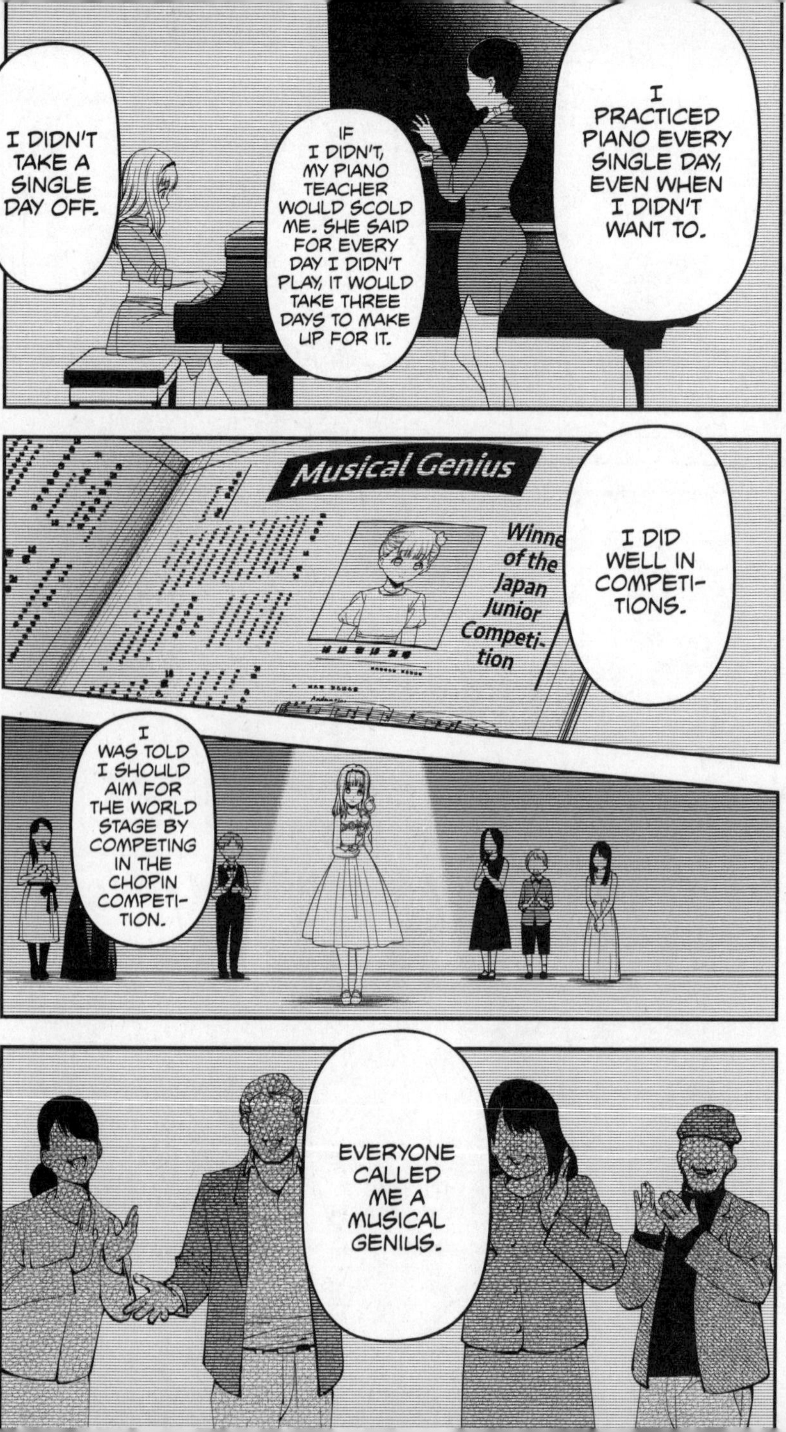
I PRACTICED PIANO EVERY SINGLE DAY, EVEN WHEN I DIDN'T WANT TO.
IF I DIDN'T, MY PIANO TEACHER WOULD SCOLD ME. SHE SAID FOR EVERY DAY I DIDN'T PLAY, IT WOULD TAKE THREE DAYS TO MAKE UP FOR IT.
I DIDN'T TAKE A SINGLE DAY OFF.
I DID WELL IN COMPETI-TIONS.
Musical Genius
Winne of the Japan Junior Competi-tion
I WAS TOLD I SHOULD AIM FOR THE WORLD STAGE BY COMPETING IN THE CHOPIN COMPETI-TION.
EVERYONE CALLED ME A MUSICAL GENIUS.

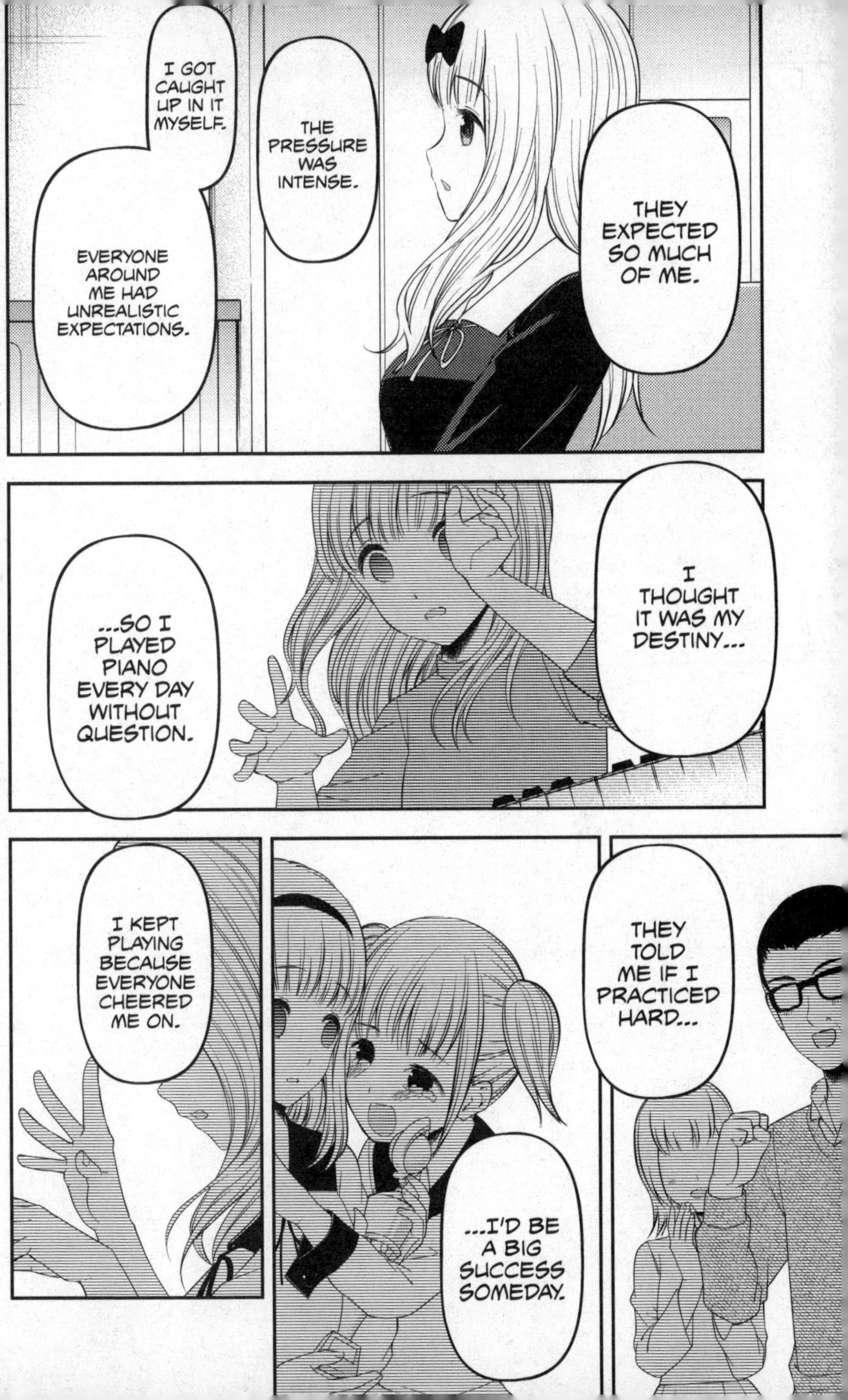
THEY EXPECTED SO MUCH OF ME.
THE PRESSURE WAS INTENSE.
I GOT CAUGHT UP IN IT MYSELF.
EVERYONE AROUND ME HAD UNREALISTIC EXPECTATIONS.
I THOUGHT IT WAS MY DESTINY...
...SO I PLAYED PIANO EVERY DAY WITHOUT QUESTION.
THEY TOLD ME IF I PRACTICED HARD...
...I'D BE A BIG SUCCESS SOMEDAY.
I KEPT PLAYING BECAUSE EVERYONE CHEERED ME ON.

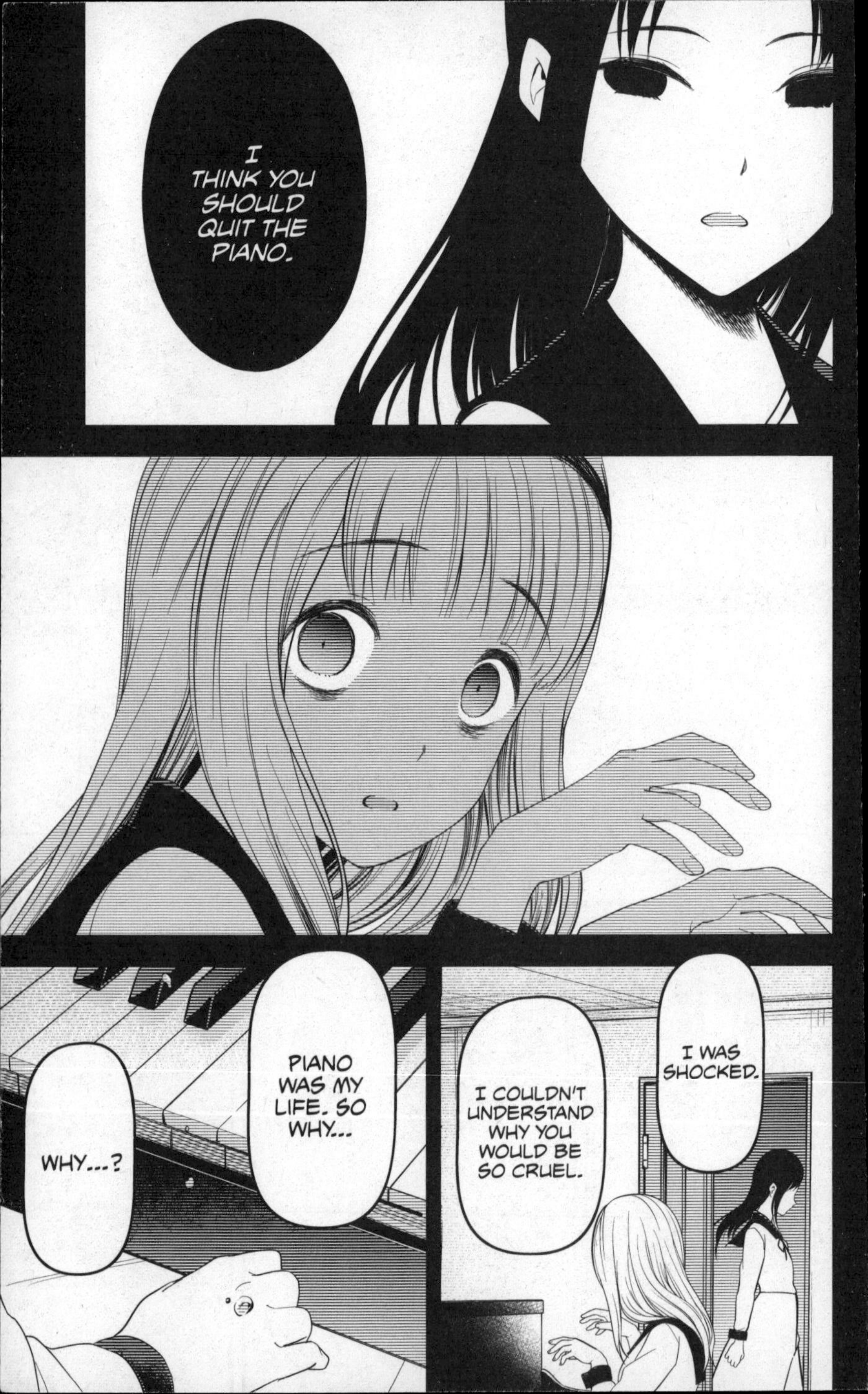
I THINK YOU SHOULD QUIT THE PIANO.
I WAS SHOCKED.
I COULDN'T UNDERSTAND WHY YOU WOULD BE SO CRUEL.
PIANO WAS MY LIFE. SO WHY...
WHY...?

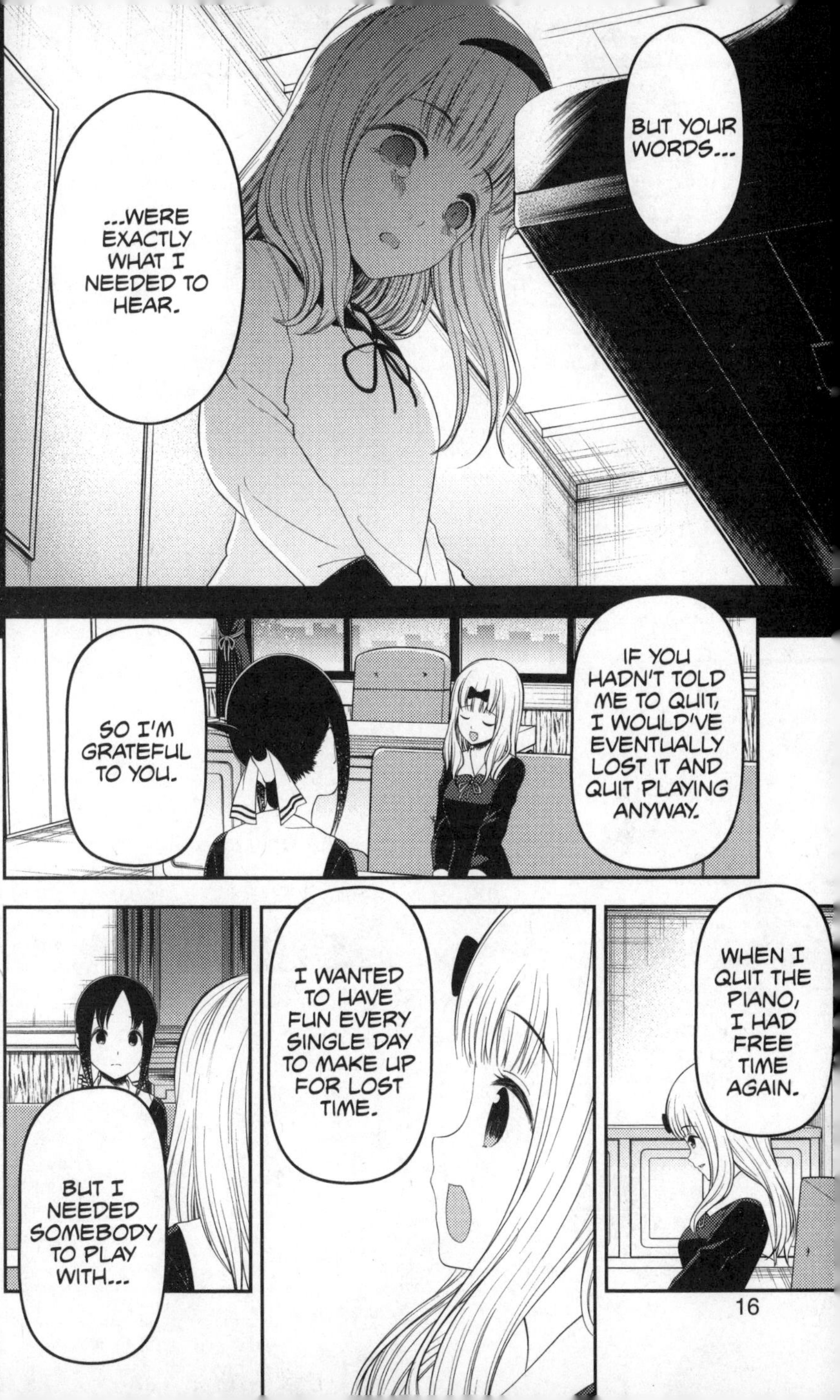
BUT YOUR WORDS...
...WERE EXACTLY WHAT I NEEDED TO HEAR.
IF YOU HADN'T TOLD ME TO QUIT, I WOULD'VE EVENTUALLY LOST IT AND QUIT PLAYING ANYWAY.
SO I'M GRATEFUL TO YOU.
WHEN I QUIT THE PIANO, I HAD FREE TIME AGAIN.
I WANTED TO HAVE FUN EVERY SINGLE DAY TO MAKE UP FOR LOST TIME.
BUT I NEEDED SOMEBODY TO PLAY WITH...

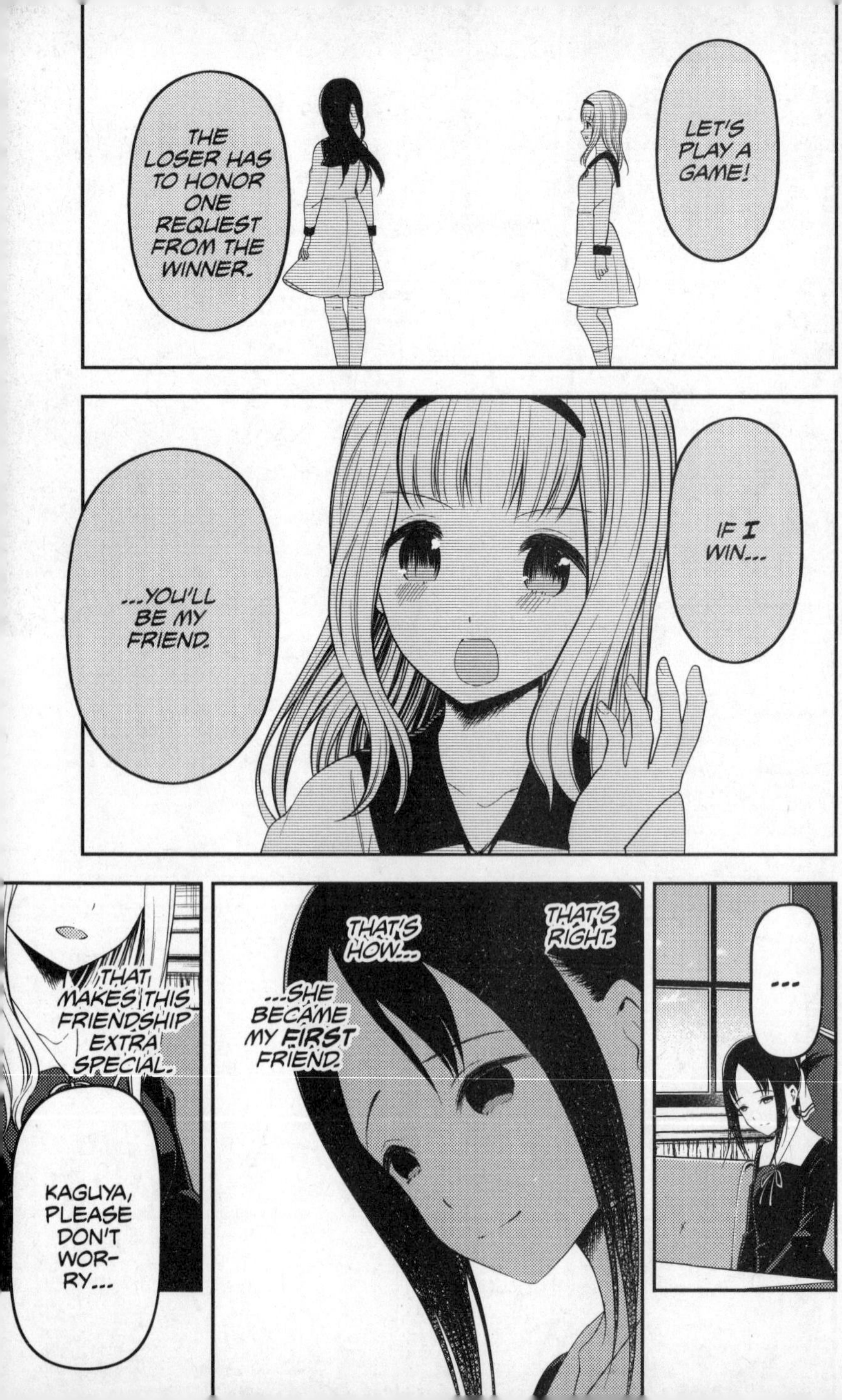
LET'S PLAY A GAME!
THE LOSER HAS TO HONOR ONE REQUEST FROM THE WINNER.
IF I WIN...
...YOU'LL BE MY FRIEND.
...
THAT'S RIGHT.
THAT'S HOW...
...SHE BECAME MY FIRST FRIEND.
THAT MAKES THIS FRIENDSHIP EXTRA SPECIAL.
KAGUYA, PLEASE DON'T WOR-RY...

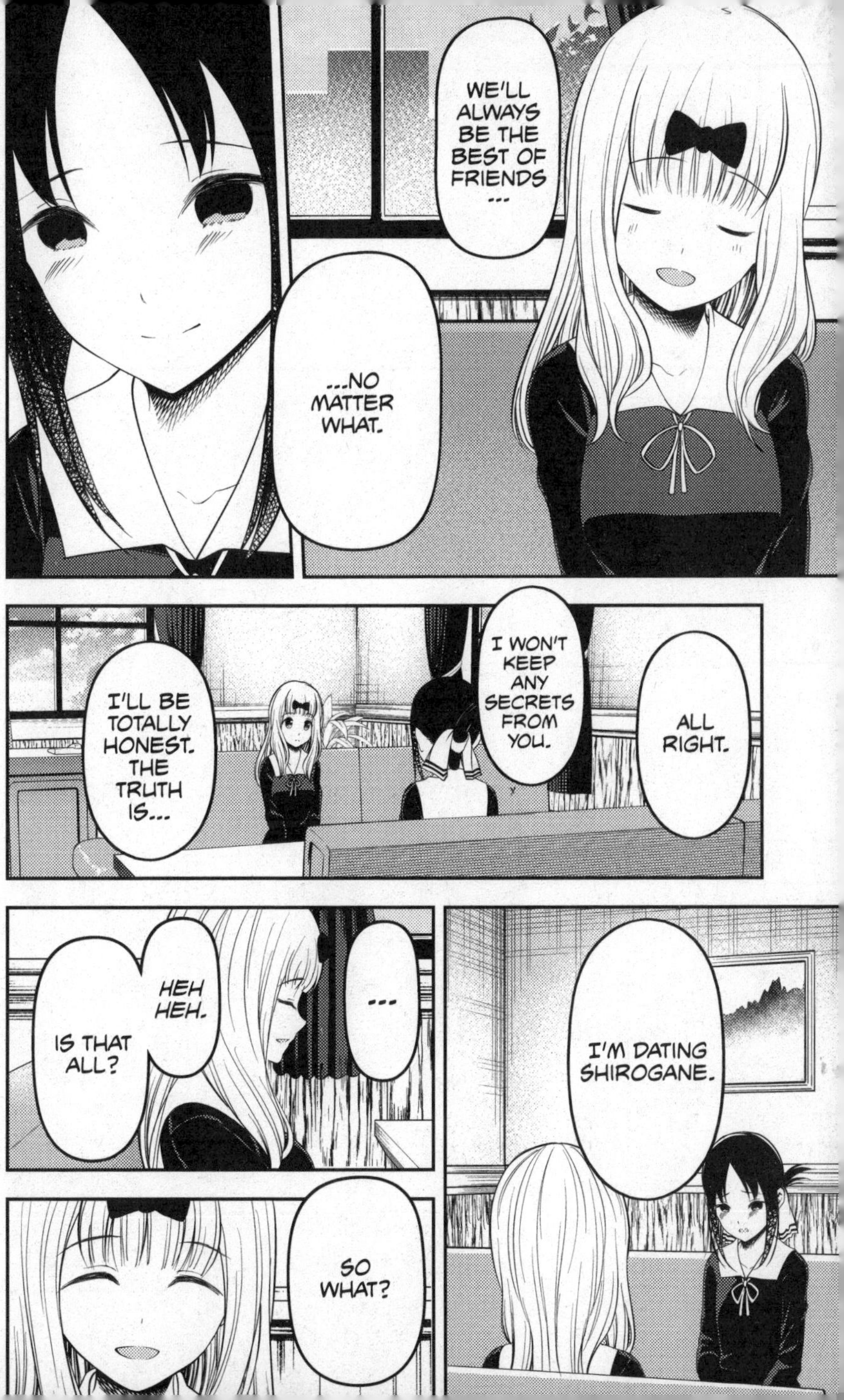
WE'LL ALWAYS BE THE BEST OF FRIENDS ...
...NO MATTER WHAT.
ALL RIGHT.
I WON'T KEEP ANY SECRETS FROM YOU.
I'LL BE TOTALLY HONEST. THE TRUTH IS...
I'M DATING SHIROGANE.
...
HEH HEH.
IS THAT ALL?
SO WHAT?

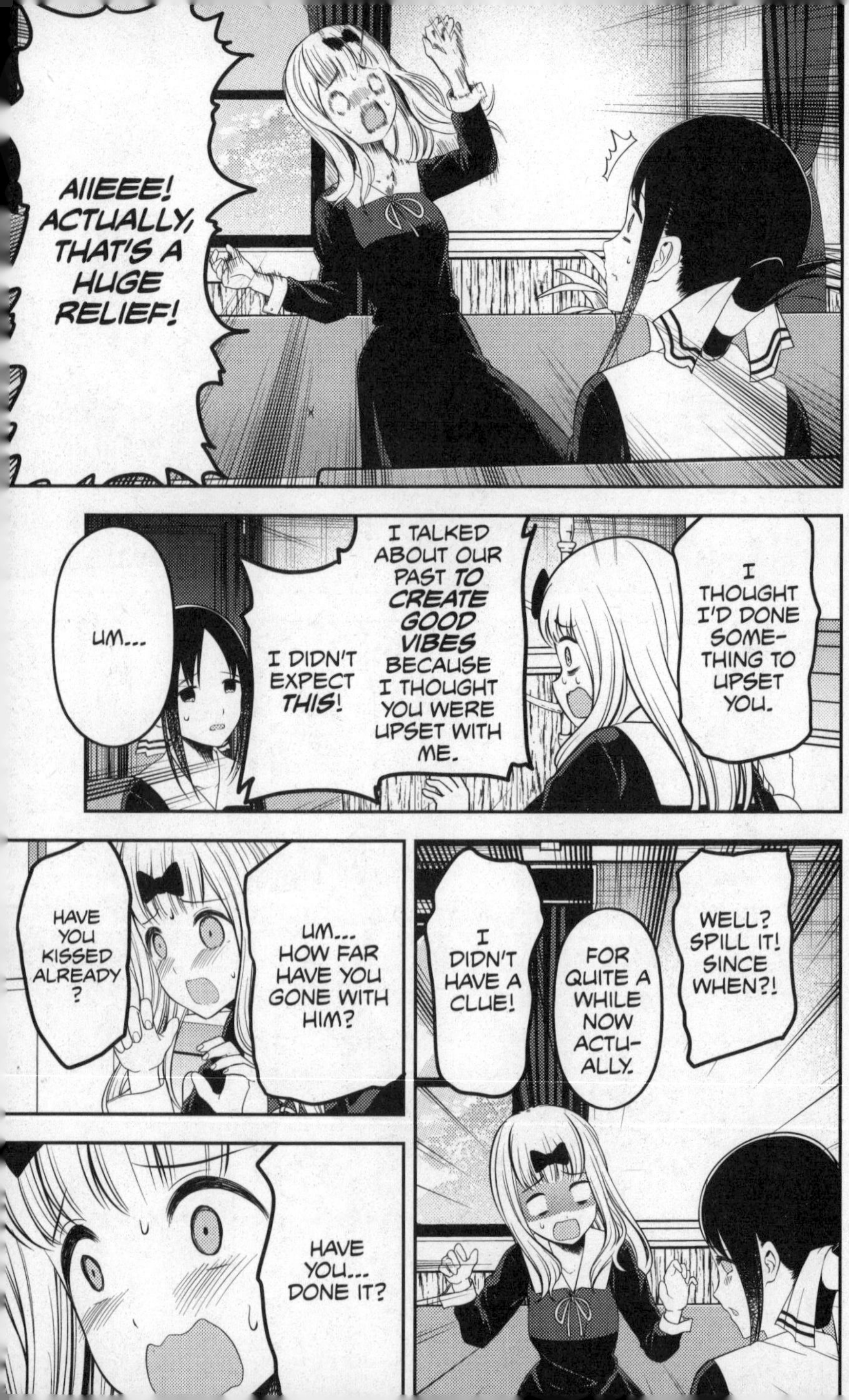
AIIEEE! ACTUALLY, THAT'S A HUGE RELIEF!
I THOUGHT I'D DONE SOME-THING TO UPSET YOU.
I TALKED ABOUT OUR PAST TO CREATE GOOD VIBES BECAUSE I THOUGHT YOU WERE UPSET WITH ME.
I DIDN'T EXPECT THIS!
UM...
WELL? SPILL IT! SINCE WHEN?!
FOR QUITE A WHILE NOW ACTU-ALLY.
I DIDN'T HAVE A CLUE!
UM... HOW FAR HAVE YOU GONE WITH HIM?
HAVE YOU KISSED ALREADY?
HAVE YOU... DONE IT?

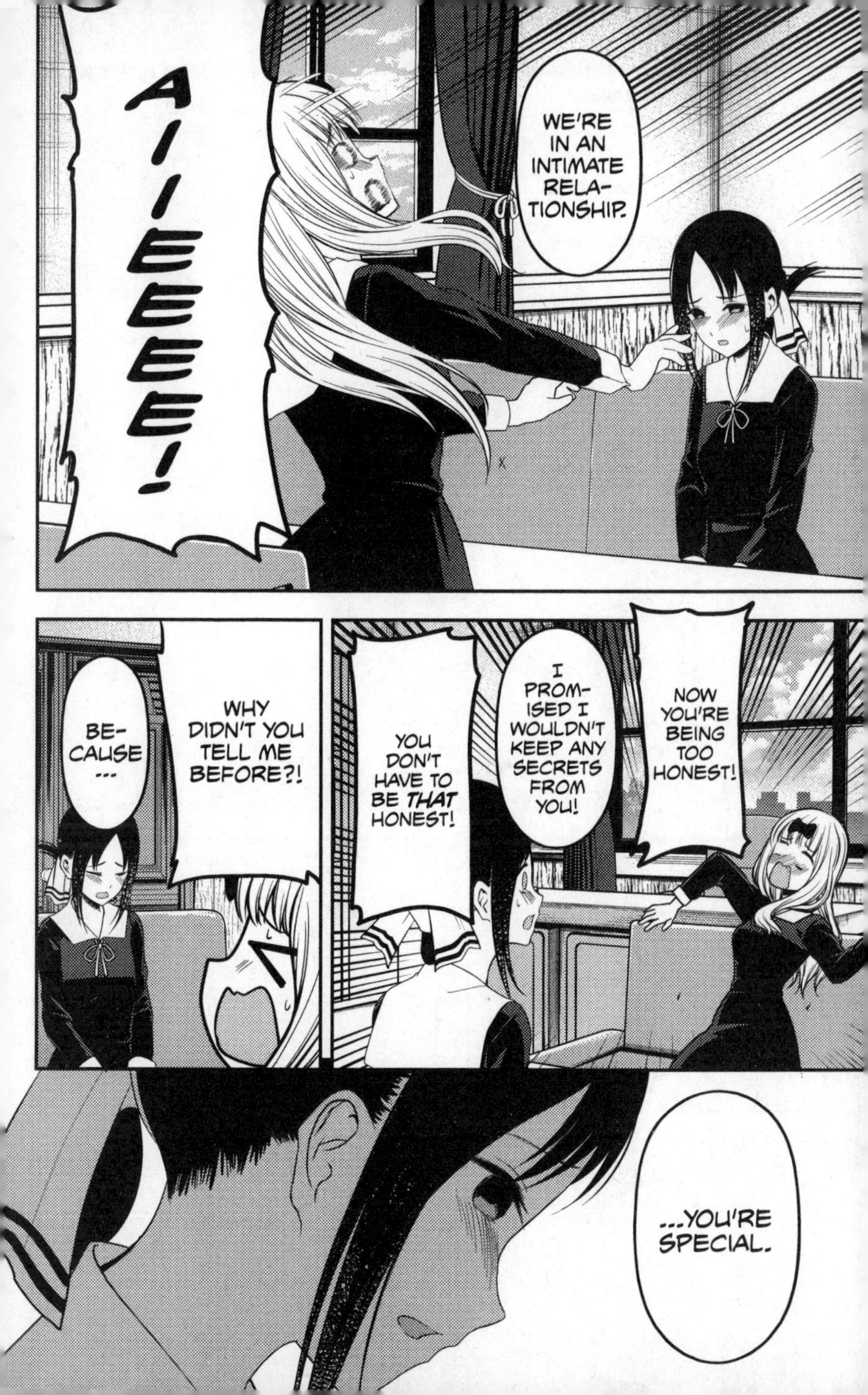

WE'RE IN AN INTIMATE RELATIONSHIP.
AIIEEEEE!
NOW YOU'RE BEING TOO HONEST!
I PROMISED I WOULDN'T KEEP ANY SECRETS FROM YOU!
YOU DON'T HAVE TO BE *THAT* HONEST!
WHY DIDN'T YOU TELL ME BEFORE?!
BECAUSE...
...YOU'RE SPECIAL.

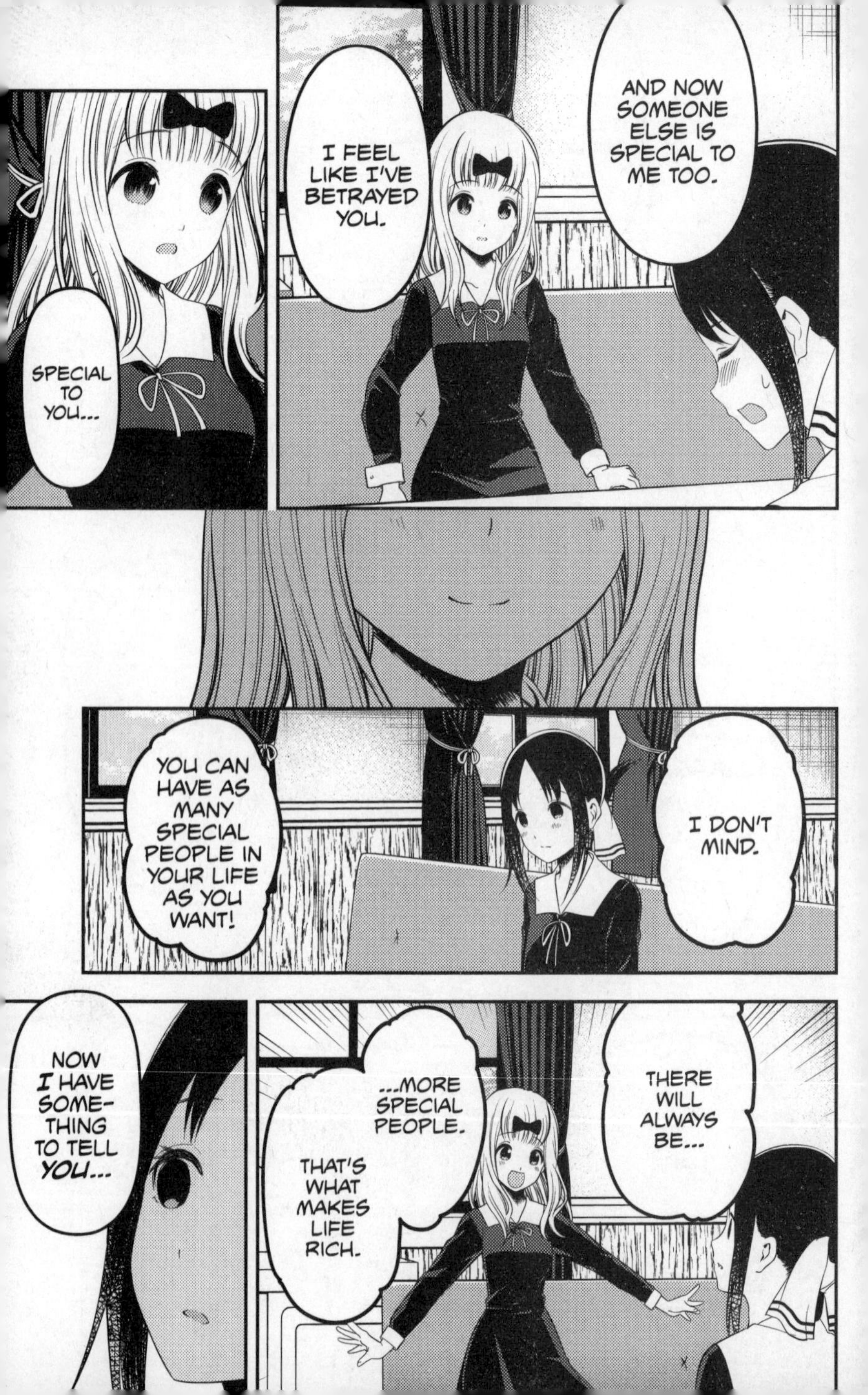
AND NOW SOMEONE ELSE IS SPECIAL TO ME TOO.
I FEEL LIKE I'VE BETRAYED YOU.
SPECIAL TO YOU...
I DON'T MIND.
YOU CAN HAVE AS MANY SPECIAL PEOPLE IN YOUR LIFE AS YOU WANT!
THERE WILL ALWAYS BE...
...MORE SPECIAL PEOPLE.
THAT'S WHAT MAKES LIFE RICH.
NOW *I* HAVE SOME-THING TO TELL *YOU*...

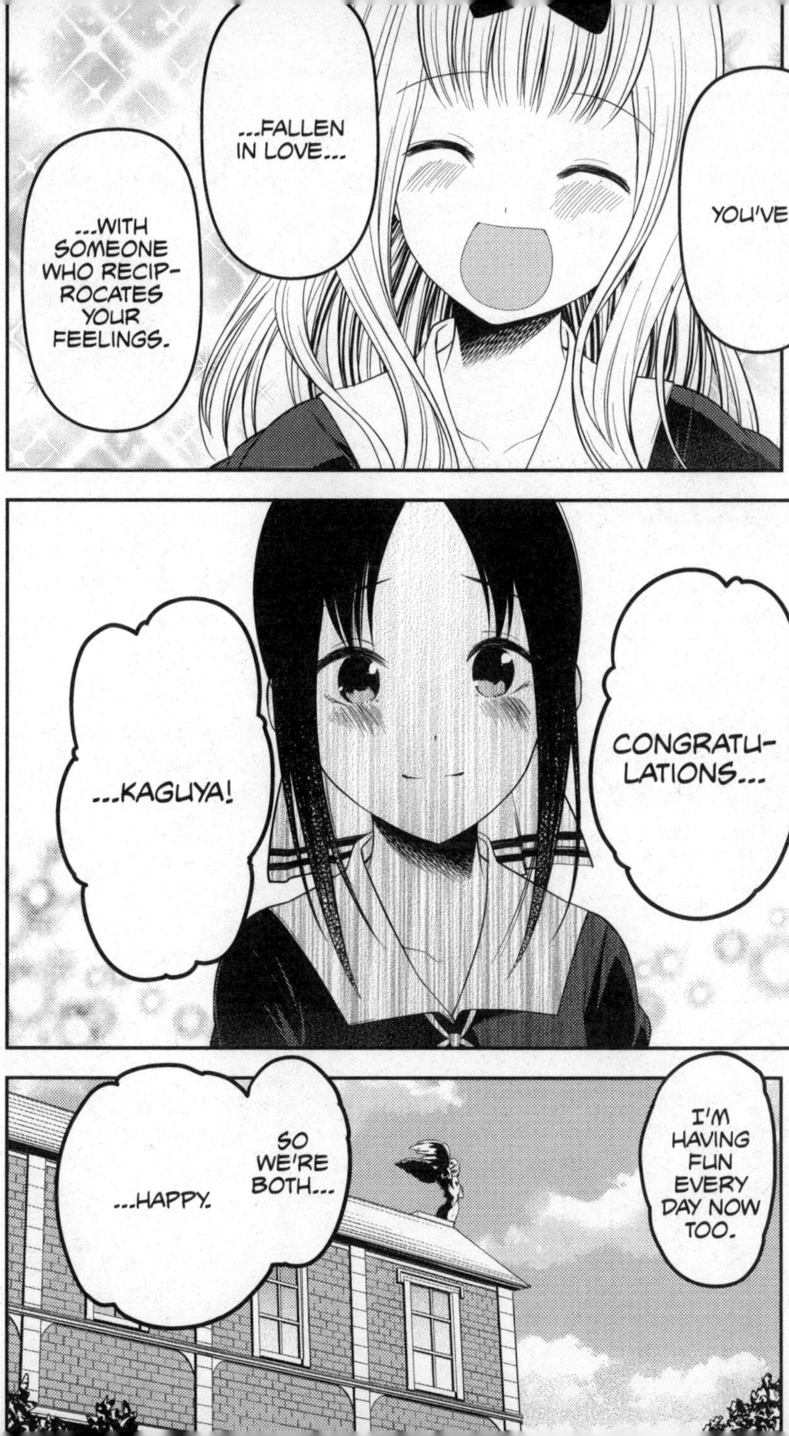
YOU'VE...
...FALLEN IN LOVE...
...WITH SOMEONE WHO RECIP-ROCATES YOUR FEELINGS.
CONGRATU-LATIONS...
...KAGUYA!
I'M HAVING FUN EVERY DAY NOW TOO.
SO WE'RE BOTH...
...HAPPY.

Lessons Student Council Members Have Taken

Kaguya: Tea ceremony, karate, Japanese koto, judo, etc.

Shirogane: Cram school, English conversation

Fujiwara: Piano, golf

Ishigami: Soccer, swimming, abacus

Ino: Piano, private tutoring

KAGUYA-SAMA
LOVE IS WAR

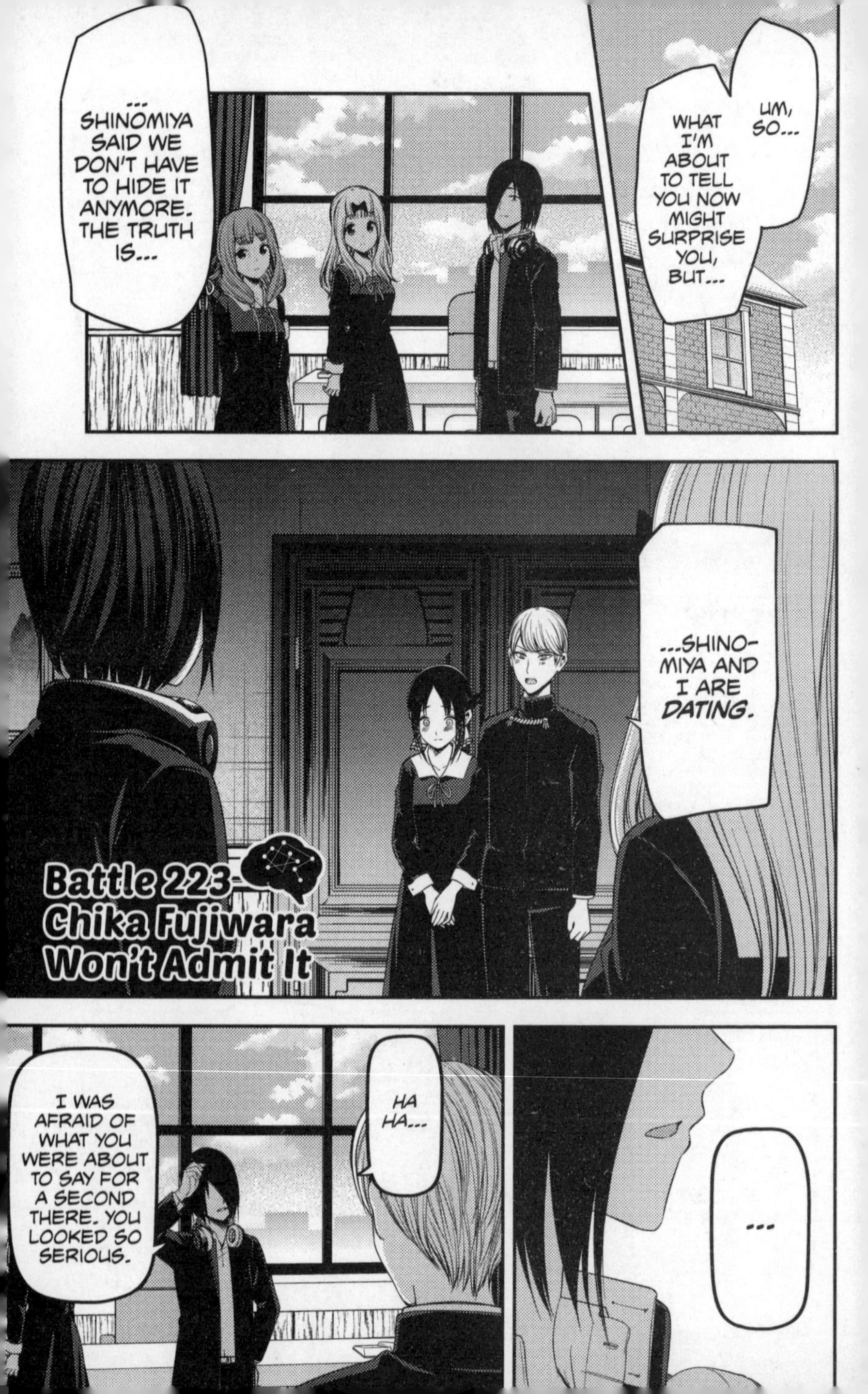
UM, SO... WHAT I'M ABOUT TO TELL YOU NOW MIGHT SURPRISE YOU, BUT...
... SHINOMIYA SAID WE DON'T HAVE TO HIDE IT ANYMORE. THE TRUTH IS...
...SHINOMIYA AND I ARE DATING.
Battle 223 Chika Fujiwara Won't Admit It
...
HA HA...
I WAS AFRAID OF WHAT YOU WERE ABOUT TO SAY FOR A SECOND THERE. YOU LOOKED SO SERIOUS.

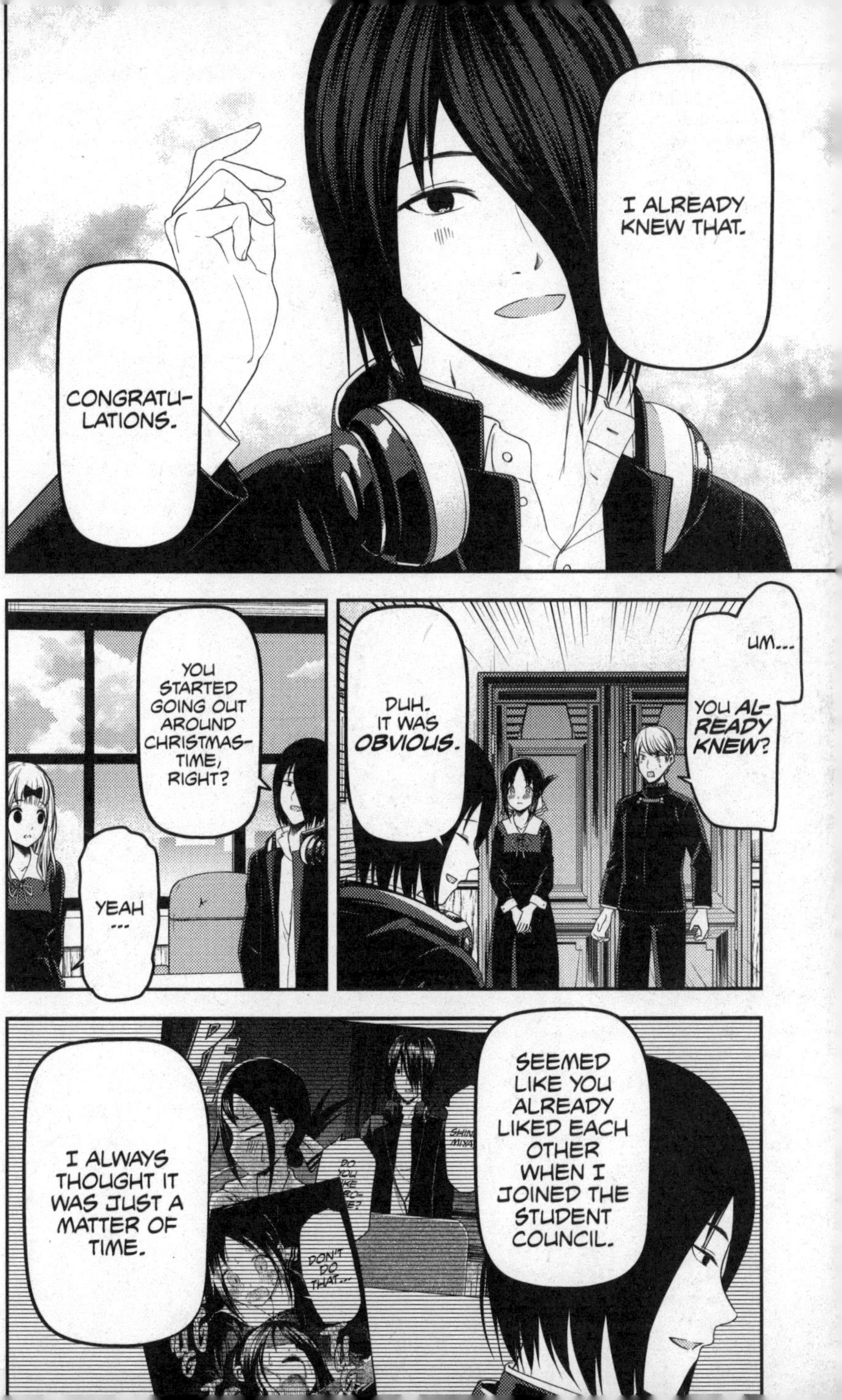
I ALREADY KNEW THAT.
CONGRATULATIONS.
UM...
YOU ALREADY KNEW?
DUH. IT WAS OBVIOUS.
YOU STARTED GOING OUT AROUND CHRISTMASTIME, RIGHT?
YEAH...
SEEMED LIKE YOU ALREADY LIKED EACH OTHER WHEN I JOINED THE STUDENT COUNCIL.
DON'T DO THAT...
I ALWAYS THOUGHT IT WAS JUST A MATTER OF TIME.

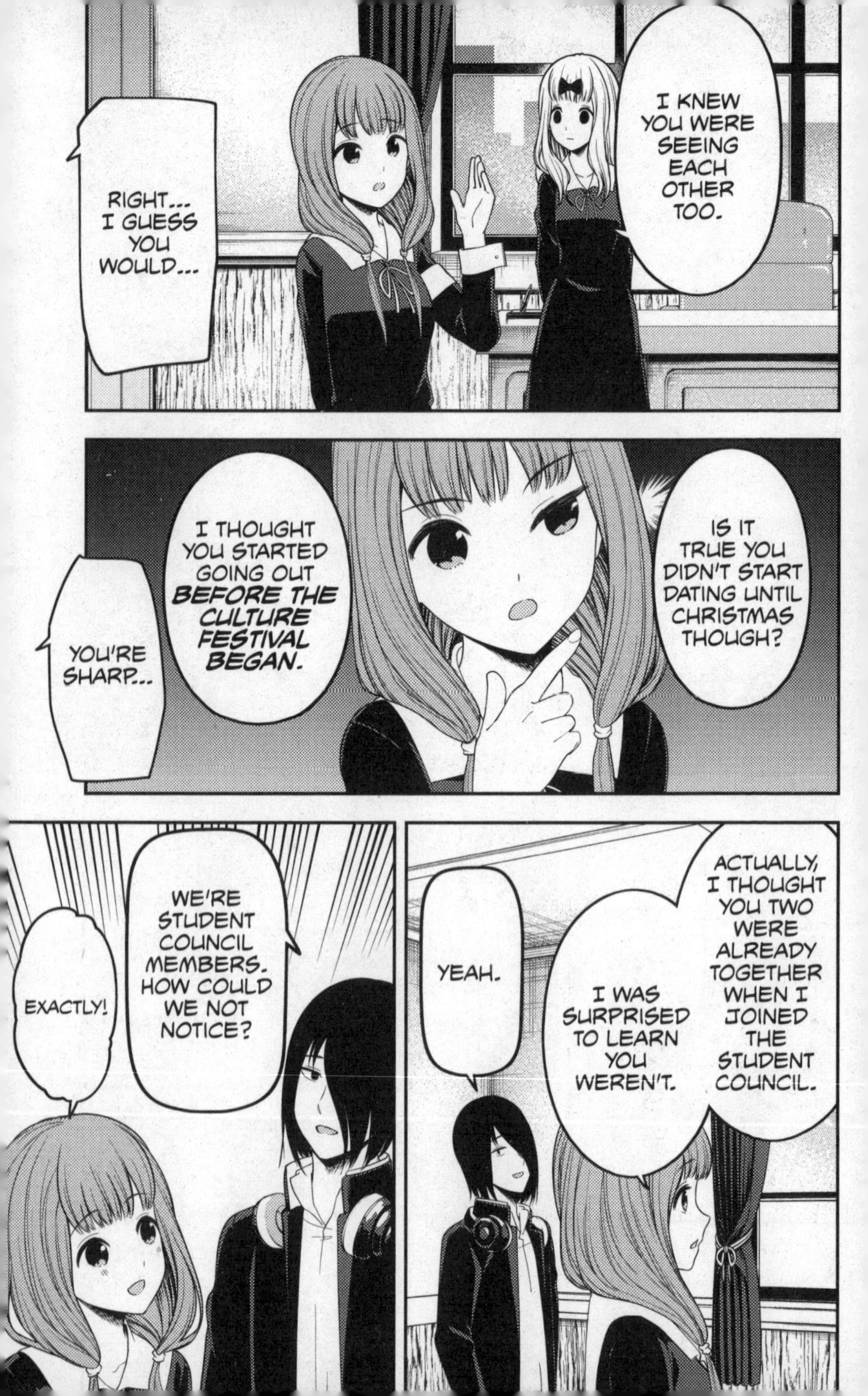
I KNEW YOU WERE SEEING EACH OTHER TOO.
RIGHT... I GUESS YOU WOULD...
IS IT TRUE YOU DIDN'T START DATING UNTIL CHRISTMAS THOUGH?
I THOUGHT YOU STARTED GOING OUT ***BEFORE THE CULTURE FESTIVAL BEGAN.***
YOU'RE SHARP...
ACTUALLY, I THOUGHT YOU TWO WERE ALREADY TOGETHER WHEN I JOINED THE STUDENT COUNCIL.
I WAS SURPRISED TO LEARN YOU WEREN'T.
YEAH.
WE'RE STUDENT COUNCIL MEMBERS. HOW COULD WE NOT NOTICE?
EXACTLY!

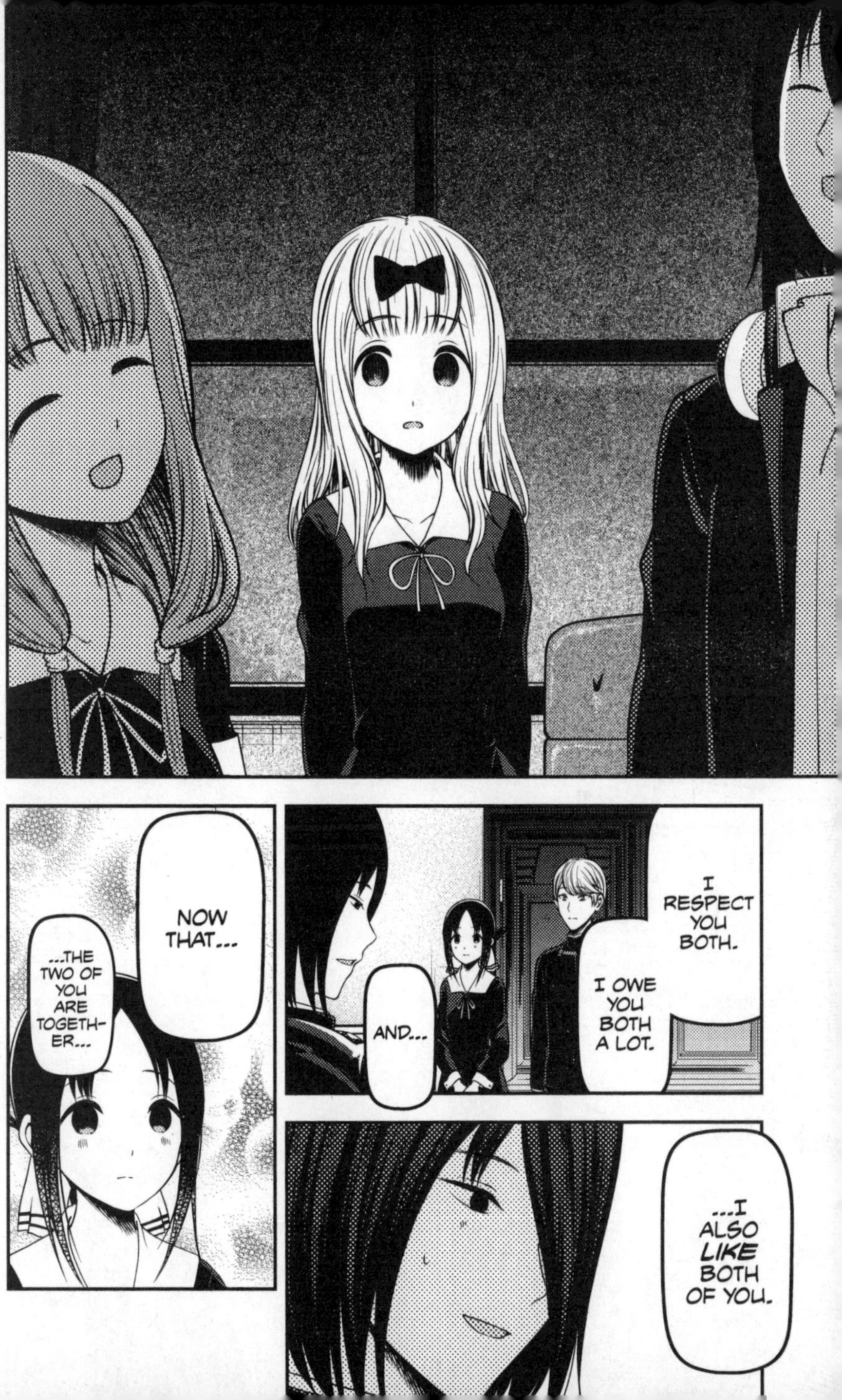
I RESPECT YOU BOTH.
I OWE YOU BOTH A LOT.
AND...
...I ALSO *LIKE* BOTH OF YOU.
NOW THAT...
...THE TWO OF YOU ARE TOGETHER...

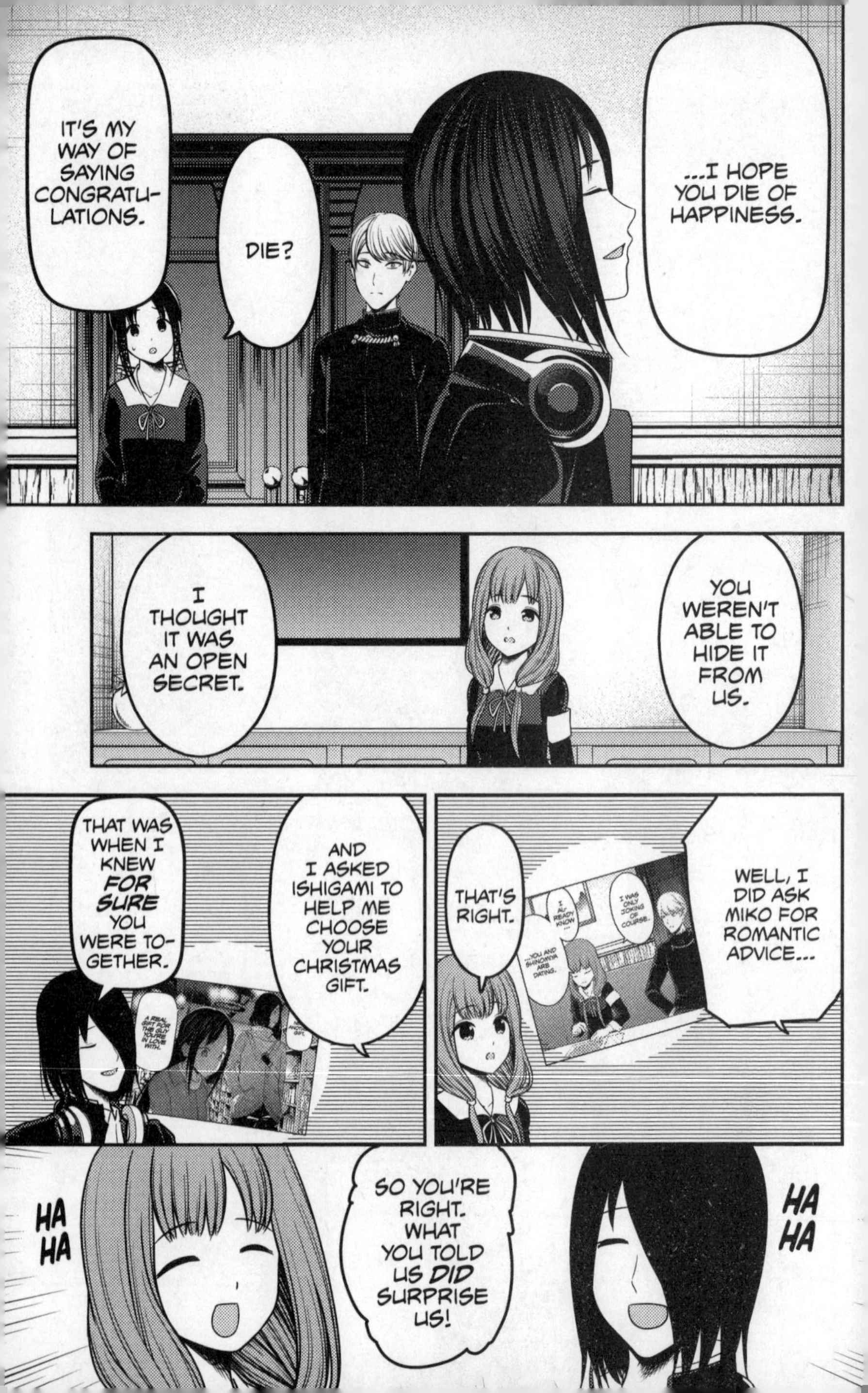
...I HOPE YOU DIE OF HAPPINESS.
DIE?
IT'S MY WAY OF SAYING CONGRATULATIONS.
YOU WEREN'T ABLE TO HIDE IT FROM US.
I THOUGHT IT WAS AN OPEN SECRET.
WELL, I DID ASK MIKO FOR ROMANTIC ADVICE...
I WAS ONLY JOKING OF COURSE.
I ALREADY KNOW...
...YOU AND SHINOMIYA ARE DATING.
THAT'S RIGHT.
AND I ASKED ISHIGAMI TO HELP ME CHOOSE YOUR CHRISTMAS GIFT.
A REAL GIFT FOR THE GUY YOU'RE IN LOVE WITH.
THAT WAS WHEN I KNEW *FOR SURE* YOU WERE TOGETHER.
HA HA
SO YOU'RE RIGHT. WHAT YOU TOLD US *DID* SURPRISE US!
HA HA

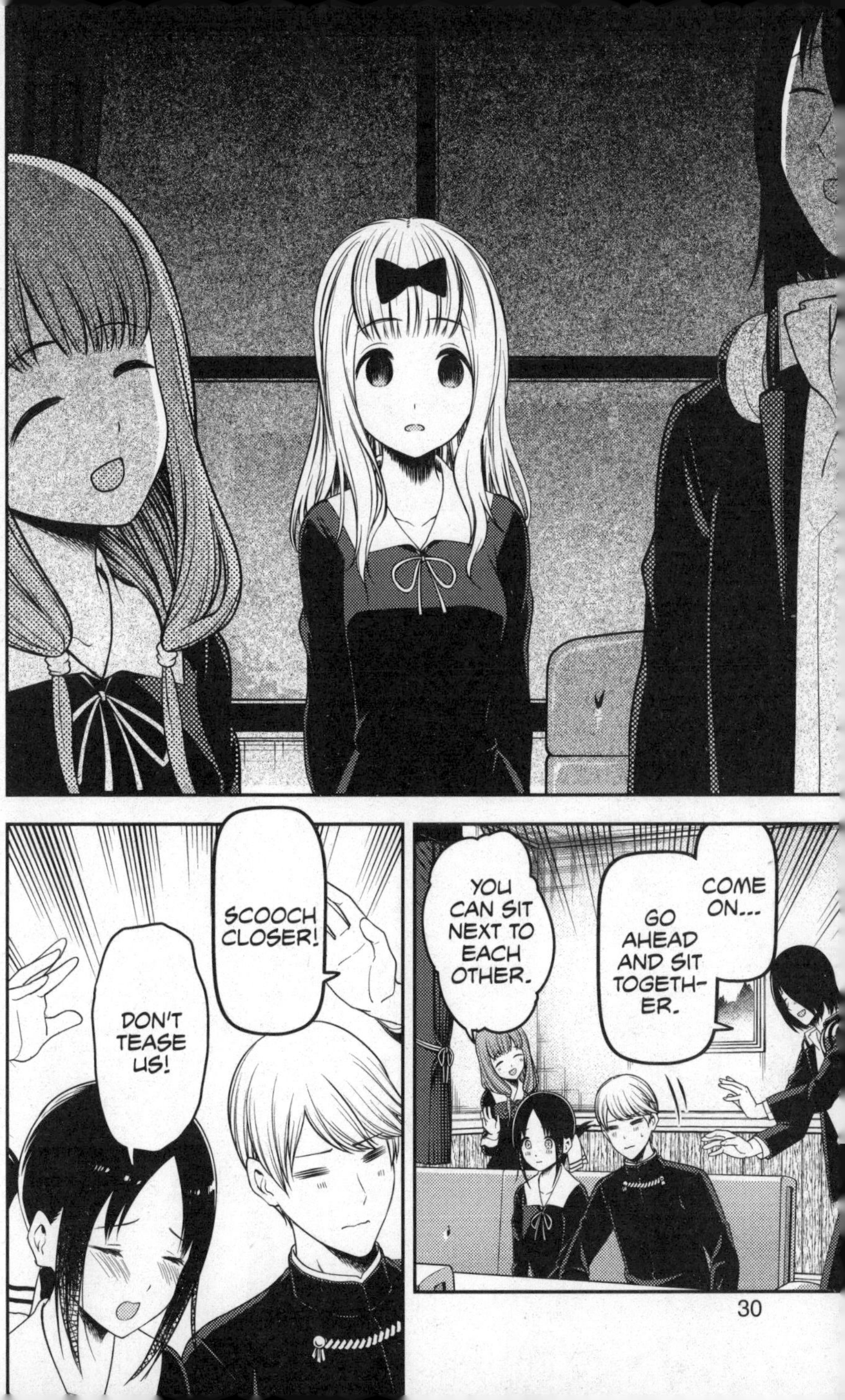
COME ON... GO AHEAD AND SIT TOGETH-ER.
YOU CAN SIT NEXT TO EACH OTHER.
SCOOCH CLOSER!
DON'T TEASE US!

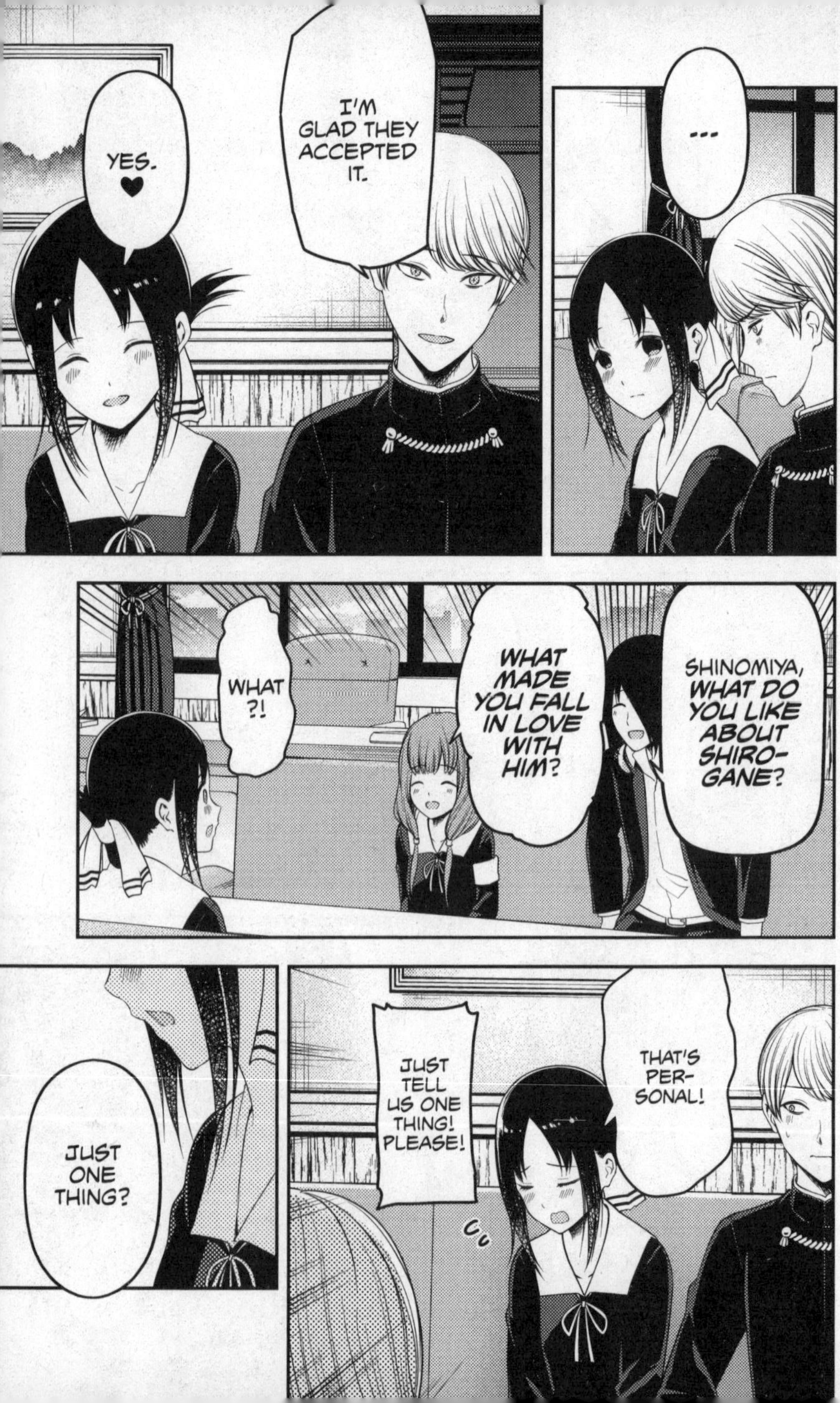
...
I'M GLAD THEY ACCEPTED IT.
YES. ♥
SHINOMIYA, WHAT DO YOU LIKE ABOUT SHIRO-GANE?
WHAT MADE YOU FALL IN LOVE WITH HIM?
WHAT ?!
THAT'S PER-SONAL!
JUST TELL US ONE THING! PLEASE!
JUST ONE THING?

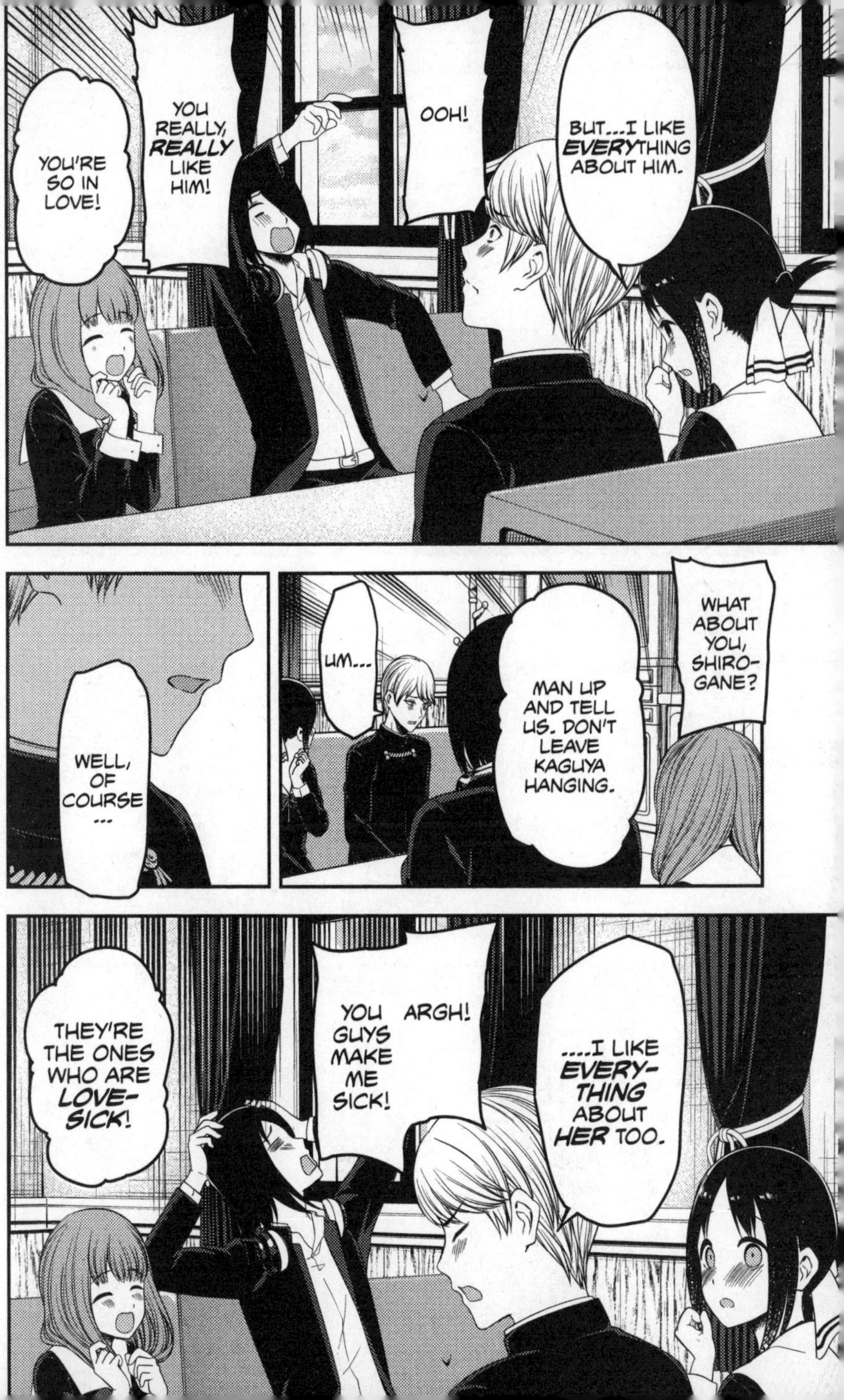
BUT...I LIKE EVERYTHING ABOUT HIM.
OOH!
YOU REALLY, REALLY LIKE HIM!
YOU'RE SO IN LOVE!
WHAT ABOUT YOU, SHIROGANE?
MAN UP AND TELL US. DON'T LEAVE KAGUYA HANGING.
UM...
WELL, OF COURSE...
....I LIKE EVERYTHING ABOUT HER TOO.
ARGH!
YOU GUYS MAKE ME SICK!
THEY'RE THE ONES WHO ARE LOVESICK!

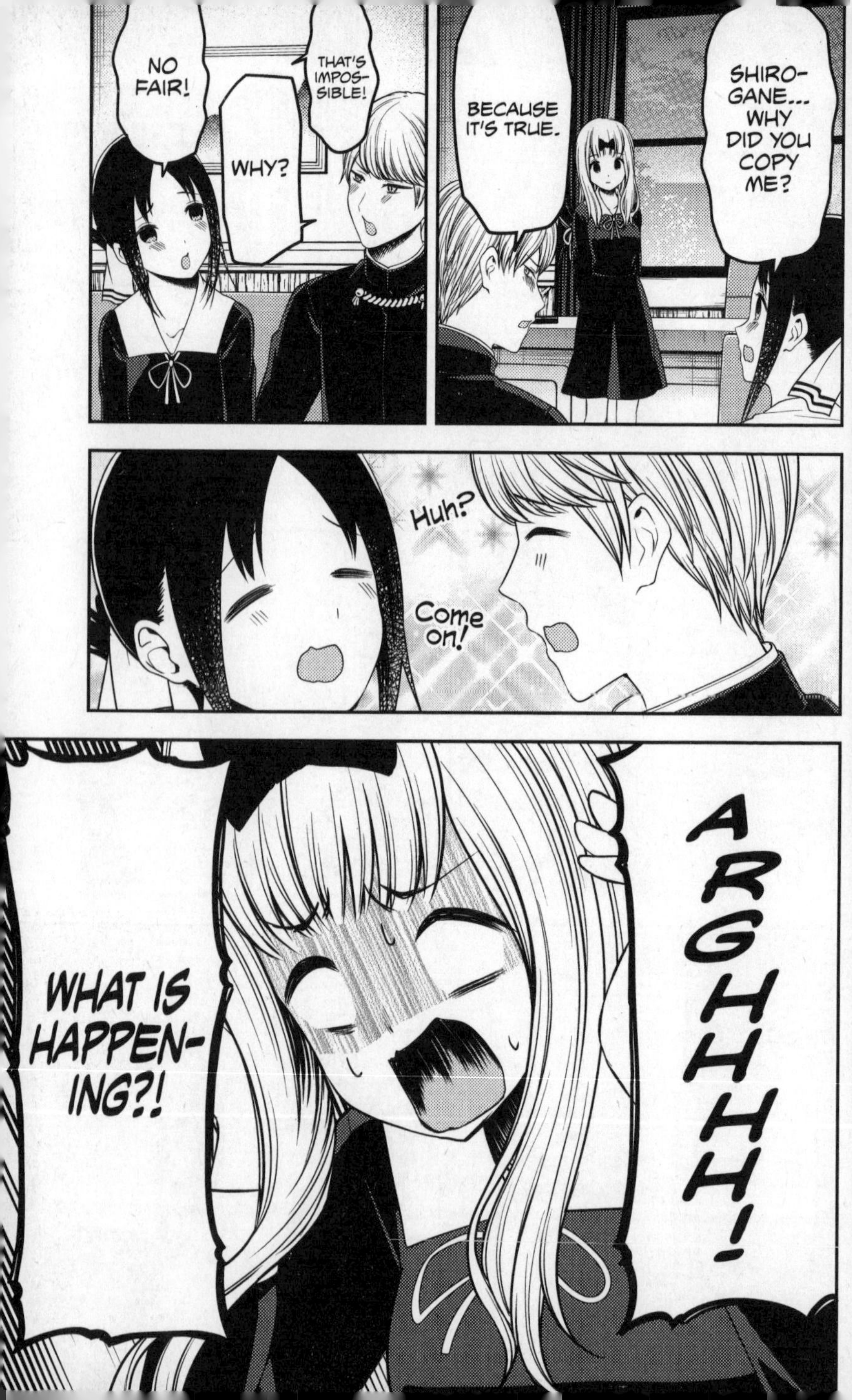
SHIRO-GANE... WHY DID YOU COPY ME?
BECAUSE IT'S TRUE.
THAT'S IMPOS-SIBLE!
NO FAIR!
WHY?
Huh?
Come on!
ARGHHH!
WHAT IS HAPPEN-ING?!

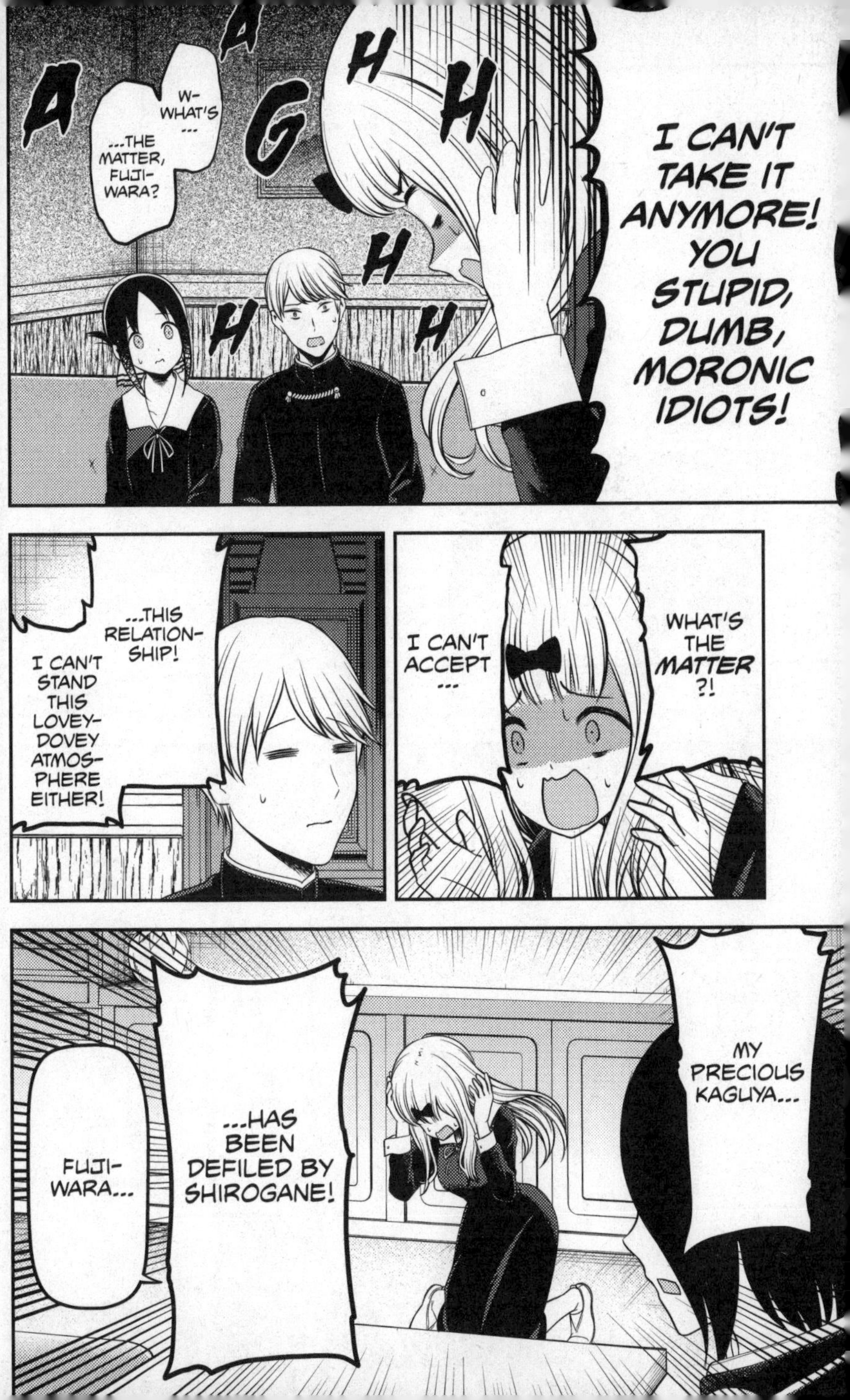

I CAN'T TAKE IT ANYMORE! YOU STUPID, DUMB, MORONIC IDIOTS!
AAGHHHHHH
W-WHAT'S... ...THE MATTER, FUJIWARA?
WHAT'S THE MATTER?!
I CAN'T ACCEPT...
...THIS RELATIONSHIP!
I CAN'T STAND THIS LOVEY-DOVEY ATMOSPHERE EITHER!
MY PRECIOUS KAGUYA...
...HAS BEEN DEFILED BY SHIROGANE!
FUJIWARA...

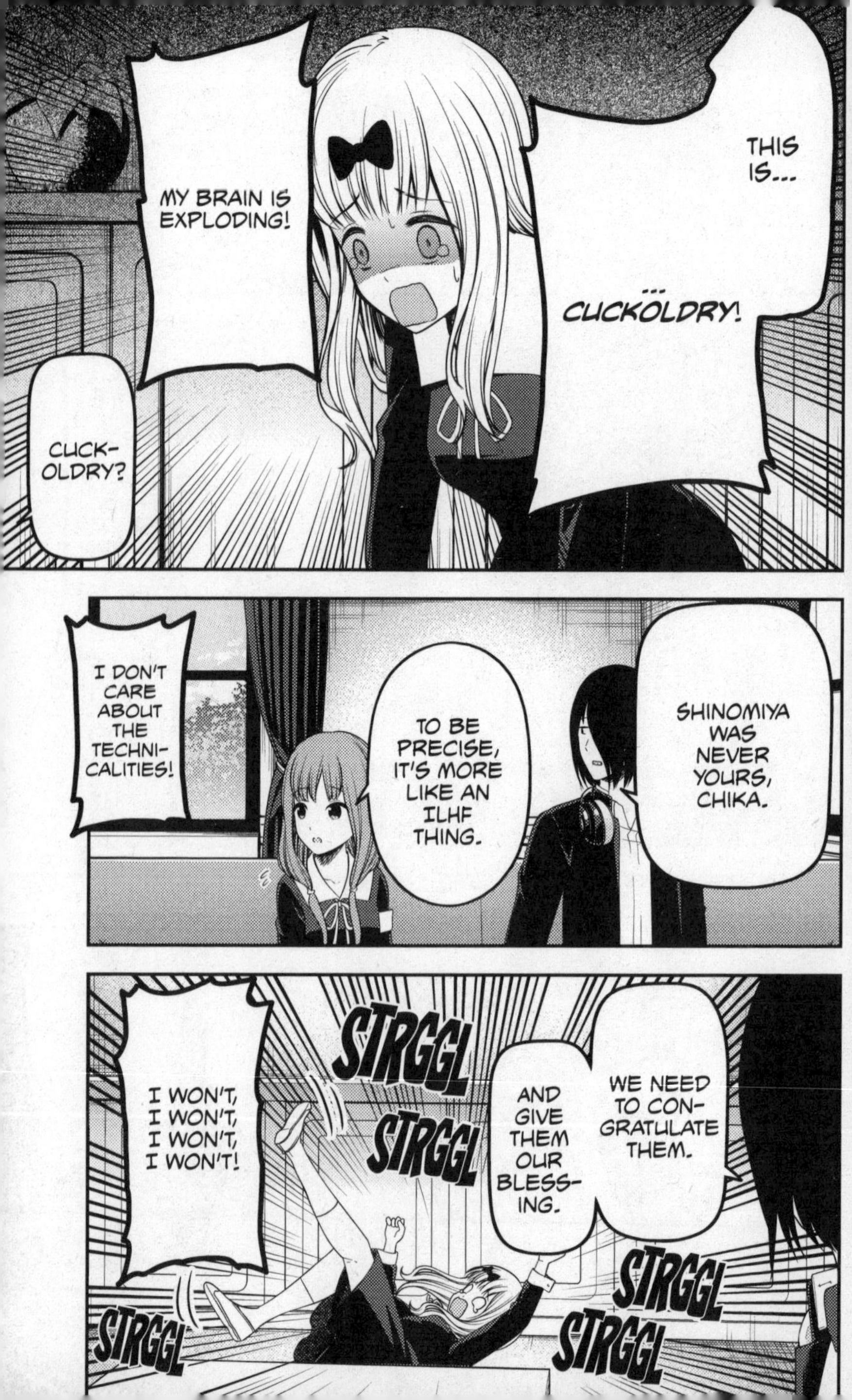
THIS IS...
...CUCKOLDRY!
MY BRAIN IS EXPLODING!
CUCKOLDRY?
SHINOMIYA WAS NEVER YOURS, CHIKA.
TO BE PRECISE, IT'S MORE LIKE AN ILHF THING.
I DON'T CARE ABOUT THE TECHNICALITIES!
WE NEED TO CONGRATULATE THEM.
AND GIVE THEM OUR BLESSING.
STRGGL
STRGGL
STRGGL
STRGGL
I WON'T, I WON'T, I WON'T, I WON'T!
STRGGL

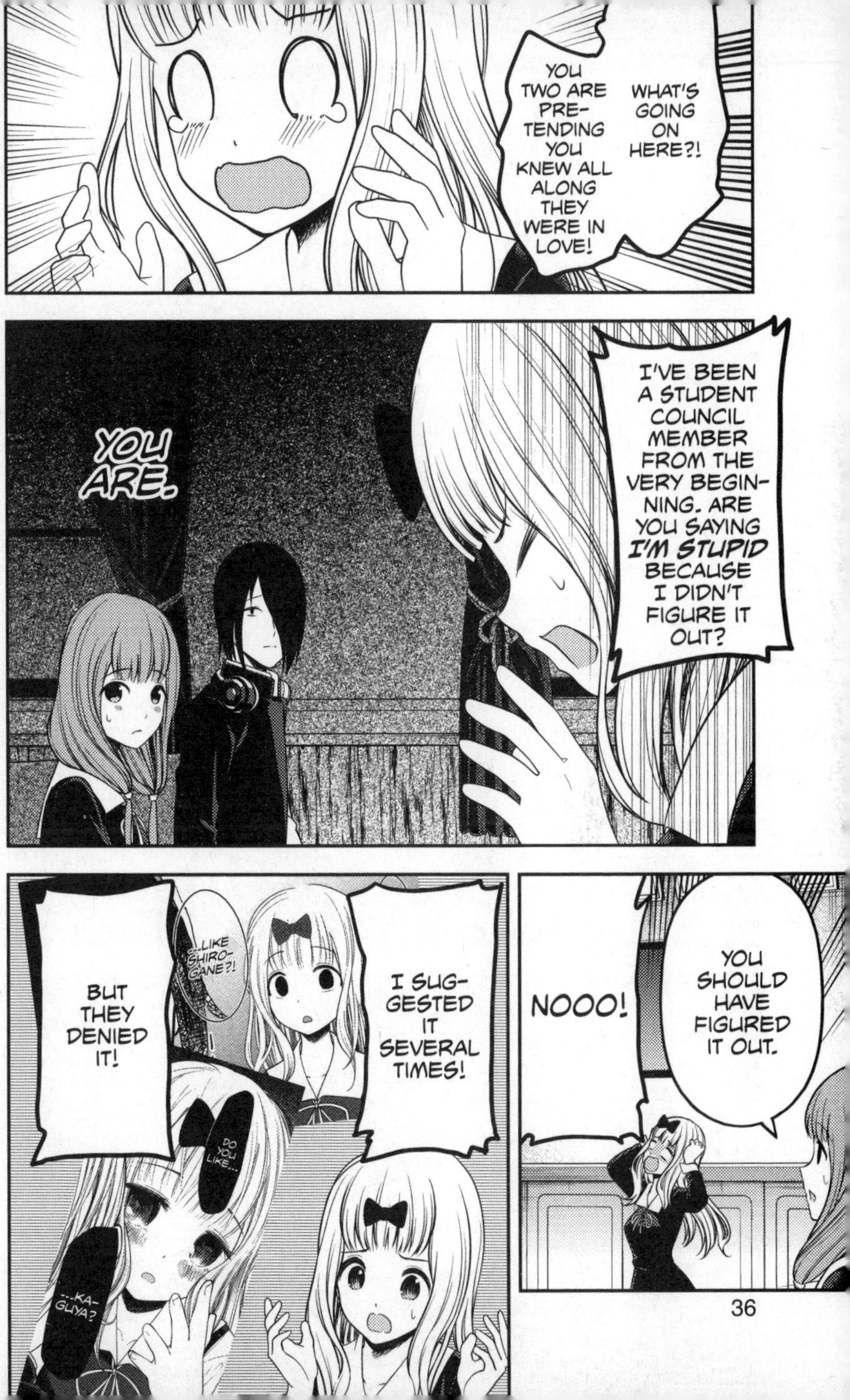
WHAT'S GOING ON HERE?!
YOU TWO ARE PRETENDING YOU KNEW ALL ALONG THEY WERE IN LOVE!
I'VE BEEN A STUDENT COUNCIL MEMBER FROM THE VERY BEGINNING. ARE YOU SAYING *I'M STUPID* BECAUSE I DIDN'T FIGURE IT OUT?
YOU ARE.
YOU SHOULD HAVE FIGURED IT OUT.
NOOO!
I SUGGESTED IT SEVERAL TIMES!
...LIKE SHIROGANE?!
BUT THEY DENIED IT!
DO YOU LIKE...
...KAGUYA?

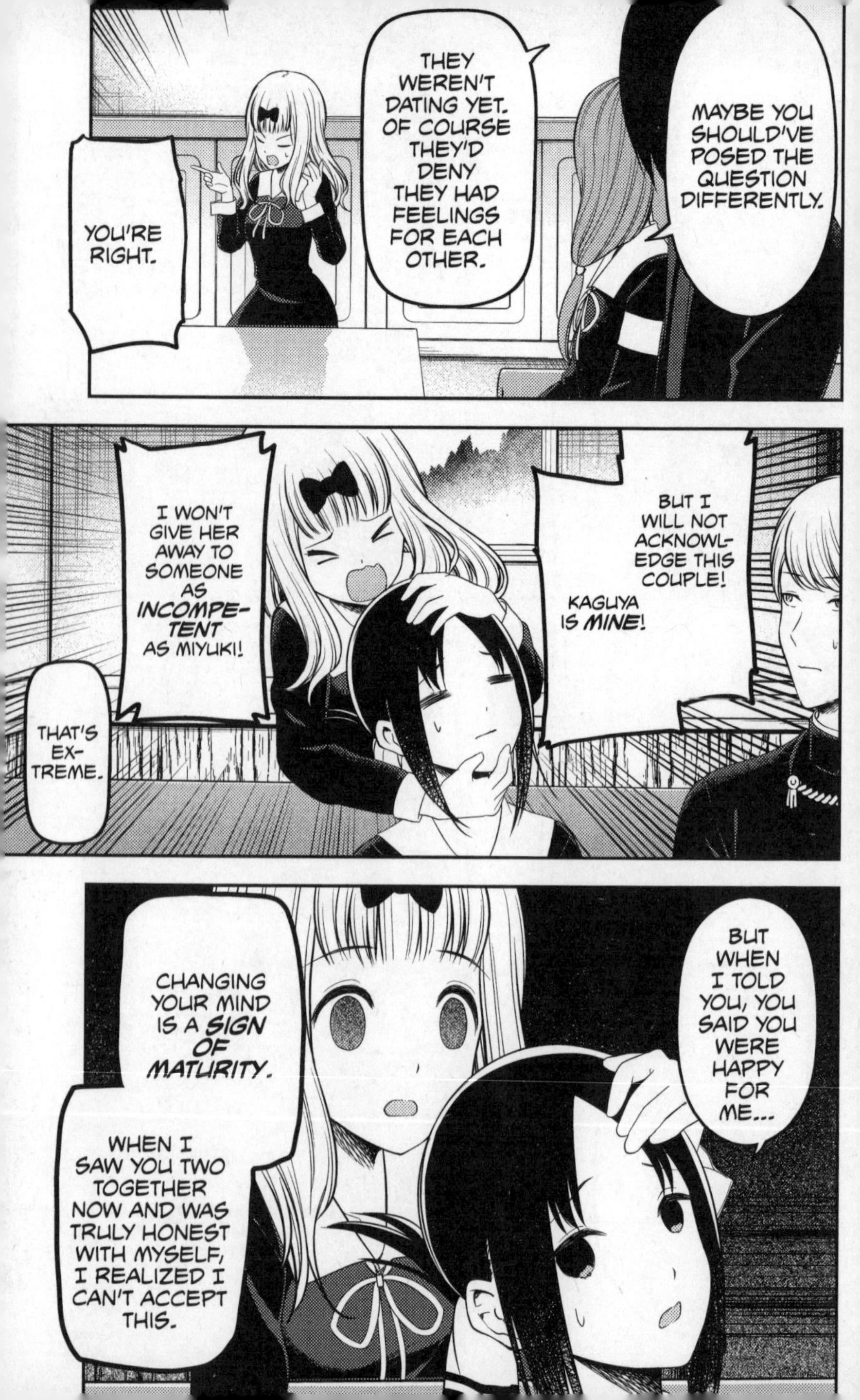
MAYBE YOU SHOULD'VE POSED THE QUESTION DIFFERENTLY.
THEY WEREN'T DATING YET. OF COURSE THEY'D DENY THEY HAD FEELINGS FOR EACH OTHER.
YOU'RE RIGHT.
BUT I WILL NOT ACKNOWLEDGE THIS COUPLE!
KAGUYA IS *MINE*!
I WON'T GIVE HER AWAY TO SOMEONE AS *INCOMPETENT* AS MIYUKI!
THAT'S EXTREME.
BUT WHEN I TOLD YOU, YOU SAID YOU WERE HAPPY FOR ME...
CHANGING YOUR MIND IS A *SIGN OF MATURITY*.
WHEN I SAW YOU TWO TOGETHER NOW AND WAS TRULY HONEST WITH MYSELF, I REALIZED I CAN'T ACCEPT THIS.

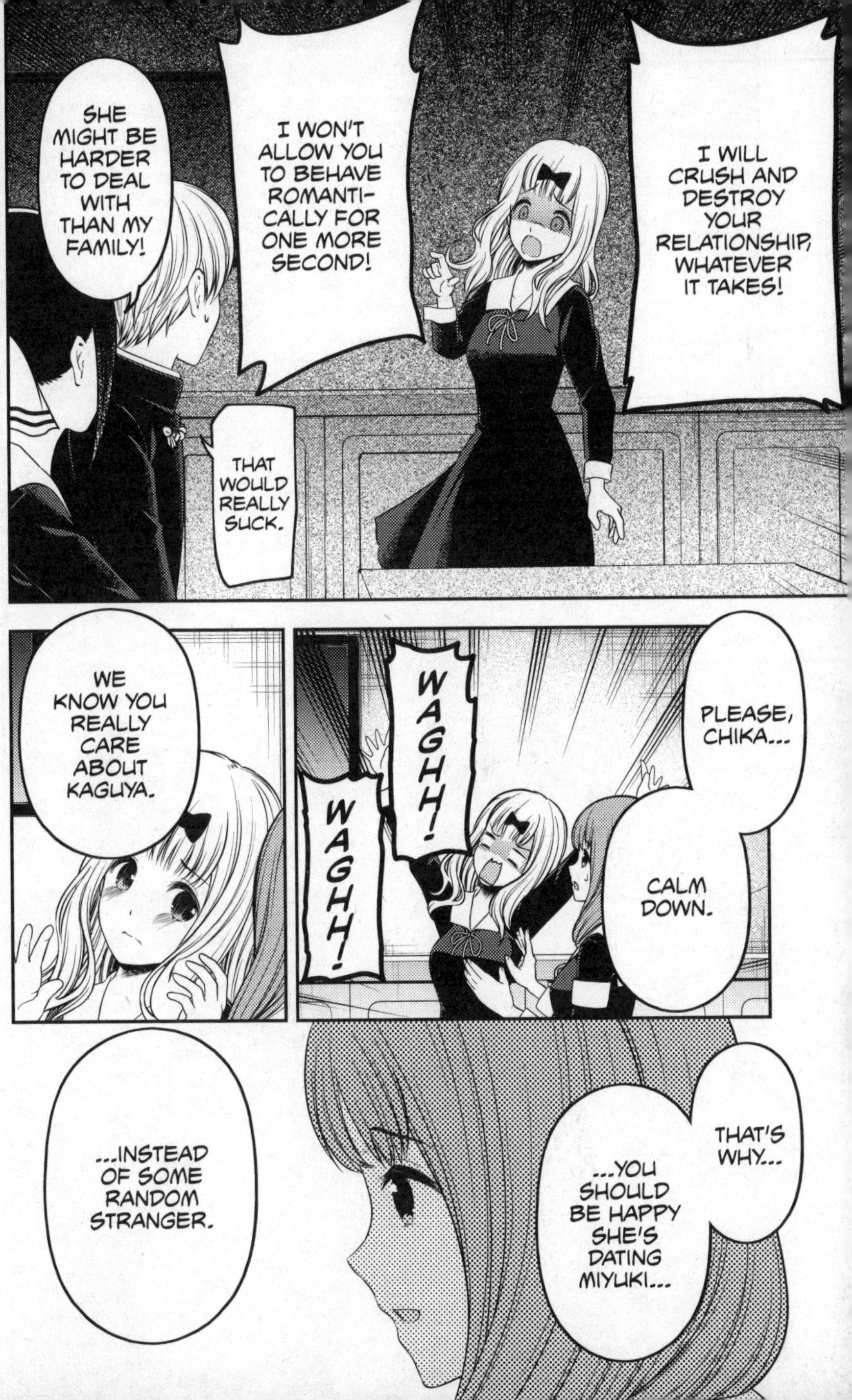
I WILL CRUSH AND DESTROY YOUR RELATIONSHIP, WHATEVER IT TAKES!
I WON'T ALLOW YOU TO BEHAVE ROMANTI-CALLY FOR ONE MORE SECOND!
SHE MIGHT BE HARDER TO DEAL WITH THAN MY FAMILY!
THAT WOULD REALLY SUCK.
PLEASE, CHIKA...
WAGHH!
CALM DOWN.
WAGHH!
WE KNOW YOU REALLY CARE ABOUT KAGUYA.
THAT'S WHY...
...YOU SHOULD BE HAPPY SHE'S DATING MIYUKI...
...INSTEAD OF SOME RANDOM STRANGER.

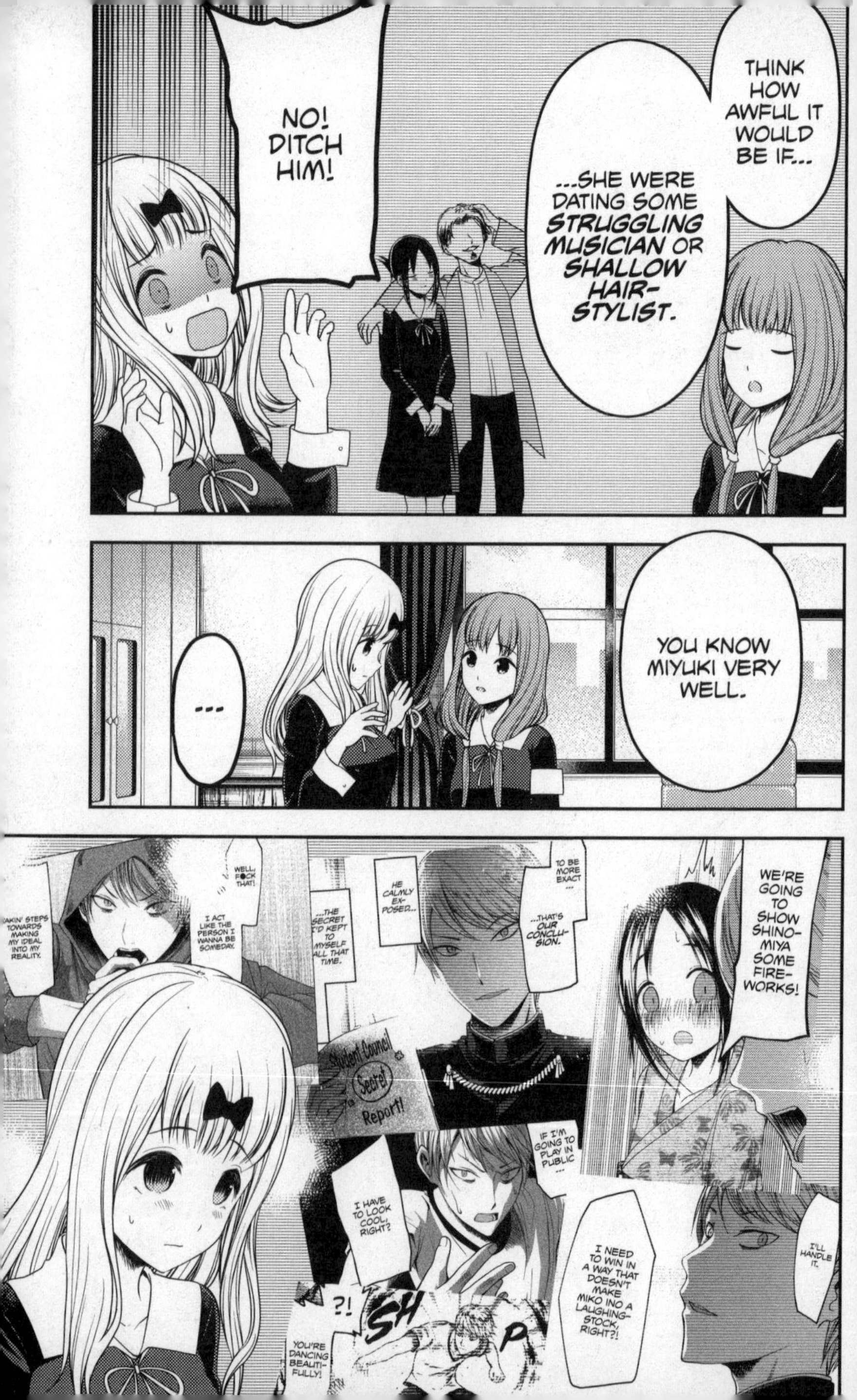
THINK HOW AWFUL IT WOULD BE IF...
...SHE WERE DATING SOME STRUGGLING MUSICIAN OR SHALLOW HAIR-STYLIST.
NO! DITCH HIM!
YOU KNOW MIYUKI VERY WELL.
...
WE'RE GOING TO SHOW SHINO-MIYA SOME FIRE-WORKS!
TO BE MORE EXACT...
...THAT'S OUR CONCLU-SION.
HE CALMLY EX-POSED...
...THE SECRET I'D KEPT TO MYSELF ALL THAT TIME.
WELL, F●CK THAT!
I ACT LIKE THE PERSON I WANNA BE SOMEDAY.
AKIN' STEPS TOWARDS MAKING MY IDEAL INTO MY REALITY.
Student Council Secret Report!
I'LL HANDLE IT.
I NEED TO WIN IN A WAY THAT DOESN'T MAKE MIKO INO A LAUGHING-STOCK, RIGHT?!
IF I'M GOING TO PLAY IN PUBLIC...
I HAVE TO LOOK COOL, RIGHT?
SH P
?!
YOU'RE DANCING BEAUTI-FULLY!

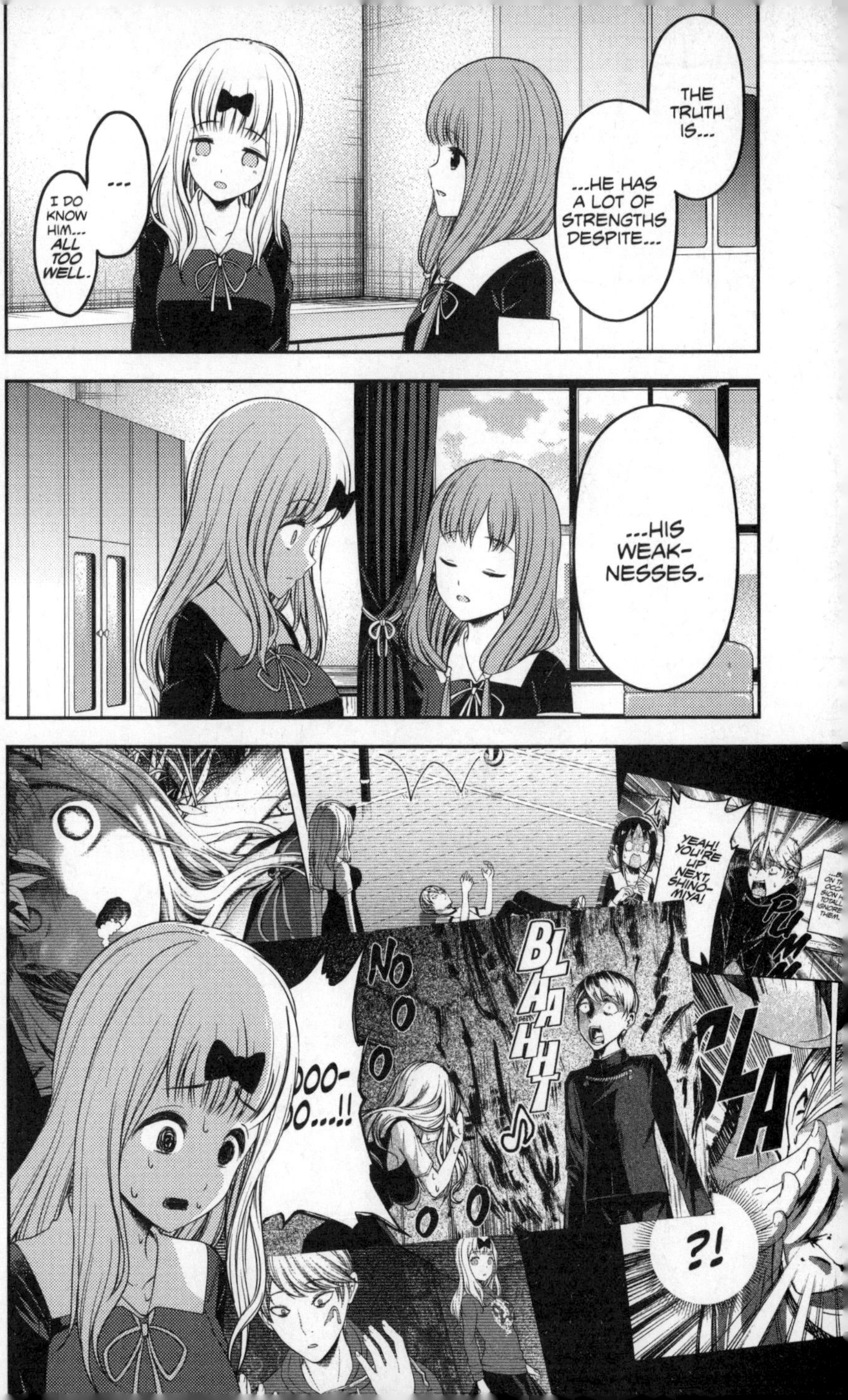
THE TRUTH IS...
...HE HAS A LOT OF STRENGTHS DESPITE...
...
I DO KNOW HIM... ALL TOO WELL.
...HIS WEAKNESSES.
YEAH! YOU'RE UP NEXT, SHINOMIYA!
BLAAAHHT ♪
NOOOOOOO
?!

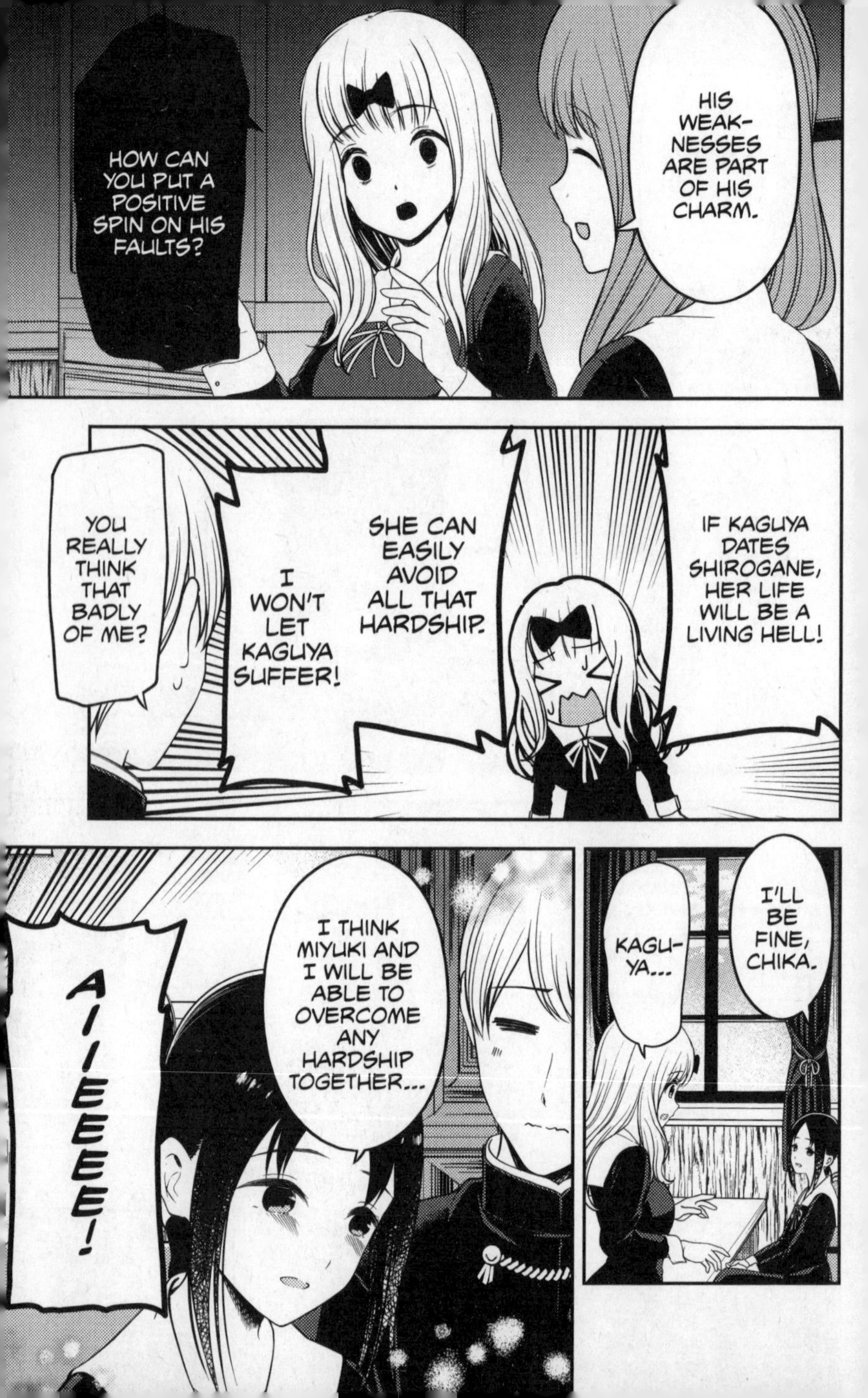
HIS WEAKNESSES ARE PART OF HIS CHARM.
HOW CAN YOU PUT A POSITIVE SPIN ON HIS FAULTS?
IF KAGUYA DATES SHIROGANE, HER LIFE WILL BE A LIVING HELL!
SHE CAN EASILY AVOID ALL THAT HARDSHIP.
I WON'T LET KAGUYA SUFFER!
YOU REALLY THINK THAT BADLY OF ME?
I'LL BE FINE, CHIKA.
KAGUYA...
I THINK MIYUKI AND I WILL BE ABLE TO OVERCOME ANY HARDSHIP TOGETHER...
AIIEEEEE!

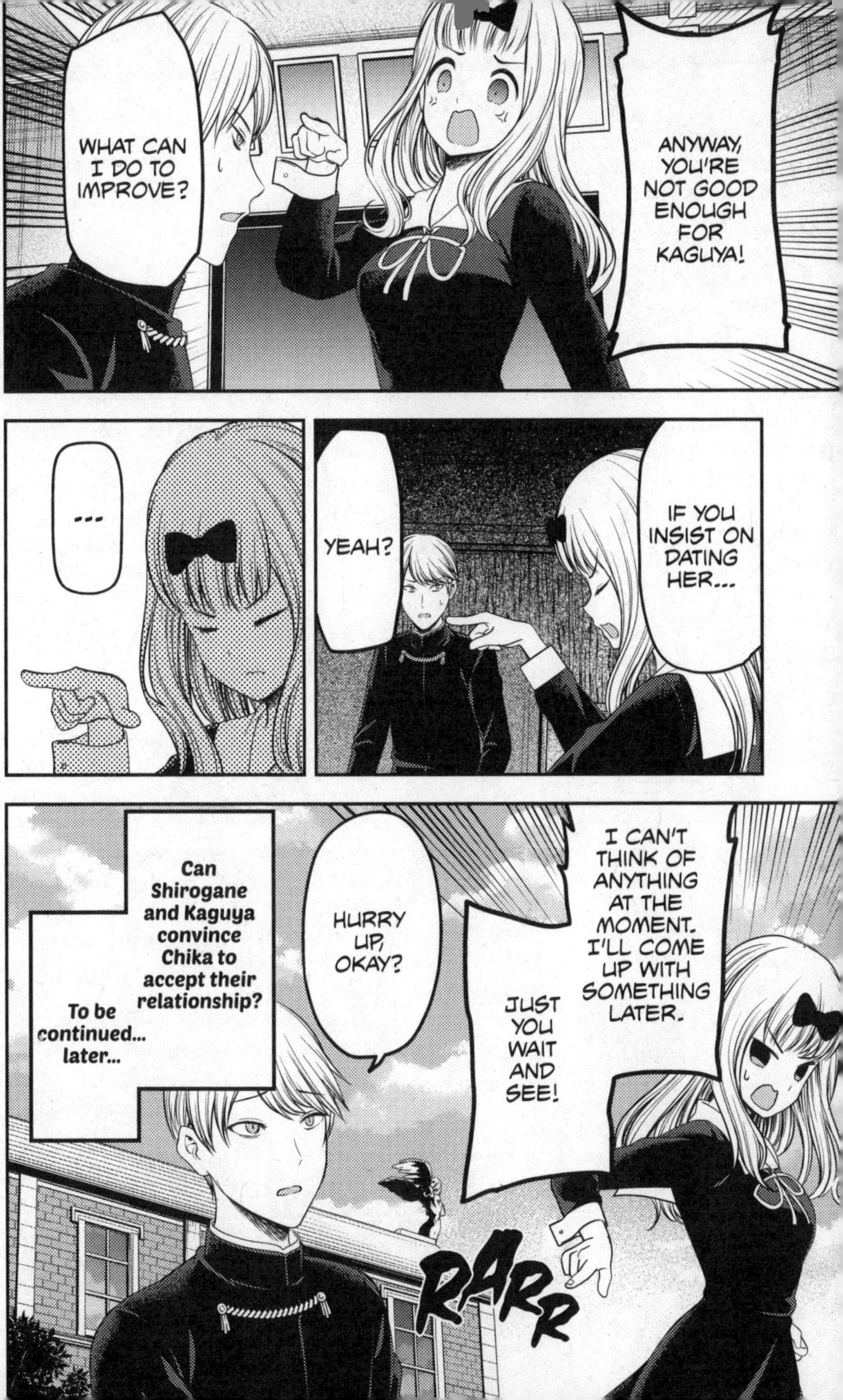
ANYWAY, YOU'RE NOT GOOD ENOUGH FOR KAGUYA!
WHAT CAN I DO TO IMPROVE?
IF YOU INSIST ON DATING HER...
YEAH?
...
I CAN'T THINK OF ANYTHING AT THE MOMENT. I'LL COME UP WITH SOMETHING LATER.
JUST YOU WAIT AND SEE!
RARR
HURRY UP, OKAY?
Can Shirogane and Kaguya convince Chika to accept their relationship?
To be continued... later...

Glossary (1)

• Cuckoldry

Having a sexual relationship with a man's lover or wife. Typical of the "warped relationship" genre. Your brain will turn to mush if you read too many stories from this genre.

• ILHF

Short for "I liked him/her first." Refers to the sense of loss you feel when the person you love (but aren't dating) starts to date someone else. Many find this genre more relatable than cuckoldry, because it's such a common experience.

KAGUYA-SAMA
LOVE IS WAR

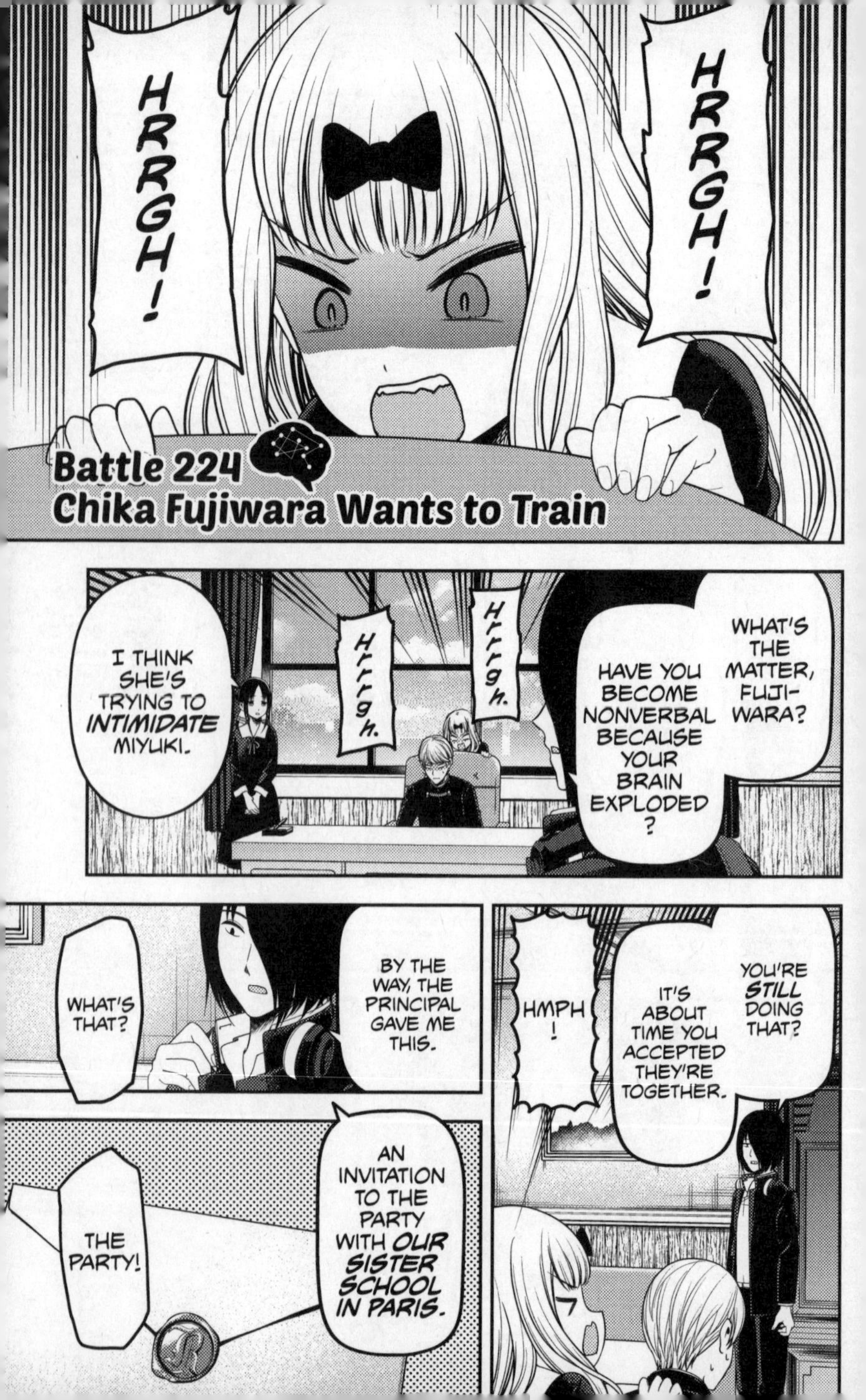
HRRGH!
HRRGH!
Battle 224 Chika Fujiwara Wants to Train
WHAT'S THE MATTER, FUJI-WARA?
HAVE YOU BECOME NONVERBAL BECAUSE YOUR BRAIN EXPLODED?
Hrrrgh.
Hrrrgh.
I THINK SHE'S TRYING TO INTIMIDATE MIYUKI.
YOU'RE STILL DOING THAT?
IT'S ABOUT TIME YOU ACCEPTED THEY'RE TOGETHER.
HMPH!
BY THE WAY, THE PRINCIPAL GAVE ME THIS.
WHAT'S THAT?
AN INVITATION TO THE PARTY WITH OUR SISTER SCHOOL IN PARIS.
THE PARTY!

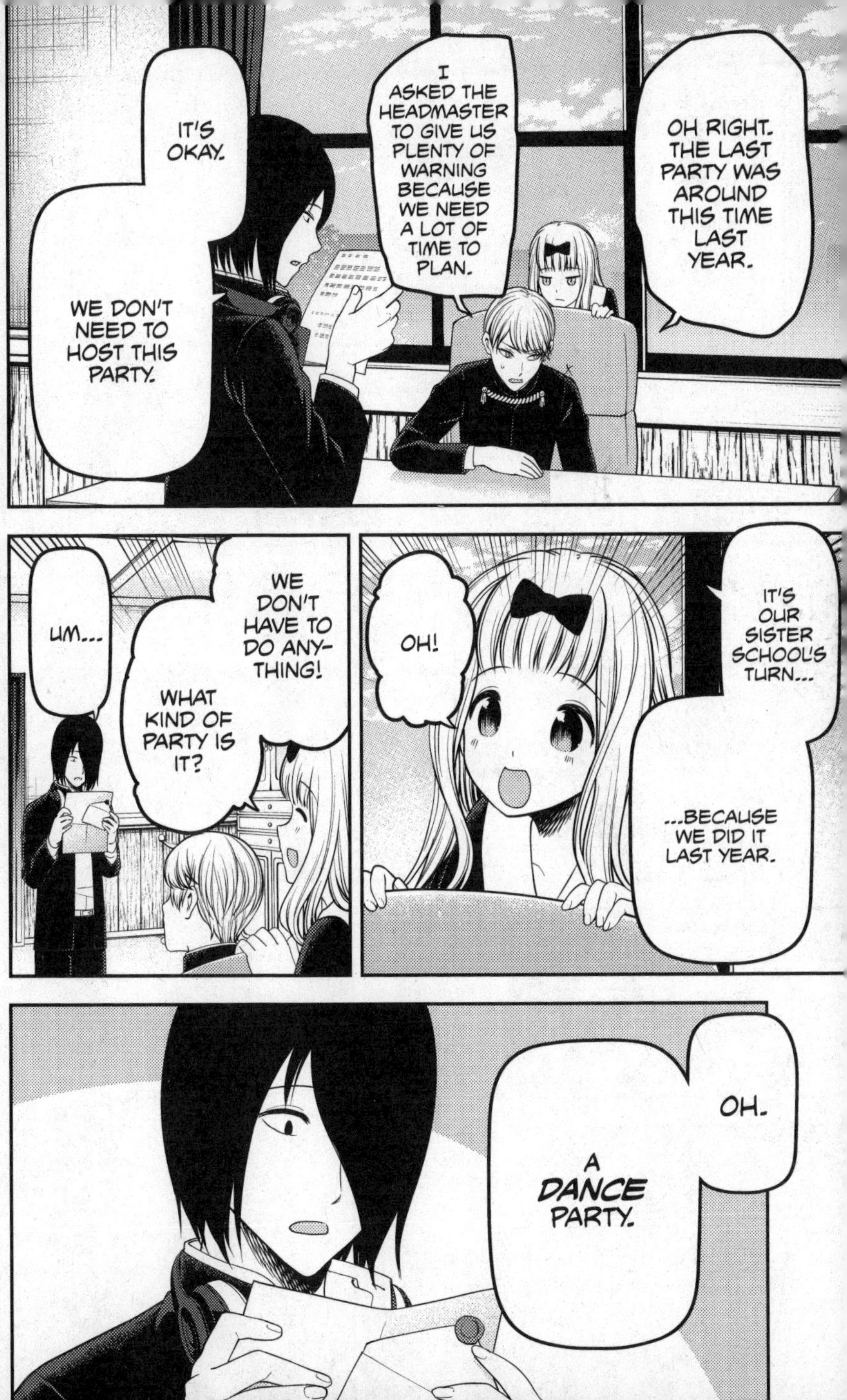
OH RIGHT. THE LAST PARTY WAS AROUND THIS TIME LAST YEAR.
I ASKED THE HEADMASTER TO GIVE US PLENTY OF WARNING BECAUSE WE NEED A LOT OF TIME TO PLAN.
IT'S OKAY.
WE DON'T NEED TO HOST THIS PARTY.
IT'S OUR SISTER SCHOOL'S TURN...
...BECAUSE WE DID IT LAST YEAR.
OH!
WE DON'T HAVE TO DO ANY-THING!
WHAT KIND OF PARTY IS IT?
UM...
OH.
A *DANCE* PARTY.

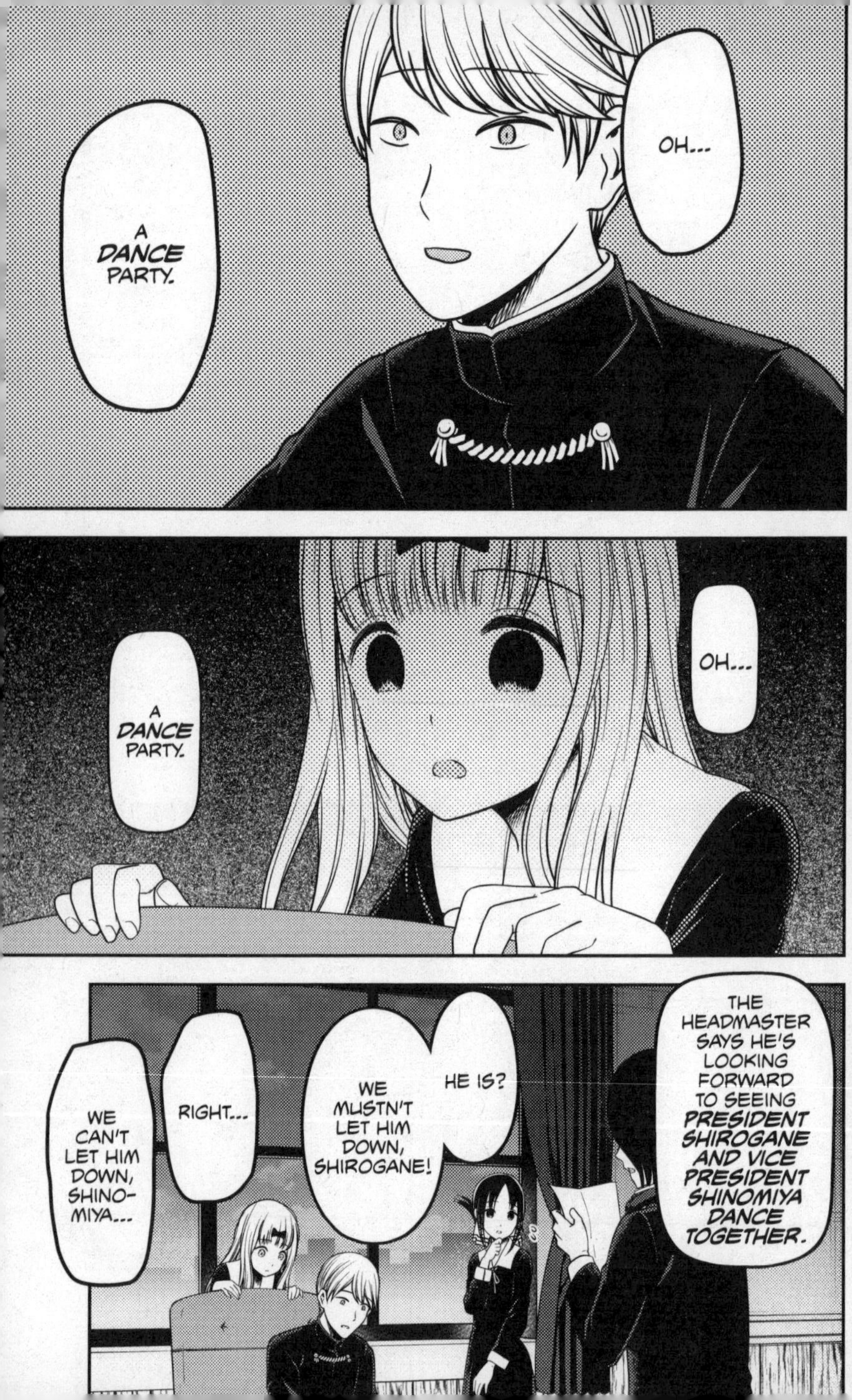
OH...
A DANCE PARTY.
OH...
A DANCE PARTY.
THE HEADMASTER SAYS HE'S LOOKING FORWARD TO SEEING PRESIDENT SHIROGANE AND VICE PRESIDENT SHINOMIYA DANCE TOGETHER.
HE IS?
WE MUSTN'T LET HIM DOWN, SHIROGANE!
RIGHT...
WE CAN'T LET HIM DOWN, SHINO-MIYA...

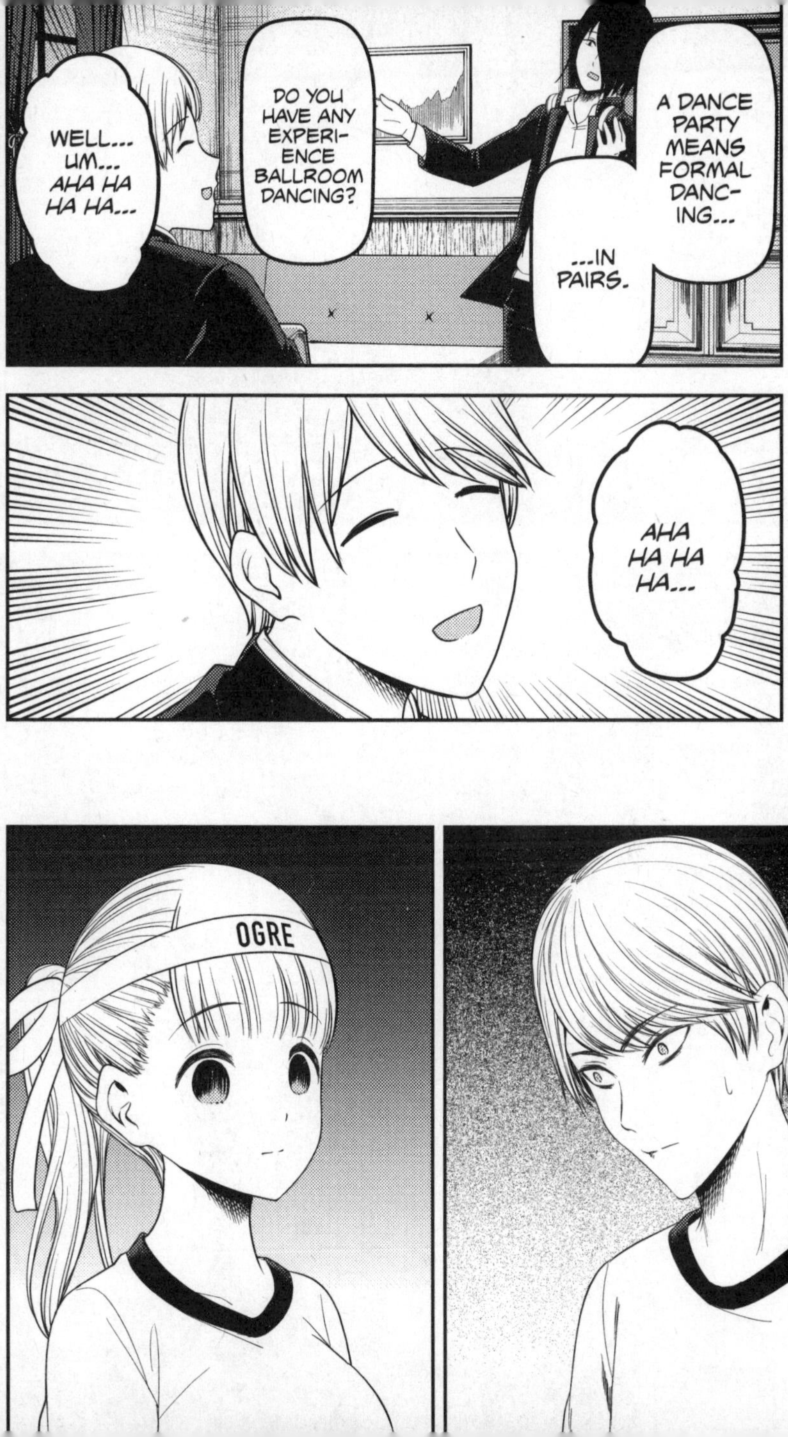
A DANCE PARTY MEANS FORMAL DANCING...
...IN PAIRS.
DO YOU HAVE ANY EXPERIENCE BALLROOM DANCING?
WELL... UM... AHA HA HA HA...
AHA HA HA HA...
OGRE

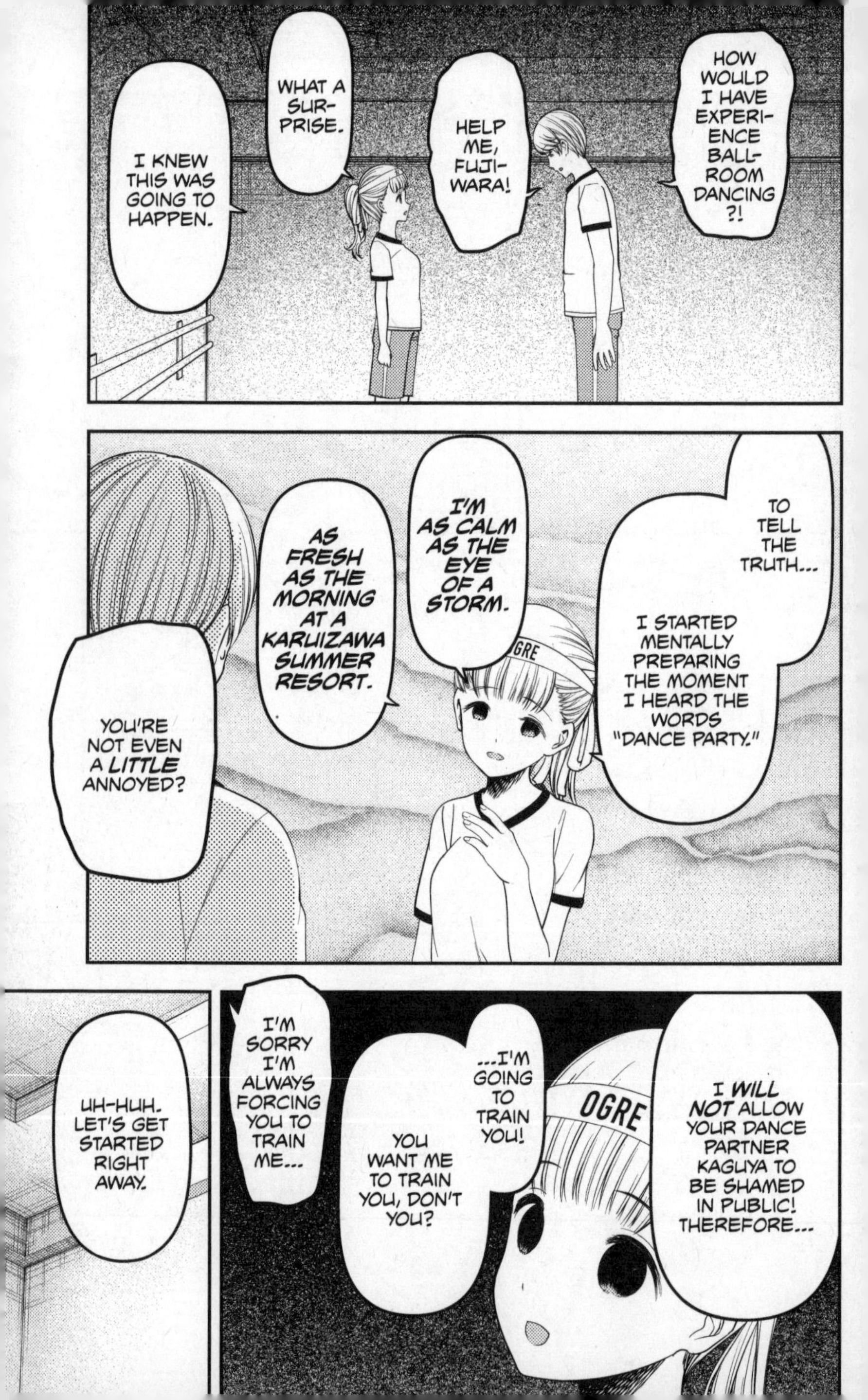
HOW WOULD I HAVE EXPERIENCE BALLROOM DANCING?!
HELP ME, FUJIWARA!
WHAT A SURPRISE.
I KNEW THIS WAS GOING TO HAPPEN.
TO TELL THE TRUTH...
I STARTED MENTALLY PREPARING THE MOMENT I HEARD THE WORDS "DANCE PARTY."
I'M AS CALM AS THE EYE OF A STORM.
AS FRESH AS THE MORNING AT A KARUIZAWA SUMMER RESORT.
OGRE
YOU'RE NOT EVEN A *LITTLE* ANNOYED?
I **WILL NOT** ALLOW YOUR DANCE PARTNER KAGUYA TO BE SHAMED IN PUBLIC! THEREFORE...
...I'M GOING TO TRAIN YOU!
OGRE
YOU WANT ME TO TRAIN YOU, DON'T YOU?
I'M SORRY I'M ALWAYS FORCING YOU TO TRAIN ME...
UH-HUH. LET'S GET STARTED RIGHT AWAY.

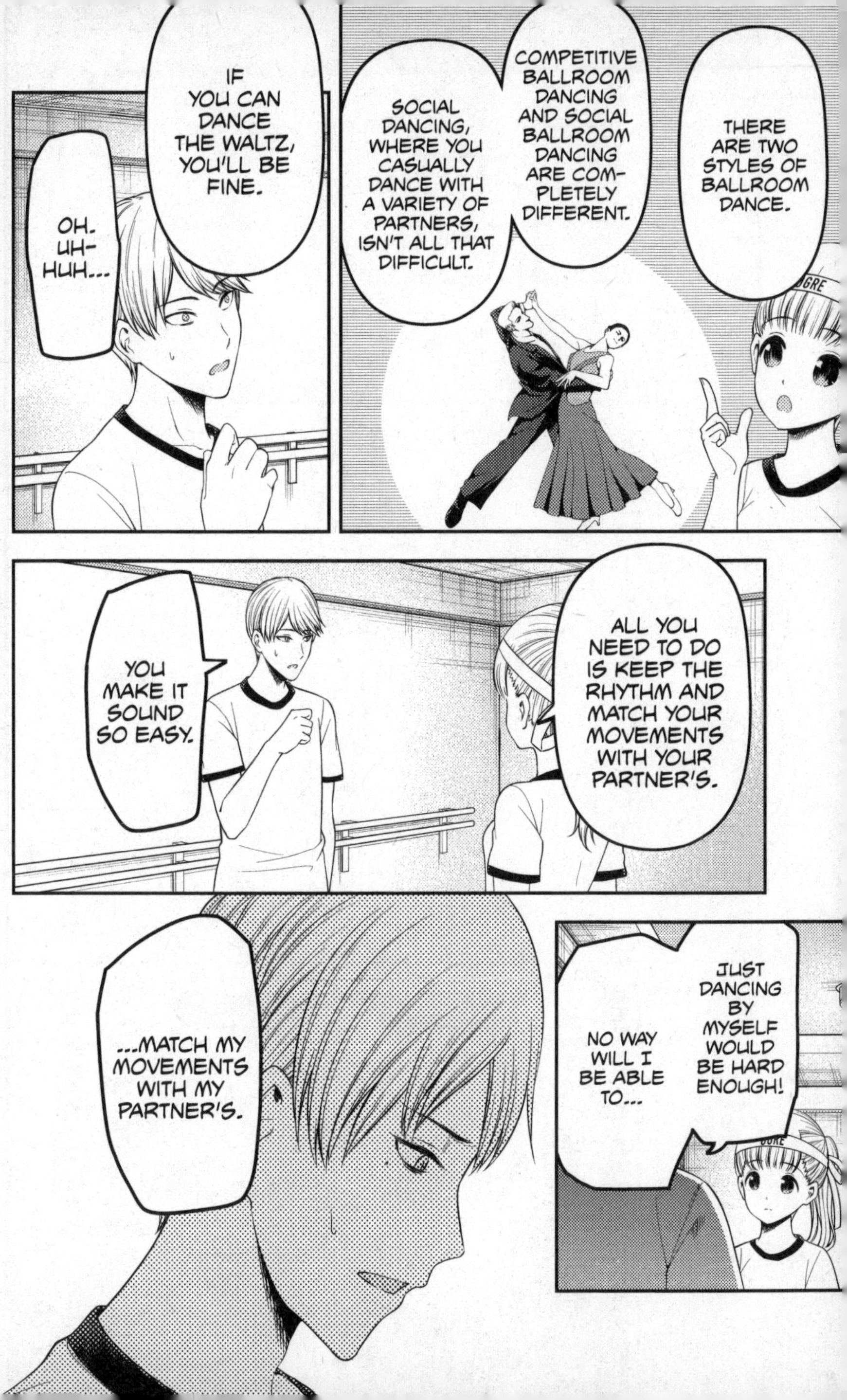
THERE ARE TWO STYLES OF BALLROOM DANCE.
COMPETITIVE BALLROOM DANCING AND SOCIAL BALLROOM DANCING ARE COMPLETELY DIFFERENT.
SOCIAL DANCING, WHERE YOU CASUALLY DANCE WITH A VARIETY OF PARTNERS, ISN'T ALL THAT DIFFICULT.
IF YOU CAN DANCE THE WALTZ, YOU'LL BE FINE.
OH. UH-HUH...
ALL YOU NEED TO DO IS KEEP THE RHYTHM AND MATCH YOUR MOVEMENTS WITH YOUR PARTNER'S.
YOU MAKE IT SOUND SO EASY.
JUST DANCING BY MYSELF WOULD BE HARD ENOUGH!
NO WAY WILL I BE ABLE TO...
...MATCH MY MOVEMENTS WITH MY PARTNER'S.

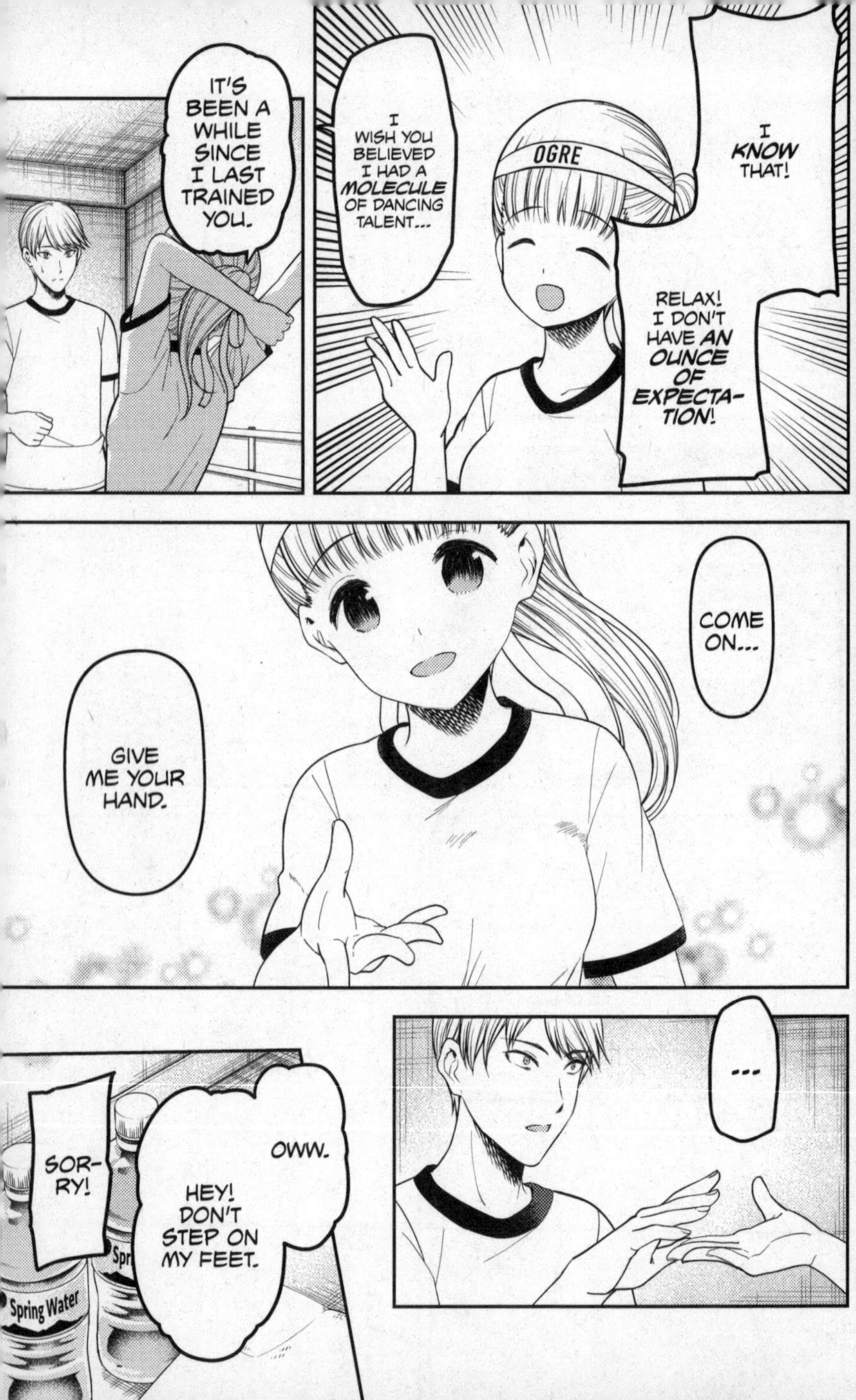
I *KNOW* THAT!
RELAX! I DON'T HAVE *AN OUNCE OF EXPECTATION!*
OGRE
I WISH YOU BELIEVED I HAD A *MOLECULE* OF DANCING TALENT...
IT'S BEEN A WHILE SINCE I LAST TRAINED YOU.
COME ON...
GIVE ME YOUR HAND.
...
OWW.
HEY! DON'T STEP ON MY FEET.
SOR-RY!
Spring Water

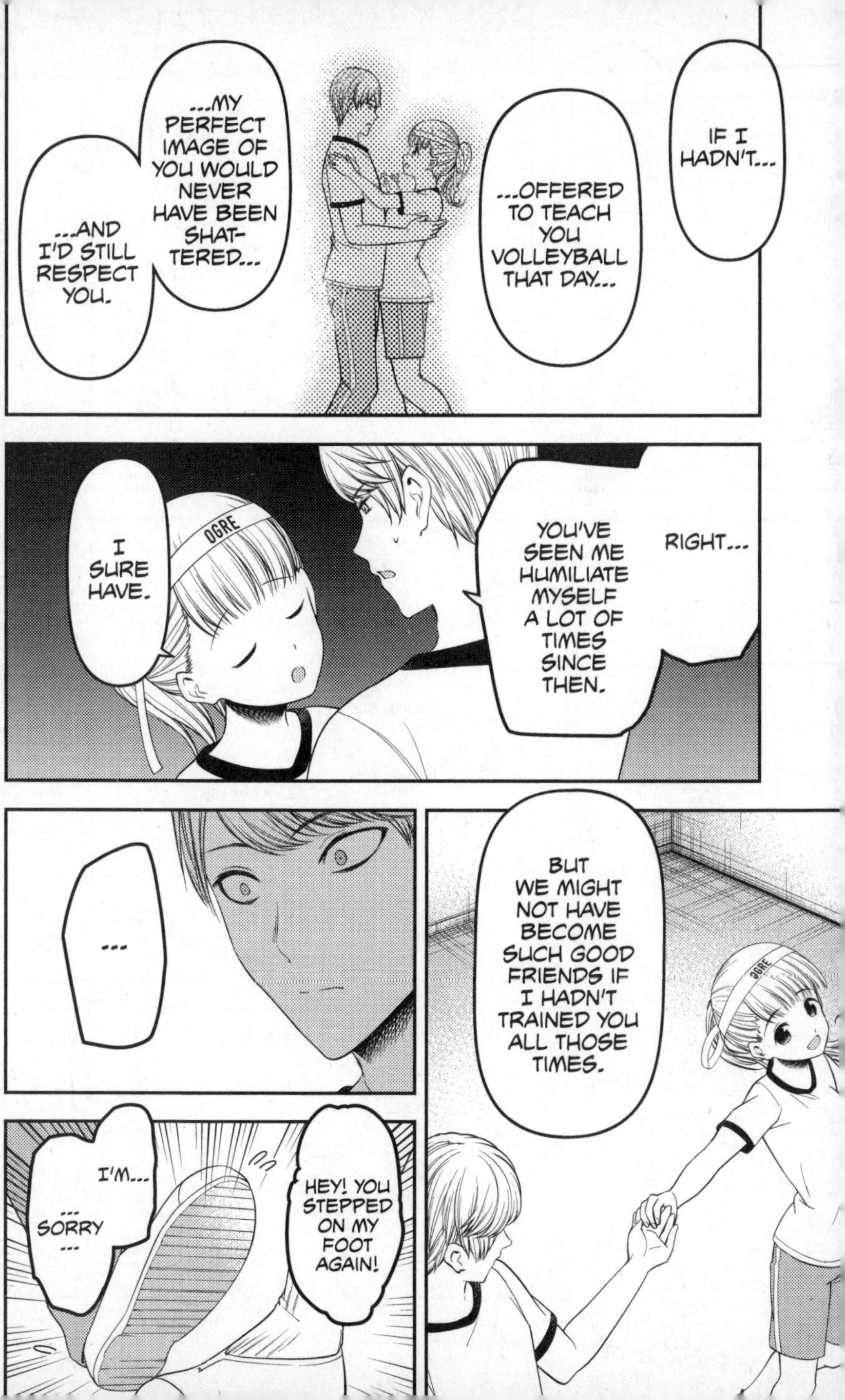
IF I HADN'T...
...OFFERED TO TEACH YOU VOLLEYBALL THAT DAY...
...MY PERFECT IMAGE OF YOU WOULD NEVER HAVE BEEN SHAT- TERED...
...AND I'D STILL RESPECT YOU.
RIGHT...
YOU'VE SEEN ME HUMILIATE MYSELF A LOT OF TIMES SINCE THEN.
OGRE
I SURE HAVE.
BUT WE MIGHT NOT HAVE BECOME SUCH GOOD FRIENDS IF I HADN'T TRAINED YOU ALL THOSE TIMES.
OGRE
...
HEY! YOU STEPPED ON MY FOOT AGAIN!
I'M...
...SORRY...

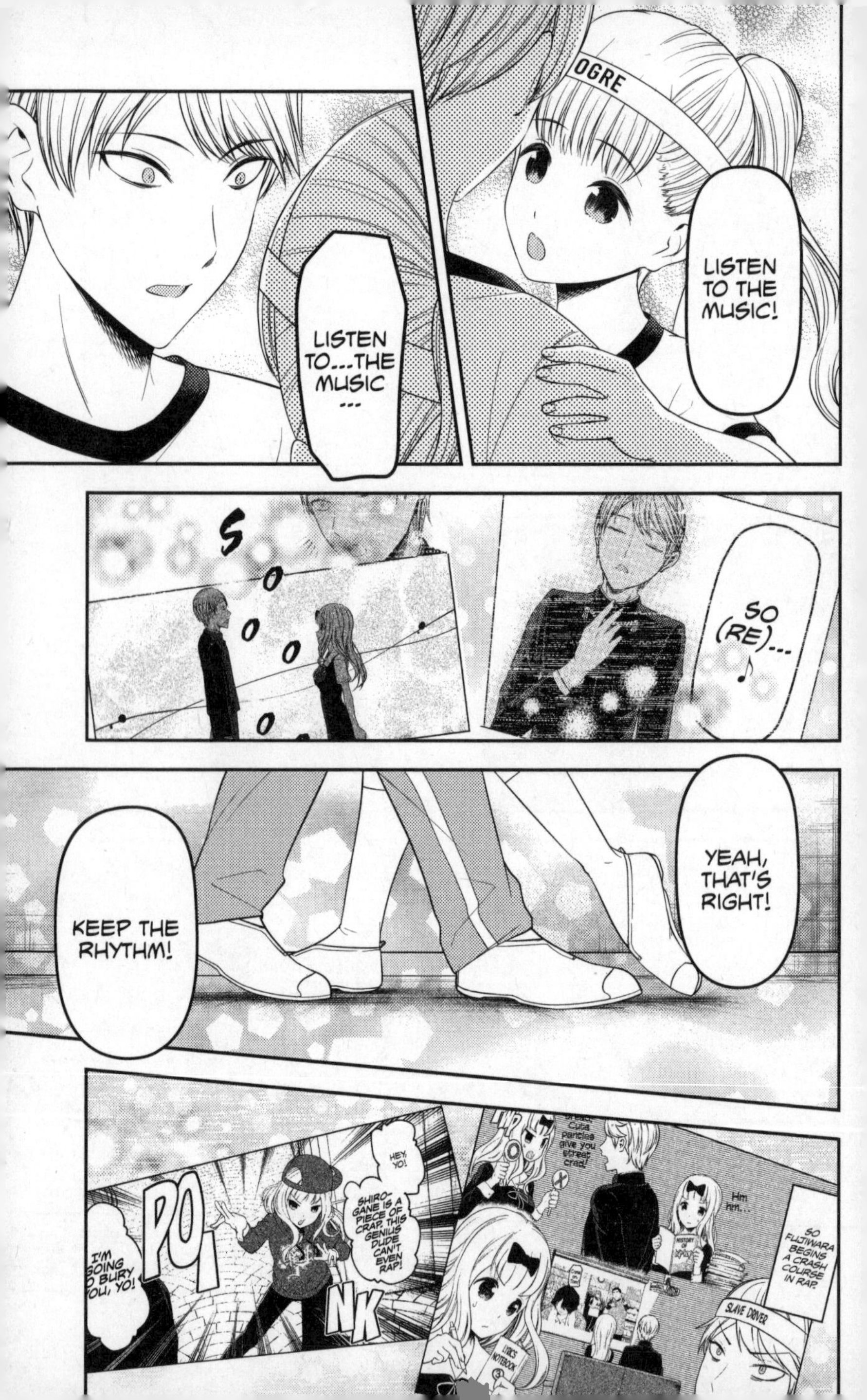
OGRE
LISTEN TO THE MUSIC!
LISTEN TO...THE MUSIC ...
SO (RE)... ♪
SOOOO
YEAH, THAT'S RIGHT!
KEEP THE RHYTHM!
SO FUJIWARA BEGINS A CRASH COURSE IN RAP.
Hm hm...
HISTORY OF
Cute particles give you street cred!
SLAVE DRIVER
LYRICS NOTEBOOK 3
HEY, YO!
SHIROGANE IS A PIECE OF CRAP. THIS GENIUS DUDE CAN'T EVEN RAP!
POINK
I'M GOING TO BURY YOU, YO!

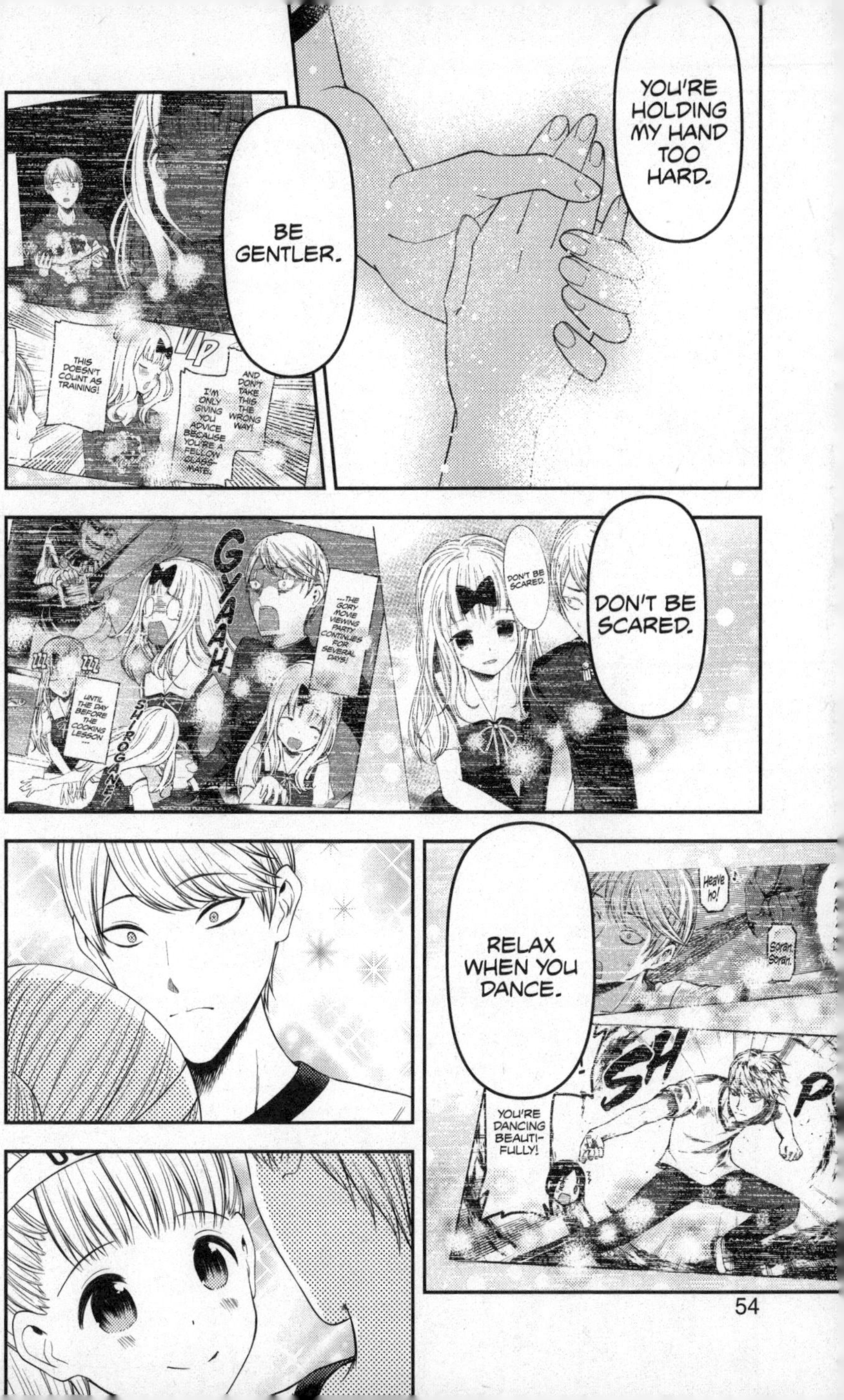
YOU'RE HOLDING MY HAND TOO HARD.
BE GENTLER.
AND DON'T TAKE THIS THE WRONG WAY!
I'M ONLY GIVING YOU ADVICE BECAUSE YOU'RE A FELLOW CLASSMATE.
THIS DOESN'T COUNT AS TRAINING!
DON'T BE SCARED.
DON'T BE SCARED.
...THE GORY MOVIE VIEWING PARTY CONTINUES FOR SEVERAL DAYS!
GYAAAH
SHIROGANE!
UNTIL THE DAY BEFORE THE COOKING LESSON...
RELAX WHEN YOU DANCE.
Heave ho!
Soran, Soran.
YOU'RE DANCING BEAUTIFULLY!

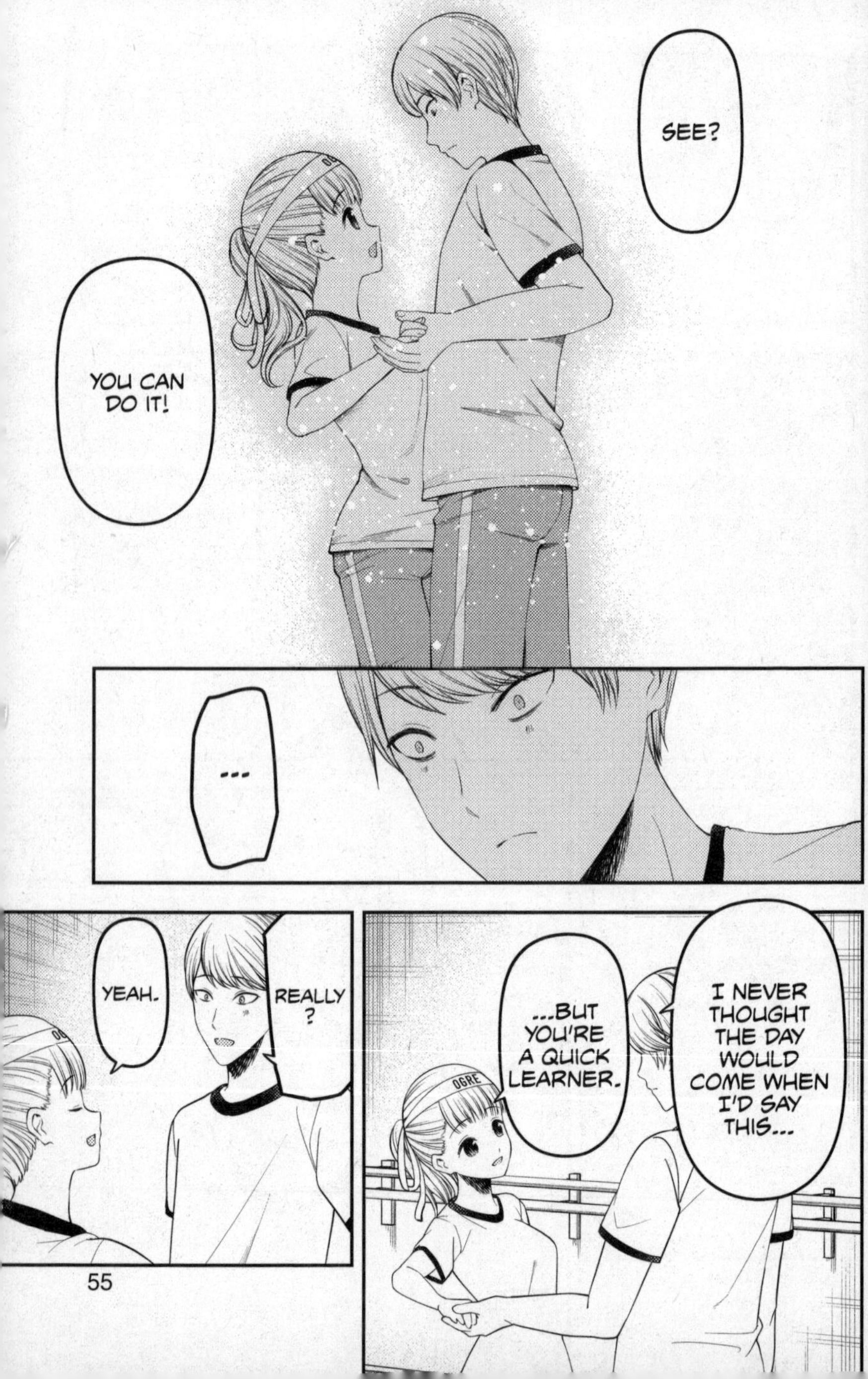
SEE?
YOU CAN DO IT!
...
I NEVER THOUGHT THE DAY WOULD COME WHEN I'D SAY THIS...
...BUT YOU'RE A QUICK LEARNER.
OGRE
REALLY?
YEAH.

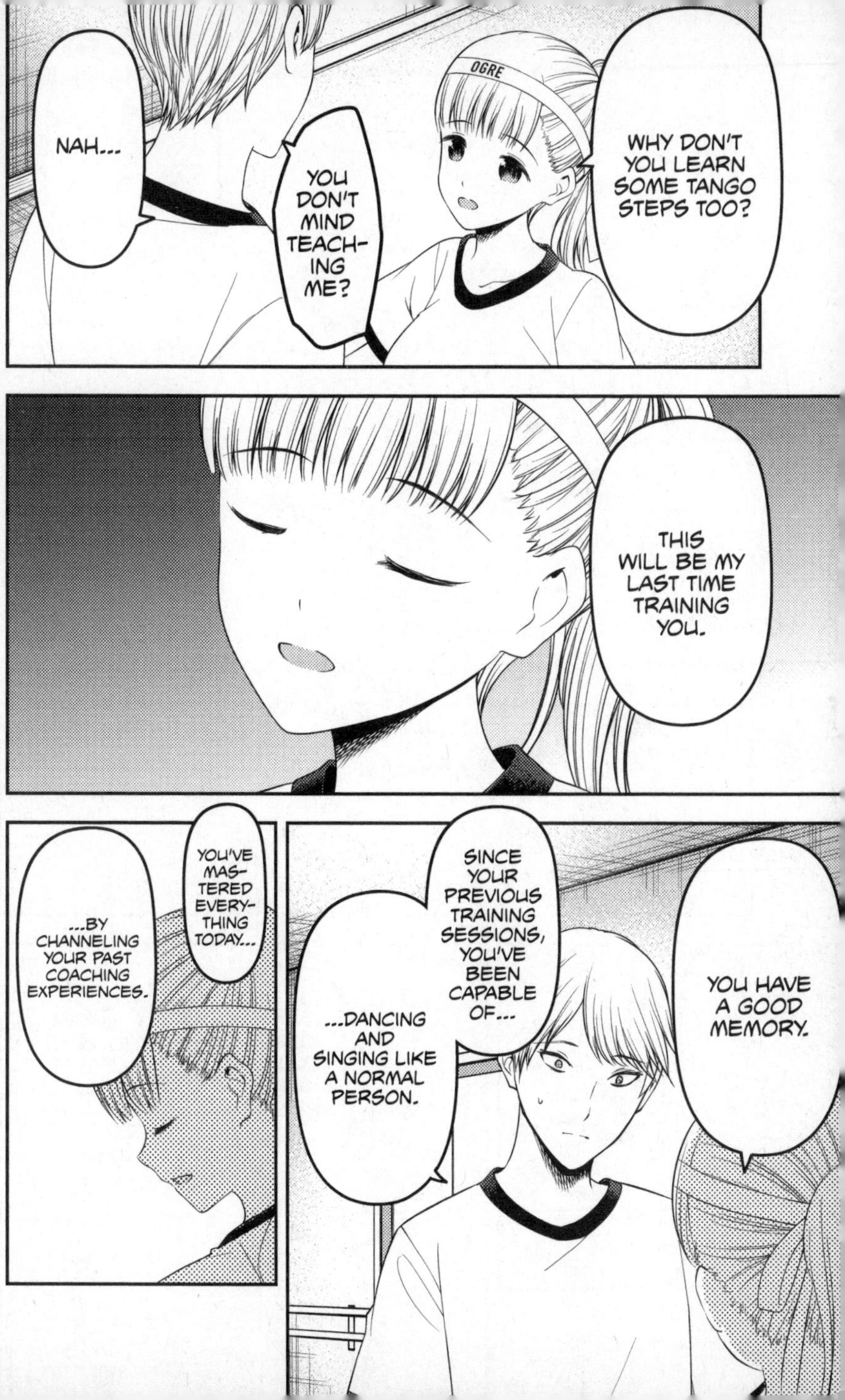
WHY DON'T YOU LEARN SOME TANGO STEPS TOO?
OGRE
YOU DON'T MIND TEACHING ME?
NAH...
THIS WILL BE MY LAST TIME TRAINING YOU.
YOU HAVE A GOOD MEMORY.
SINCE YOUR PREVIOUS TRAINING SESSIONS, YOU'VE BEEN CAPABLE OF...
...DANCING AND SINGING LIKE A NORMAL PERSON.
YOU'VE MASTERED EVERYTHING TODAY...
...BY CHANNELING YOUR PAST COACHING EXPERIENCES.

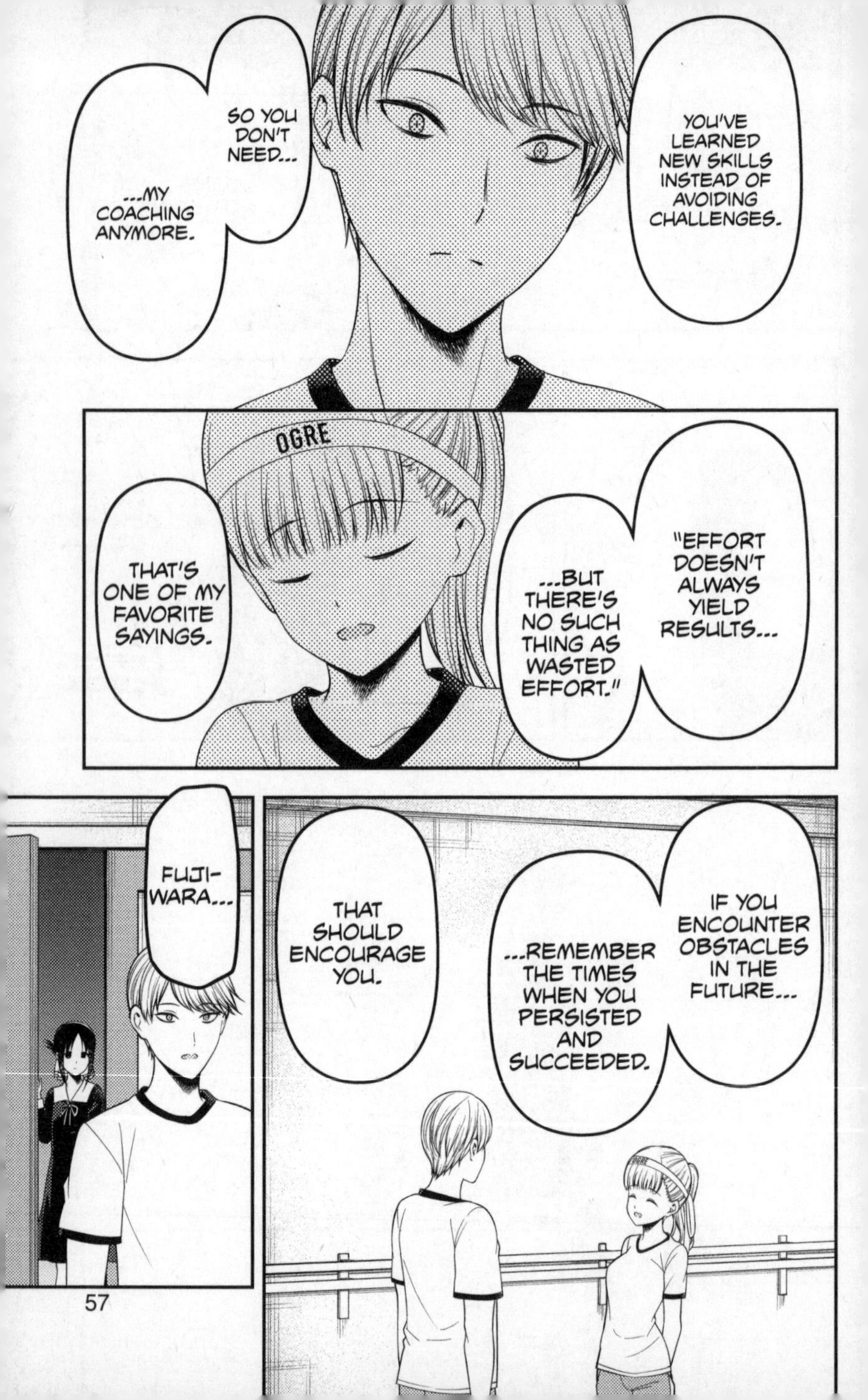
YOU'VE LEARNED NEW SKILLS INSTEAD OF AVOIDING CHALLENGES.
SO YOU DON'T NEED...
...MY COACHING ANYMORE.
"EFFORT DOESN'T ALWAYS YIELD RESULTS...
...BUT THERE'S NO SUCH THING AS WASTED EFFORT."
THAT'S ONE OF MY FAVORITE SAYINGS.
OGRE
IF YOU ENCOUNTER OBSTACLES IN THE FUTURE...
...REMEMBER THE TIMES WHEN YOU PERSISTED AND SUCCEEDED.
THAT SHOULD ENCOURAGE YOU.
OGRE
FUJI-WARA...

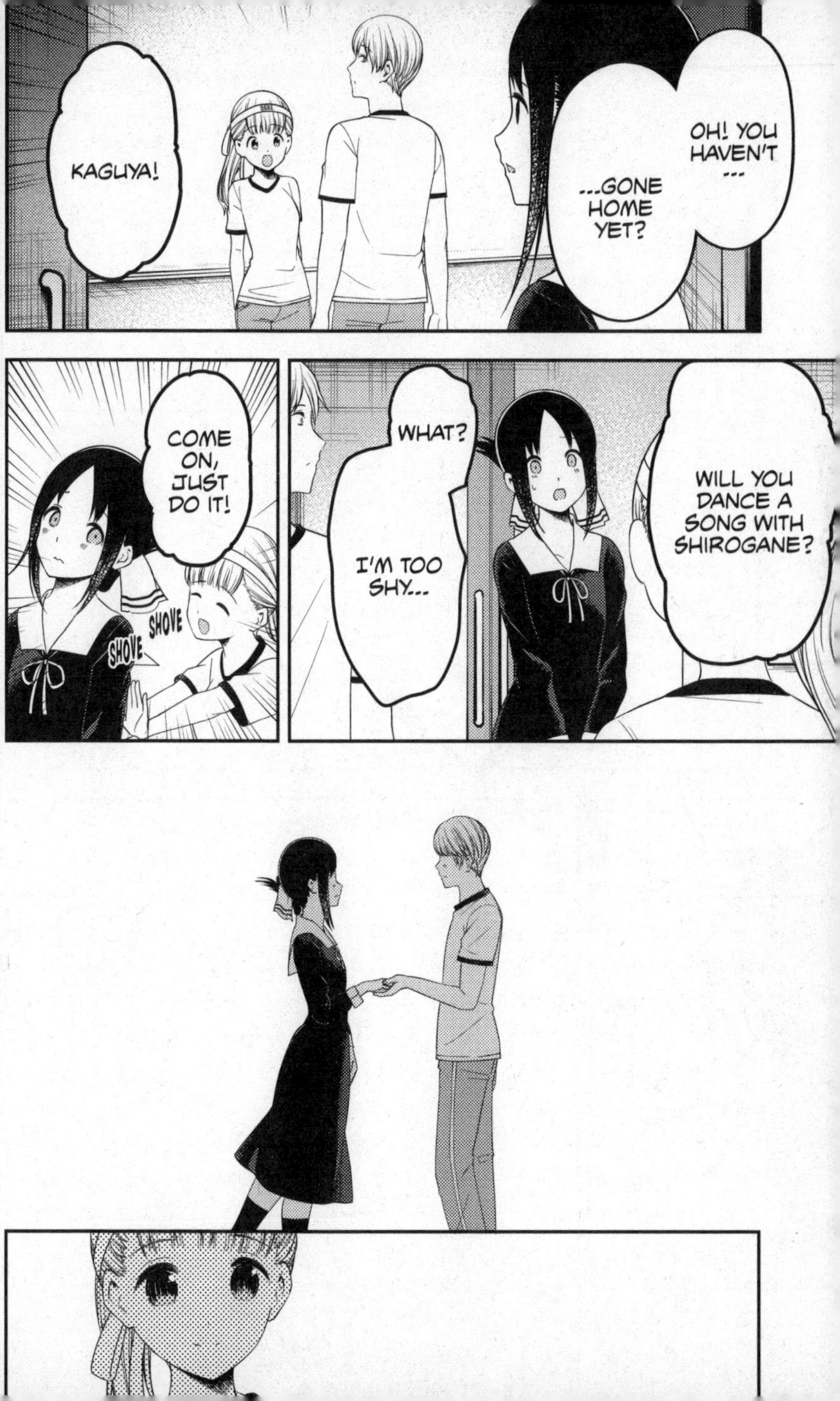
OH! YOU HAVEN'T ---
...GONE HOME YET?
KAGUYA!
WILL YOU DANCE A SONG WITH SHIROGANE?
WHAT?
I'M TOO SHY...
COME ON, JUST DO IT!
SHOVE
SHOVE

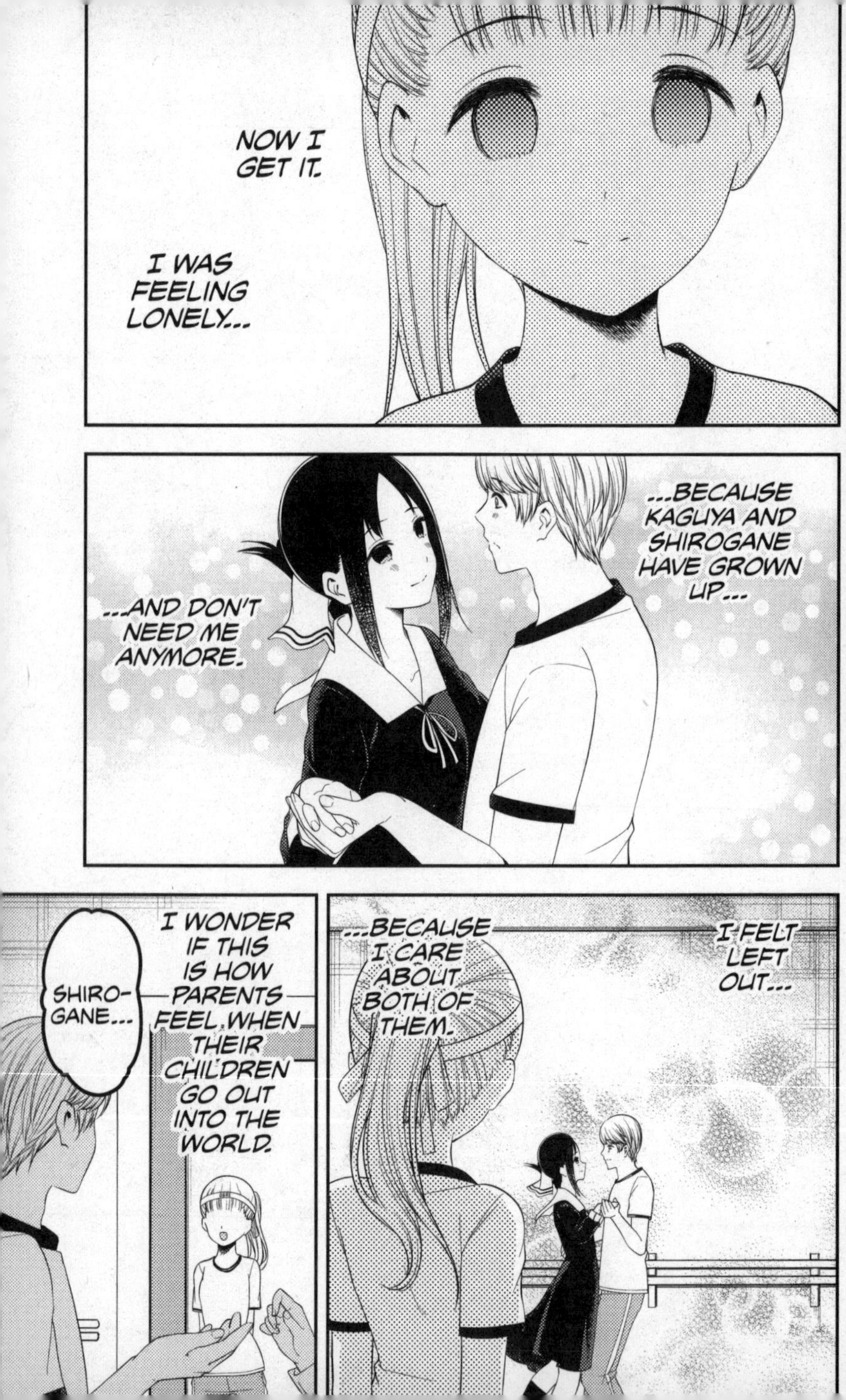
NOW I GET IT.
I WAS FEELING LONELY...
...BECAUSE KAGUYA AND SHIROGANE HAVE GROWN UP...
...AND DON'T NEED ME ANYMORE.
I FELT LEFT OUT...
...BECAUSE I CARE ABOUT BOTH OF THEM.
I WONDER IF THIS IS HOW PARENTS FEEL WHEN THEIR CHILDREN GO OUT INTO THE WORLD.
SHIRO-GANE...

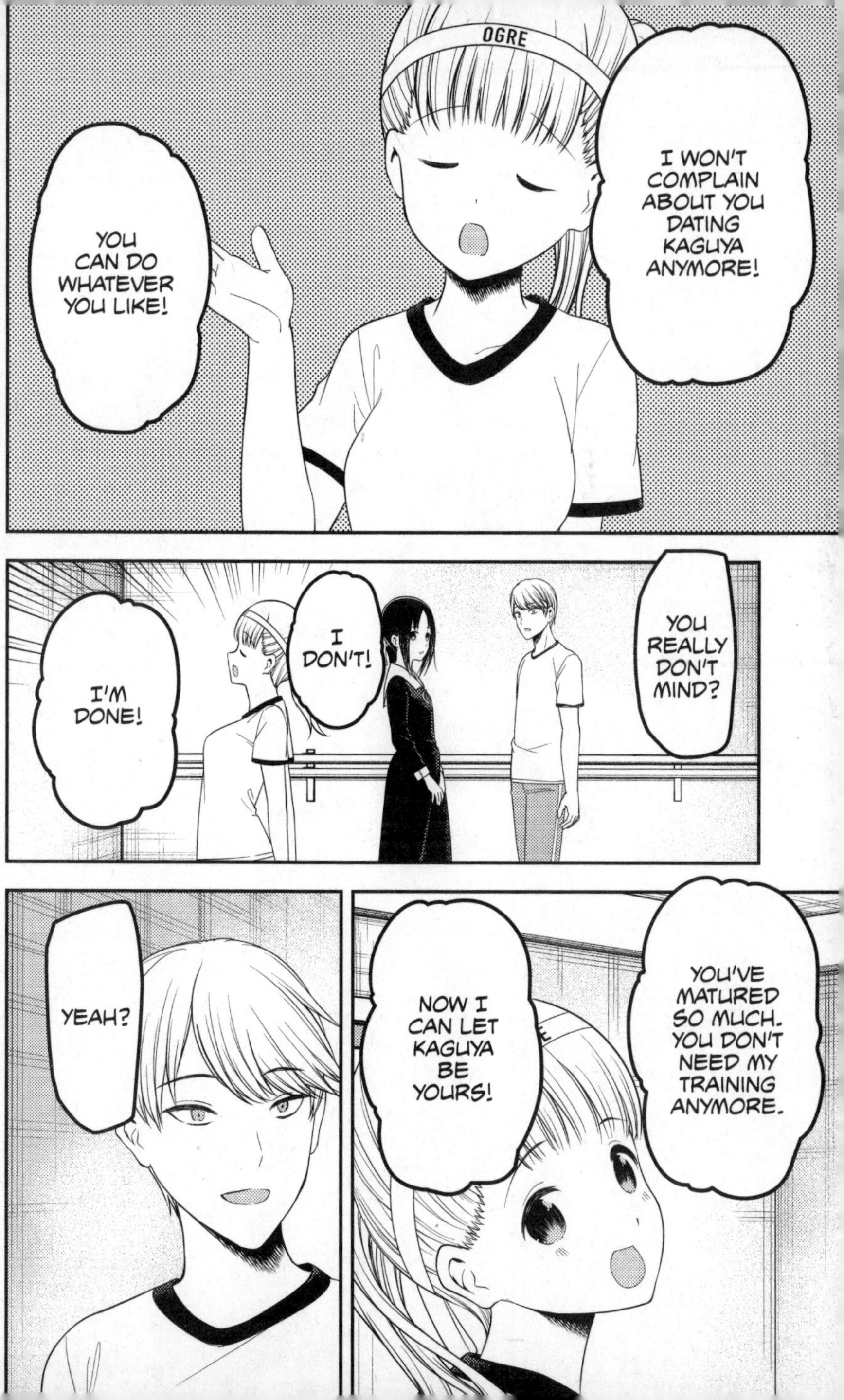
OGRE
I WON'T COMPLAIN ABOUT YOU DATING KAGUYA ANYMORE!
YOU CAN DO WHATEVER YOU LIKE!
YOU REALLY DON'T MIND?
I DON'T!
I'M DONE!
YOU'VE MATURED SO MUCH. YOU DON'T NEED MY TRAINING ANYMORE.
NOW I CAN LET KAGUYA BE YOURS!
YEAH?

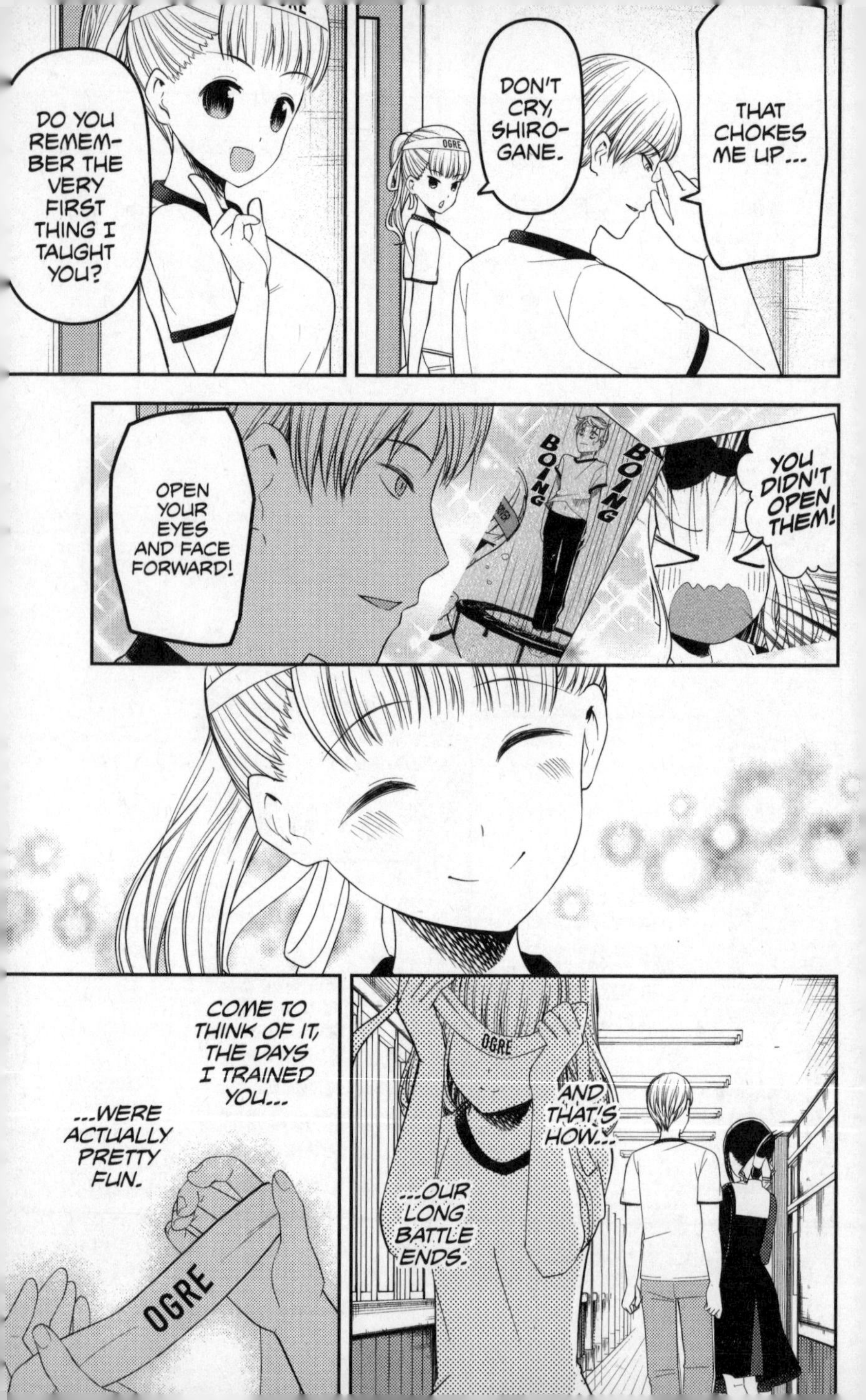
THAT CHOKES ME UP...
DON'T CRY, SHIRO-GANE.
DO YOU REMEMBER THE VERY FIRST THING I TAUGHT YOU?
YOU DIDN'T OPEN THEM!
BOING
BOING
OPEN YOUR EYES AND FACE FORWARD!
OGRE
AND THAT'S HOW...
...OUR LONG BATTLE ENDS.
COME TO THINK OF IT, THE DAYS I TRAINED YOU...
...WERE ACTUALLY PRETTY FUN.
OGRE

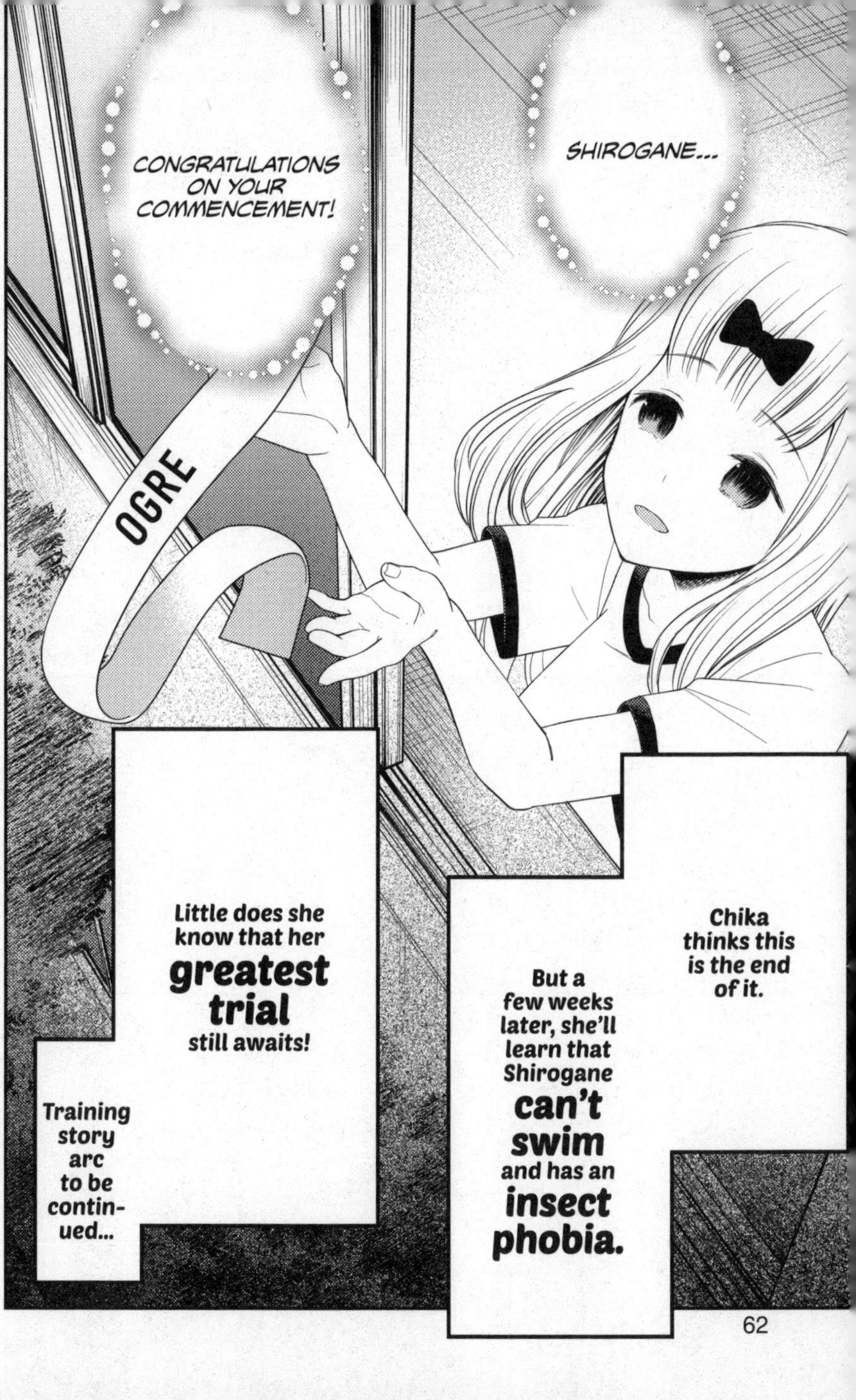
SHIROGANE...
CONGRATULATIONS ON YOUR COMMENCEMENT!
OGRE
Chika thinks this is the end of it.
But a few weeks later, she'll learn that Shirogane can't swim and has an insect phobia.
Little does she know that her greatest trial still awaits!
Training story arc to be contin-ued...

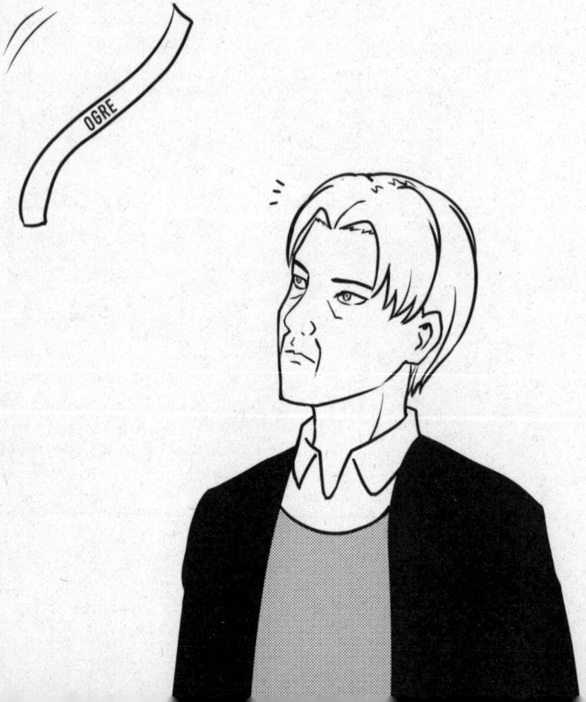
OGRE

KAGUYA-SAMA
LOVE IS WAR

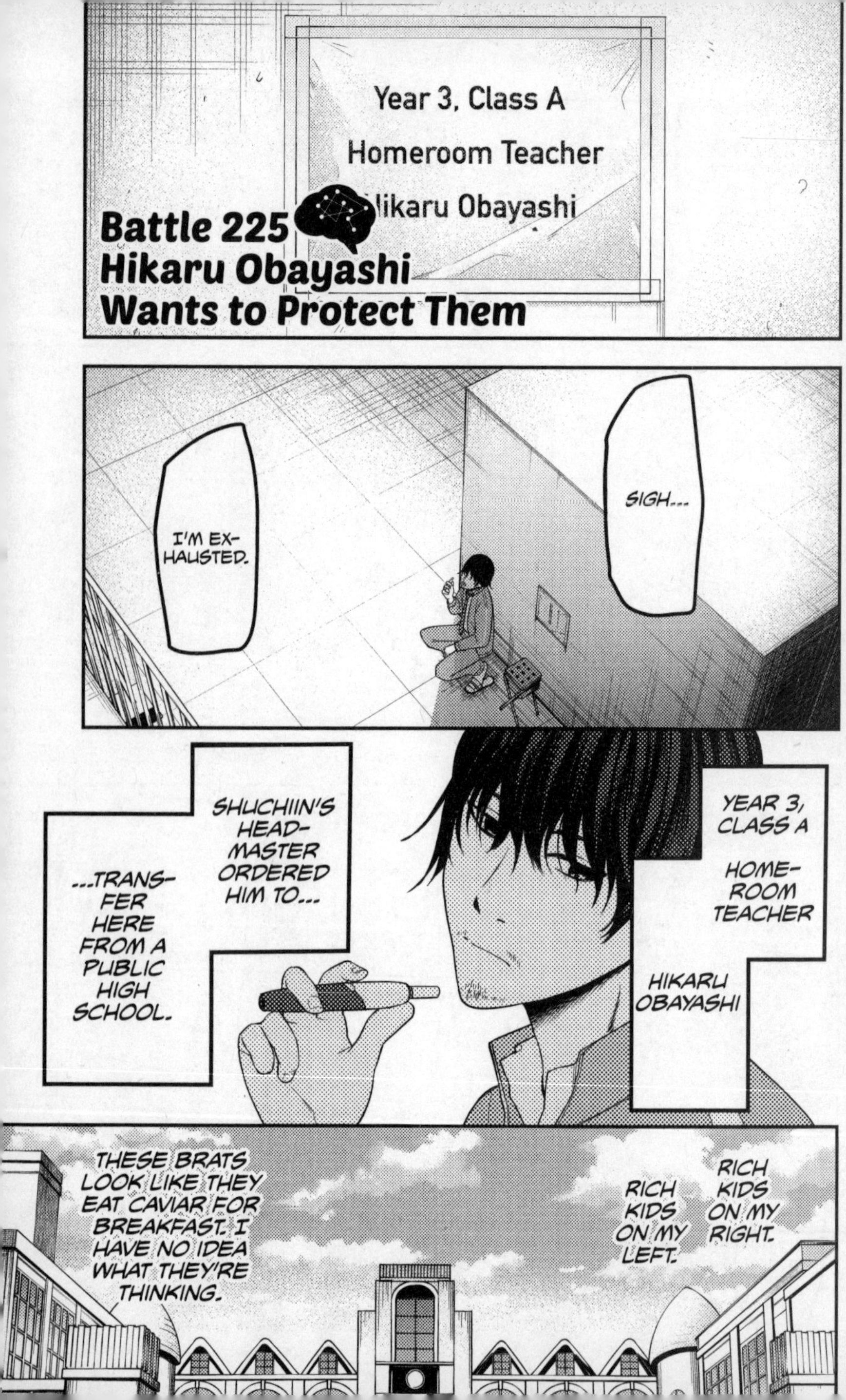
Year 3, Class A
Homeroom Teacher
Hikaru Obayashi
Battle 225 Hikaru Obayashi Wants to Protect Them
SIGH...
I'M EXHAUSTED.
YEAR 3, CLASS A HOMEROOM TEACHER
HIKARU OBAYASHI
SHUCHIIN'S HEADMASTER ORDERED HIM TO...
...TRANSFER HERE FROM A PUBLIC HIGH SCHOOL.
RICH KIDS ON MY RIGHT.
RICH KIDS ON MY LEFT.
THESE BRATS LOOK LIKE THEY EAT CAVIAR FOR BREAKFAST. I HAVE NO IDEA WHAT THEY'RE THINKING.

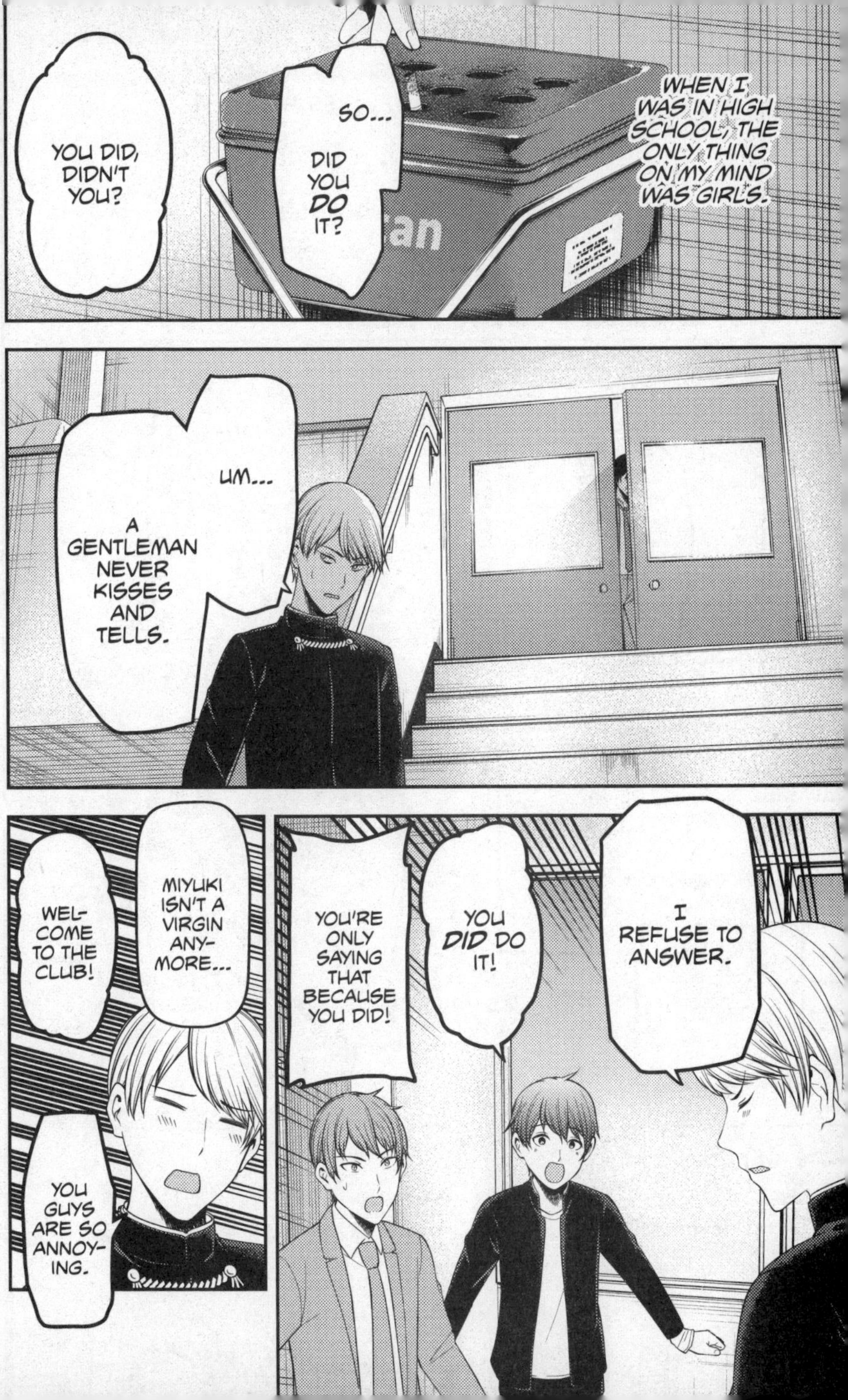
WHEN I WAS IN HIGH SCHOOL, THE ONLY THING ON MY MIND WAS GIRLS.
SO... DID YOU DO IT?
YOU DID, DIDN'T YOU?
UM... A GENTLEMAN NEVER KISSES AND TELLS.
I REFUSE TO ANSWER.
YOU DID DO IT!
YOU'RE ONLY SAYING THAT BECAUSE YOU DID!
MIYUKI ISN'T A VIRGIN ANY-MORE...
WEL-COME TO THE CLUB!
YOU GUYS ARE SO ANNOY-ING.

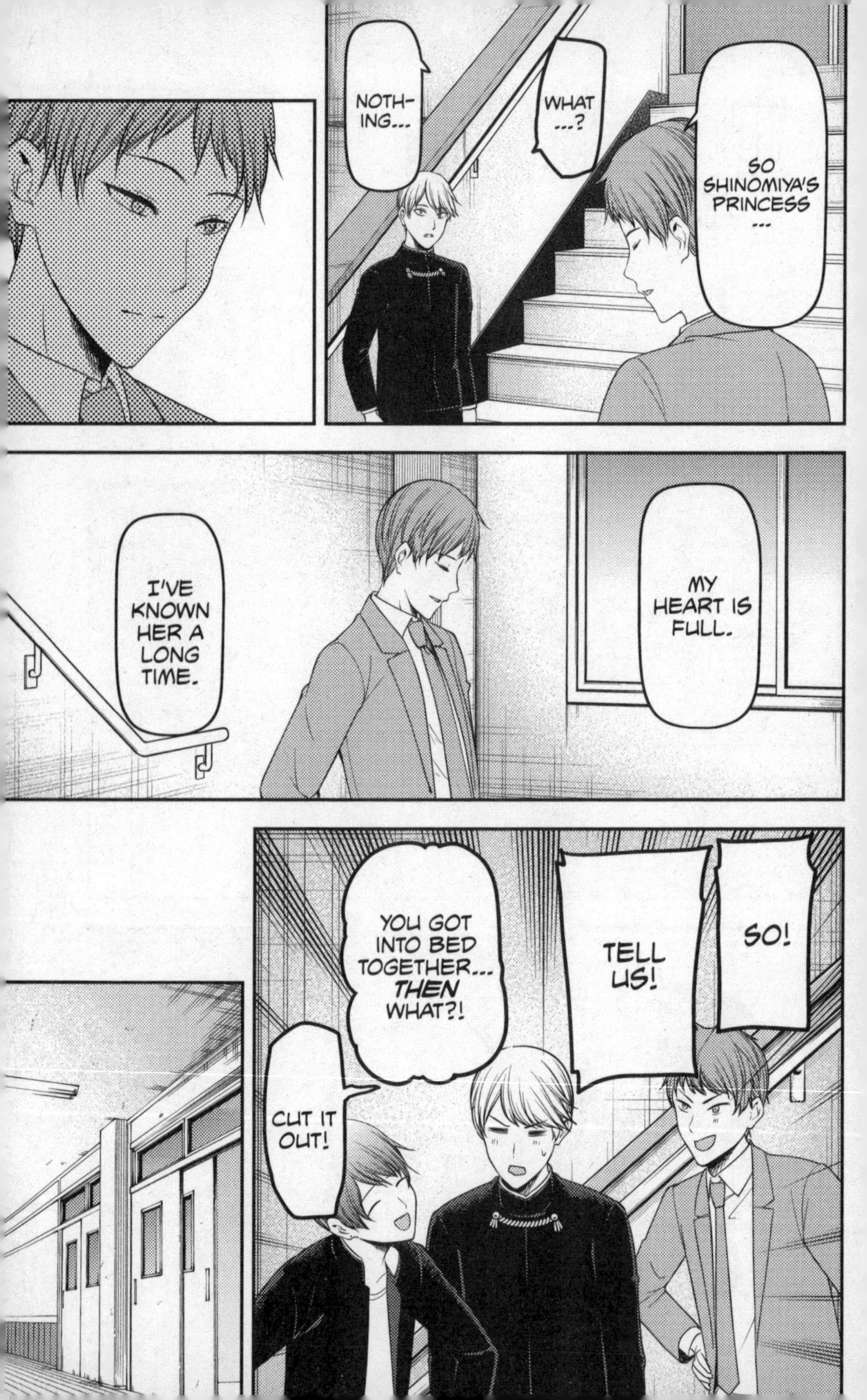
SO SHINOMIYA'S PRINCESS ...
WHAT ...?
NOTH-ING...
MY HEART IS FULL.
I'VE KNOWN HER A LONG TIME.
SO!
TELL US!
YOU GOT INTO BED TOGETHER... *THEN* WHAT?!
CUT IT OUT!

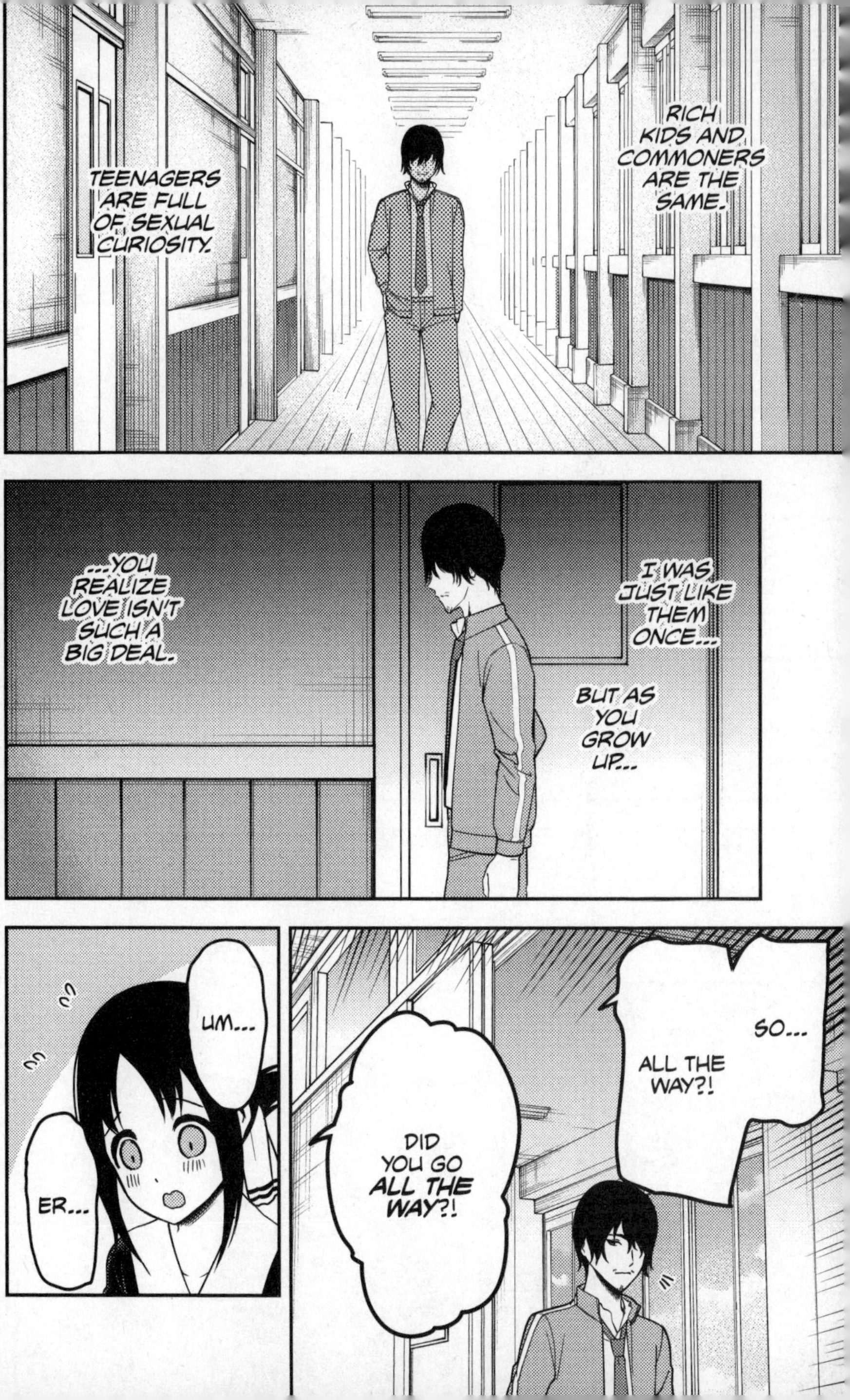
RICH KIDS AND COMMONERS ARE THE SAME.
TEENAGERS ARE FULL OF SEXUAL CURIOSITY.
I WAS JUST LIKE THEM ONCE...
BUT AS YOU GROW UP...
...YOU REALIZE LOVE ISN'T SUCH A BIG DEAL.
SO... ALL THE WAY?!
DID YOU GO ALL THE WAY?!
UM...
ER...

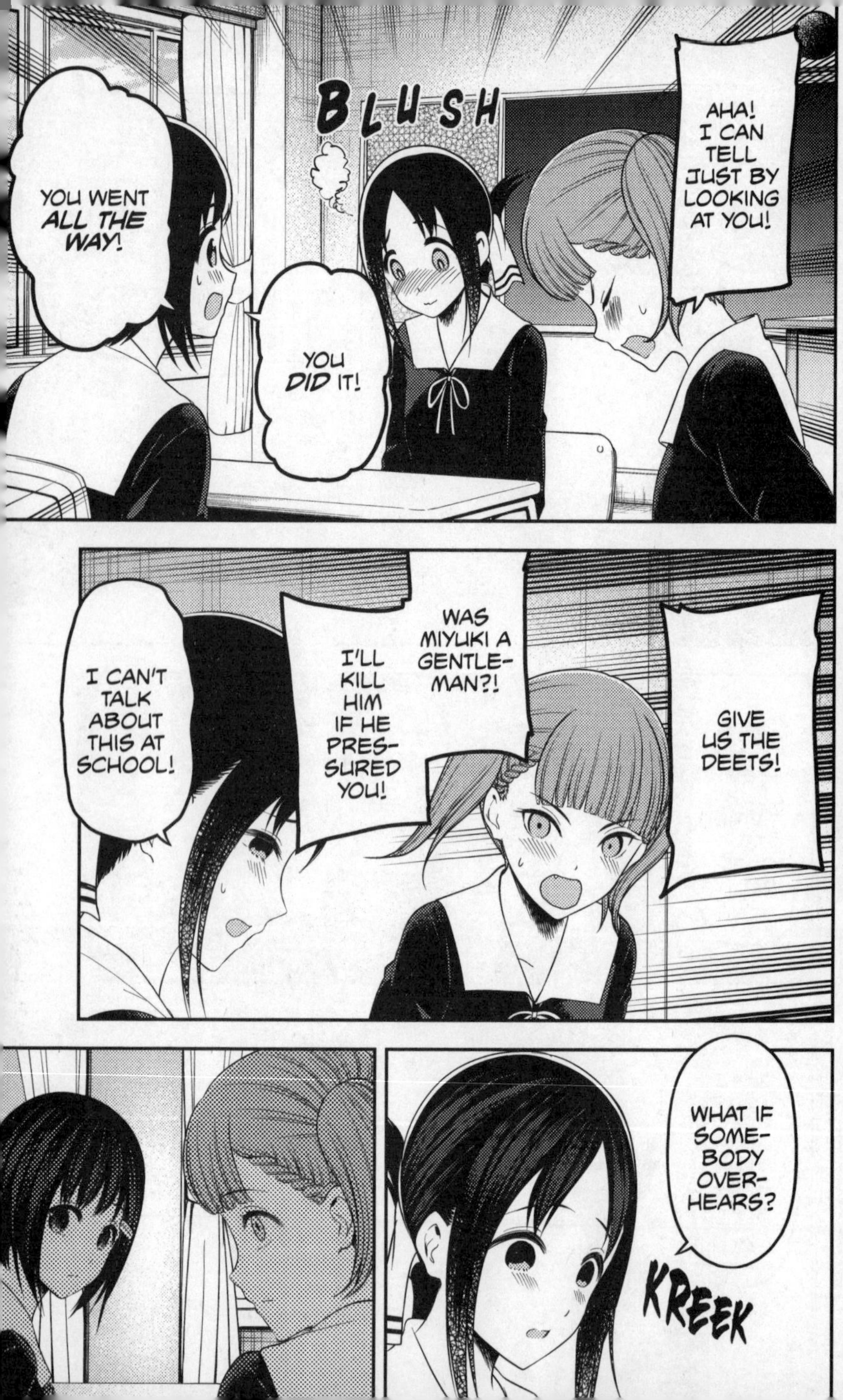
AHA! I CAN TELL JUST BY LOOKING AT YOU!
BLUSH
YOU WENT ALL THE WAY!
YOU DID IT!
GIVE US THE DEETS!
WAS MIYUKI A GENTLEMAN?!
I'LL KILL HIM IF HE PRESSURED YOU!
I CAN'T TALK ABOUT THIS AT SCHOOL!
WHAT IF SOMEBODY OVERHEARS?
KREEK

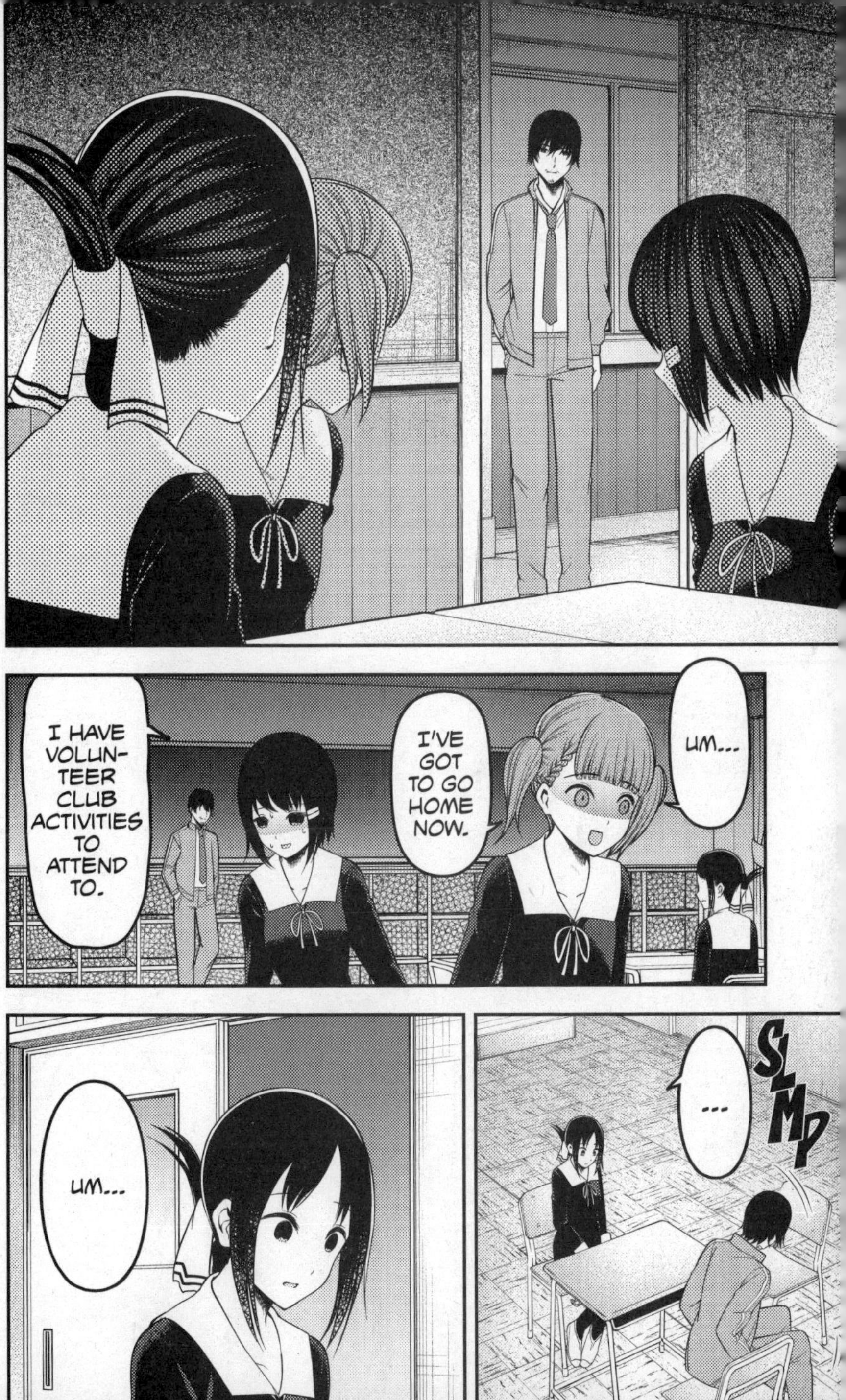
UM...
I'VE GOT TO GO HOME NOW.
I HAVE VOLUNTEER CLUB ACTIVITIES TO ATTEND TO.
...
SLMP
UM...

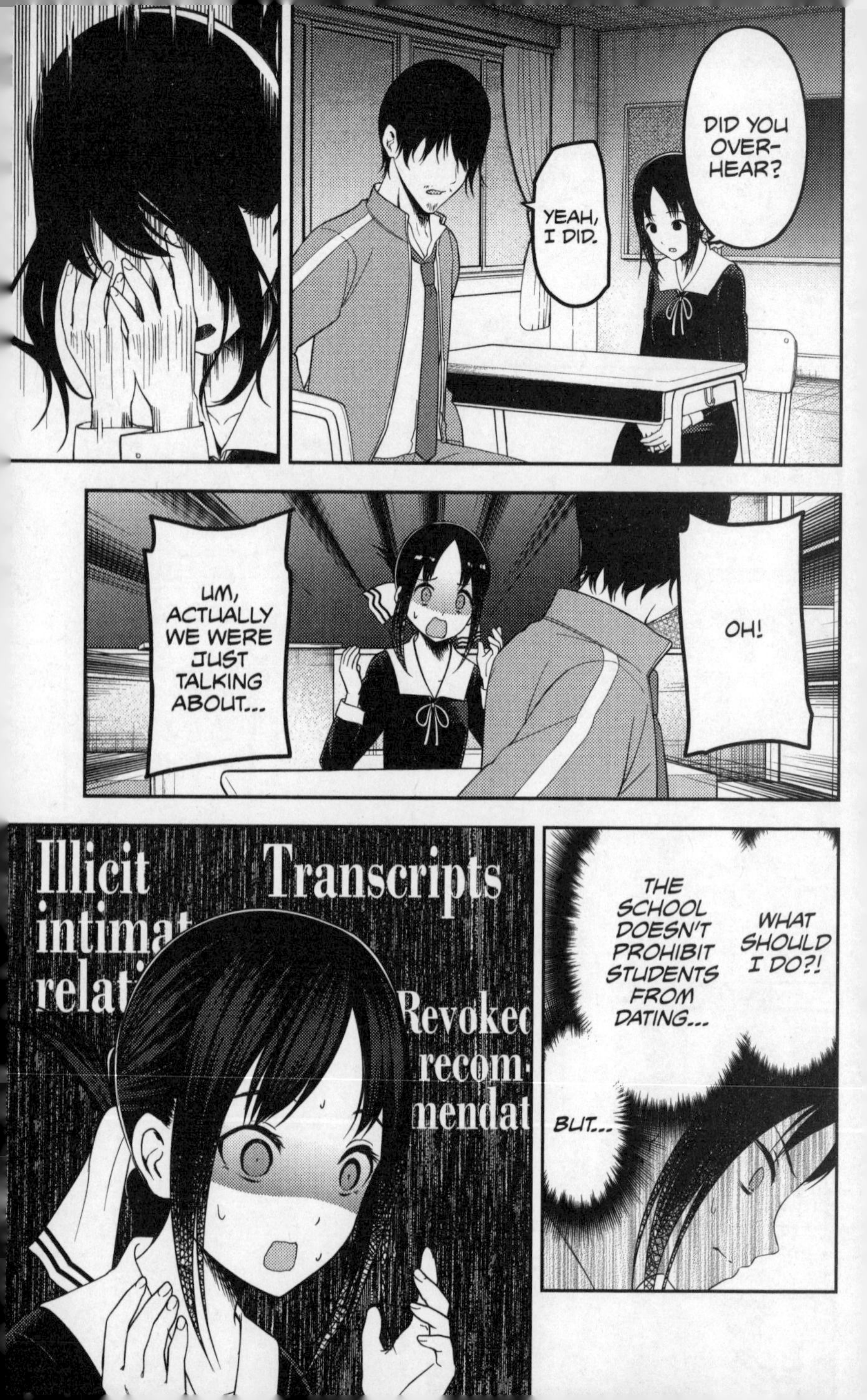
DID YOU OVER-HEAR?
YEAH, I DID.
OH!
UM, ACTUALLY WE WERE JUST TALKING ABOUT...
WHAT SHOULD I DO?!
THE SCHOOL DOESN'T PROHIBIT STUDENTS FROM DATING...
BUT...
Transcripts
Illicit intimat relat
Revokec recom-mendat

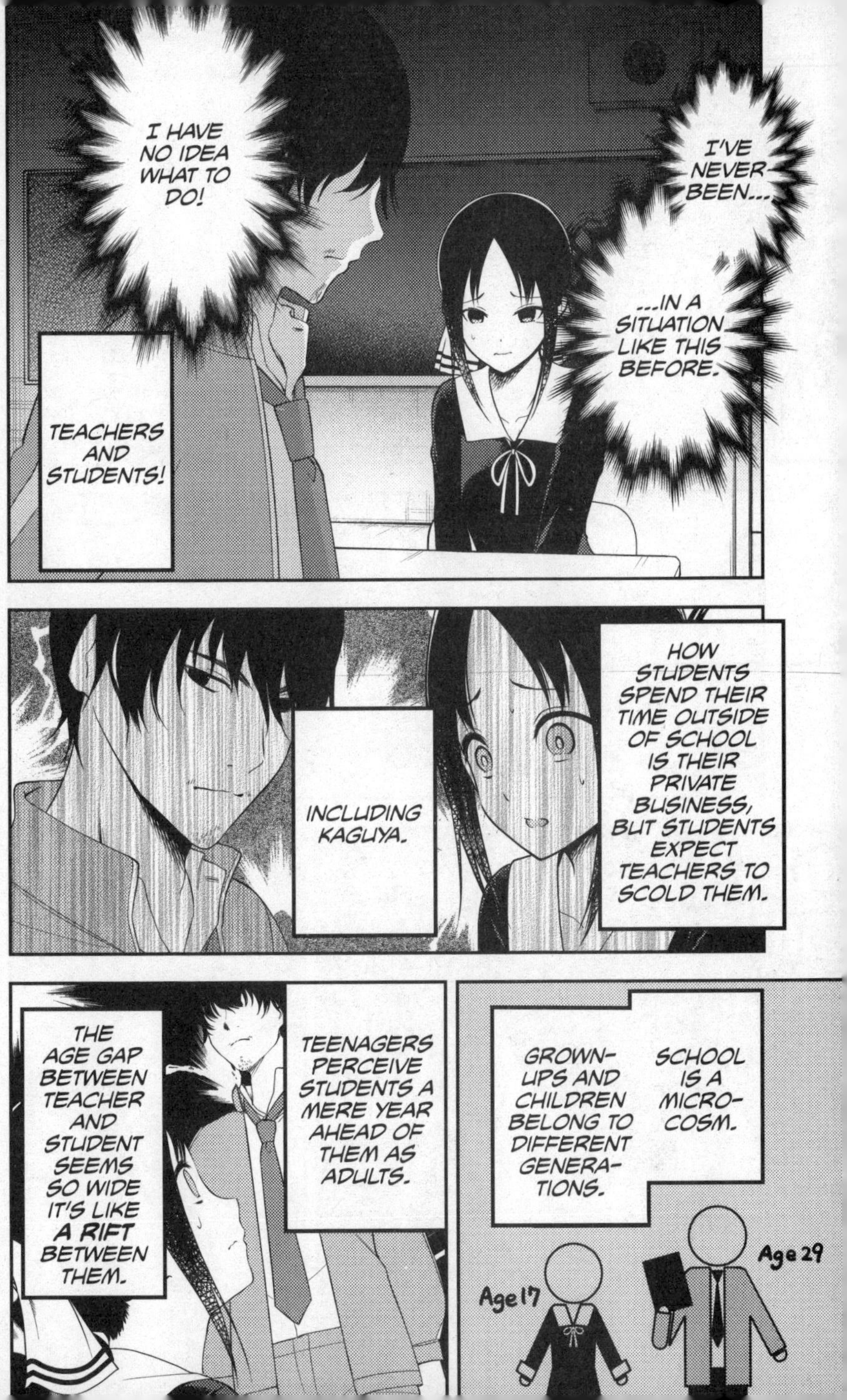
I'VE NEVER BEEN...
...IN A SITUATION LIKE THIS BEFORE.
I HAVE NO IDEA WHAT TO DO!
TEACHERS AND STUDENTS!
HOW STUDENTS SPEND THEIR TIME OUTSIDE OF SCHOOL IS THEIR PRIVATE BUSINESS, BUT STUDENTS EXPECT TEACHERS TO SCOLD THEM.
INCLUDING KAGUYA.
SCHOOL IS A MICRO-COSM.
GROWN-UPS AND CHILDREN BELONG TO DIFFERENT GENERA-TIONS.
Age 29
Age 17
TEENAGERS PERCEIVE STUDENTS A MERE YEAR AHEAD OF THEM AS ADULTS.
THE AGE GAP BETWEEN TEACHER AND STUDENT SEEMS SO WIDE IT'S LIKE A RIFT BETWEEN THEM.

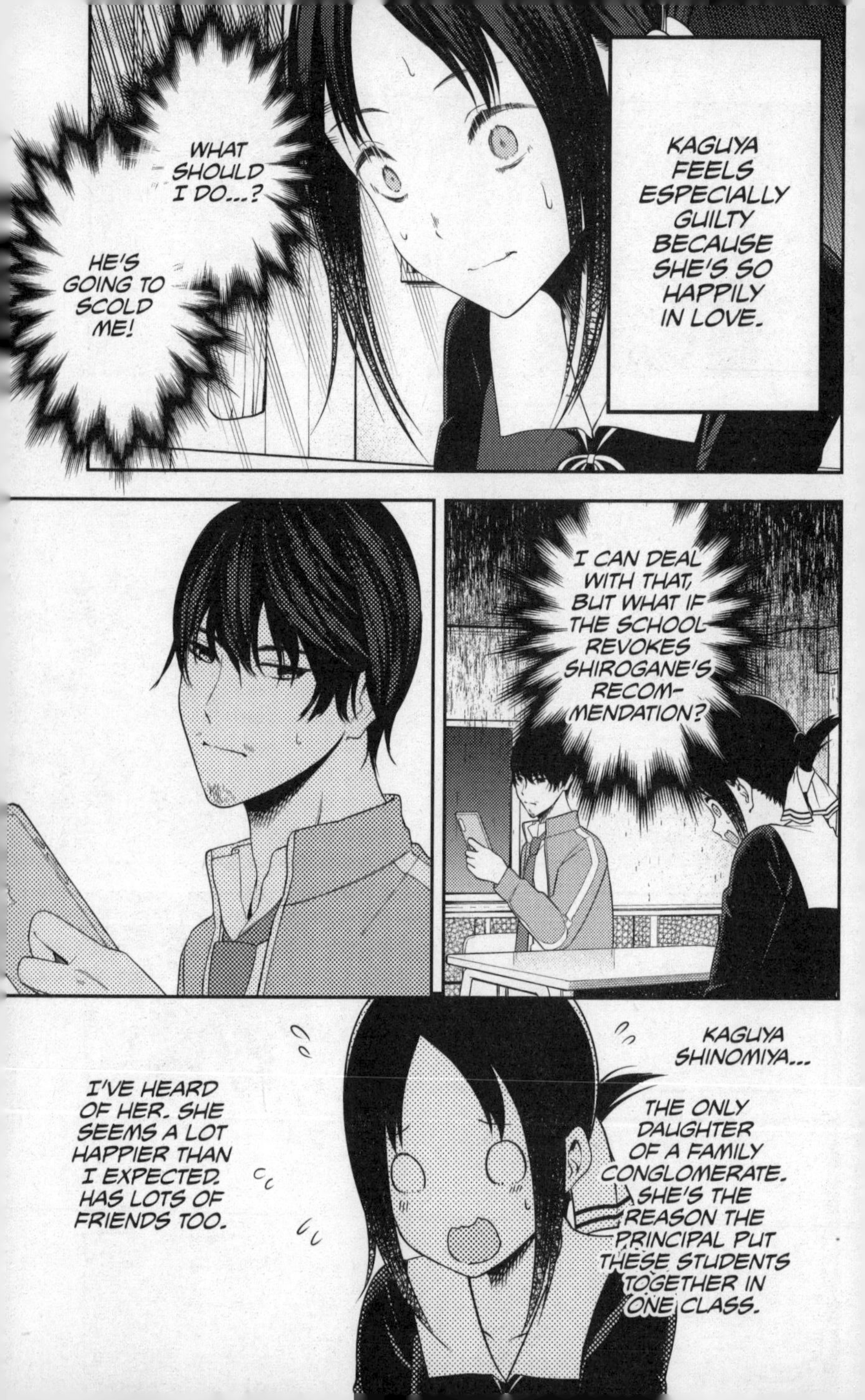
KAGUYA FEELS ESPECIALLY GUILTY BECAUSE SHE'S SO HAPPILY IN LOVE.
WHAT SHOULD I DO...?
HE'S GOING TO SCOLD ME!
I CAN DEAL WITH THAT, BUT WHAT IF THE SCHOOL REVOKES SHIROGANE'S RECOM-MENDATION?
KAGUYA SHINOMIYA...
THE ONLY DAUGHTER OF A FAMILY CONGLOMERATE. SHE'S THE REASON THE PRINCIPAL PUT THESE STUDENTS TOGETHER IN ONE CLASS.
I'VE HEARD OF HER. SHE SEEMS A LOT HAPPIER THAN I EXPECTED. HAS LOTS OF FRIENDS TOO.

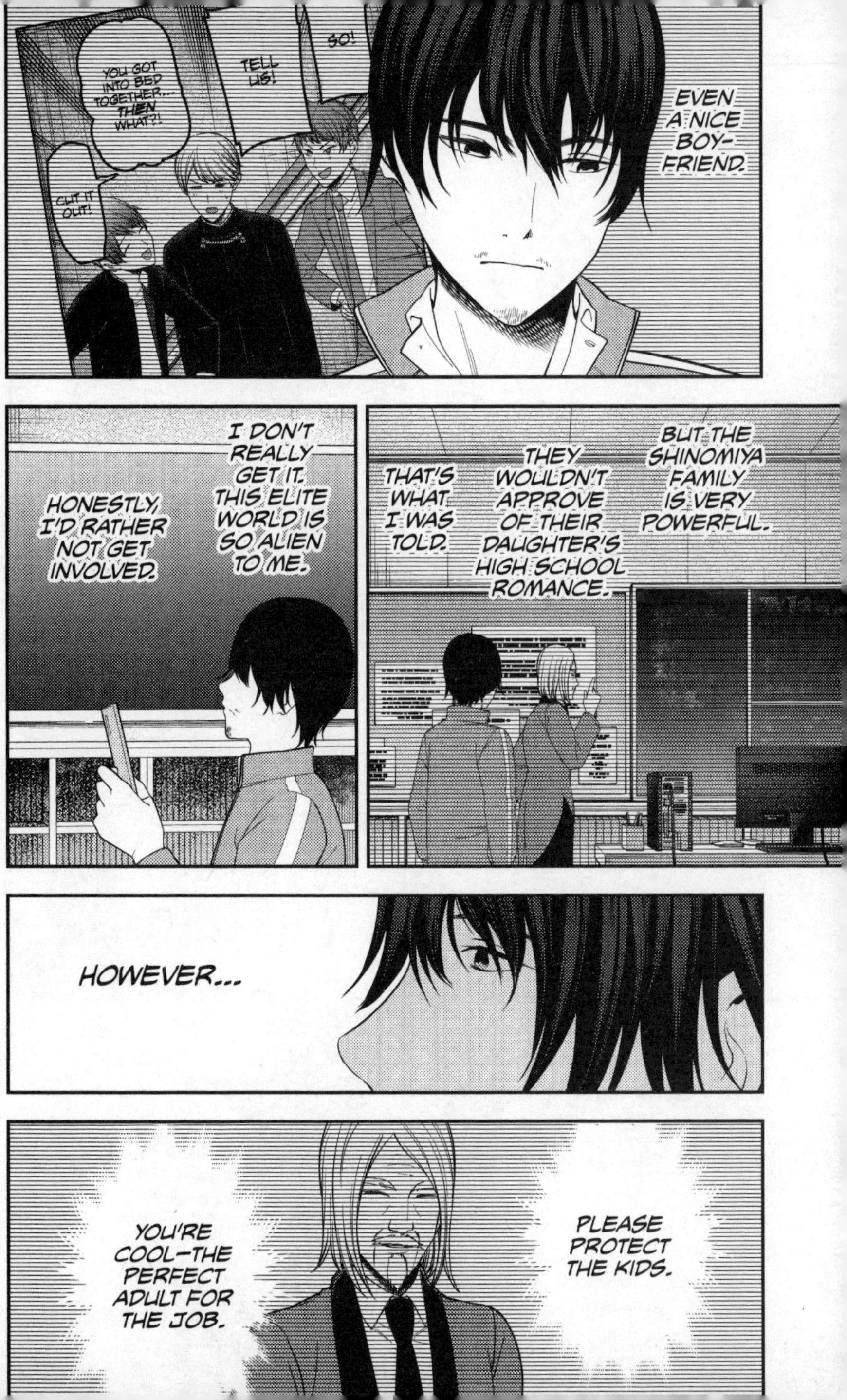
EVEN A NICE BOYFRIEND.
SO!
TELL US!
YOU GOT INTO BED TOGETHER... THEN WHAT?!
CUT IT OUT!
BUT THE SHINOMIYA FAMILY IS VERY POWERFUL.
THEY WOULDN'T APPROVE OF THEIR DAUGHTER'S HIGH SCHOOL ROMANCE.
THAT'S WHAT I WAS TOLD.
I DON'T REALLY GET IT. THIS ELITE WORLD IS SO ALIEN TO ME.
HONESTLY, I'D RATHER NOT GET INVOLVED.
HOWEVER...
PLEASE PROTECT THE KIDS.
YOU'RE COOL—THE PERFECT ADULT FOR THE JOB.

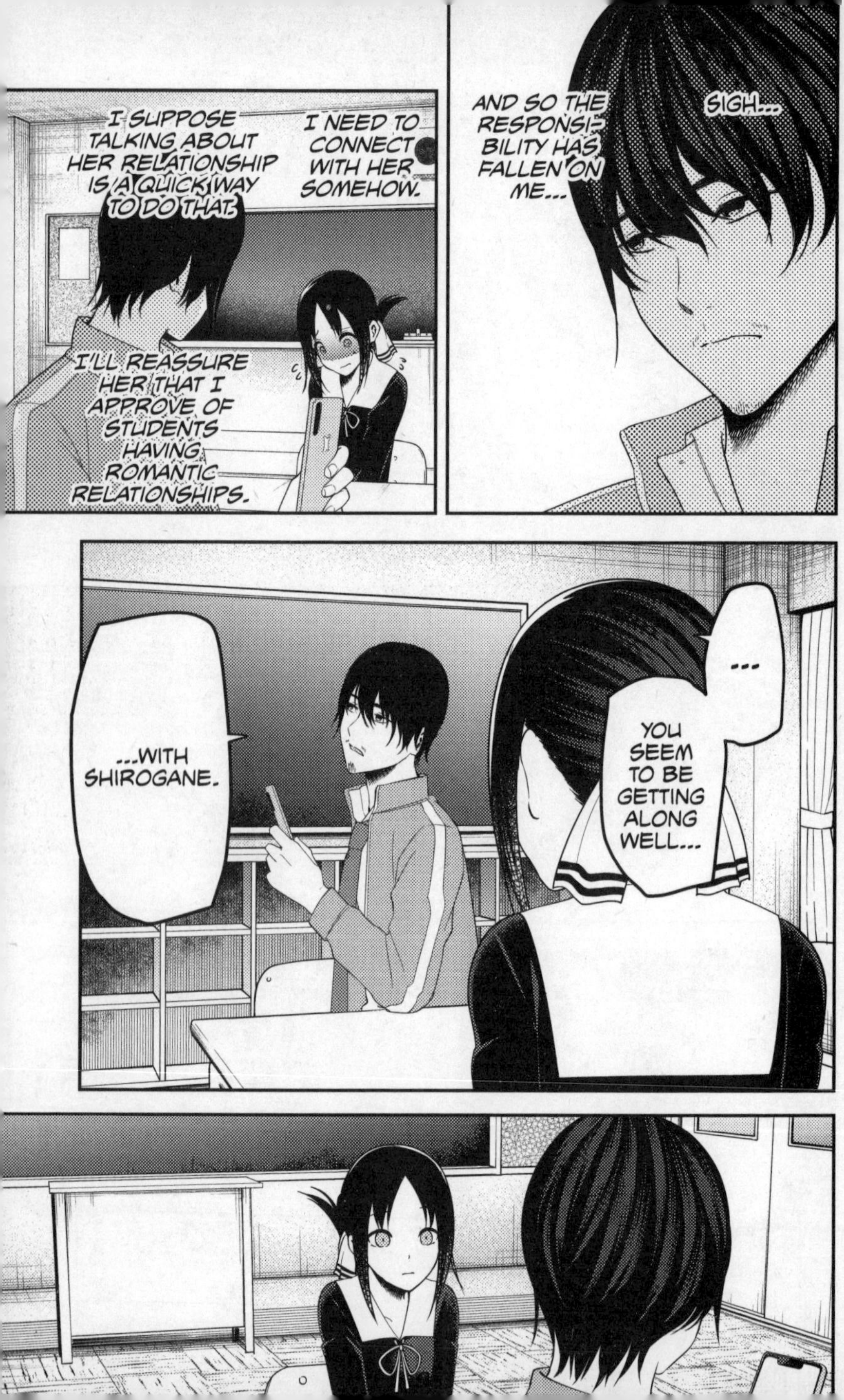
SIGH...
AND SO THE RESPONSIBILITY HAS FALLEN ON ME...
I NEED TO CONNECT WITH HER SOMEHOW.
I SUPPOSE TALKING ABOUT HER RELATIONSHIP IS A QUICK WAY TO DO THAT.
I'LL REASSURE HER THAT I APPROVE OF STUDENTS HAVING ROMANTIC RELATIONSHIPS.
...
YOU SEEM TO BE GETTING ALONG WELL...
...WITH SHIROGANE.

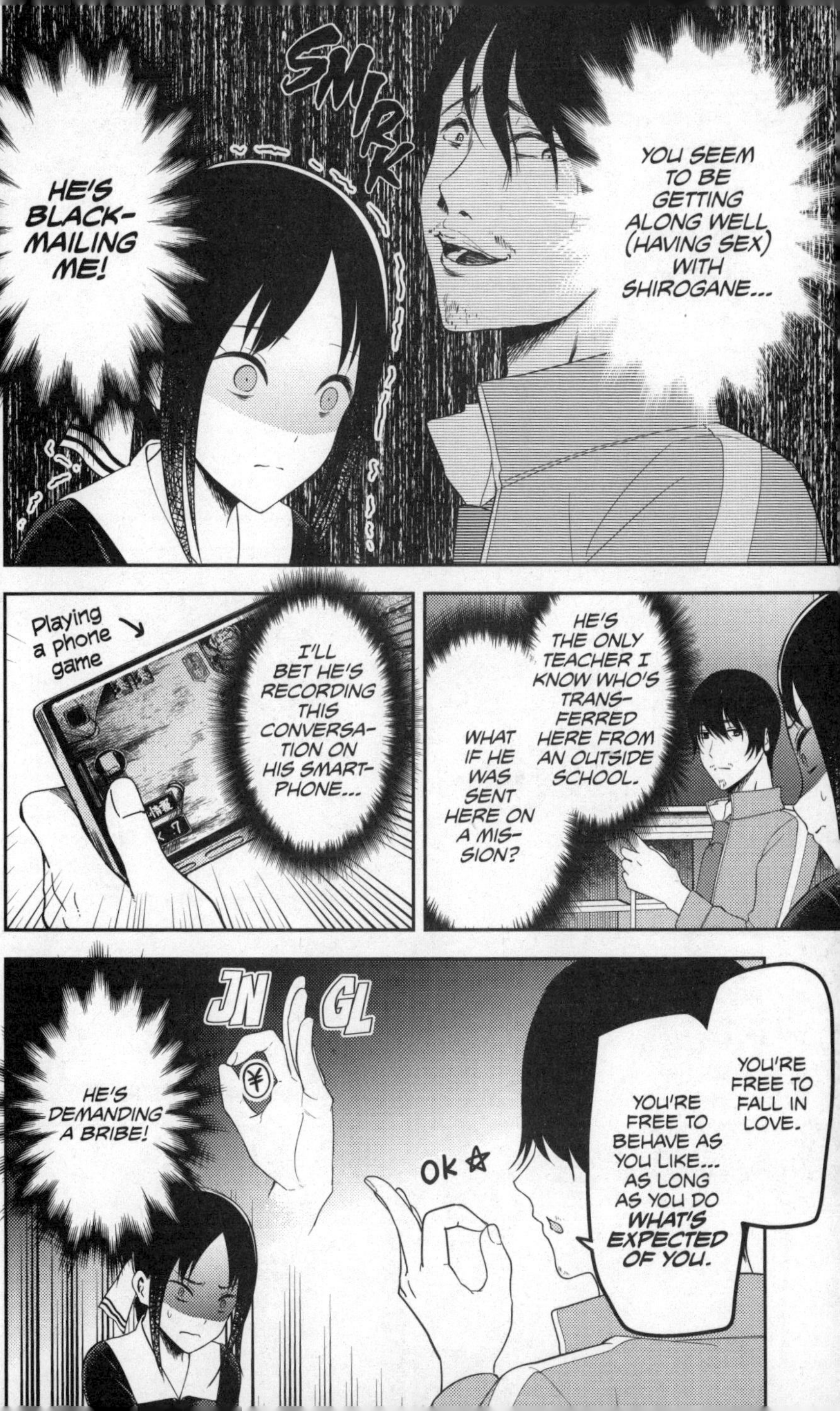
YOU SEEM TO BE GETTING ALONG WELL (HAVING SEX) WITH SHIROGANE...
SMRK
HE'S BLACK-MAILING ME!
HE'S THE ONLY TEACHER I KNOW WHO'S TRANS-FERRED HERE FROM AN OUTSIDE SCHOOL.
WHAT IF HE WAS SENT HERE ON A MIS-SION?
I'LL BET HE'S RECORDING THIS CONVERSA-TION ON HIS SMART-PHONE...
Playing a phone game
YOU'RE FREE TO FALL IN LOVE.
YOU'RE FREE TO BEHAVE AS YOU LIKE... AS LONG AS YOU DO WHAT'S EXPECTED OF YOU.
OK☆
JNGL
HE'S DEMANDING A BRIBE!

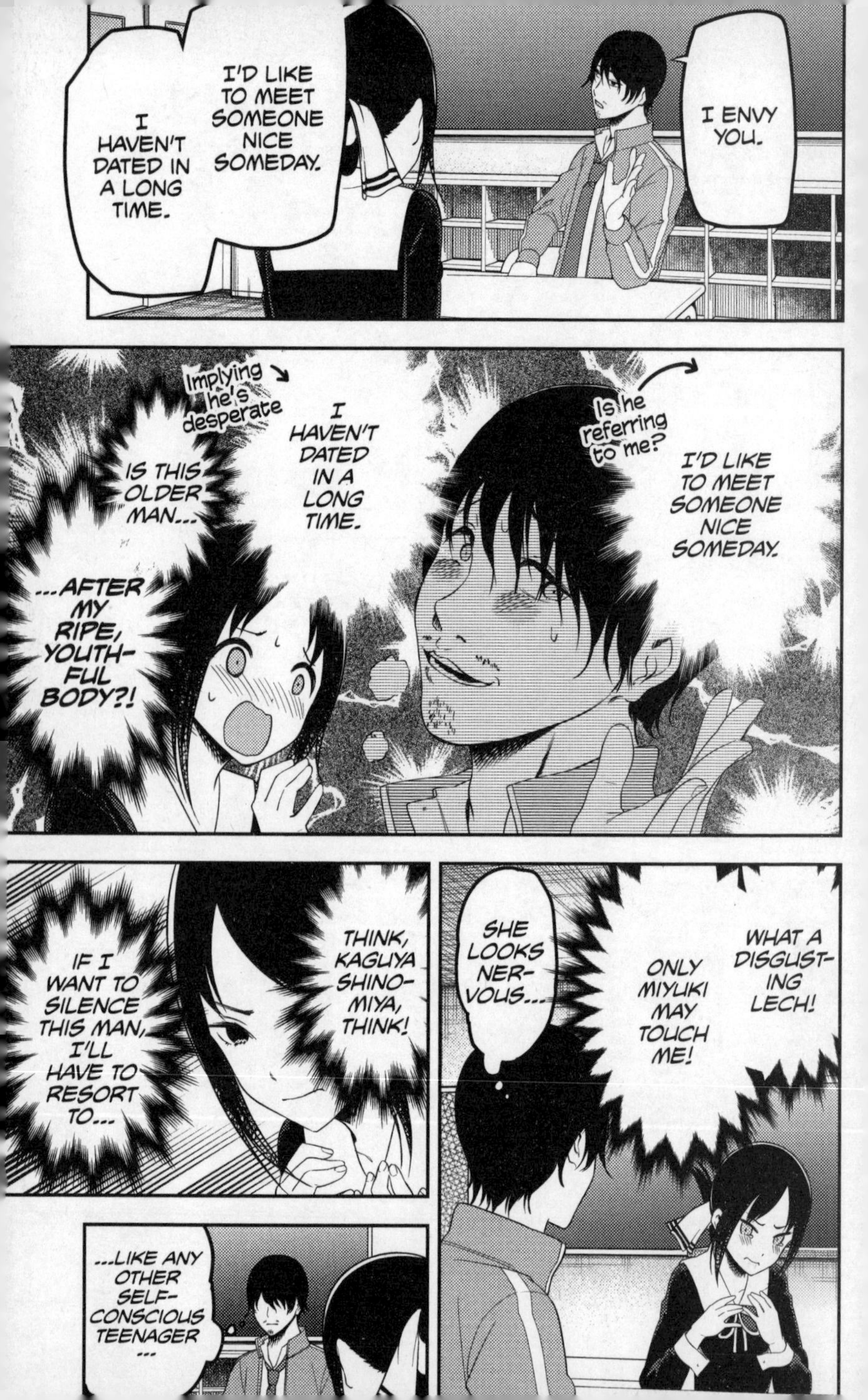
I ENVY YOU.
I HAVEN'T DATED IN A LONG TIME.
I'D LIKE TO MEET SOMEONE NICE SOMEDAY.
I'D LIKE TO MEET SOMEONE NICE SOMEDAY.
Is he referring to me?
I HAVEN'T DATED IN A LONG TIME.
Implying he's desperate
IS THIS OLDER MAN...
...AFTER MY RIPE, YOUTH-FUL BODY?!
WHAT A DISGUST-ING LECH!
ONLY MIYUKI MAY TOUCH ME!
SHE LOOKS NER-VOUS...
THINK, KAGUYA SHINO-MIYA, THINK!
IF I WANT TO SILENCE THIS MAN, I'LL HAVE TO RESORT TO...
...LIKE ANY OTHER SELF-CONSCIOUS TEENAGER...

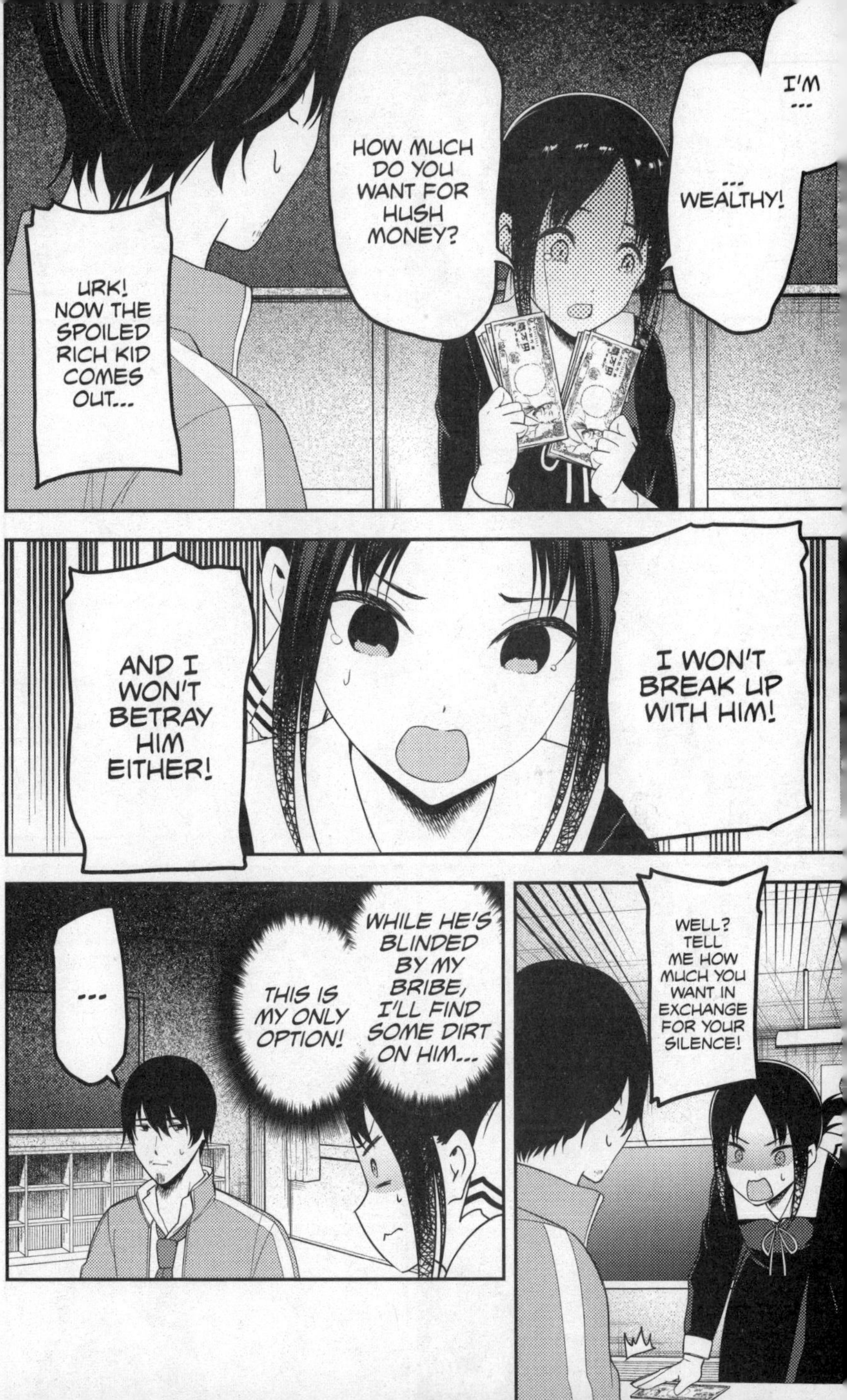
I'M ...
... WEALTHY!
HOW MUCH DO YOU WANT FOR HUSH MONEY?
URK! NOW THE SPOILED RICH KID COMES OUT...
I WON'T BREAK UP WITH HIM!
AND I WON'T BETRAY HIM EITHER!
WELL? TELL ME HOW MUCH YOU WANT IN EXCHANGE FOR YOUR SILENCE!
WHILE HE'S BLINDED BY MY BRIBE, I'LL FIND SOME DIRT ON HIM...
THIS IS MY ONLY OPTION!
...

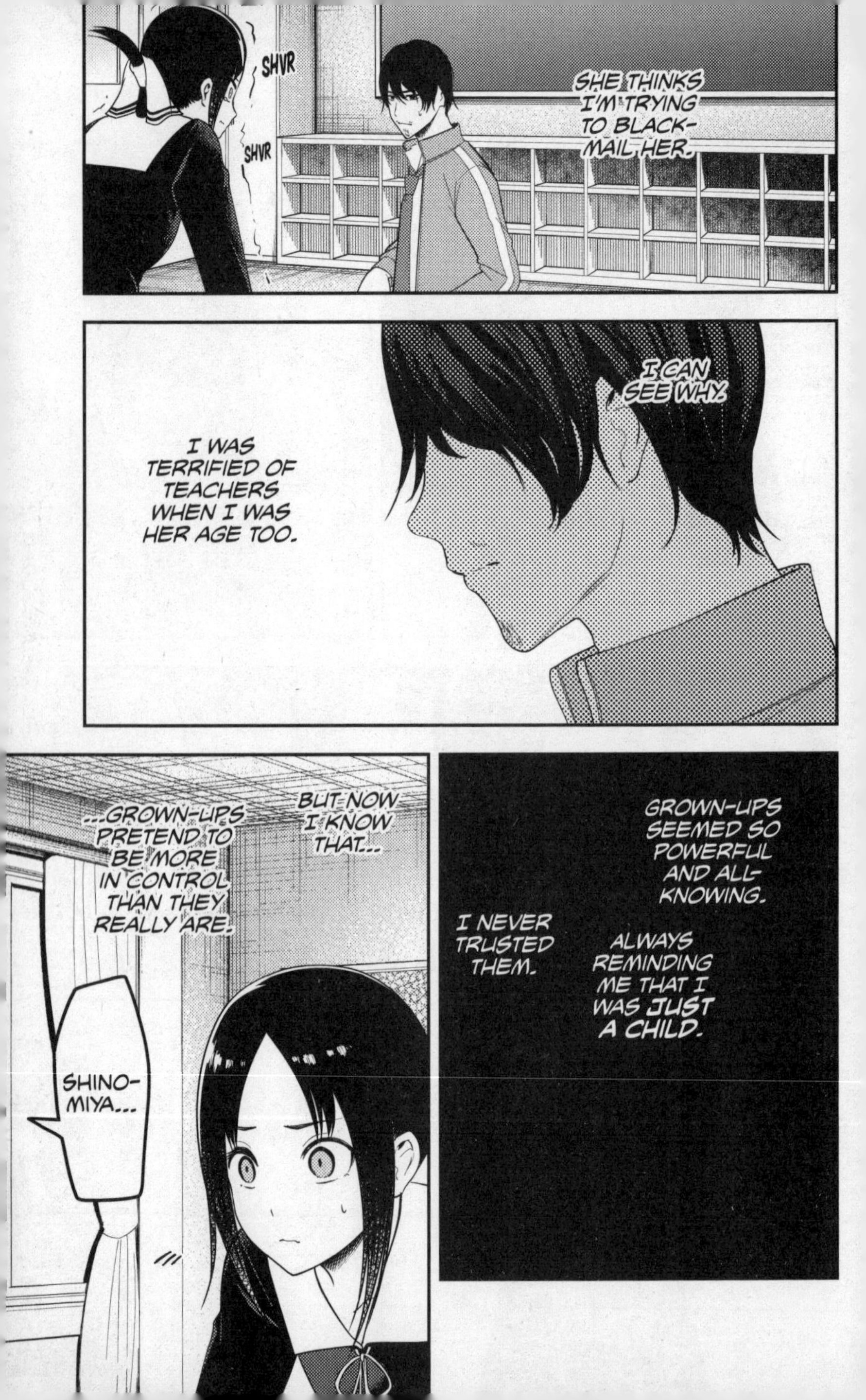
SHE THINKS I'M TRYING TO BLACK-MAIL HER.
SHVR
SHVR
I CAN SEE WHY.
I WAS TERRIFIED OF TEACHERS WHEN I WAS HER AGE TOO.
GROWN-UPS SEEMED SO POWERFUL AND ALL-KNOWING.
ALWAYS REMINDING ME THAT I WAS JUST A CHILD.
I NEVER TRUSTED THEM.
BUT NOW I KNOW THAT...
...GROWN-UPS PRETEND TO BE MORE IN CONTROL THAN THEY REALLY ARE.
SHINO-MIYA...

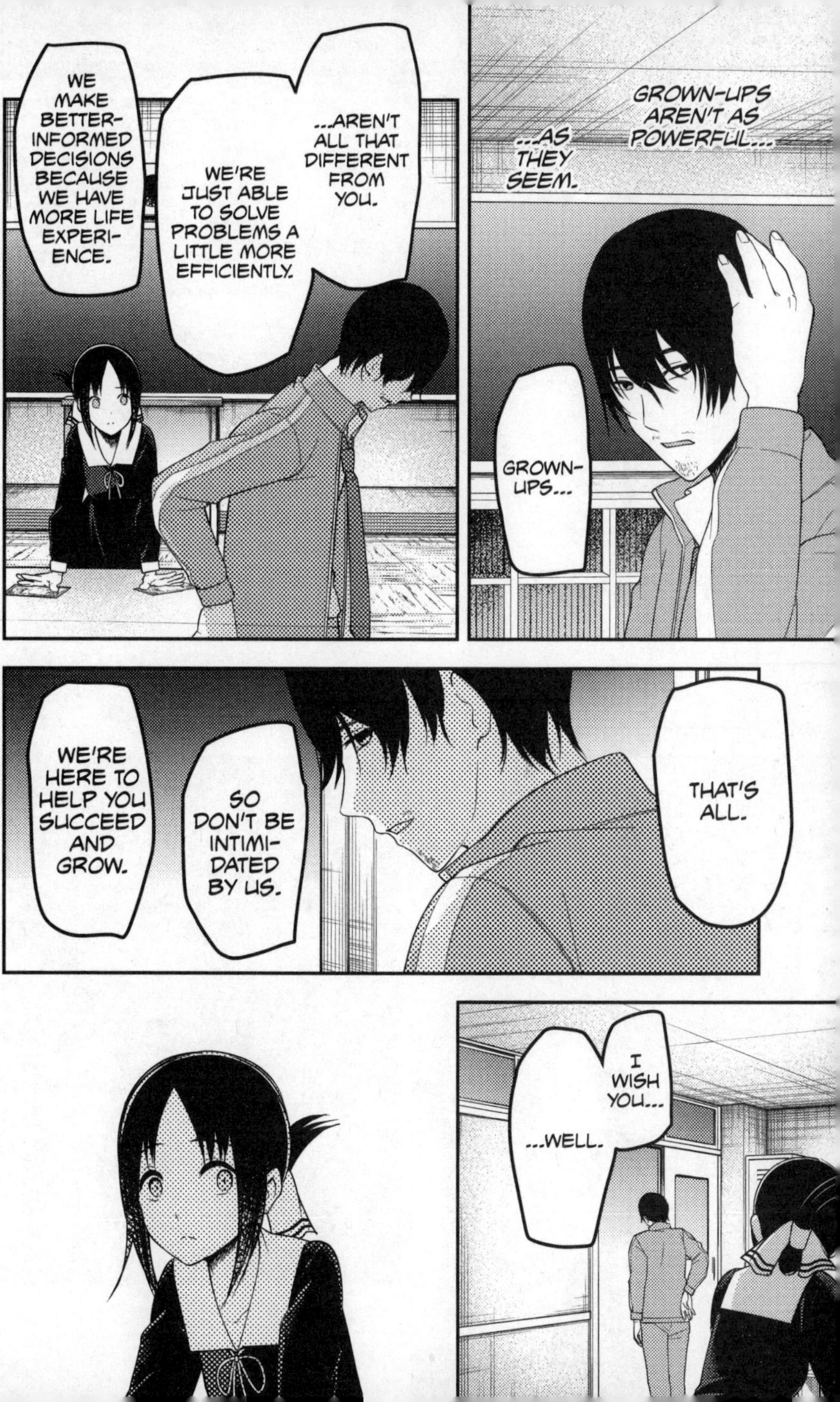
GROWN-UPS AREN'T AS POWERFUL...
...AS THEY SEEM.
GROWN-UPS...
...AREN'T ALL THAT DIFFERENT FROM YOU.
WE'RE JUST ABLE TO SOLVE PROBLEMS A LITTLE MORE EFFICIENTLY.
WE MAKE BETTER-INFORMED DECISIONS BECAUSE WE HAVE MORE LIFE EXPERI-ENCE.
THAT'S ALL.
SO DON'T BE INTIMI-DATED BY US.
WE'RE HERE TO HELP YOU SUCCEED AND GROW.
I WISH YOU...
...WELL.

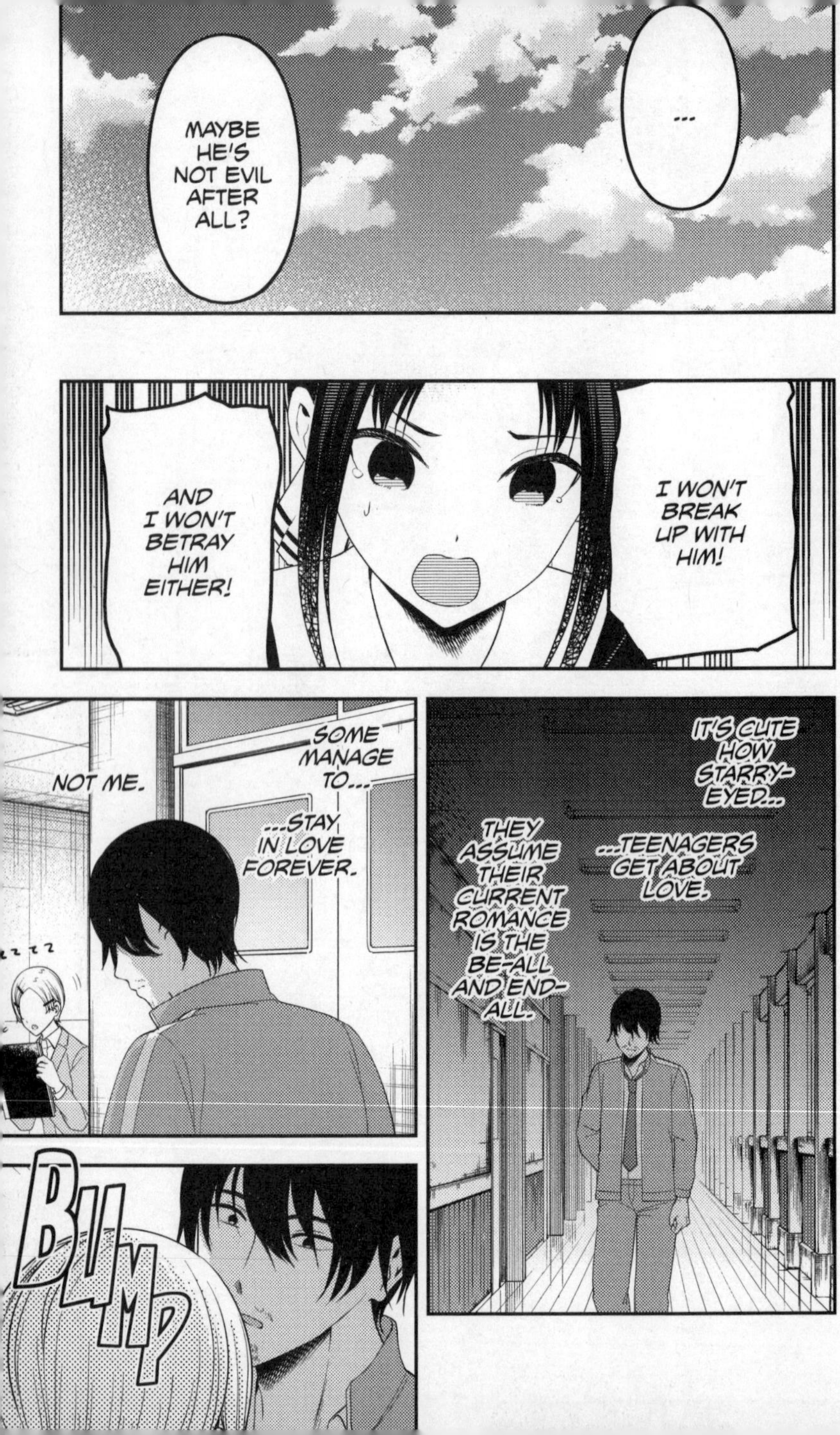
...
MAYBE HE'S NOT EVIL AFTER ALL?
I WON'T BREAK UP WITH HIM!
AND I WON'T BETRAY HIM EITHER!
IT'S CUTE HOW STARRY-EYED...
...TEENAGERS GET ABOUT LOVE.
THEY ASSUME THEIR CURRENT ROMANCE IS THE BE-ALL AND END-ALL.
SOME MANAGE TO...
...STAY IN LOVE FOREVER.
NOT ME.
BUMP

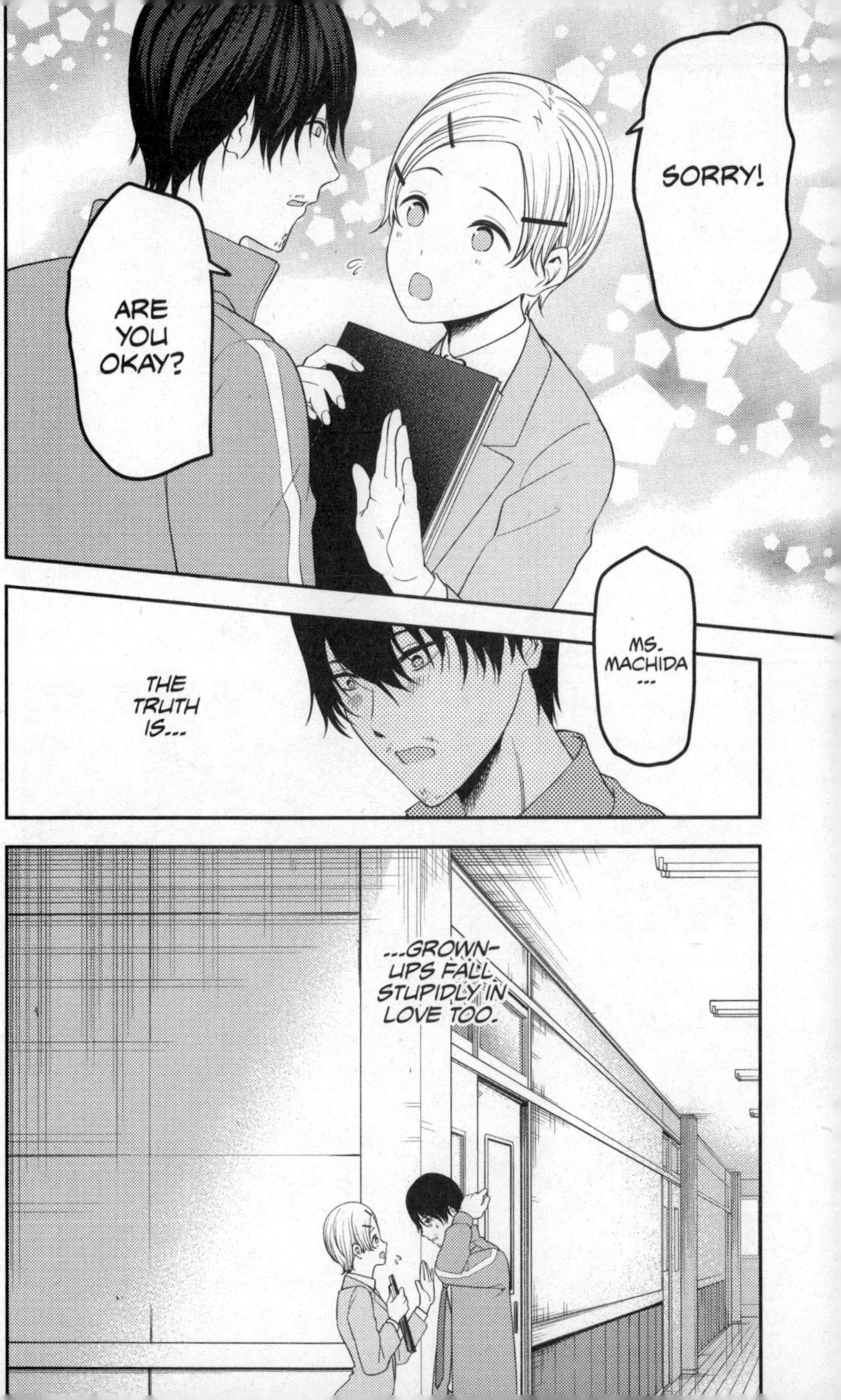
SORRY!
ARE YOU OKAY?
MS. MACHIDA...
THE TRUTH IS...
...GROWN-UPS FALL STUPIDLY IN LOVE TOO.

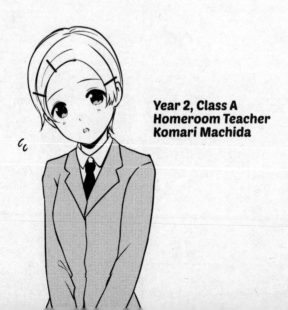

Year 2, Class A
Homeroom Teacher
Komari Machida

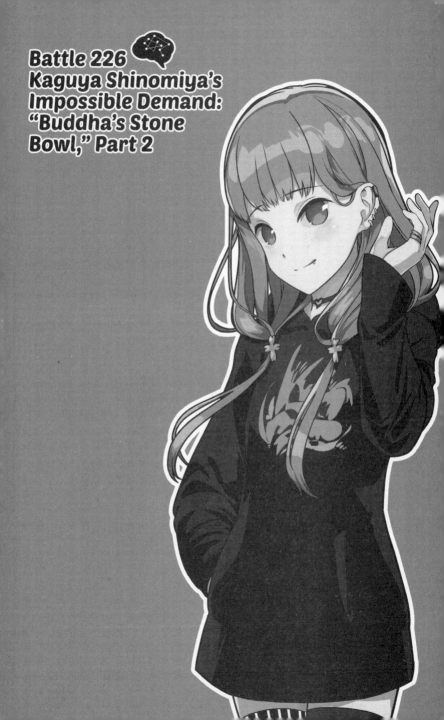

Battle 226
Kaguya Shinomiya's Impossible Demand: "Buddha's Stone Bowl," Part 2

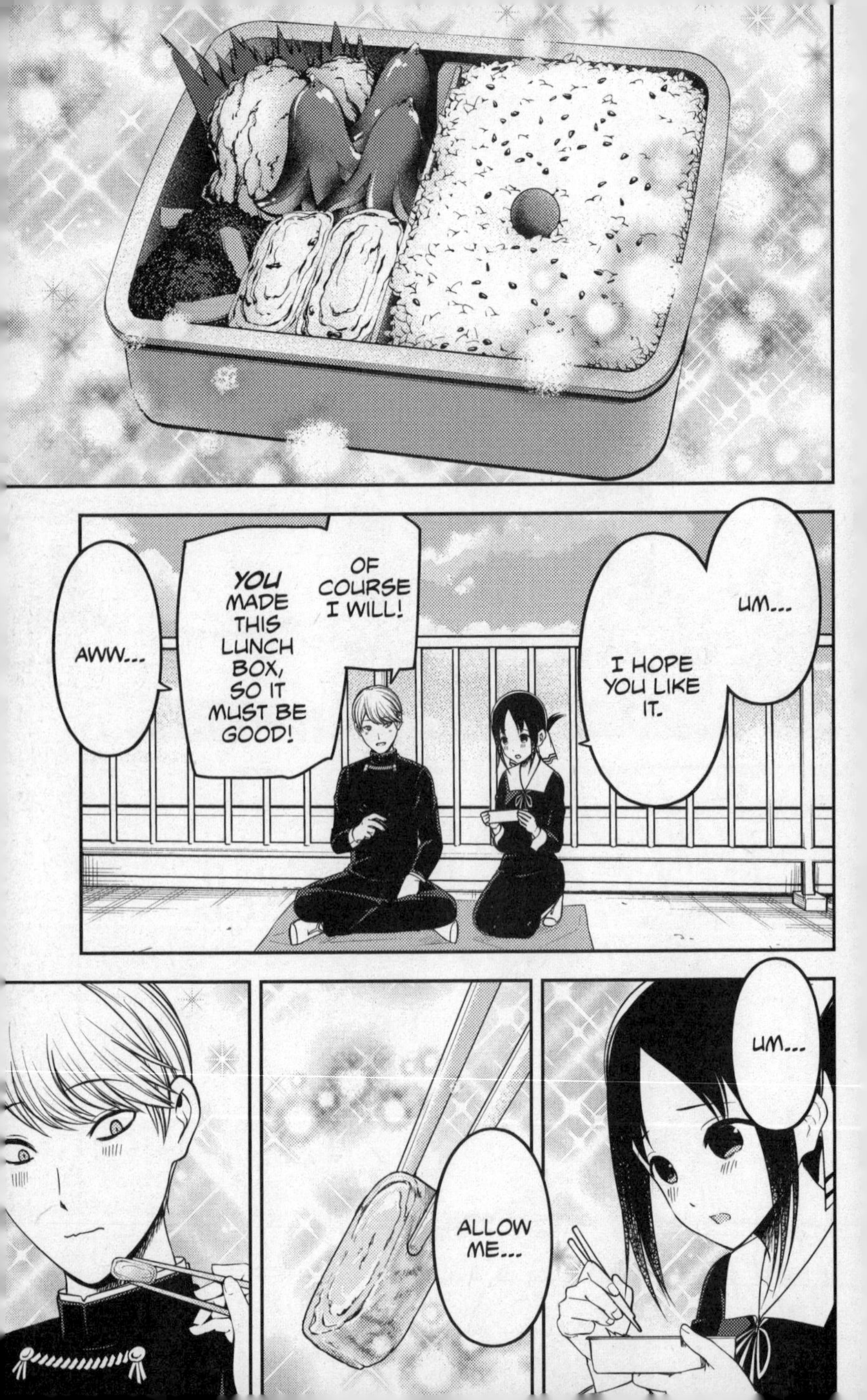
UM...
I HOPE YOU LIKE IT.
OF COURSE I WILL!
YOU MADE THIS LUNCH BOX, SO IT MUST BE GOOD!
AWW...
UM...
ALLOW ME...

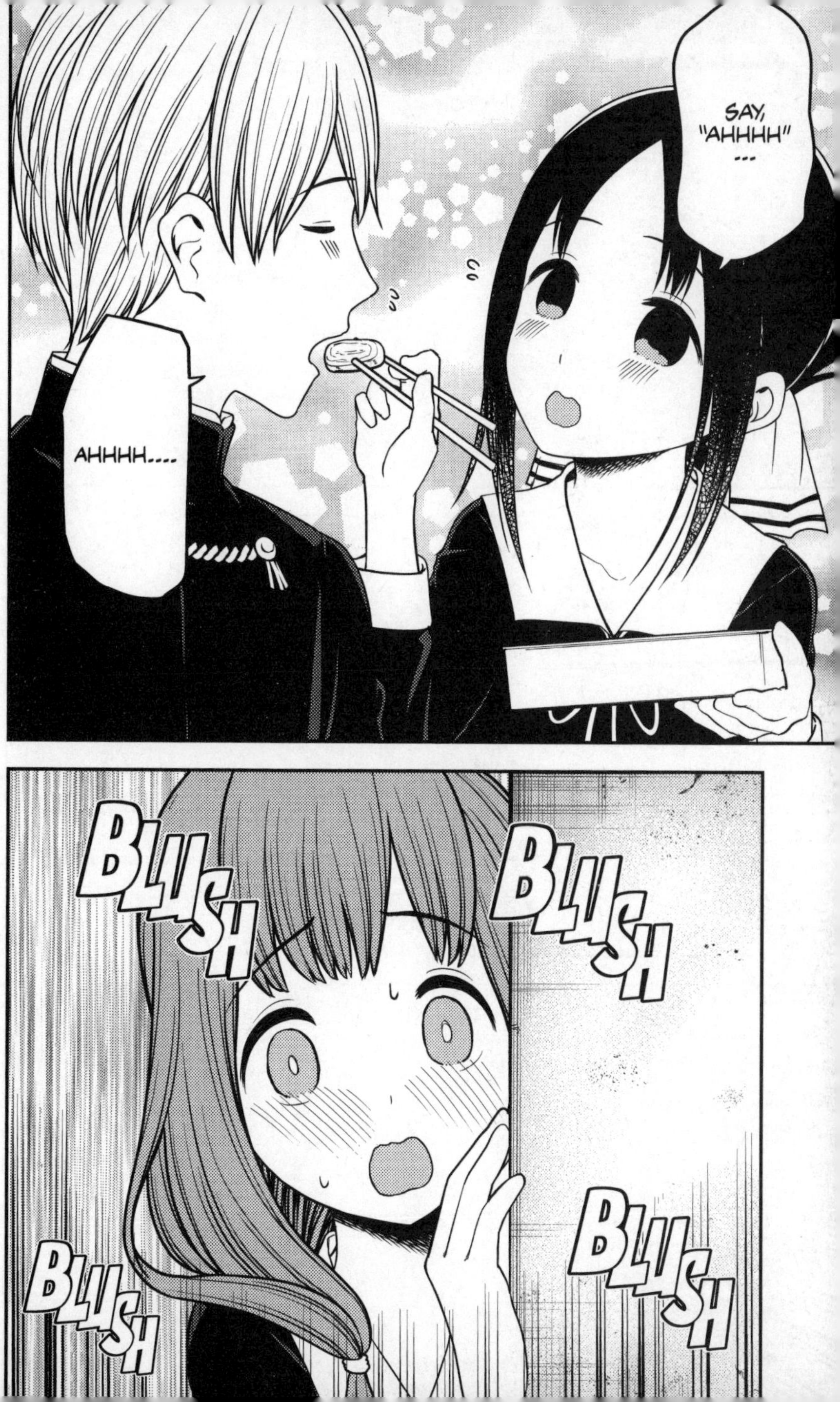
SAY, "AHHHH" ---
AHHHH....
BLUSH
BLUSH
BLUSH
BLUSH

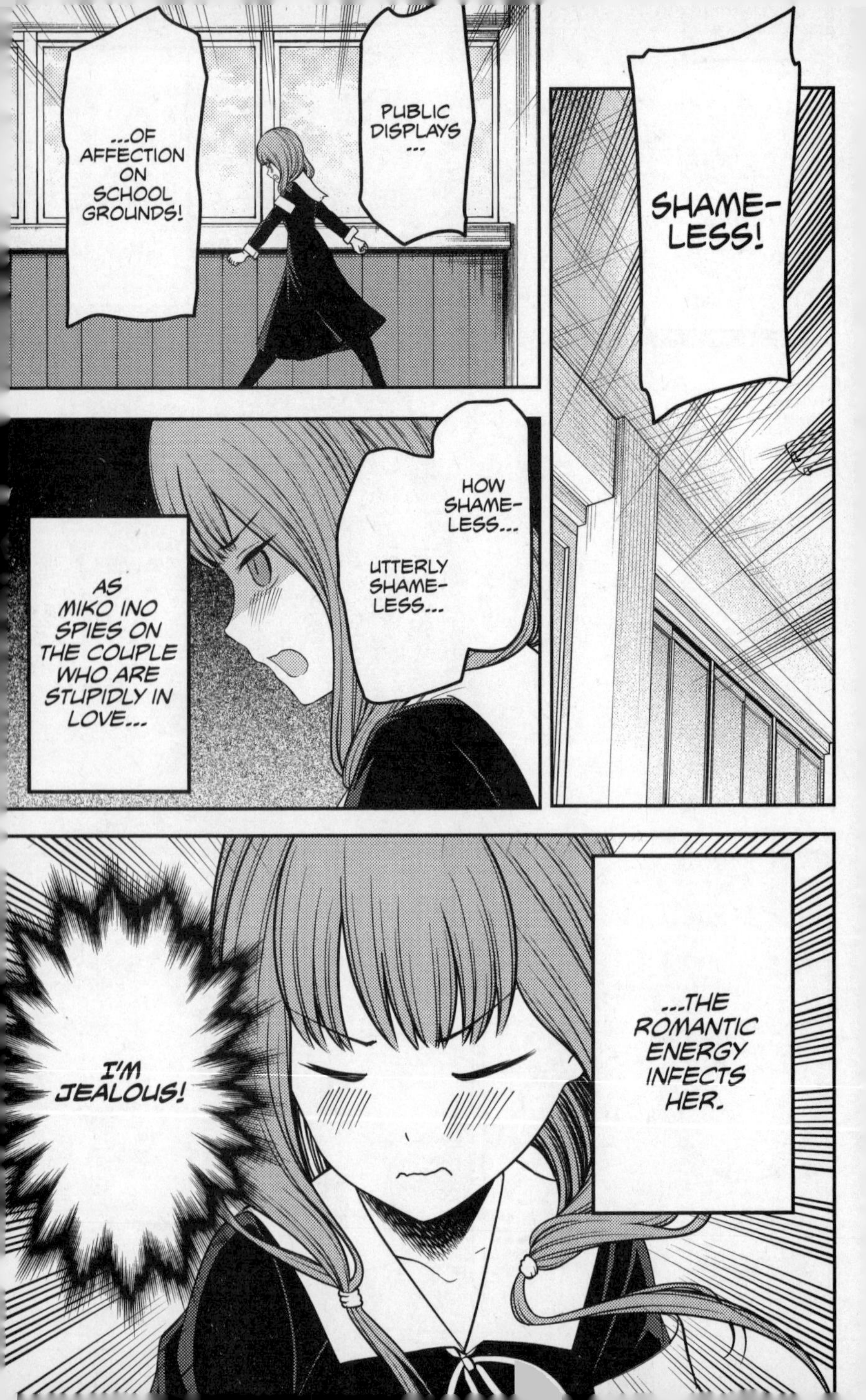
SHAME-LESS!
PUBLIC DISPLAYS...
...OF AFFECTION ON SCHOOL GROUNDS!
HOW SHAME-LESS...
UTTERLY SHAME-LESS...
AS MIKO INO SPIES ON THE COUPLE WHO ARE STUPIDLY IN LOVE...
...THE ROMANTIC ENERGY INFECTS HER.
I'M JEALOUS!

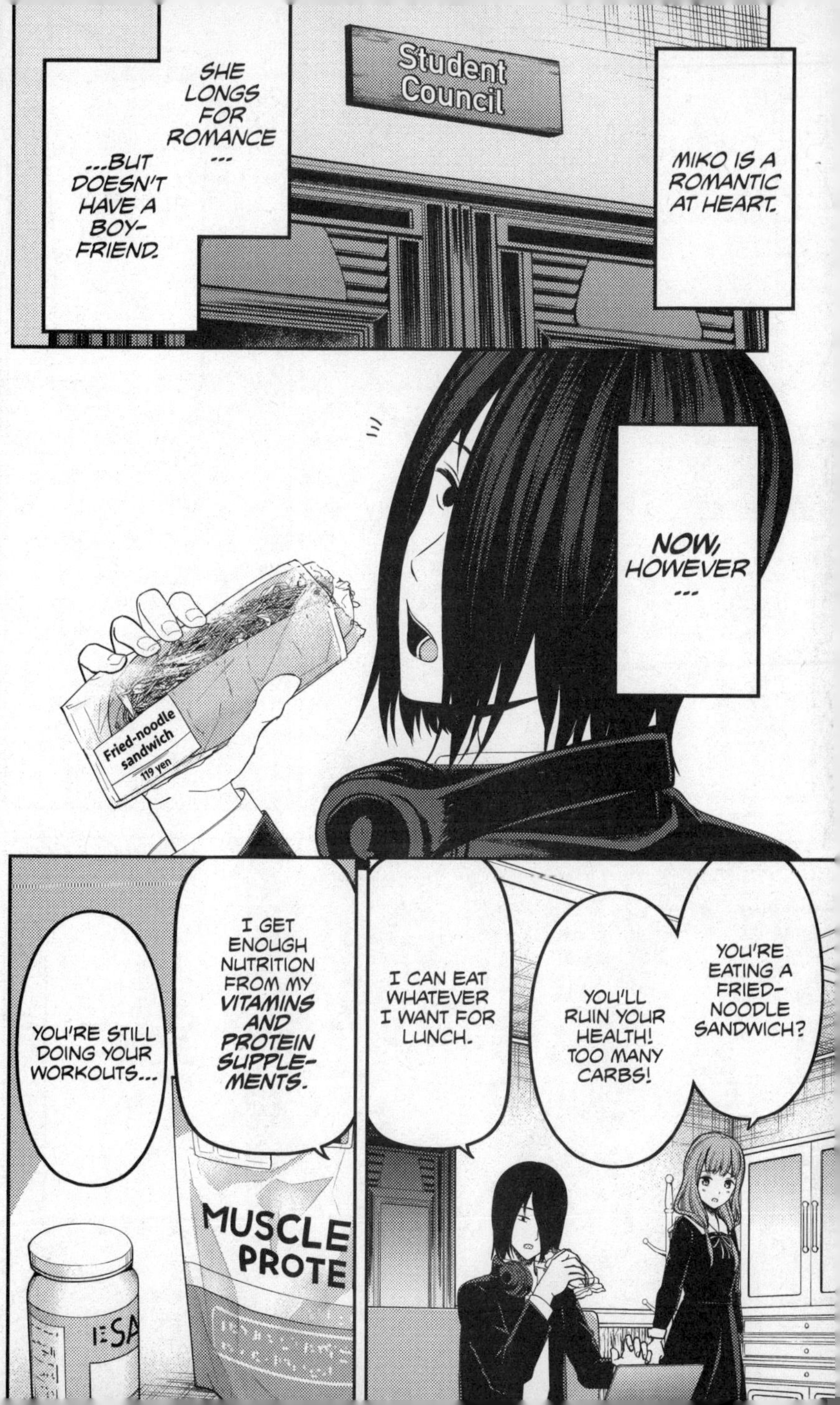
Student Council
MIKO IS A ROMANTIC AT HEART.
SHE LONGS FOR ROMANCE...
...BUT DOESN'T HAVE A BOYFRIEND.
NOW, HOWEVER...
Fried-noodle sandwich 119 yen
YOU'RE EATING A FRIED-NOODLE SANDWICH?
YOU'LL RUIN YOUR HEALTH! TOO MANY CARBS!
I CAN EAT WHATEVER I WANT FOR LUNCH.
I GET ENOUGH NUTRITION FROM MY *VITAMINS AND PROTEIN SUPPLEMENTS.*
YOU'RE STILL DOING YOUR WORKOUTS...
MUSCLE PROTE

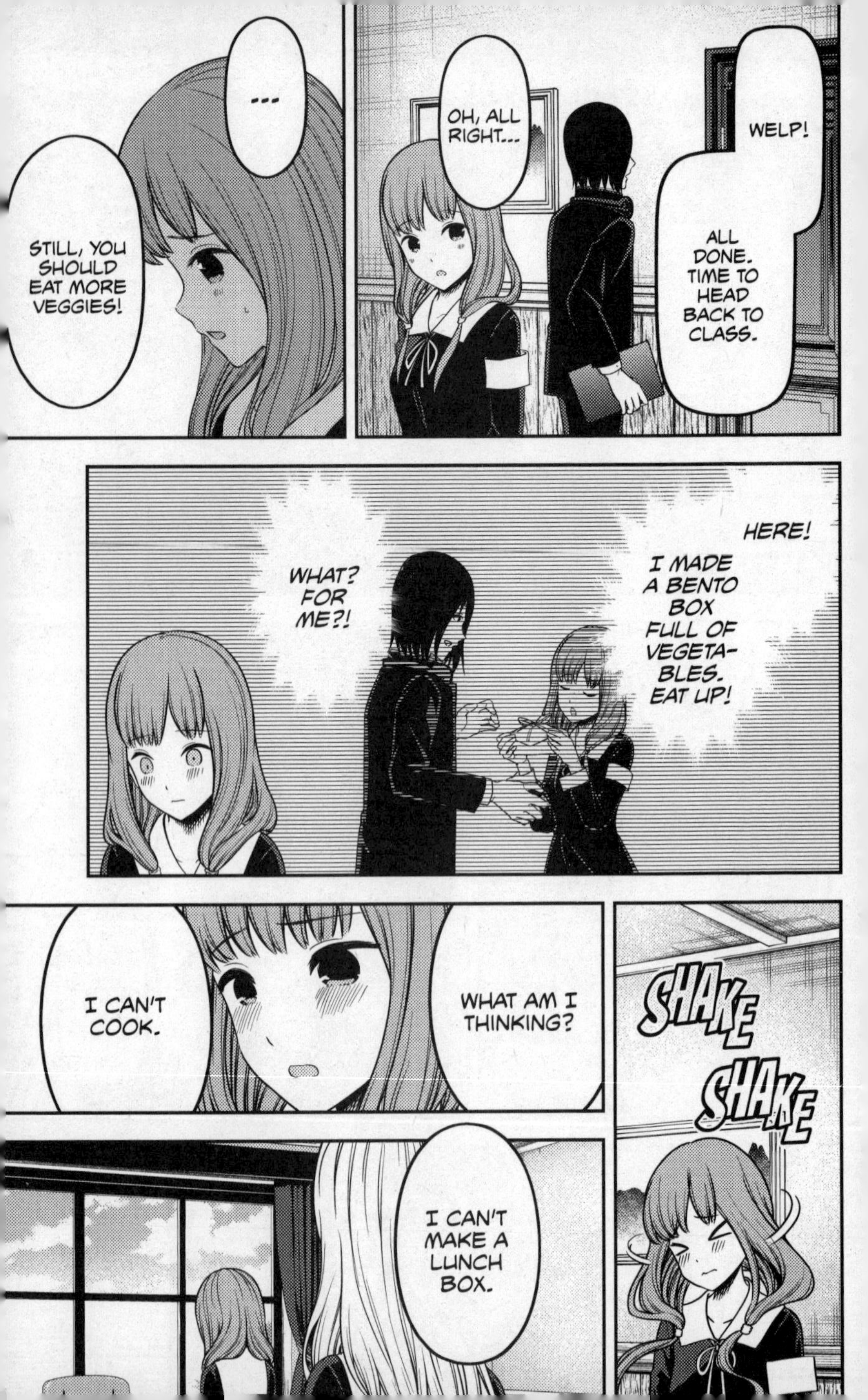
WELP!
ALL DONE. TIME TO HEAD BACK TO CLASS.
OH, ALL RIGHT...
...
STILL, YOU SHOULD EAT MORE VEGGIES!
HERE!
I MADE A BENTO BOX FULL OF VEGETA-BLES. EAT UP!
WHAT? FOR ME?!
SHAKE
SHAKE
WHAT AM I THINKING?
I CAN'T COOK.
I CAN'T MAKE A LUNCH BOX.

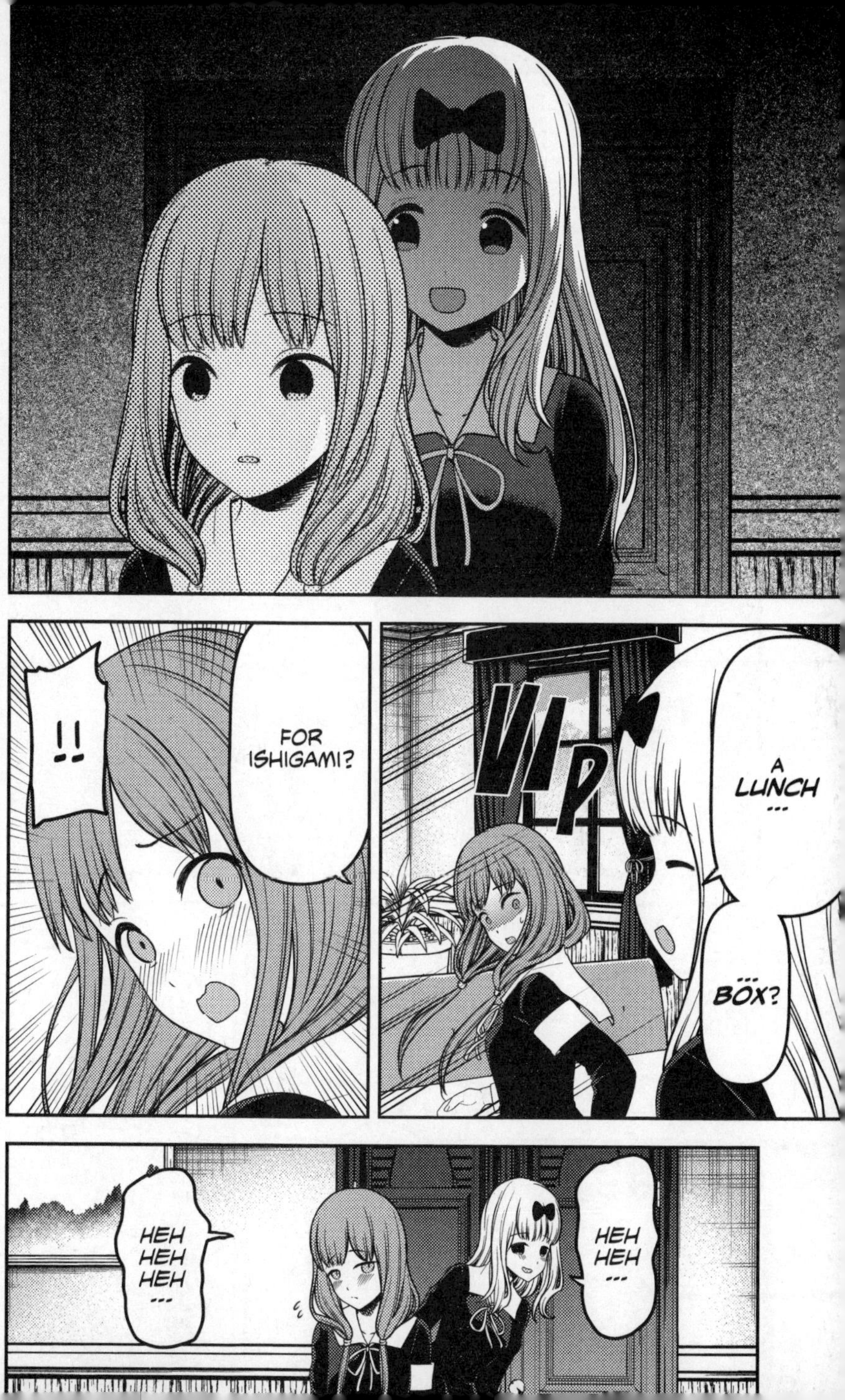
A LUNCH ...
VIP
... BÖX?
FOR ISHIGAMI?
!!
HEH HEH ...
HEH HEH HEH ...

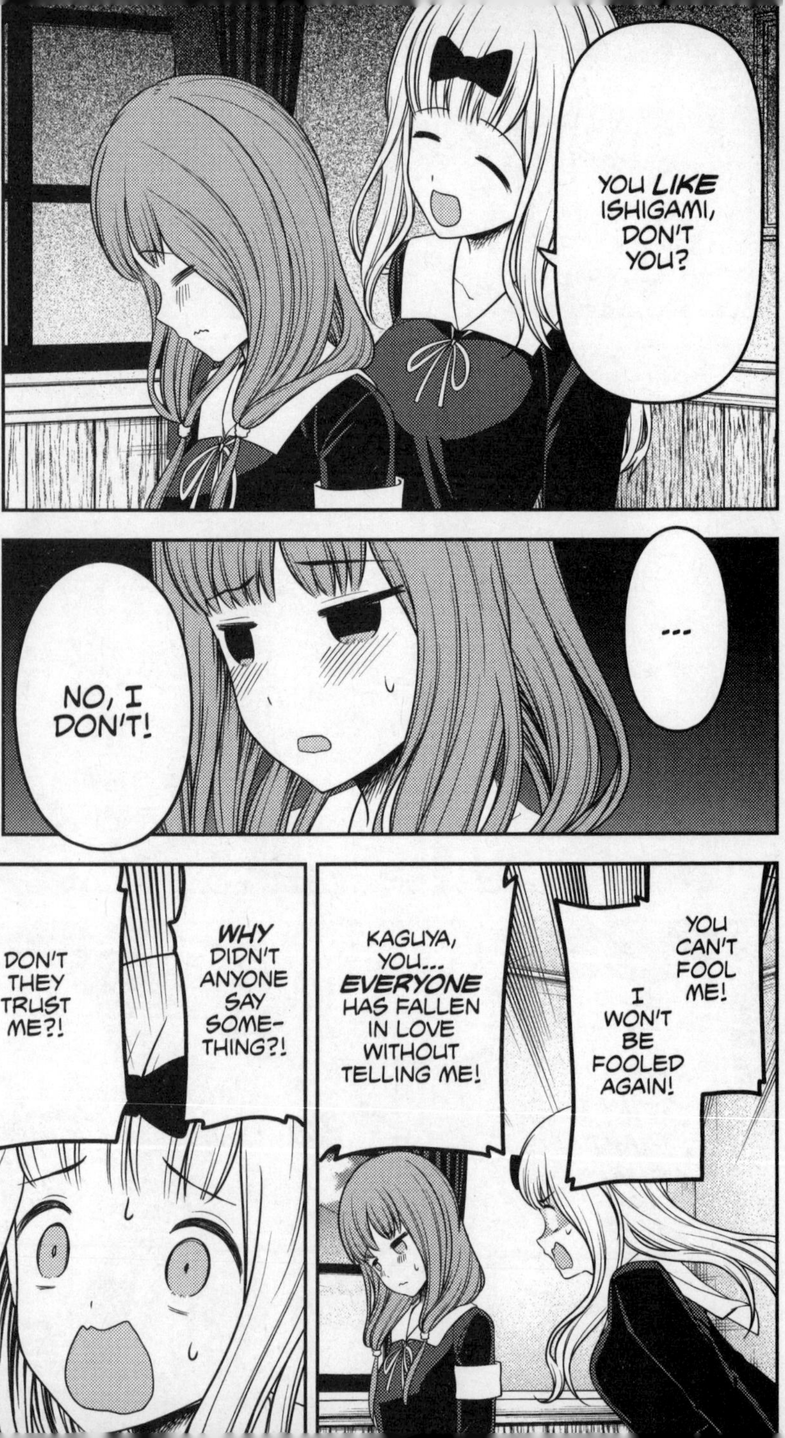
YOU LIKE ISHIGAMI, DON'T YOU?
...
NO, I DON'T!
YOU CAN'T FOOL ME!
I WON'T BE FOOLED AGAIN!
KAGUYA, YOU... EVERYONE HAS FALLEN IN LOVE WITHOUT TELLING ME!
WHY DIDN'T ANYONE SAY SOME-THING?!
DON'T THEY TRUST ME?!

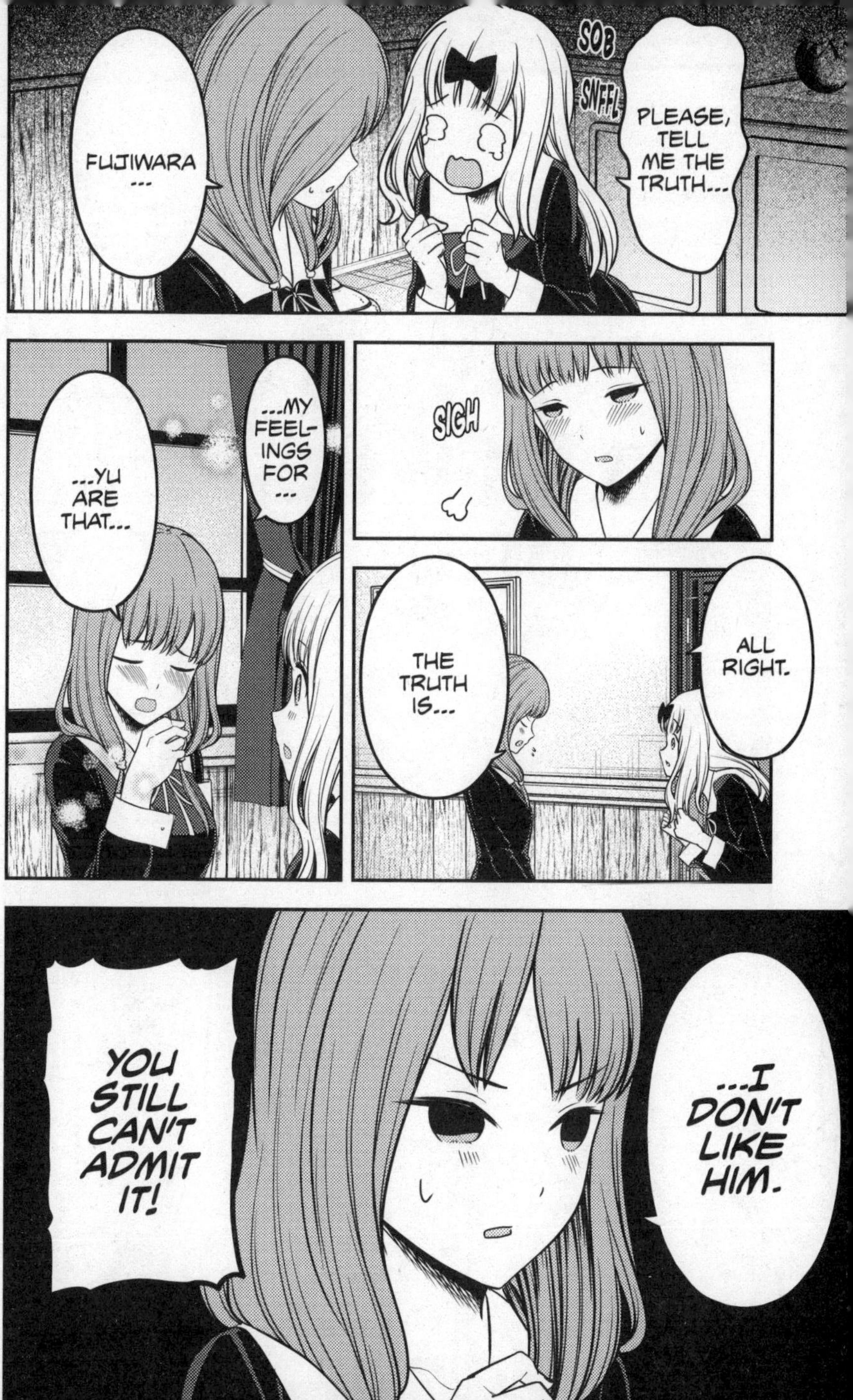
SOB
SNFFL
PLEASE, TELL ME THE TRUTH...
FUJIWARA...
SIGH
ALL RIGHT.
THE TRUTH IS...
...MY FEEL-INGS FOR...
...YU ARE THAT...
...I DON'T LIKE HIM.
YOU STILL CAN'T ADMIT IT!

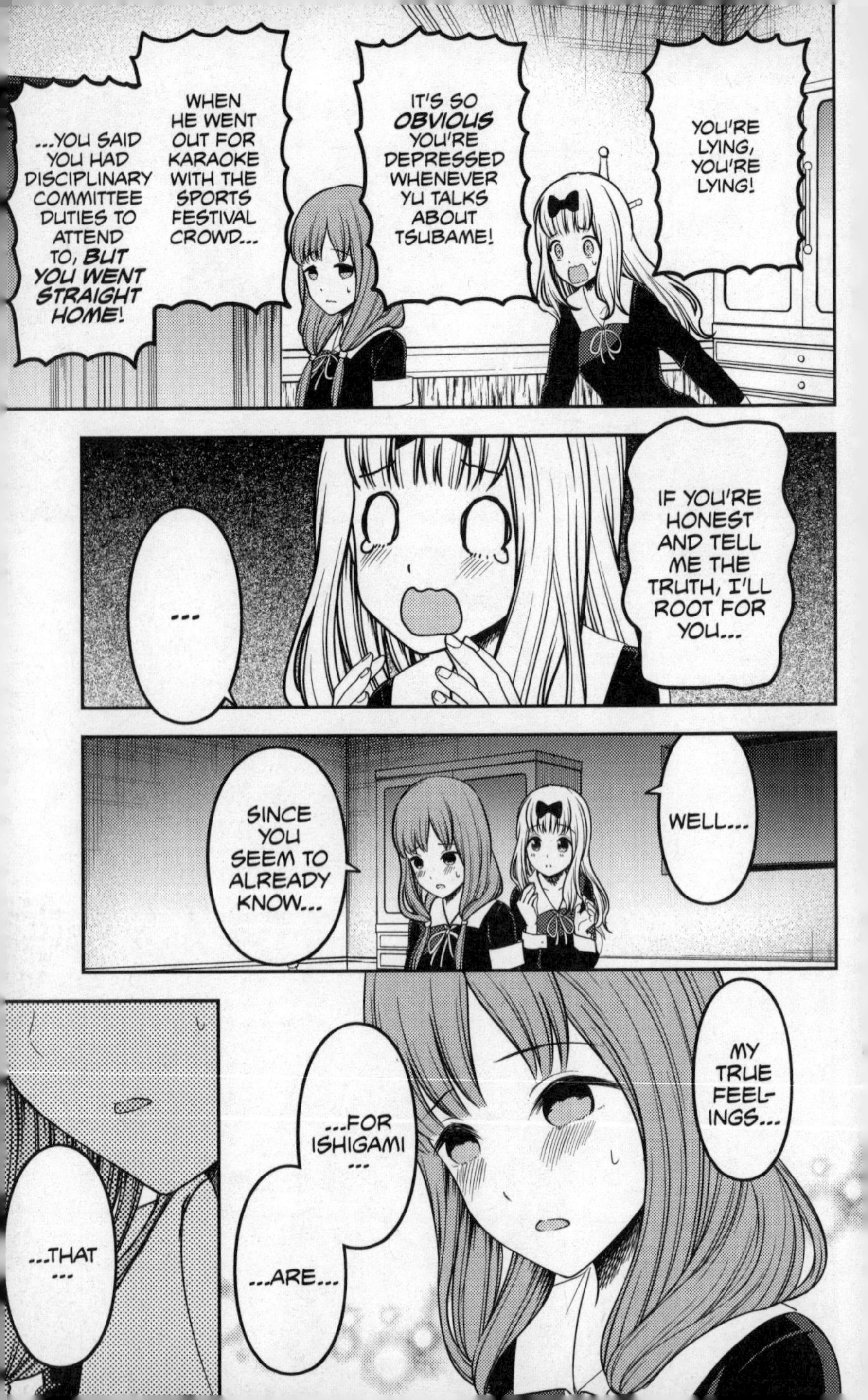
YOU'RE LYING, YOU'RE LYING!
IT'S SO OBVIOUS YOU'RE DEPRESSED WHENEVER YU TALKS ABOUT TSUBAME!
WHEN HE WENT OUT FOR KARAOKE WITH THE SPORTS FESTIVAL CROWD...
...YOU SAID YOU HAD DISCIPLINARY COMMITTEE DUTIES TO ATTEND TO, BUT YOU WENT STRAIGHT HOME!
IF YOU'RE HONEST AND TELL ME THE TRUTH, I'LL ROOT FOR YOU...
...
WELL...
SINCE YOU SEEM TO ALREADY KNOW...
MY TRUE FEEL-INGS...
...FOR ISHIGAMI ...
...ARE...
...THAT ...

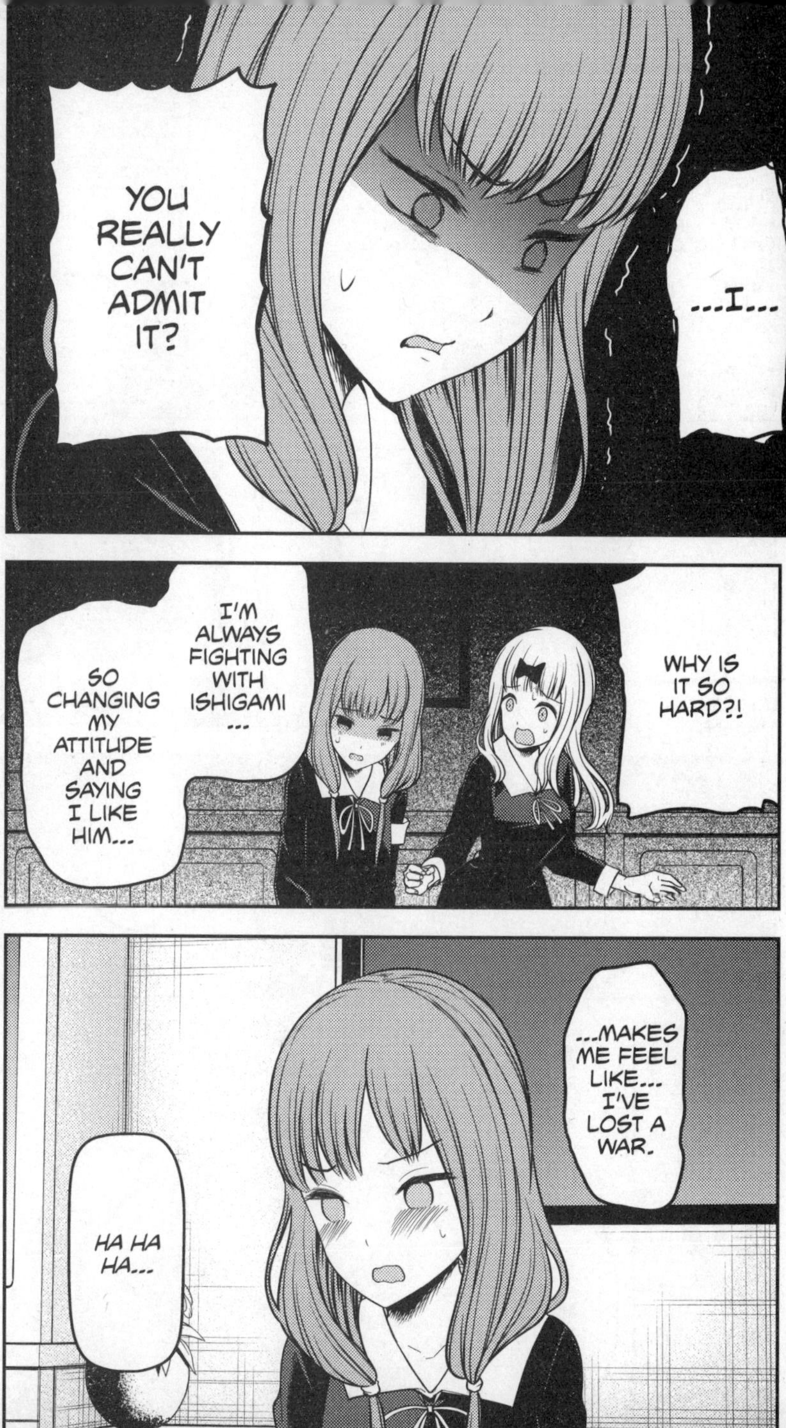
...I...
YOU REALLY CAN'T ADMIT IT?
WHY IS IT SO HARD?!
I'M ALWAYS FIGHTING WITH ISHIGAMI ...
SO CHANGING MY ATTITUDE AND SAYING I LIKE HIM...
...MAKES ME FEEL LIKE... I'VE LOST A WAR.
HA HA HA...

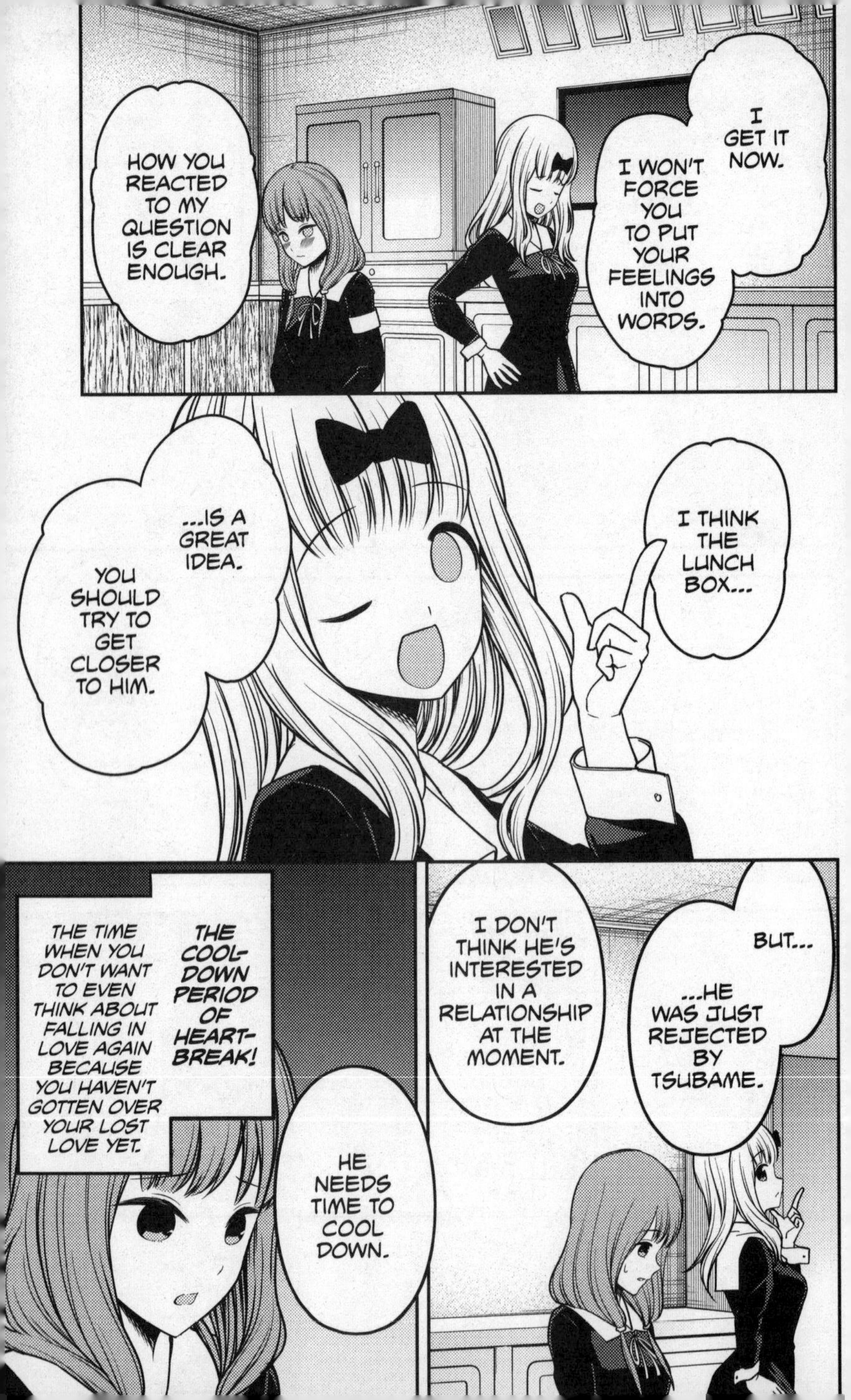
I GET IT NOW.
I WON'T FORCE YOU TO PUT YOUR FEELINGS INTO WORDS.
HOW YOU REACTED TO MY QUESTION IS CLEAR ENOUGH.
I THINK THE LUNCH BOX...
...IS A GREAT IDEA.
YOU SHOULD TRY TO GET CLOSER TO HIM.
BUT...
...HE WAS JUST REJECTED BY TSUBAME.
I DON'T THINK HE'S INTERESTED IN A RELATIONSHIP AT THE MOMENT.
HE NEEDS TIME TO COOL DOWN.
THE COOL-DOWN PERIOD OF HEART-BREAK!
THE TIME WHEN YOU DON'T WANT TO EVEN THINK ABOUT FALLING IN LOVE AGAIN BECAUSE YOU HAVEN'T GOTTEN OVER YOUR LOST LOVE YET.

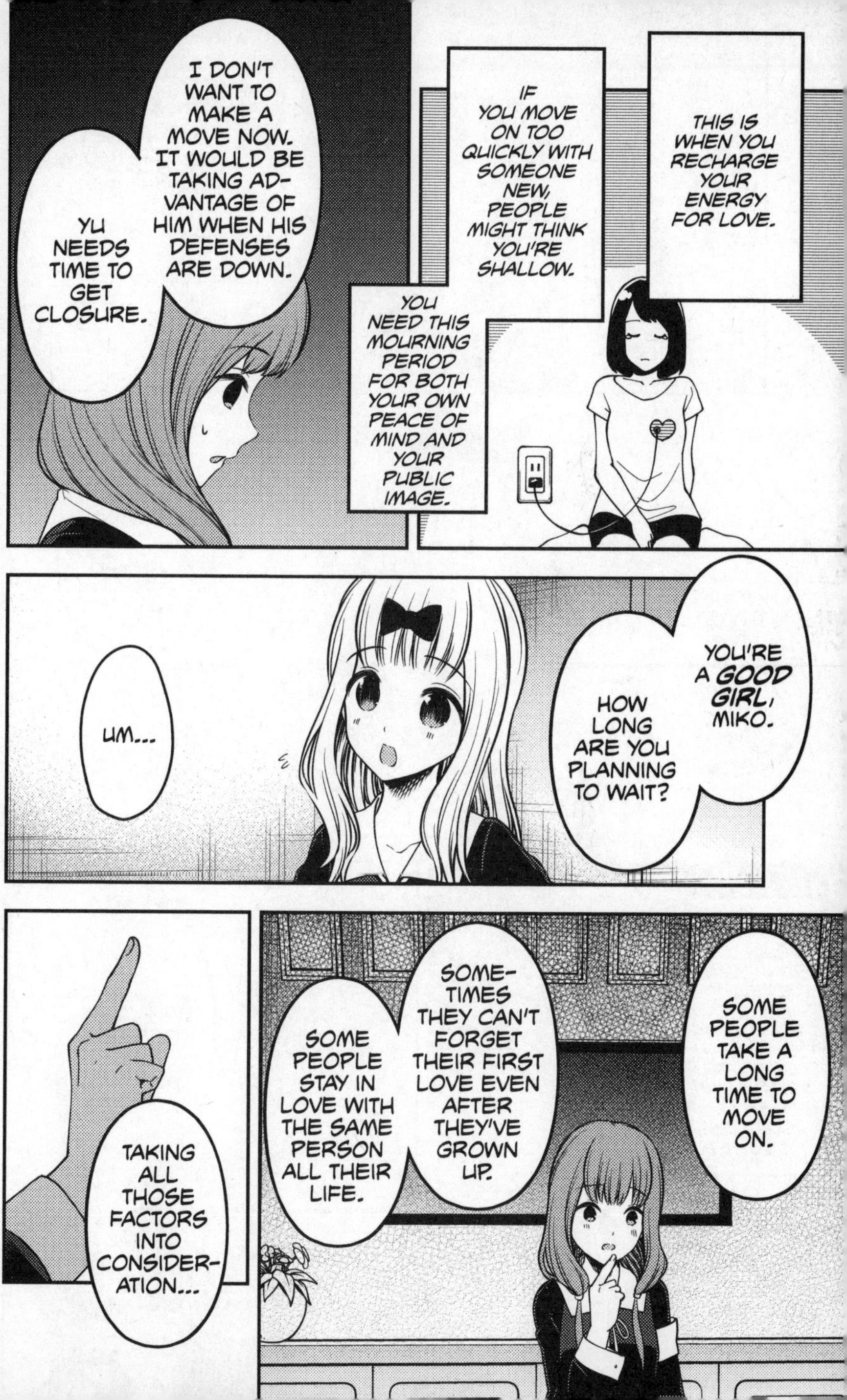
THIS IS WHEN YOU RECHARGE YOUR ENERGY FOR LOVE.
IF YOU MOVE ON TOO QUICKLY WITH SOMEONE NEW, PEOPLE MIGHT THINK YOU'RE SHALLOW.
YOU NEED THIS MOURNING PERIOD FOR BOTH YOUR OWN PEACE OF MIND AND YOUR PUBLIC IMAGE.
I DON'T WANT TO MAKE A MOVE NOW. IT WOULD BE TAKING ADVANTAGE OF HIM WHEN HIS DEFENSES ARE DOWN.
YU NEEDS TIME TO GET CLOSURE.
YOU'RE A GOOD GIRL, MIKO.
HOW LONG ARE YOU PLANNING TO WAIT?
UM...
SOME PEOPLE TAKE A LONG TIME TO MOVE ON.
SOMETIMES THEY CAN'T FORGET THEIR FIRST LOVE EVEN AFTER THEY'VE GROWN UP.
SOME PEOPLE STAY IN LOVE WITH THE SAME PERSON ALL THEIR LIFE.
TAKING ALL THOSE FACTORS INTO CONSIDERATION...

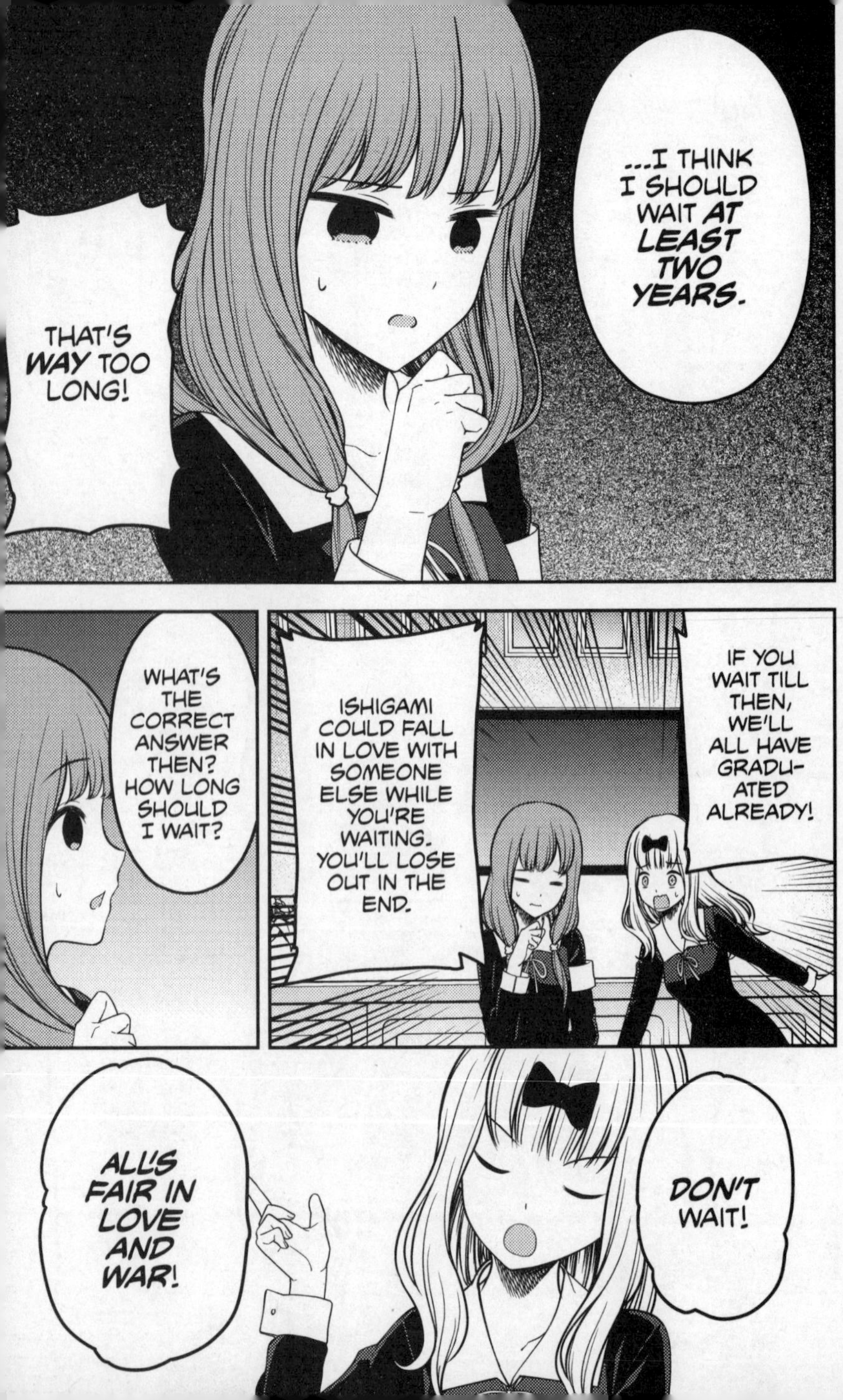
...I THINK I SHOULD WAIT AT LEAST TWO YEARS.
THAT'S WAY TOO LONG!
IF YOU WAIT TILL THEN, WE'LL ALL HAVE GRADU-ATED ALREADY!
ISHIGAMI COULD FALL IN LOVE WITH SOMEONE ELSE WHILE YOU'RE WAITING. YOU'LL LOSE OUT IN THE END.
WHAT'S THE CORRECT ANSWER THEN? HOW LONG SHOULD I WAIT?
DON'T WAIT!
ALL'S FAIR IN LOVE AND WAR!

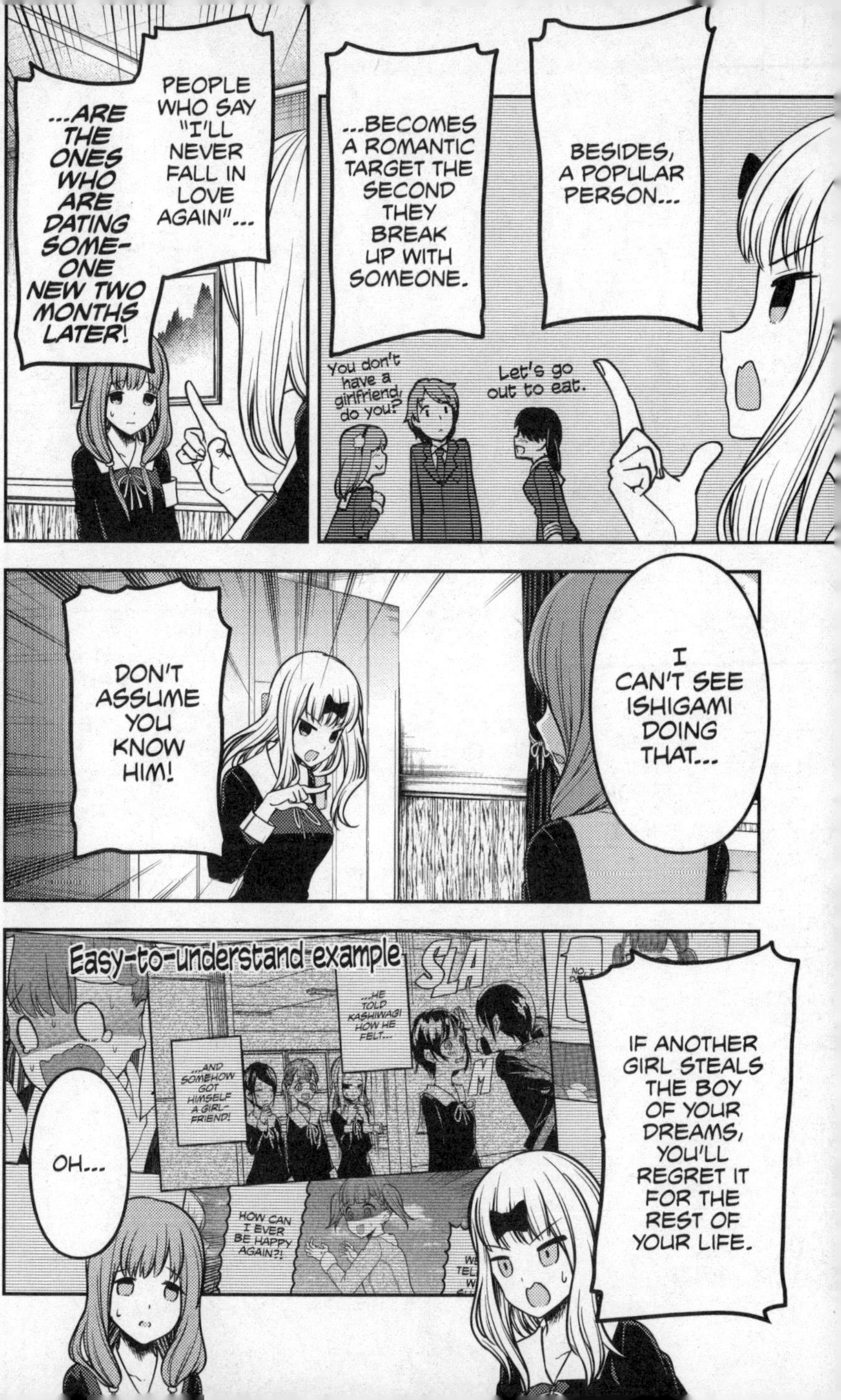
BESIDES, A POPULAR PERSON...
...BECOMES A ROMANTIC TARGET THE SECOND THEY BREAK UP WITH SOMEONE.
Let's go out to eat.
You don't have a girlfriend, do you?
PEOPLE WHO SAY "I'LL NEVER FALL IN LOVE AGAIN"...
...ARE THE ONES WHO ARE DATING SOMEONE NEW TWO MONTHS LATER!
I CAN'T SEE ISHIGAMI DOING THAT...
DON'T ASSUME YOU KNOW HIM!
IF ANOTHER GIRL STEALS THE BOY OF YOUR DREAMS, YOU'LL REGRET IT FOR THE REST OF YOUR LIFE.
Easy-to-understand example
SLA
...HE TOLD KASHIWAGI HOW HE FELT...
...AND SOMEHOW GOT HIMSELF A GIRLFRIEND!
HOW CAN I EVER BE HAPPY AGAIN?!
OH...

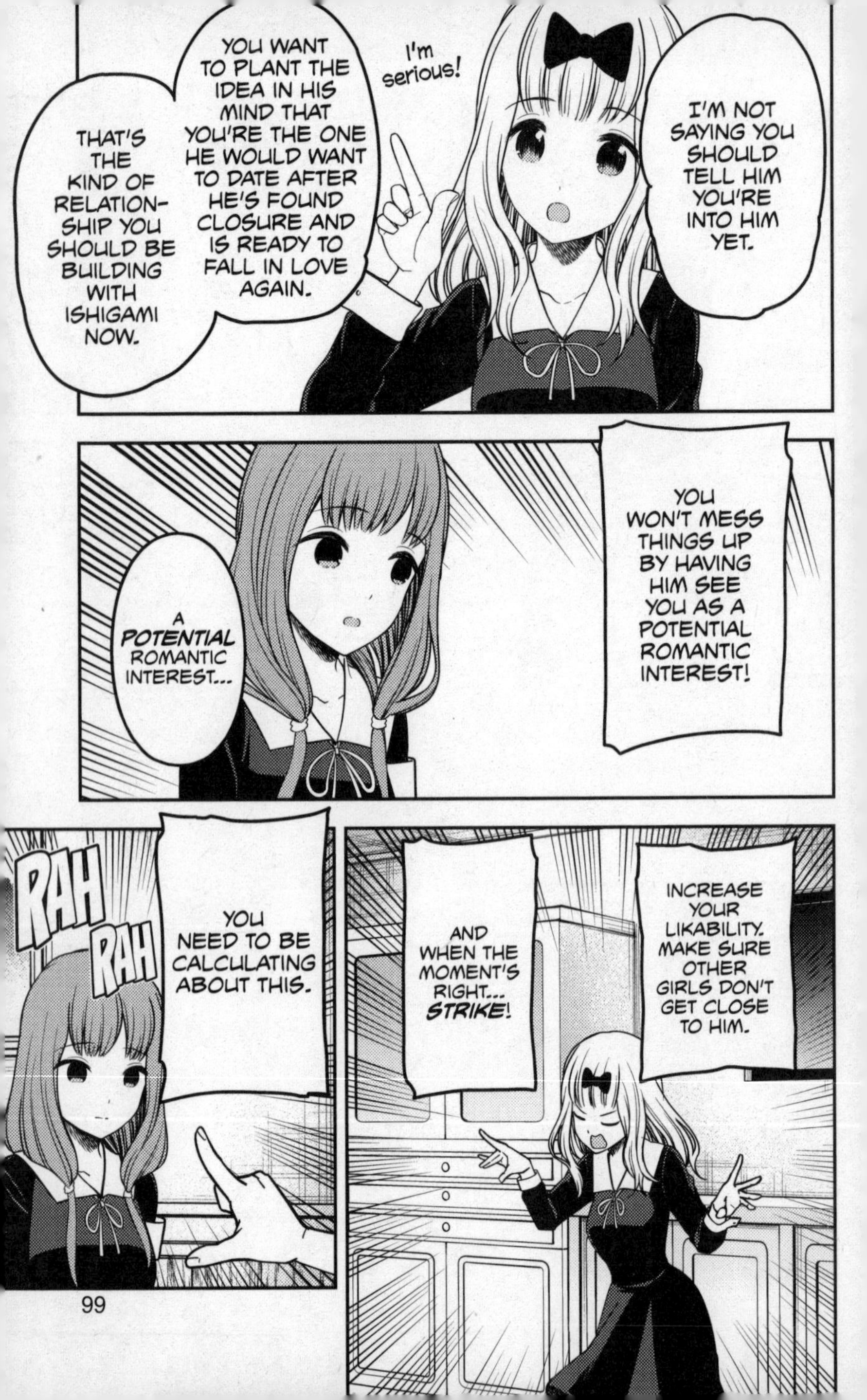
I'M NOT SAYING YOU SHOULD TELL HIM YOU'RE INTO HIM YET.
I'm serious!
YOU WANT TO PLANT THE IDEA IN HIS MIND THAT YOU'RE THE ONE HE WOULD WANT TO DATE AFTER HE'S FOUND CLOSURE AND IS READY TO FALL IN LOVE AGAIN.
THAT'S THE KIND OF RELATION-SHIP YOU SHOULD BE BUILDING WITH ISHIGAMI NOW.
YOU WON'T MESS THINGS UP BY HAVING HIM SEE YOU AS A POTENTIAL ROMANTIC INTEREST!
A *POTENTIAL* ROMANTIC INTEREST...
INCREASE YOUR LIKABILITY. MAKE SURE OTHER GIRLS DON'T GET CLOSE TO HIM.
AND WHEN THE MOMENT'S RIGHT... *STRIKE*!
YOU NEED TO BE CALCULATING ABOUT THIS.
RAH RAH

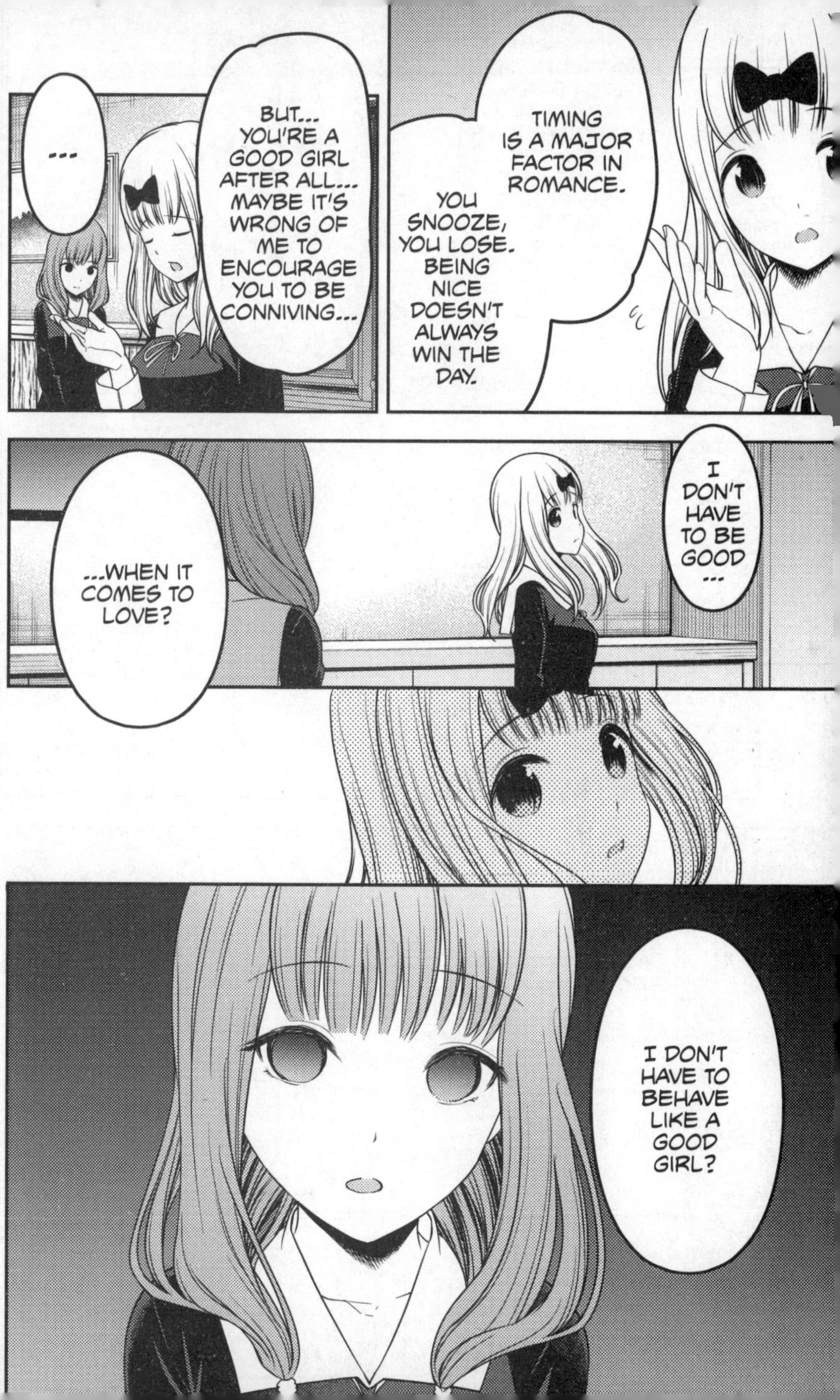
TIMING IS A MAJOR FACTOR IN ROMANCE.
YOU SNOOZE, YOU LOSE. BEING NICE DOESN'T ALWAYS WIN THE DAY.
BUT... YOU'RE A GOOD GIRL AFTER ALL... MAYBE IT'S WRONG OF ME TO ENCOURAGE YOU TO BE CONNIVING...
...
I DON'T HAVE TO BE GOOD...
...WHEN IT COMES TO LOVE?
I DON'T HAVE TO BEHAVE LIKE A GOOD GIRL?

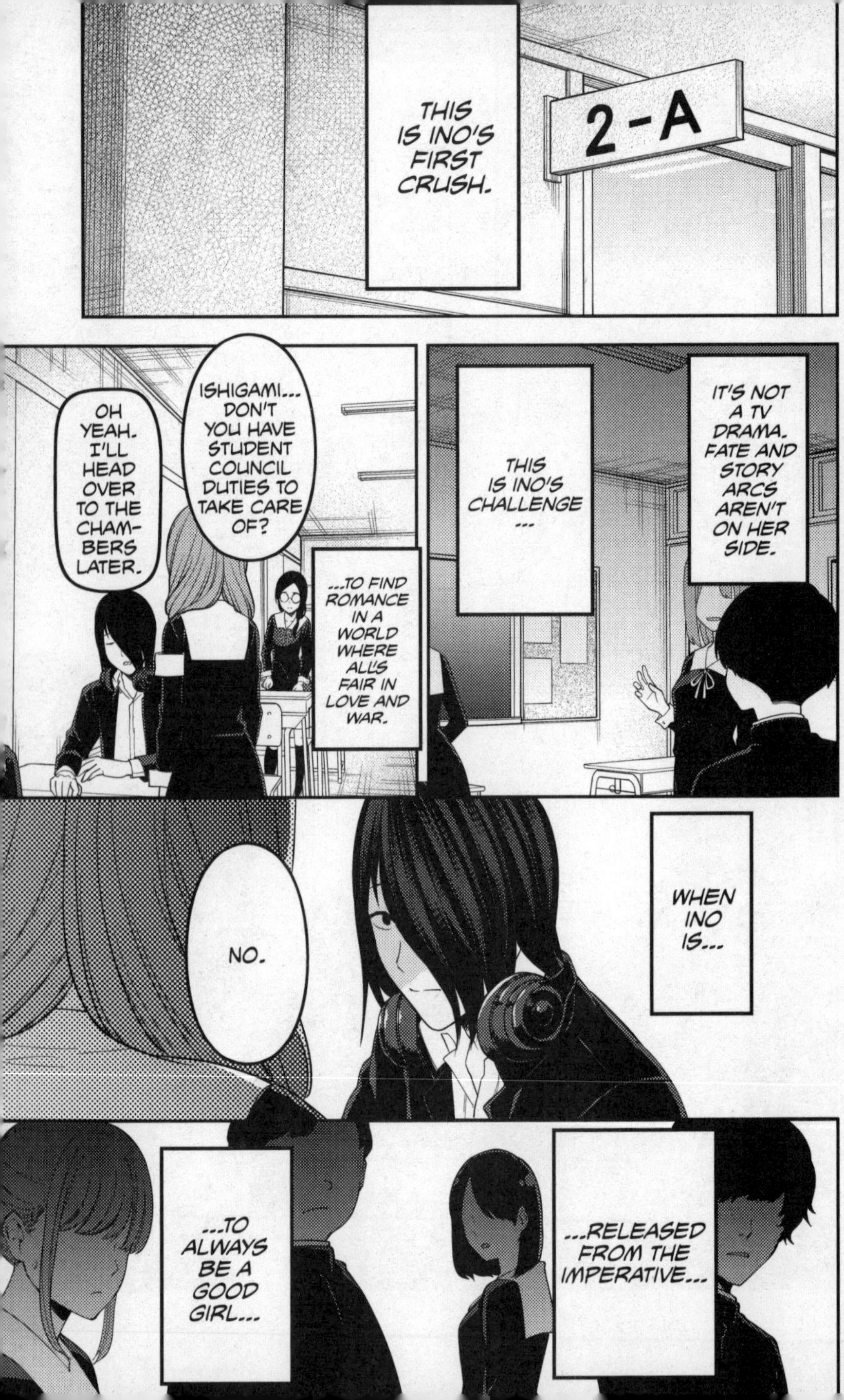
2-A
THIS IS INO'S FIRST CRUSH.
IT'S NOT A TV DRAMA. FATE AND STORY ARCS AREN'T ON HER SIDE.
THIS IS INO'S CHALLENGE...
...TO FIND ROMANCE IN A WORLD WHERE ALL'S FAIR IN LOVE AND WAR.
ISHIGAMI... DON'T YOU HAVE STUDENT COUNCIL DUTIES TO TAKE CARE OF?
OH YEAH. I'LL HEAD OVER TO THE CHAMBERS LATER.
WHEN INO IS...
NO.
...RELEASED FROM THE IMPERATIVE...
...TO ALWAYS BE A GOOD GIRL...

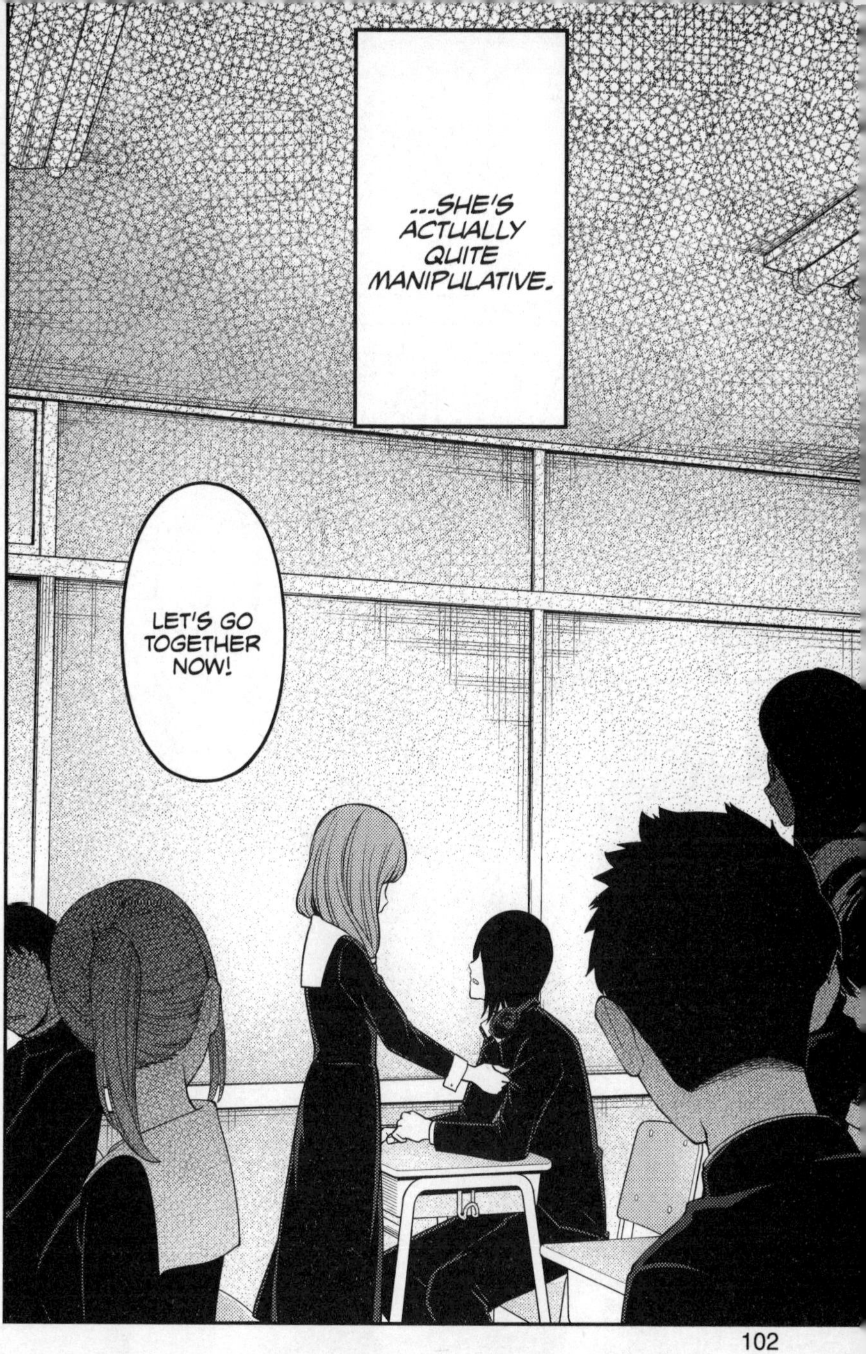
...SHE'S ACTUALLY QUITE MANIPULATIVE.
LET'S GO TOGETHER NOW!

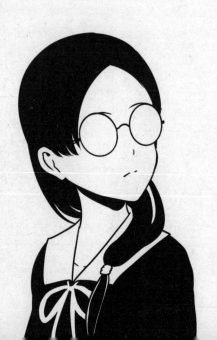

KAGUYA-SAMA
LOVE IS WAR

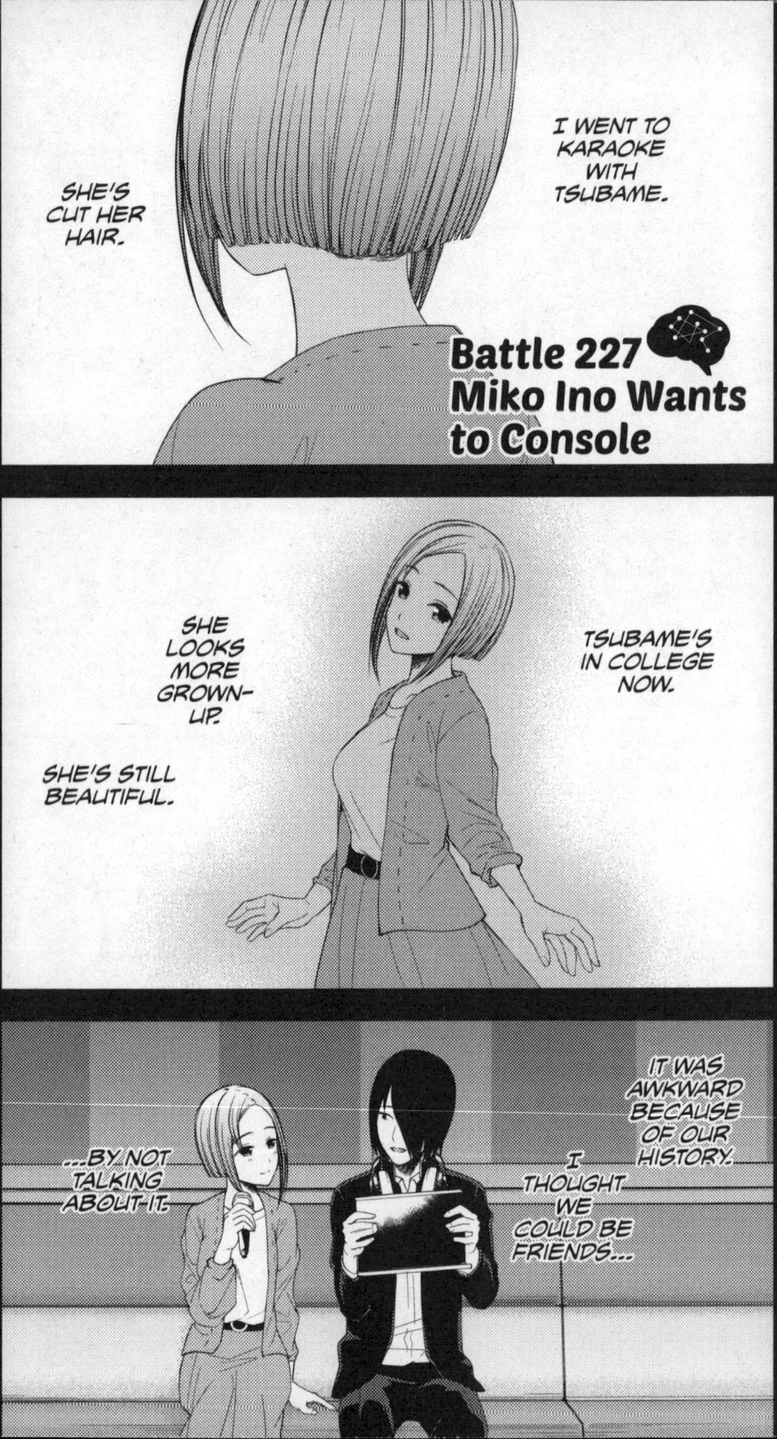
I WENT TO KARAOKE WITH TSUBAME.
SHE'S CUT HER HAIR.
Battle 227 Miko Ino Wants to Console
TSUBAME'S IN COLLEGE NOW.
SHE LOOKS MORE GROWN-UP.
SHE'S STILL BEAUTIFUL.
IT WAS AWKWARD BECAUSE OF OUR HISTORY.
I THOUGHT WE COULD BE FRIENDS...
...BY NOT TALKING ABOUT IT.

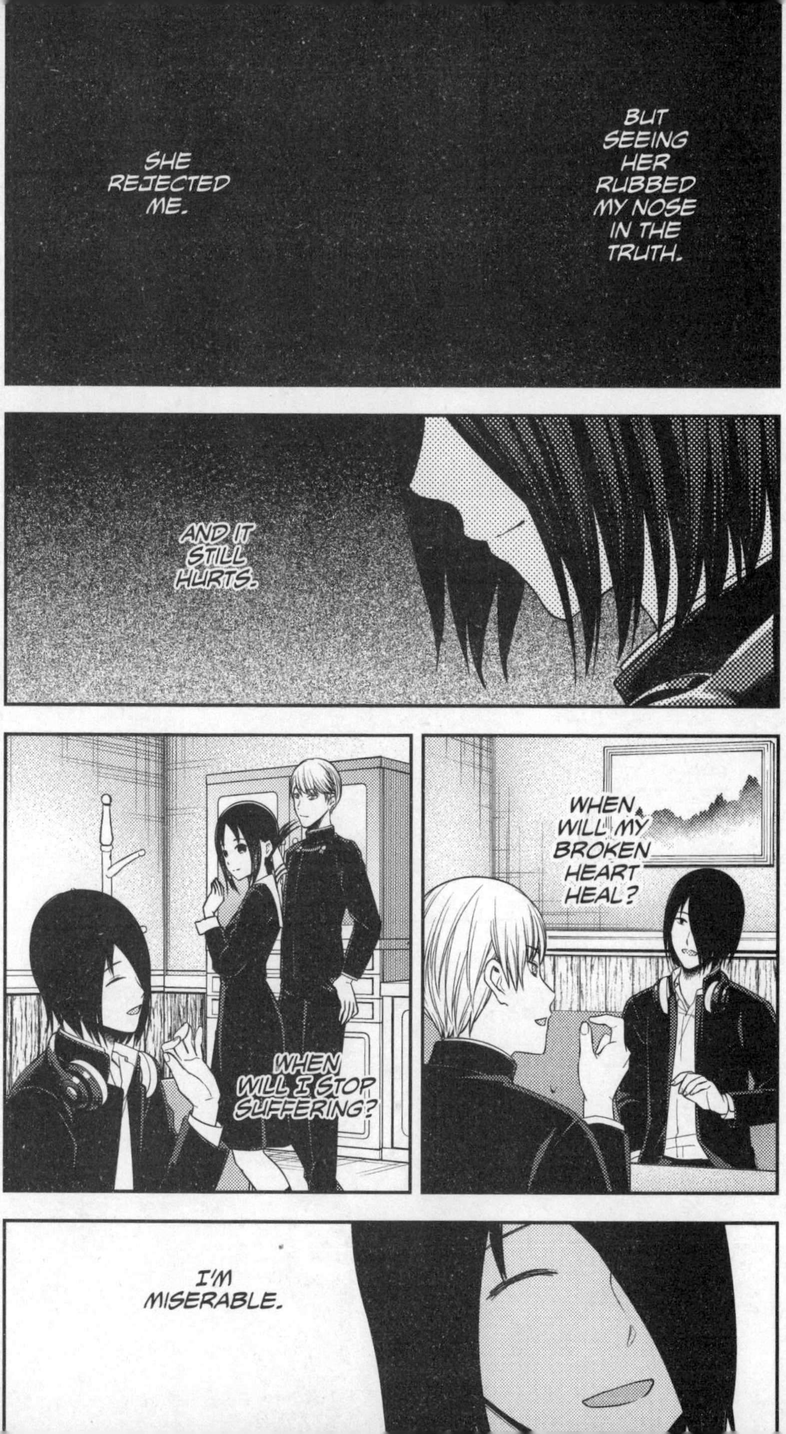
BUT SEEING HER RUBBED MY NOSE IN THE TRUTH.
SHE REJECTED ME.
AND IT STILL HURTS.
WHEN WILL MY BROKEN HEART HEAL?
WHEN WILL I STOP SUFFERING?
I'M MISERABLE.

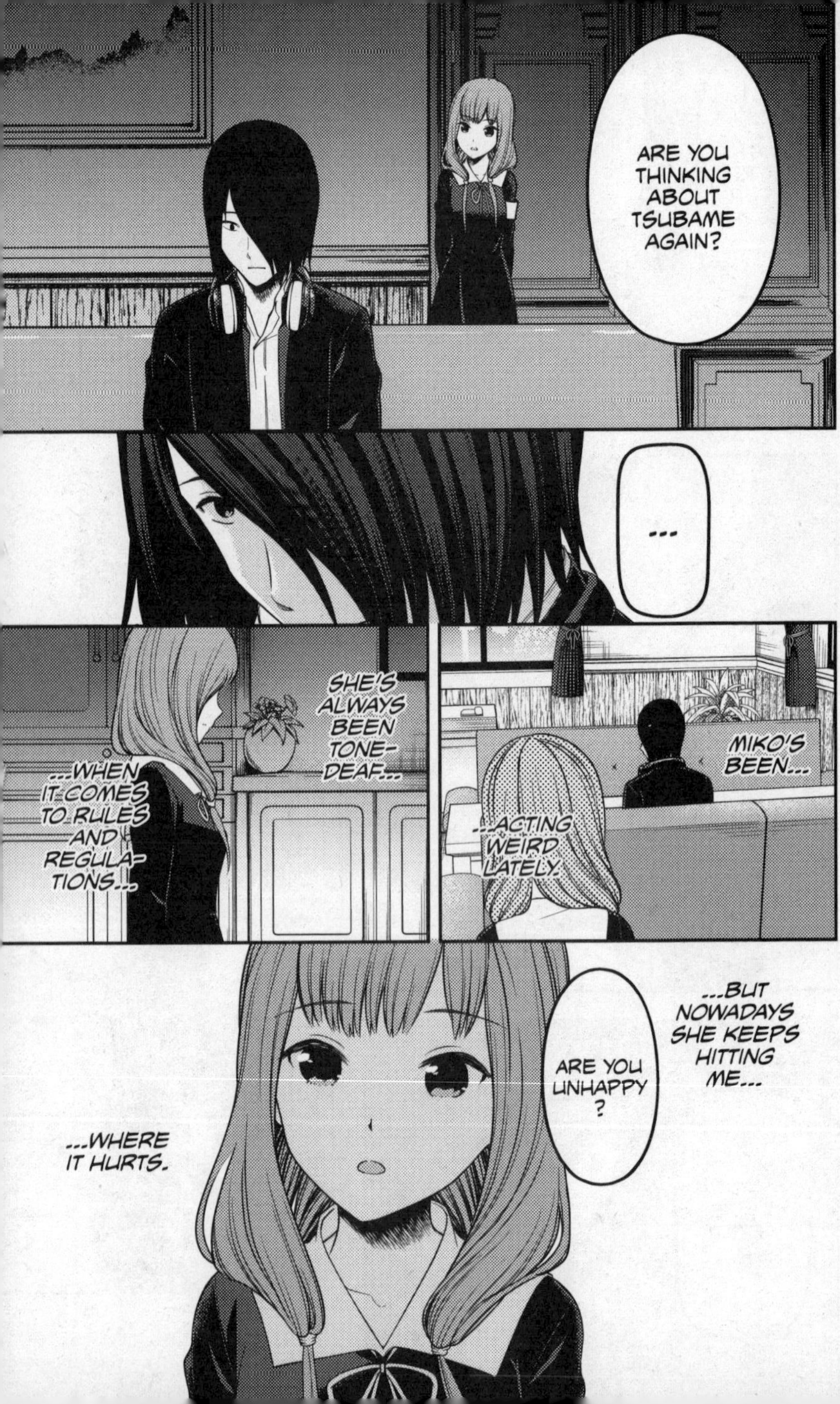
ARE YOU THINKING ABOUT TSUBAME AGAIN?
...
MIKO'S BEEN...
...ACTING WEIRD LATELY.
SHE'S ALWAYS BEEN TONE-DEAF...
...WHEN IT COMES TO RULES AND REGULATIONS...
...BUT NOWADAYS SHE KEEPS HITTING ME...
ARE YOU UNHAPPY?
...WHERE IT HURTS.

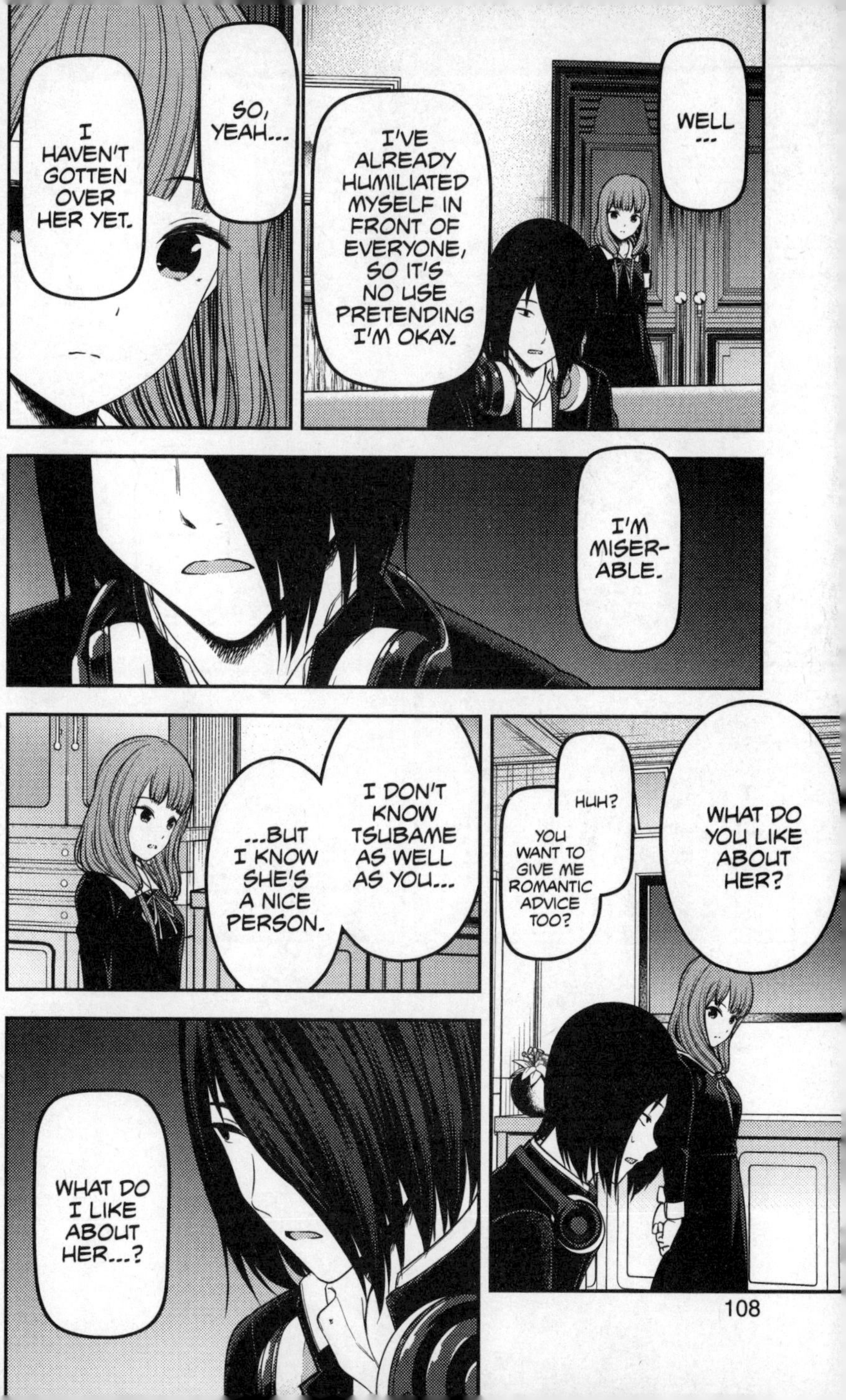
WELL...
I'VE ALREADY HUMILIATED MYSELF IN FRONT OF EVERYONE, SO IT'S NO USE PRETENDING I'M OKAY.
SO, YEAH...
I HAVEN'T GOTTEN OVER HER YET.
I'M MISER-ABLE.
WHAT DO YOU LIKE ABOUT HER?
HUH?
YOU WANT TO GIVE ME ROMANTIC ADVICE TOO?
I DON'T KNOW TSUBAME AS WELL AS YOU...
...BUT I KNOW SHE'S A NICE PERSON.
WHAT DO I LIKE ABOUT HER...?

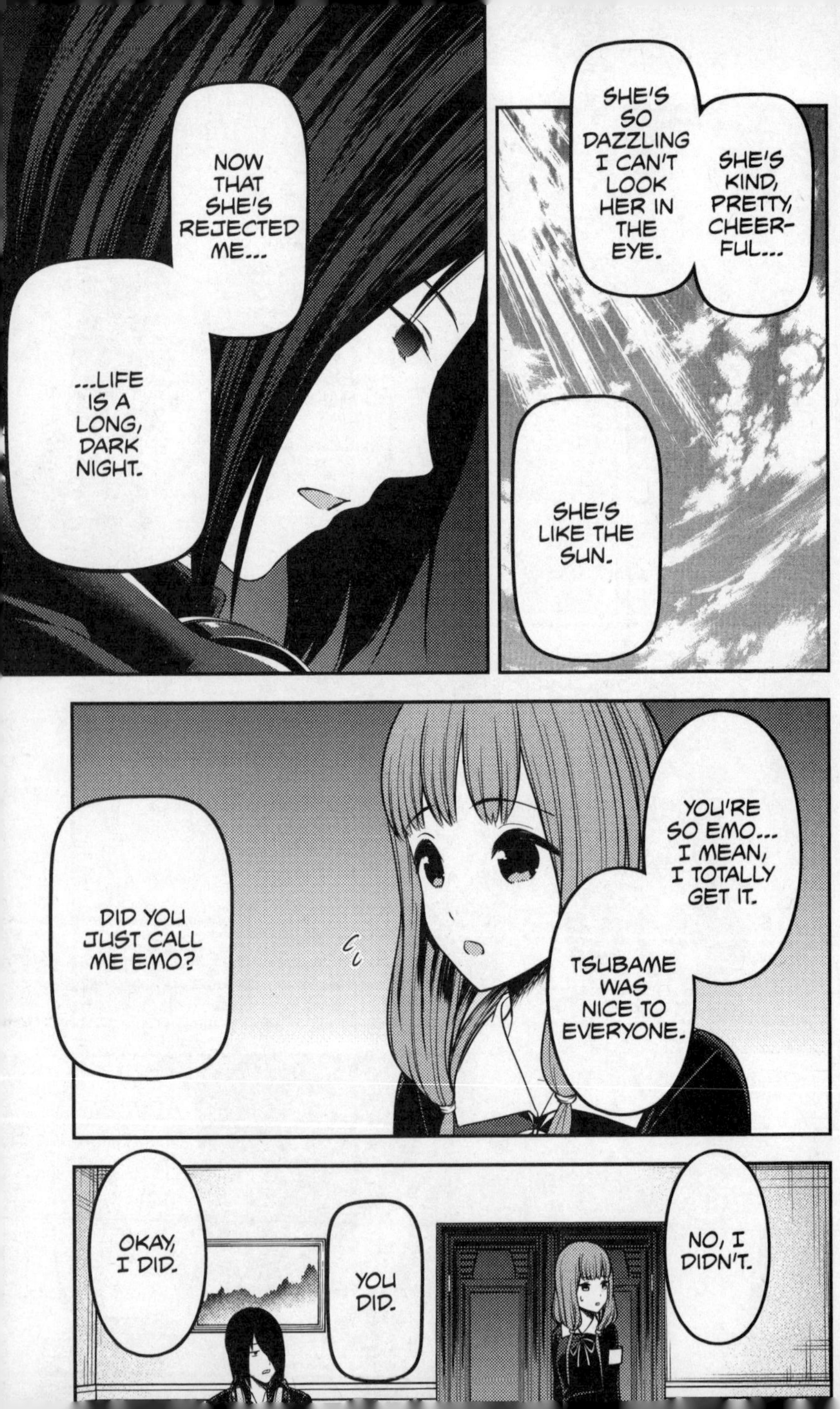
SHE'S KIND, PRETTY, CHEERFUL...
SHE'S SO DAZZLING I CAN'T LOOK HER IN THE EYE.
SHE'S LIKE THE SUN.
NOW THAT SHE'S REJECTED ME...
...LIFE IS A LONG, DARK NIGHT.
YOU'RE SO EMO... I MEAN, I TOTALLY GET IT.
TSUBAME WAS NICE TO EVERYONE.
DID YOU JUST CALL ME EMO?
NO, I DIDN'T.
YOU DID.
OKAY, I DID.

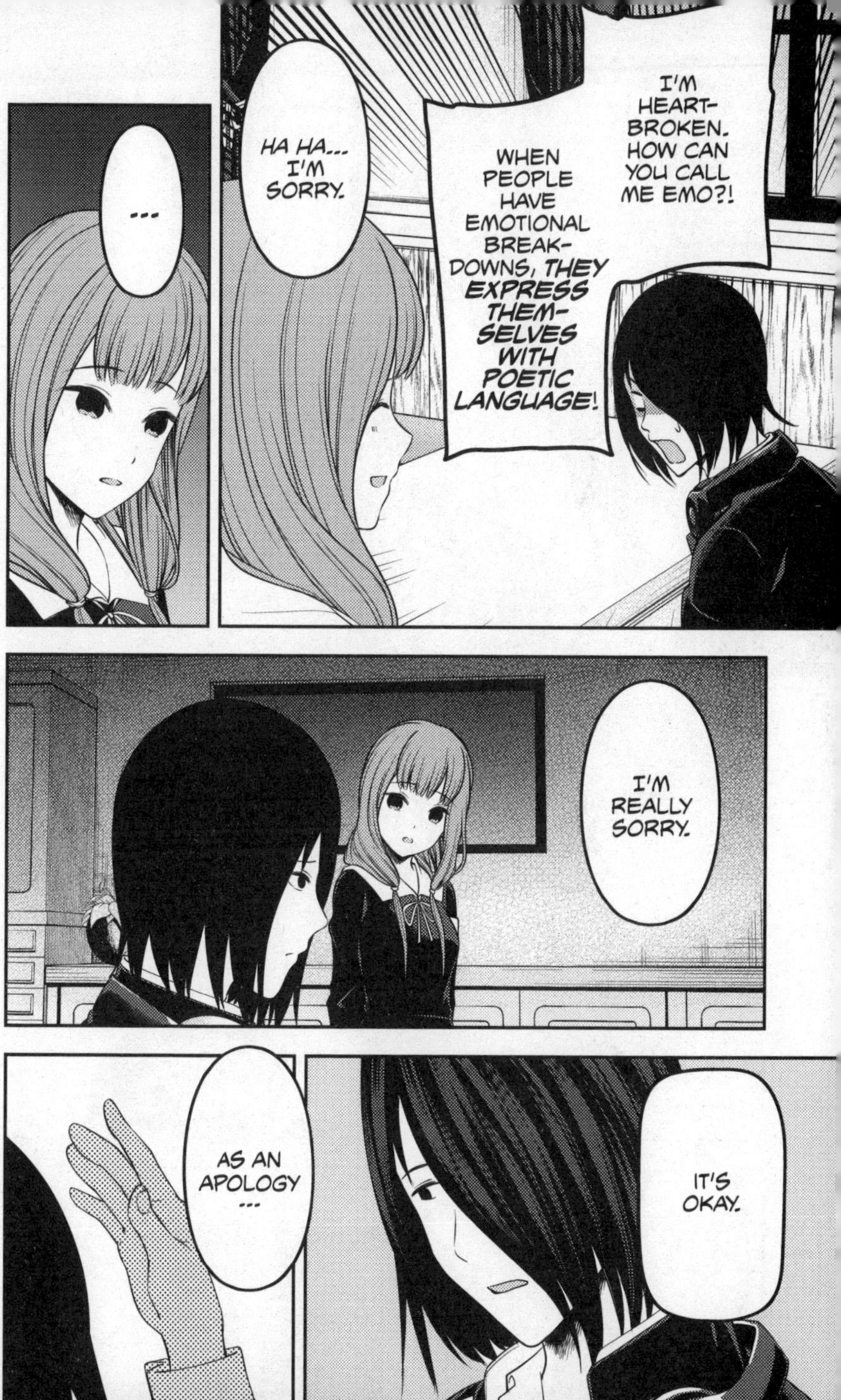
I'M HEART-BROKEN. HOW CAN YOU CALL ME EMO?!
WHEN PEOPLE HAVE EMOTIONAL BREAK-DOWNS, THEY EXPRESS THEM-SELVES WITH POETIC LANGUAGE!
HA HA... I'M SORRY.
...
I'M REALLY SORRY.
IT'S OKAY.
AS AN APOLOGY...

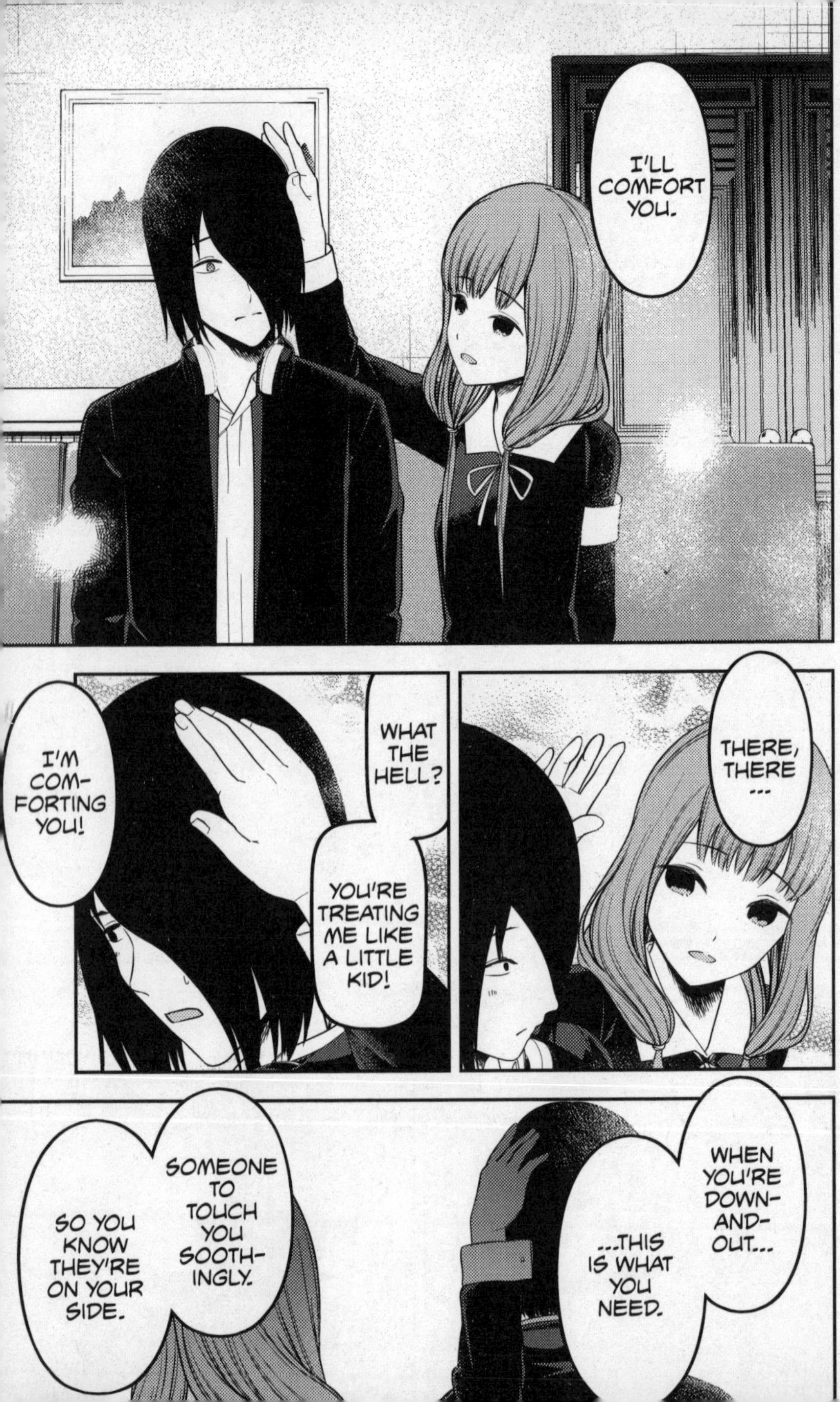
I'LL COMFORT YOU.
THERE, THERE ...
WHAT THE HELL?
YOU'RE TREATING ME LIKE A LITTLE KID!
I'M COM-FORTING YOU!
WHEN YOU'RE DOWN-AND-OUT...
...THIS IS WHAT YOU NEED.
SOMEONE TO TOUCH YOU SOOTH-INGLY.
SO YOU KNOW THEY'RE ON YOUR SIDE.

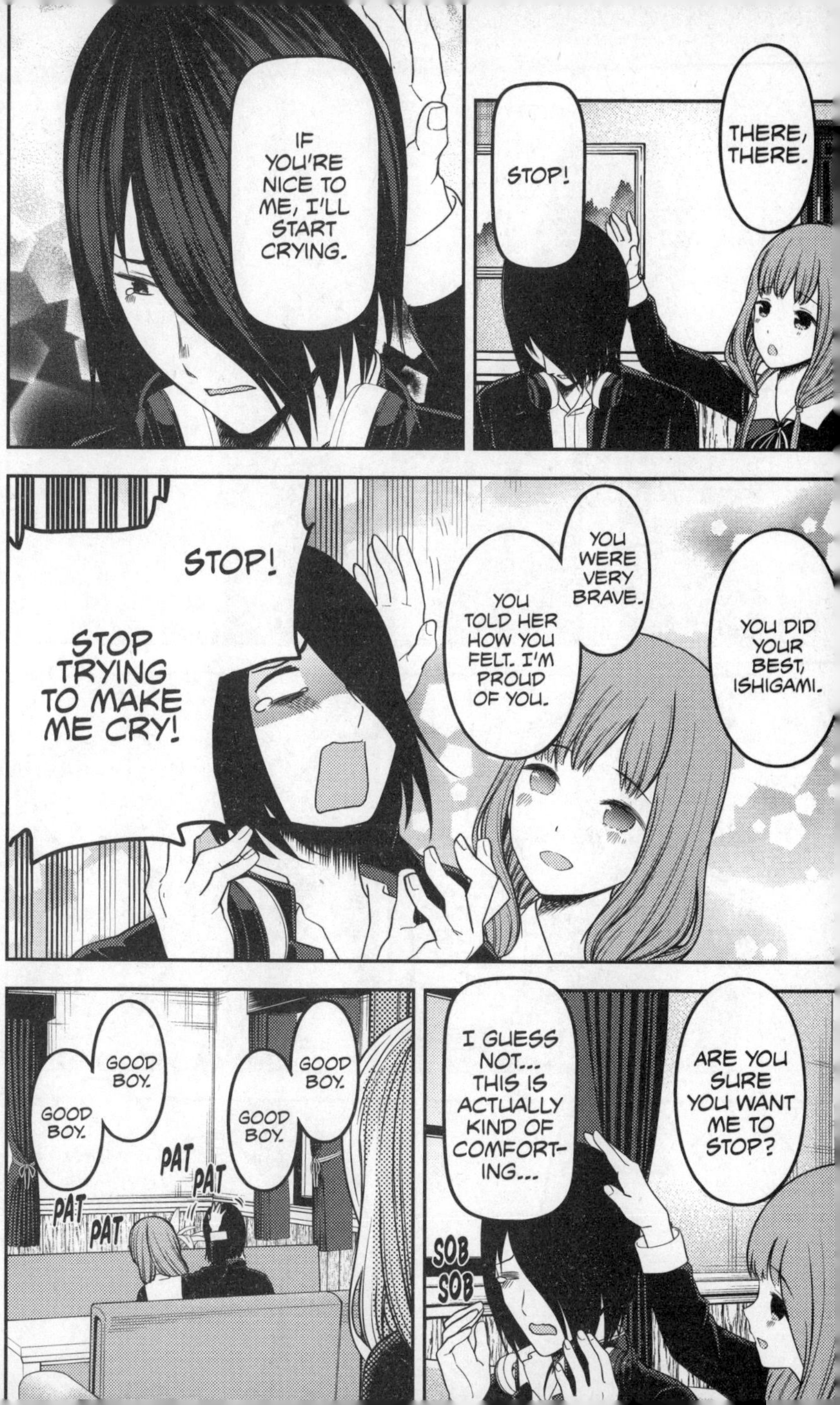
THERE, THERE.
STOP!
IF YOU'RE NICE TO ME, I'LL START CRYING.
YOU DID YOUR BEST, ISHIGAMI.
YOU WERE VERY BRAVE.
YOU TOLD HER HOW YOU FELT. I'M PROUD OF YOU.
STOP!
STOP TRYING TO MAKE ME CRY!
ARE YOU SURE YOU WANT ME TO STOP?
I GUESS NOT... THIS IS ACTUALLY KIND OF COMFORTING...
SOB
SOB
GOOD BOY.
GOOD BOY.
GOOD BOY.
GOOD BOY.
PAT
PAT
PAT
PAT

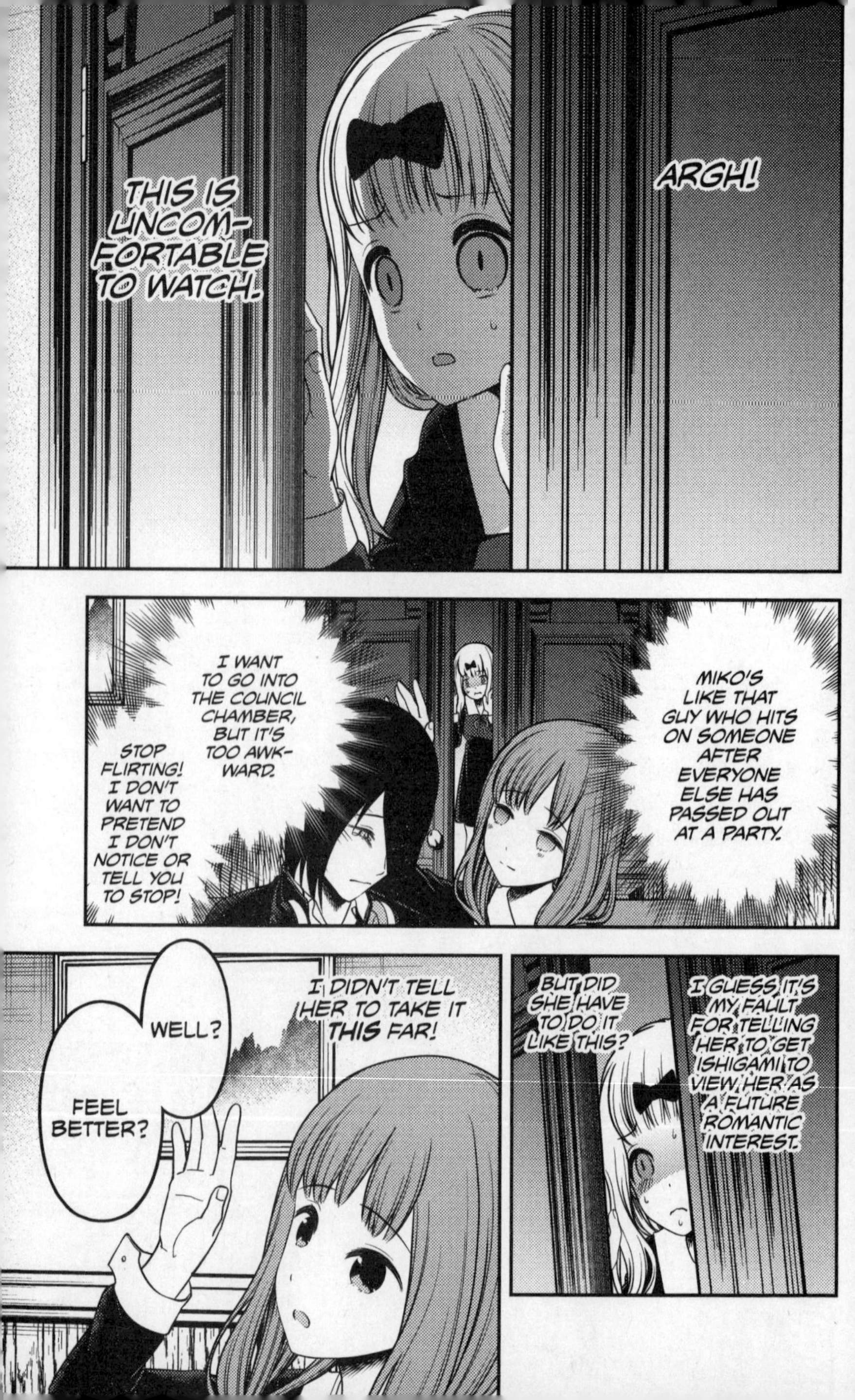
ARGH!
THIS IS UNCOMFORTABLE TO WATCH.
MIKO'S LIKE THAT GUY WHO HITS ON SOMEONE AFTER EVERYONE ELSE HAS PASSED OUT AT A PARTY.
I WANT TO GO INTO THE COUNCIL CHAMBER, BUT IT'S TOO AWKWARD.
STOP FLIRTING! I DON'T WANT TO PRETEND I DON'T NOTICE OR TELL YOU TO STOP!
I GUESS IT'S MY FAULT FOR TELLING HER TO GET ISHIGAMI TO VIEW HER AS A FUTURE ROMANTIC INTEREST.
BUT DID SHE HAVE TO DO IT LIKE THIS?
I DIDN'T TELL HER TO TAKE IT THIS FAR!
WELL?
FEEL BETTER?

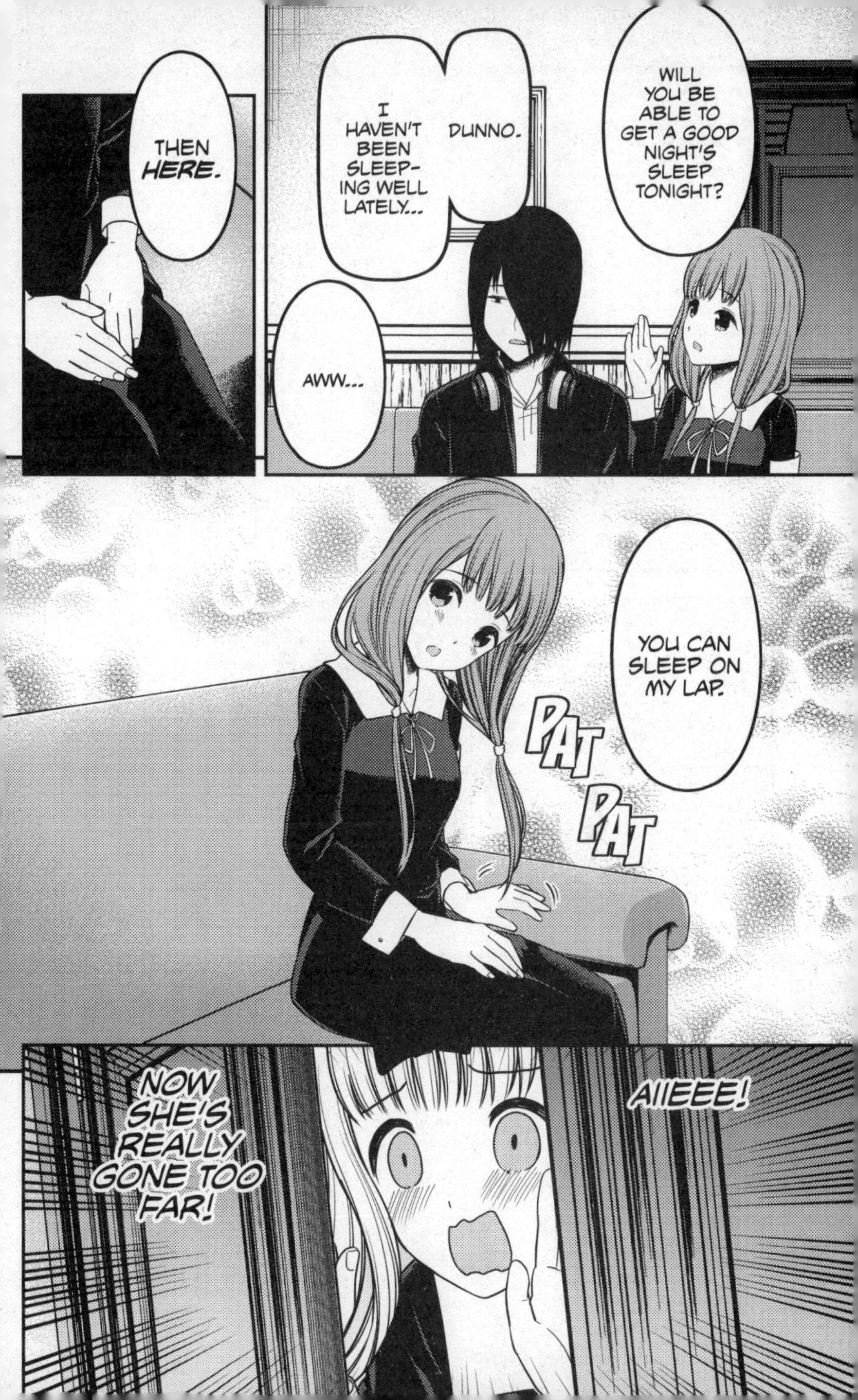
WILL YOU BE ABLE TO GET A GOOD NIGHT'S SLEEP TONIGHT?
DUNNO.
I HAVEN'T BEEN SLEEP-ING WELL LATELY...
AWW...
THEN *HERE*.
YOU CAN SLEEP ON MY LAP.
PAT PAT
AIIEEE!
NOW SHE'S REALLY GONE TOO FAR!

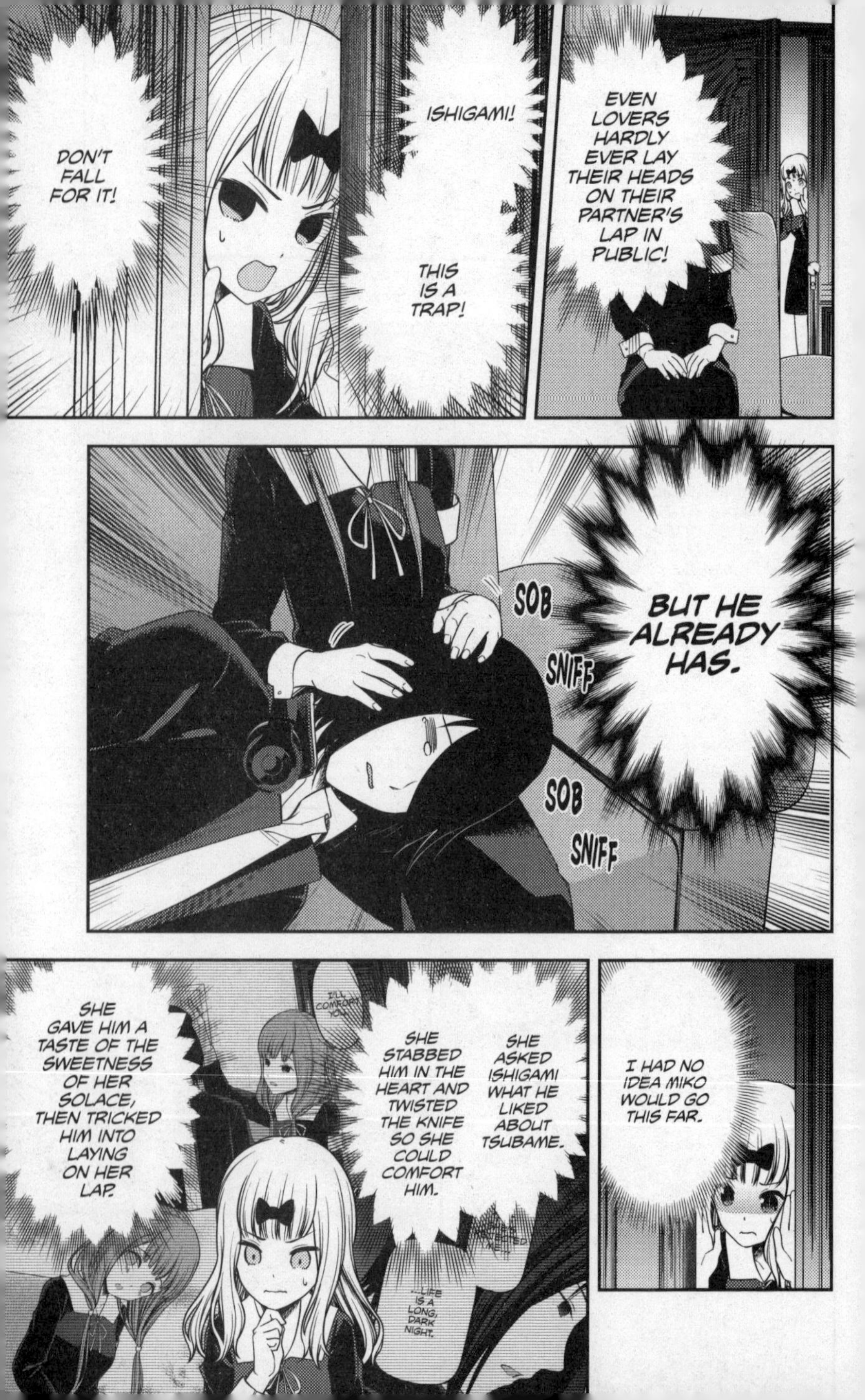
EVEN LOVERS HARDLY EVER LAY THEIR HEADS ON THEIR PARTNER'S LAP IN PUBLIC!
ISHIGAMI!
THIS IS A TRAP!
DON'T FALL FOR IT!
BUT HE ALREADY HAS.
SOB
SNIFF
SOB
SNIFF
I HAD NO IDEA MIKO WOULD GO THIS FAR.
SHE ASKED ISHIGAMI WHAT HE LIKED ABOUT TSUBAME.
SHE STABBED HIM IN THE HEART AND TWISTED THE KNIFE SO SHE COULD COMFORT HIM.
I'LL COMFORT YOU
SHE GAVE HIM A TASTE OF THE SWEETNESS OF HER SOLACE, THEN TRICKED HIM INTO LAYING ON HER LAP.
...LIFE IS A LONG, DARK NIGHT.

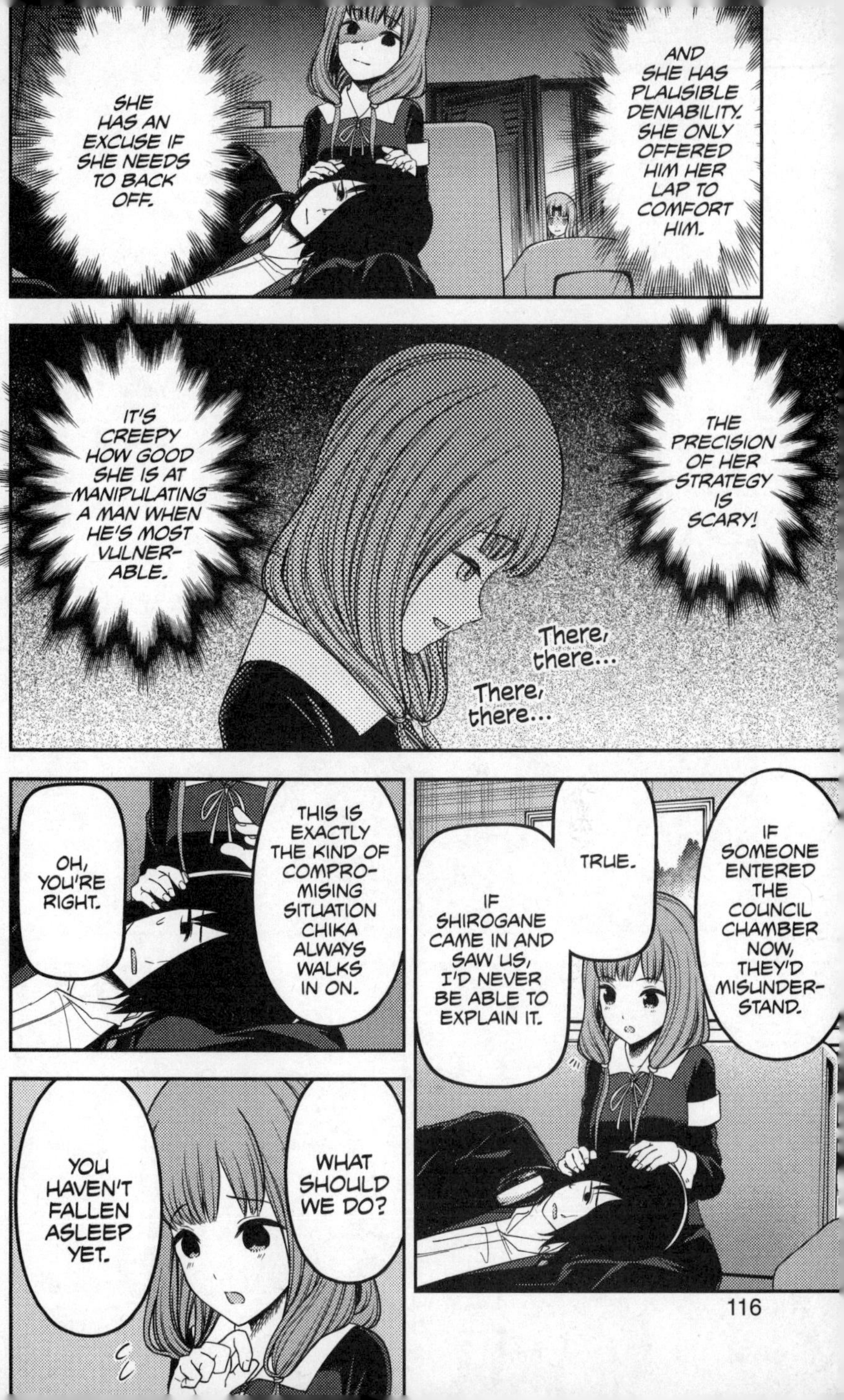

AND SHE HAS PLAUSIBLE DENIABILITY. SHE ONLY OFFERED HIM HER LAP TO COMFORT HIM.
SHE HAS AN EXCUSE IF SHE NEEDS TO BACK OFF.
THE PRECISION OF HER STRATEGY IS SCARY!
IT'S CREEPY HOW GOOD SHE IS AT MANIPULATING A MAN WHEN HE'S MOST VULNER-ABLE.
There, there...
There, there...
IF SOMEONE ENTERED THE COUNCIL CHAMBER NOW, THEY'D MISUNDER-STAND.
TRUE.
IF SHIROGANE CAME IN AND SAW US, I'D NEVER BE ABLE TO EXPLAIN IT.
THIS IS EXACTLY THE KIND OF COMPRO-MISING SITUATION CHIKA ALWAYS WALKS IN ON.
OH, YOU'RE RIGHT.
WHAT SHOULD WE DO?
YOU HAVEN'T FALLEN ASLEEP YET.

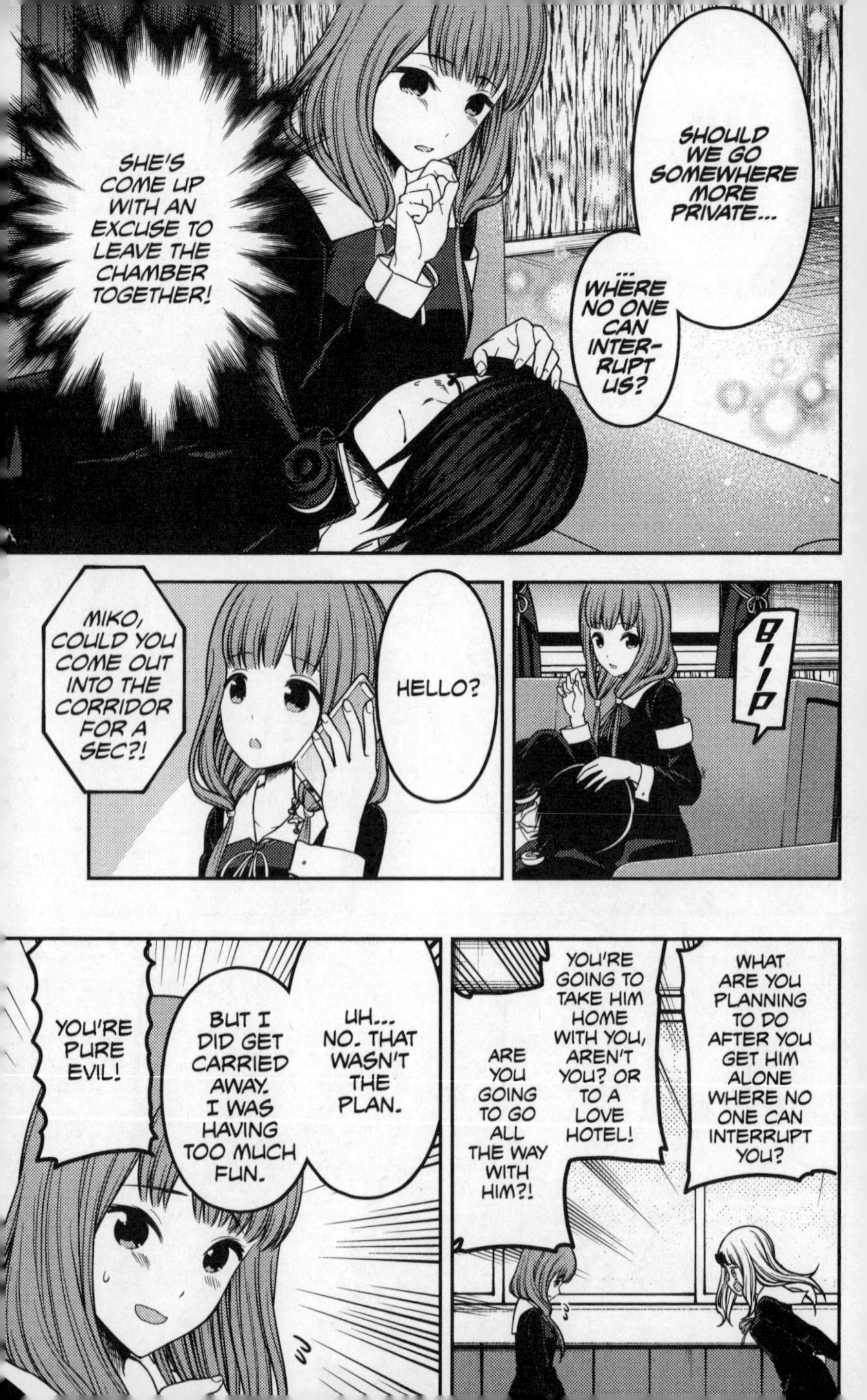
SHOULD WE GO SOMEWHERE MORE PRIVATE...
...WHERE NO ONE CAN INTER-RUPT US?
SHE'S COME UP WITH AN EXCUSE TO LEAVE THE CHAMBER TOGETHER!
BIIP
HELLO?
MIKO, COULD YOU COME OUT INTO THE CORRIDOR FOR A SEC?!
WHAT ARE YOU PLANNING TO DO AFTER YOU GET HIM ALONE WHERE NO ONE CAN INTERRUPT YOU?
YOU'RE GOING TO TAKE HIM HOME WITH YOU, AREN'T YOU? OR TO A LOVE HOTEL!
ARE YOU GOING TO GO ALL THE WAY WITH HIM?!
UH... NO. THAT WASN'T THE PLAN.
BUT I DID GET CARRIED AWAY. I WAS HAVING TOO MUCH FUN.
YOU'RE PURE EVIL!

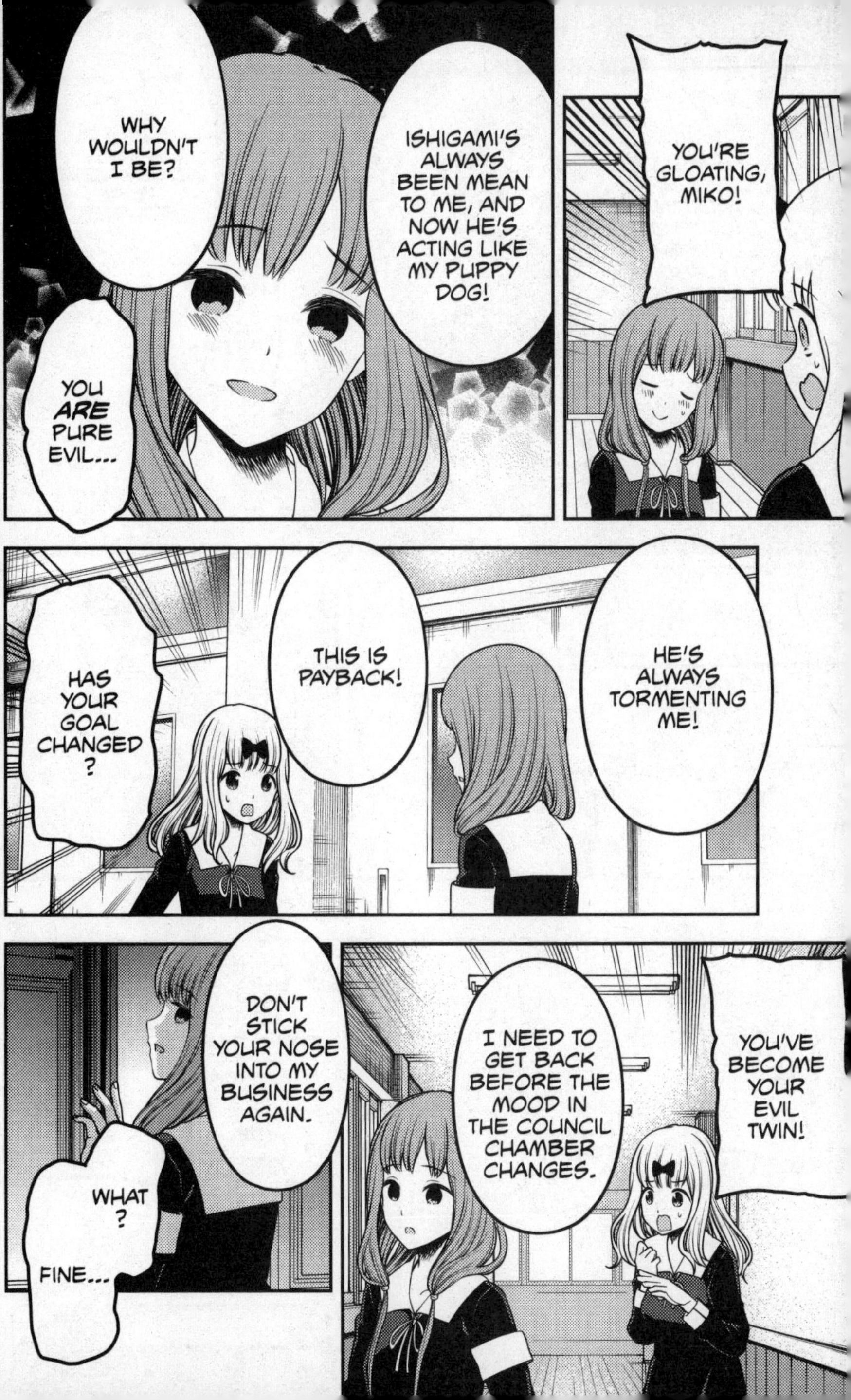
YOU'RE GLOATING, MIKO!
WHY WOULDN'T I BE?
ISHIGAMI'S ALWAYS BEEN MEAN TO ME, AND NOW HE'S ACTING LIKE MY PUPPY DOG!
YOU ARE PURE EVIL...
HE'S ALWAYS TORMENTING ME!
THIS IS PAYBACK!
HAS YOUR GOAL CHANGED?
YOU'VE BECOME YOUR EVIL TWIN!
I NEED TO GET BACK BEFORE THE MOOD IN THE COUNCIL CHAMBER CHANGES.
DON'T STICK YOUR NOSE INTO MY BUSINESS AGAIN.
WHAT?
FINE...

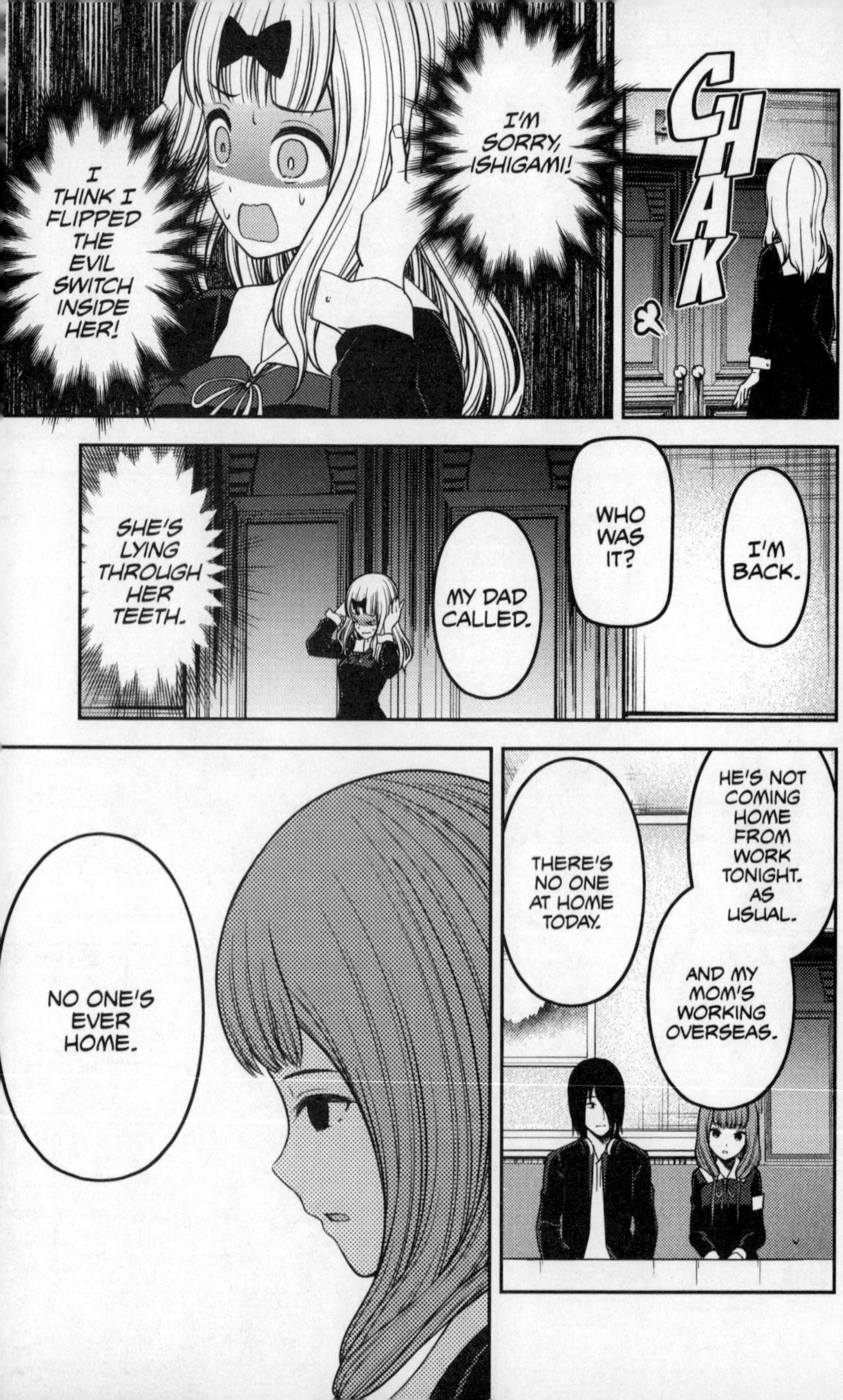
CHAK
I'M SORRY, ISHIGAMI!
I THINK I FLIPPED THE EVIL SWITCH INSIDE HER!
I'M BACK.
WHO WAS IT?
MY DAD CALLED.
SHE'S LYING THROUGH HER TEETH.
HE'S NOT COMING HOME FROM WORK TONIGHT. AS USUAL.
THERE'S NO ONE AT HOME TODAY.
AND MY MOM'S WORKING OVERSEAS.
NO ONE'S EVER HOME.

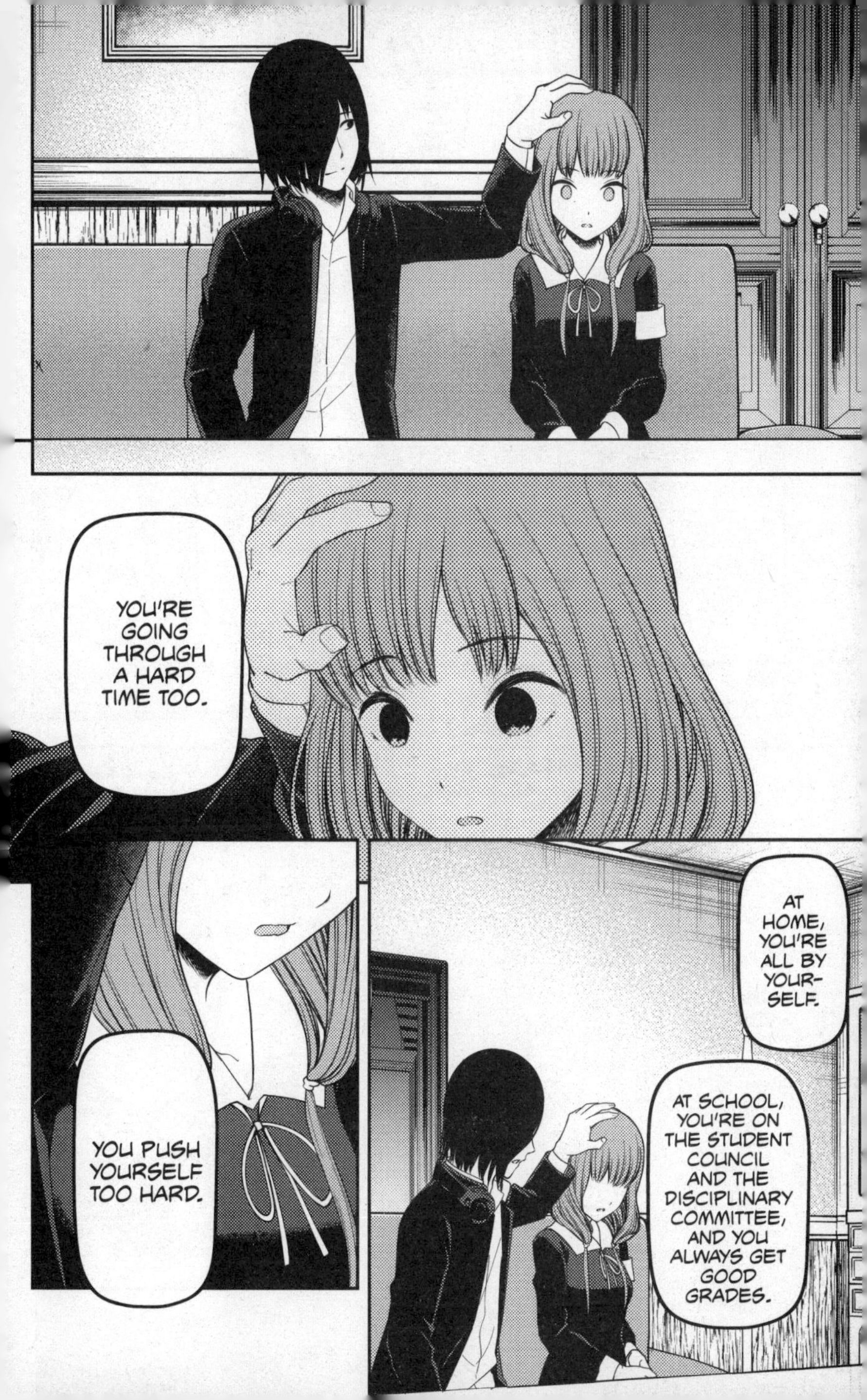
YOU'RE GOING THROUGH A HARD TIME TOO.
AT HOME, YOU'RE ALL BY YOUR-SELF.
AT SCHOOL, YOU'RE ON THE STUDENT COUNCIL AND THE DISCIPLINARY COMMITTEE, AND YOU ALWAYS GET GOOD GRADES.
YOU PUSH YOURSELF TOO HARD.

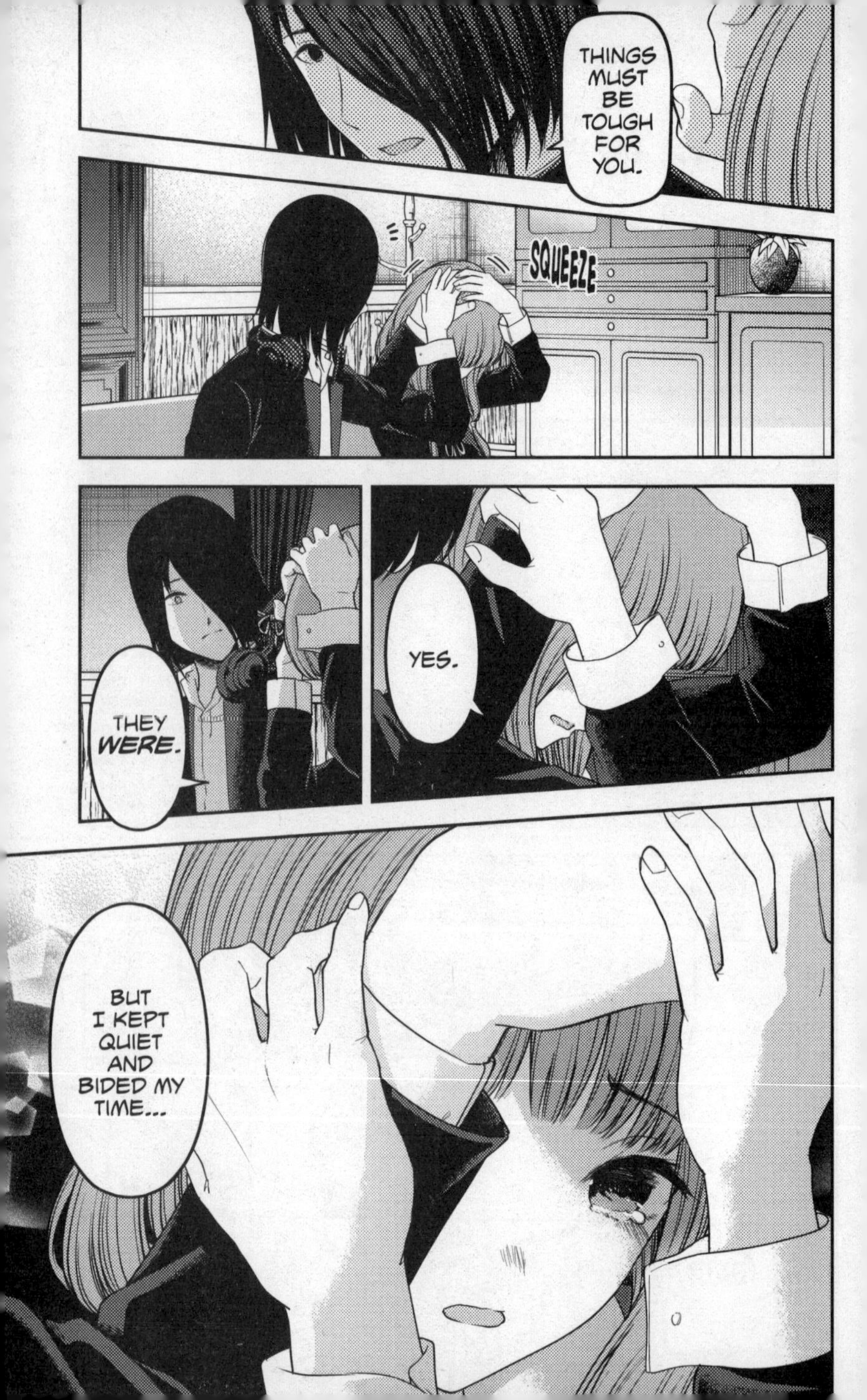
THINGS MUST BE TOUGH FOR YOU.
SQUEEZE
YES.
THEY WERE.
BUT I KEPT QUIET AND BIDED MY TIME...

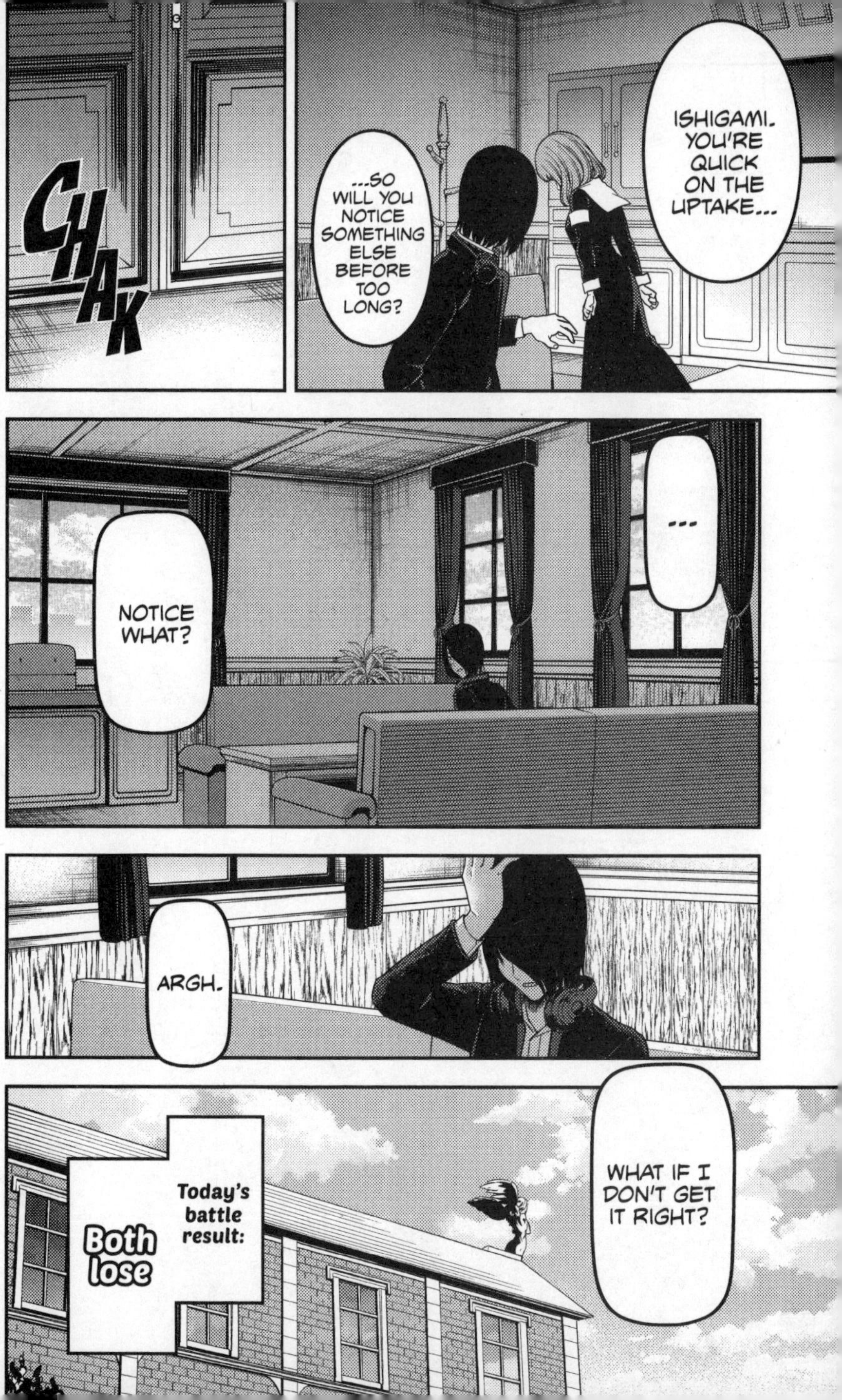
ISHIGAMI. YOU'RE QUICK ON THE UPTAKE...
...SO WILL YOU NOTICE SOMETHING ELSE BEFORE TOO LONG?
CHAK
...
NOTICE WHAT?
ARGH.
WHAT IF I DON'T GET IT RIGHT?
Today's battle result:
Both lose

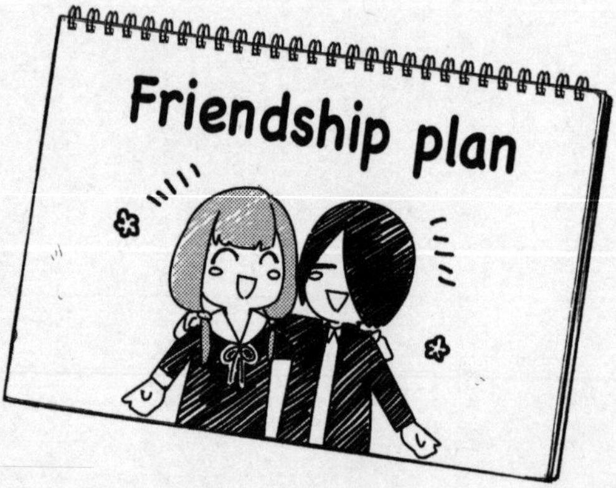
Friendship plan

KAGUYA-SAMA
LOVE IS WAR

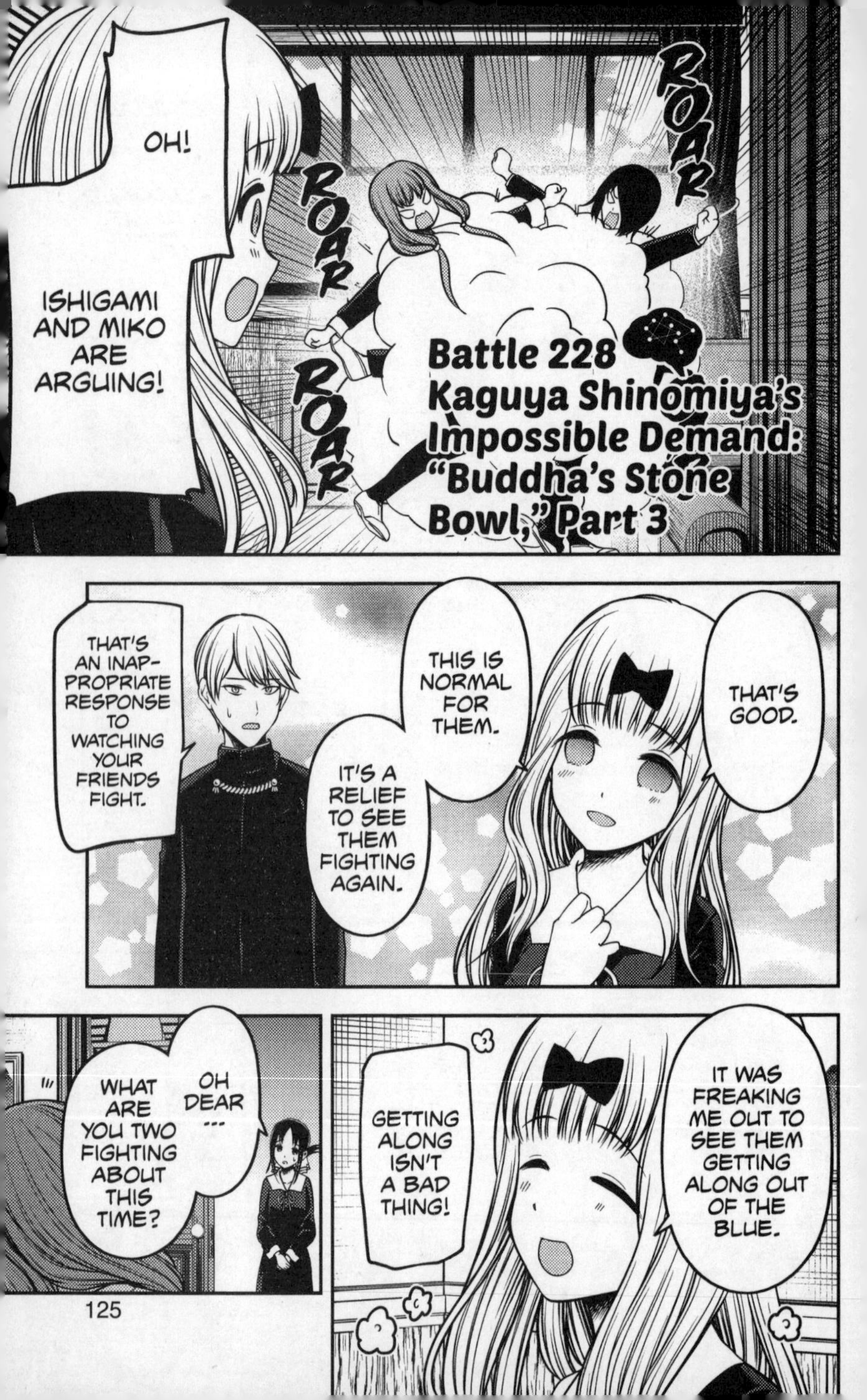
ROAR
ROAR
ROAR
Battle 228 Kaguya Shinomiya's Impossible Demand: "Buddha's Stone Bowl," Part 3
OH!
ISHIGAMI AND MIKO ARE ARGUING!
THAT'S GOOD.
THIS IS NORMAL FOR THEM.
IT'S A RELIEF TO SEE THEM FIGHTING AGAIN.
THAT'S AN INAPPROPRIATE RESPONSE TO WATCHING YOUR FRIENDS FIGHT.
IT WAS FREAKING ME OUT TO SEE THEM GETTING ALONG OUT OF THE BLUE.
GETTING ALONG ISN'T A BAD THING!
OH DEAR ...
WHAT ARE YOU TWO FIGHTING ABOUT THIS TIME?

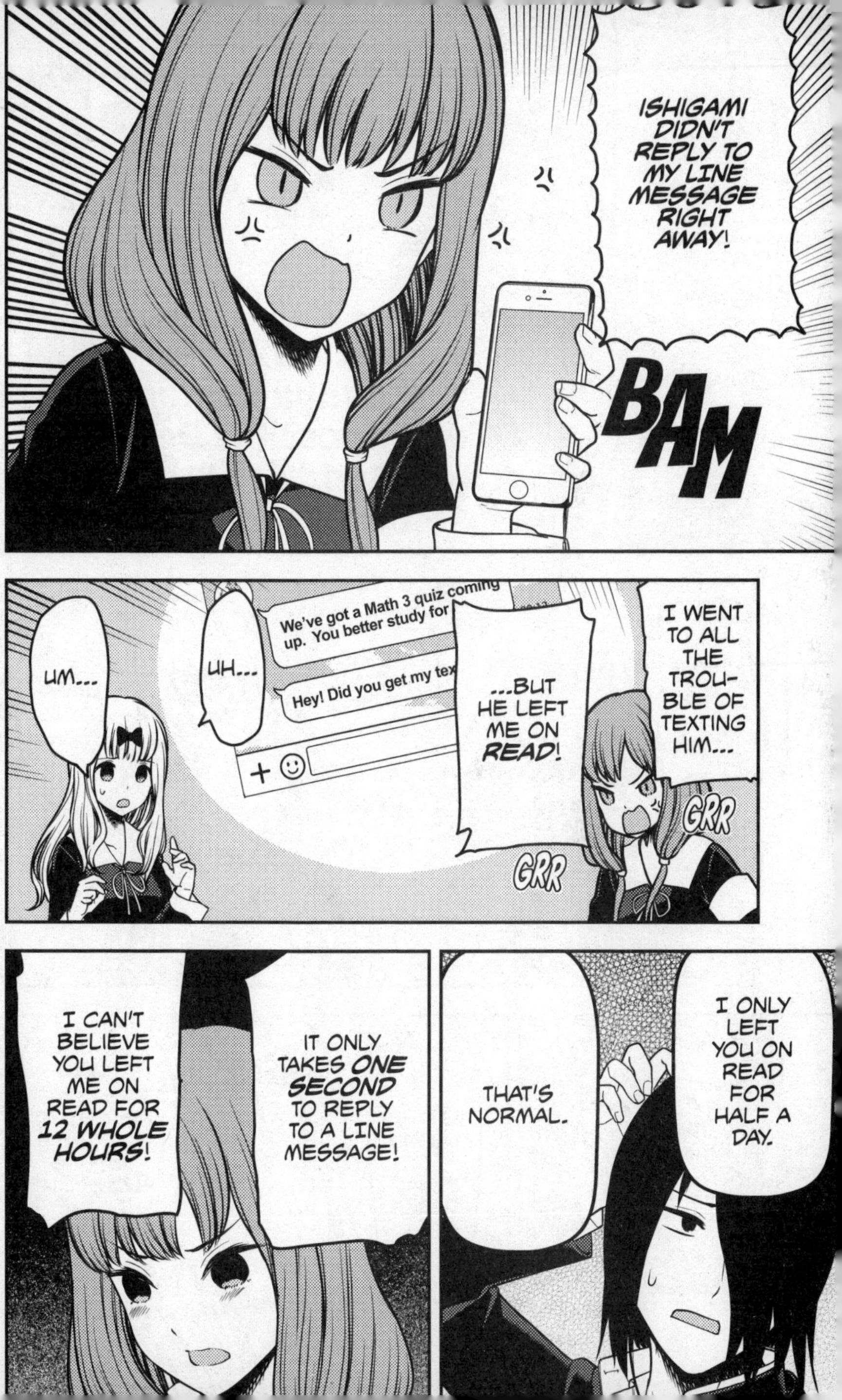
ISHIGAMI DIDN'T REPLY TO MY LINE MESSAGE RIGHT AWAY!
BAM
I WENT TO ALL THE TROUBLE OF TEXTING HIM...
...BUT HE LEFT ME ON READ!
GRR
GRR
We've got a Math 3 quiz coming up. You better study for
Hey! Did you get my tex
UH...
UM...
I ONLY LEFT YOU ON READ FOR HALF A DAY.
THAT'S NORMAL.
IT ONLY TAKES ONE SECOND TO REPLY TO A LINE MESSAGE!
I CAN'T BELIEVE YOU LEFT ME ON READ FOR 12 WHOLE HOURS!

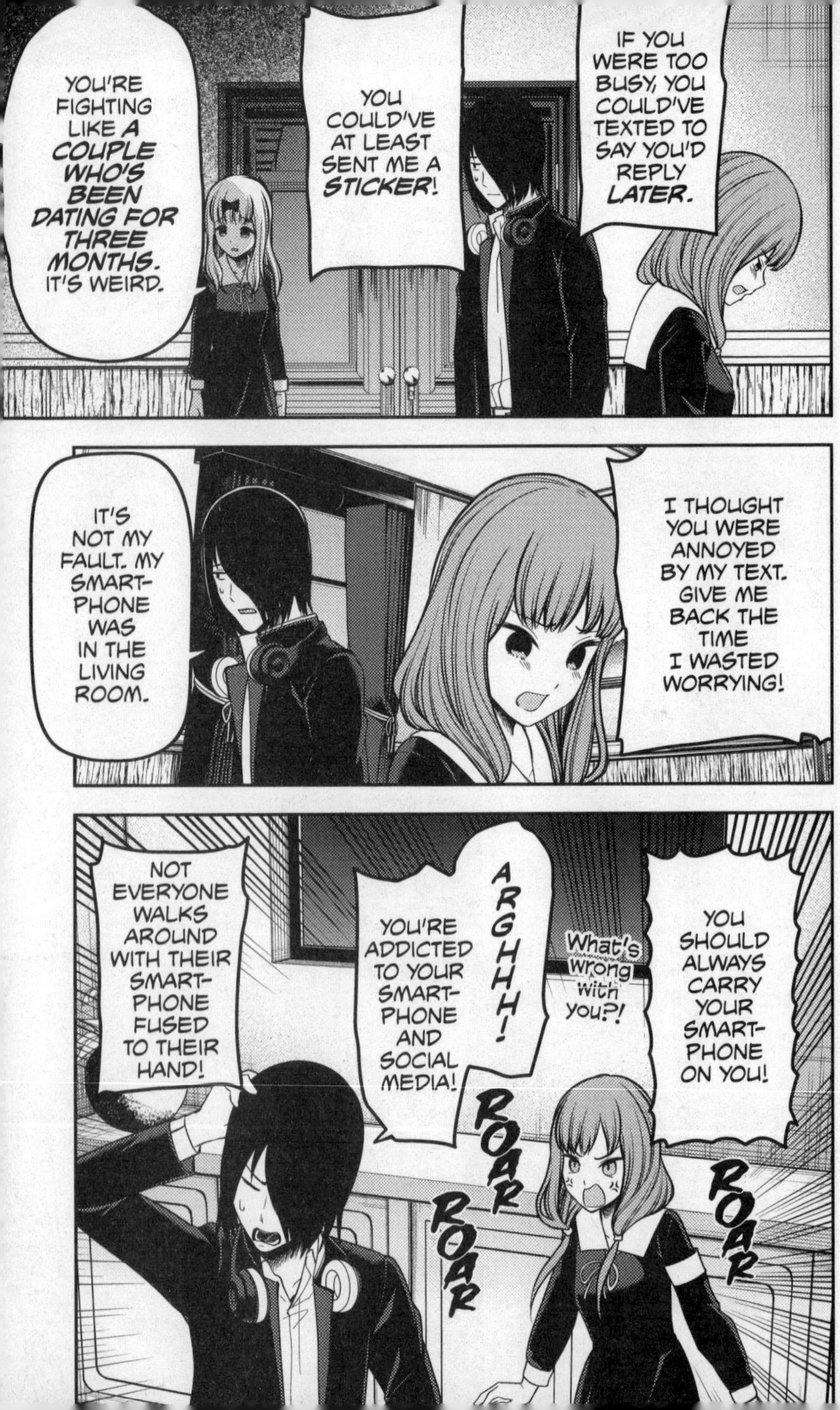
IF YOU WERE TOO BUSY, YOU COULD'VE TEXTED TO SAY YOU'D REPLY LATER.
YOU COULD'VE AT LEAST SENT ME A STICKER!
YOU'RE FIGHTING LIKE A COUPLE WHO'S BEEN DATING FOR THREE MONTHS. IT'S WEIRD.
I THOUGHT YOU WERE ANNOYED BY MY TEXT. GIVE ME BACK THE TIME I WASTED WORRYING!
IT'S NOT MY FAULT. MY SMARTPHONE WAS IN THE LIVING ROOM.
YOU SHOULD ALWAYS CARRY YOUR SMARTPHONE ON YOU!
ROAR
What's wrong with you?!
ARGHHH!
YOU'RE ADDICTED TO YOUR SMARTPHONE AND SOCIAL MEDIA!
ROAR
ROAR
NOT EVERYONE WALKS AROUND WITH THEIR SMARTPHONE FUSED TO THEIR HAND!

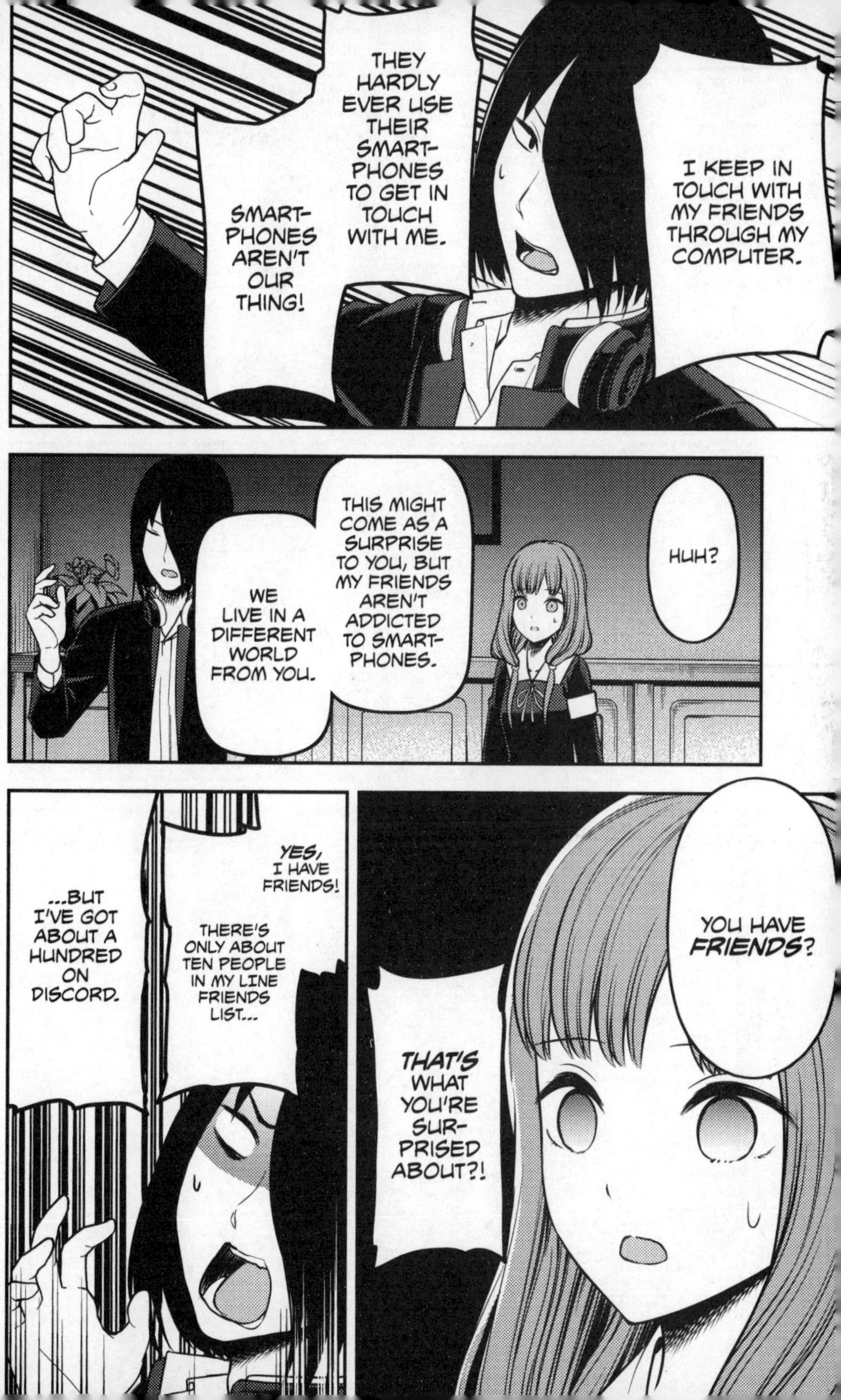
I KEEP IN TOUCH WITH MY FRIENDS THROUGH MY COMPUTER.
THEY HARDLY EVER USE THEIR SMART-PHONES TO GET IN TOUCH WITH ME.
SMART-PHONES AREN'T OUR THING!
HUH?
THIS MIGHT COME AS A SURPRISE TO YOU, BUT MY FRIENDS AREN'T ADDICTED TO SMART-PHONES.
WE LIVE IN A DIFFERENT WORLD FROM YOU.
YOU HAVE *FRIENDS*?
THAT'S WHAT YOU'RE SUR-PRISED ABOUT?!
YES, I HAVE FRIENDS!
THERE'S ONLY ABOUT TEN PEOPLE IN MY LINE FRIENDS LIST...
...BUT I'VE GOT ABOUT A HUNDRED ON DISCORD.

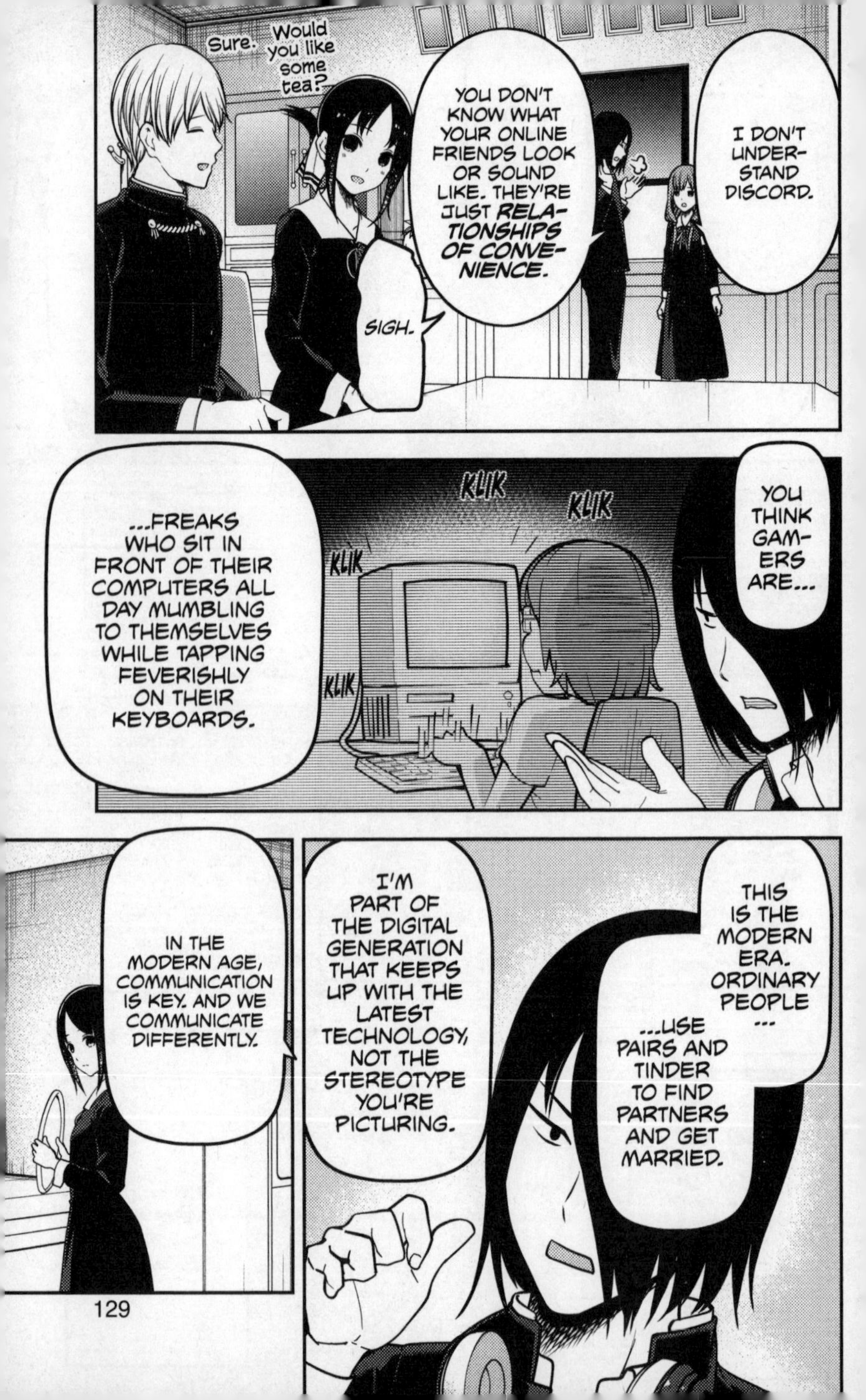
I DON'T UNDERSTAND DISCORD.
YOU DON'T KNOW WHAT YOUR ONLINE FRIENDS LOOK OR SOUND LIKE. THEY'RE JUST *RELATIONSHIPS OF CONVENIENCE*.
SIGH.
Would you like some tea?
Sure.
YOU THINK GAMERS ARE...
KLIK
KLIK
KLIK
KLIK
...FREAKS WHO SIT IN FRONT OF THEIR COMPUTERS ALL DAY MUMBLING TO THEMSELVES WHILE TAPPING FEVERISHLY ON THEIR KEYBOARDS.
THIS IS THE MODERN ERA. ORDINARY PEOPLE ...
...USE PAIRS AND TINDER TO FIND PARTNERS AND GET MARRIED.
I'M PART OF THE DIGITAL GENERATION THAT KEEPS UP WITH THE LATEST TECHNOLOGY, NOT THE STEREOTYPE YOU'RE PICTURING.
IN THE MODERN AGE, COMMUNICATION IS KEY. AND WE COMMUNICATE DIFFERENTLY.

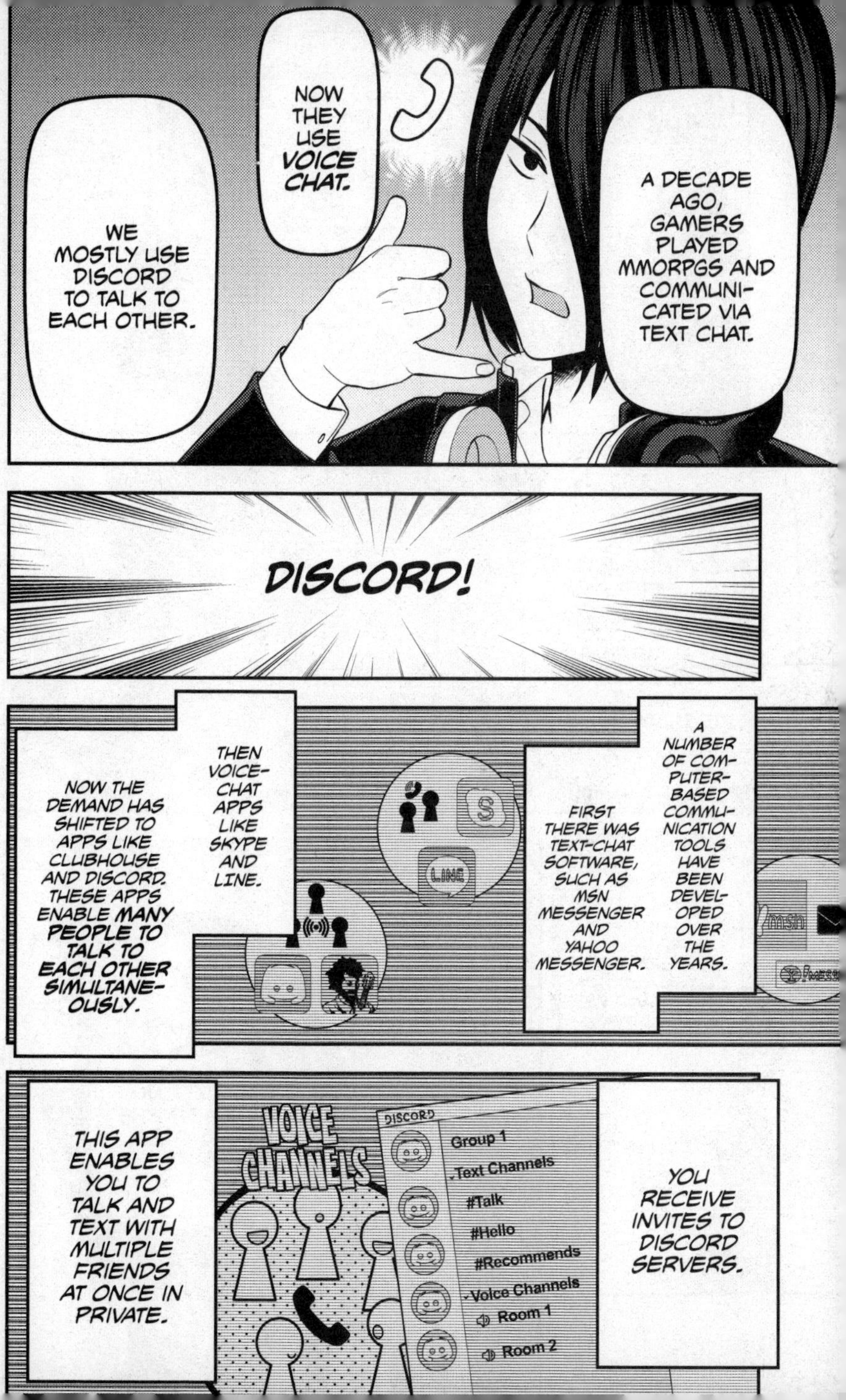
A DECADE AGO, GAMERS PLAYED MMORPGS AND COMMUNICATED VIA TEXT CHAT.
NOW THEY USE VOICE CHAT.
WE MOSTLY USE DISCORD TO TALK TO EACH OTHER.
DISCORD!
A NUMBER OF COMPUTER-BASED COMMUNICATION TOOLS HAVE BEEN DEVELOPED OVER THE YEARS.
msn
FIRST THERE WAS TEXT-CHAT SOFTWARE, SUCH AS MSN MESSENGER AND YAHOO MESSENGER.
LINE
THEN VOICE-CHAT APPS LIKE SKYPE AND LINE.
NOW THE DEMAND HAS SHIFTED TO APPS LIKE CLUBHOUSE AND DISCORD. THESE APPS ENABLE MANY PEOPLE TO TALK TO EACH OTHER SIMULTANEOUSLY.
YOU RECEIVE INVITES TO DISCORD SERVERS.
DISCORD
Group 1
Text Channels
#Talk
#Hello
#Recommends
Voice Channels
Room 1
Room 2
VOICE CHANNELS
THIS APP ENABLES YOU TO TALK AND TEXT WITH MULTIPLE FRIENDS AT ONCE IN PRIVATE.

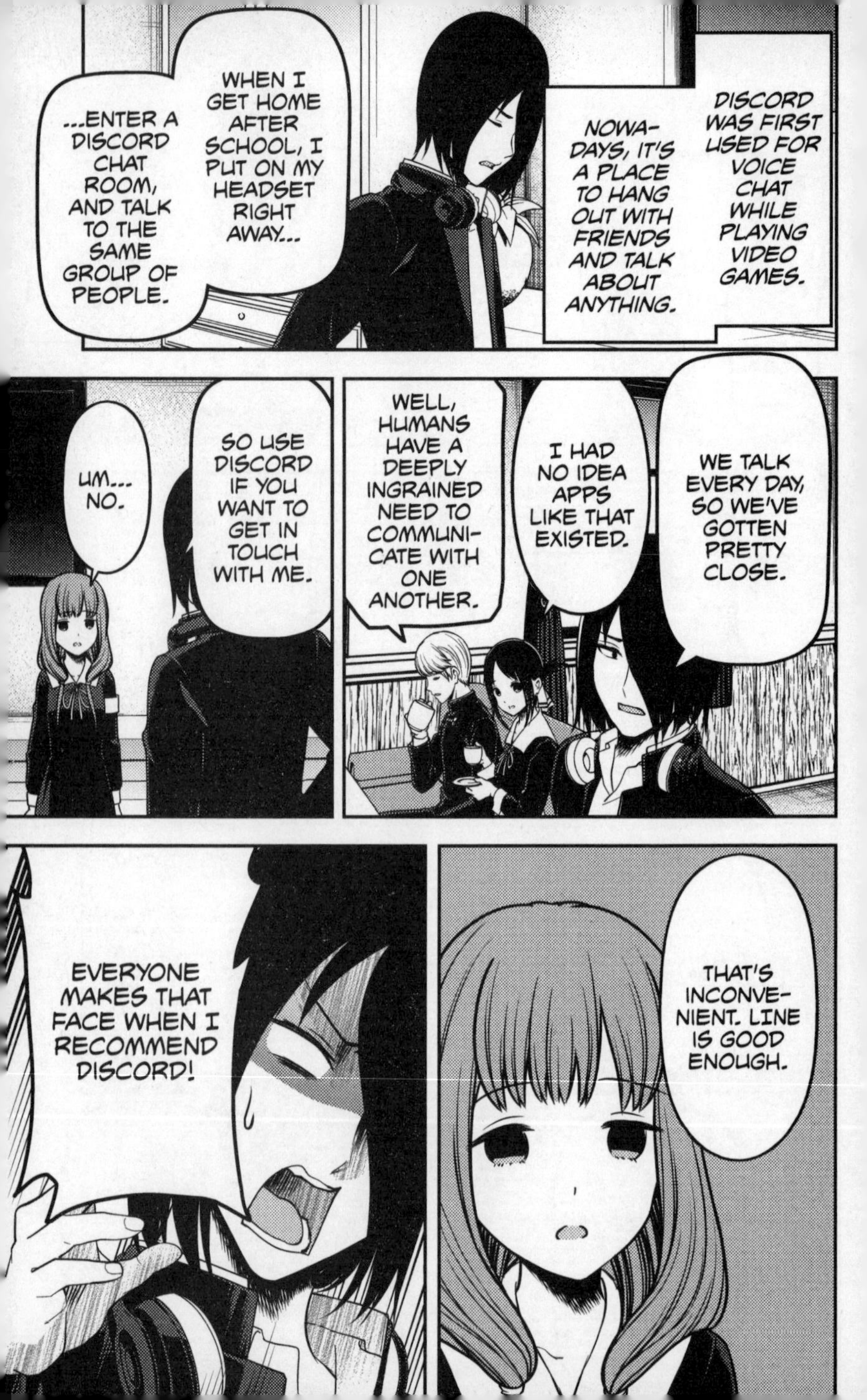
DISCORD WAS FIRST USED FOR VOICE CHAT WHILE PLAYING VIDEO GAMES.
NOWA-DAYS, IT'S A PLACE TO HANG OUT WITH FRIENDS AND TALK ABOUT ANYTHING.
WHEN I GET HOME AFTER SCHOOL, I PUT ON MY HEADSET RIGHT AWAY...
...ENTER A DISCORD CHAT ROOM, AND TALK TO THE SAME GROUP OF PEOPLE.
WE TALK EVERY DAY, SO WE'VE GOTTEN PRETTY CLOSE.
I HAD NO IDEA APPS LIKE THAT EXISTED.
WELL, HUMANS HAVE A DEEPLY INGRAINED NEED TO COMMUNI-CATE WITH ONE ANOTHER.
SO USE DISCORD IF YOU WANT TO GET IN TOUCH WITH ME.
UM... NO.
THAT'S INCONVE-NIENT. LINE IS GOOD ENOUGH.
EVERYONE MAKES THAT FACE WHEN I RECOMMEND DISCORD!

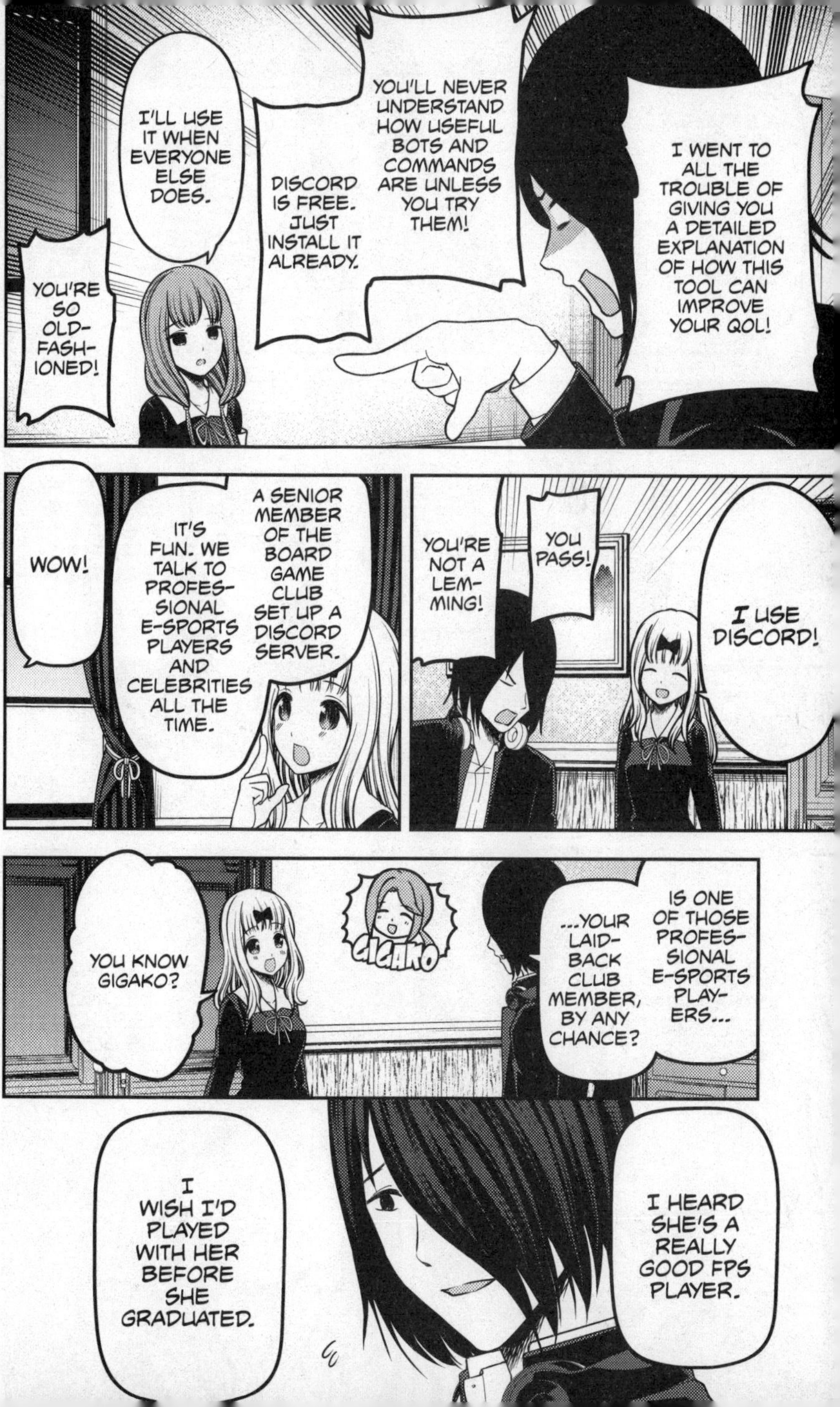
I WENT TO ALL THE TROUBLE OF GIVING YOU A DETAILED EXPLANATION OF HOW THIS TOOL CAN IMPROVE YOUR QOL!
YOU'LL NEVER UNDERSTAND HOW USEFUL BOTS AND COMMANDS ARE UNLESS YOU TRY THEM!
DISCORD IS FREE. JUST INSTALL IT ALREADY.
I'LL USE IT WHEN EVERYONE ELSE DOES.
YOU'RE SO OLD-FASHIONED!
I USE DISCORD!
YOU PASS!
YOU'RE NOT A LEMMING!
A SENIOR MEMBER OF THE BOARD GAME CLUB SET UP A DISCORD SERVER.
IT'S FUN. WE TALK TO PROFESSIONAL E-SPORTS PLAYERS AND CELEBRITIES ALL THE TIME.
WOW!
IS ONE OF THOSE PROFESSIONAL E-SPORTS PLAYERS...
...YOUR LAID-BACK CLUB MEMBER, BY ANY CHANCE?
GIGAKO
YOU KNOW GIGAKO?
I HEARD SHE'S A REALLY GOOD FPS PLAYER.
I WISH I'D PLAYED WITH HER BEFORE SHE GRADUATED.

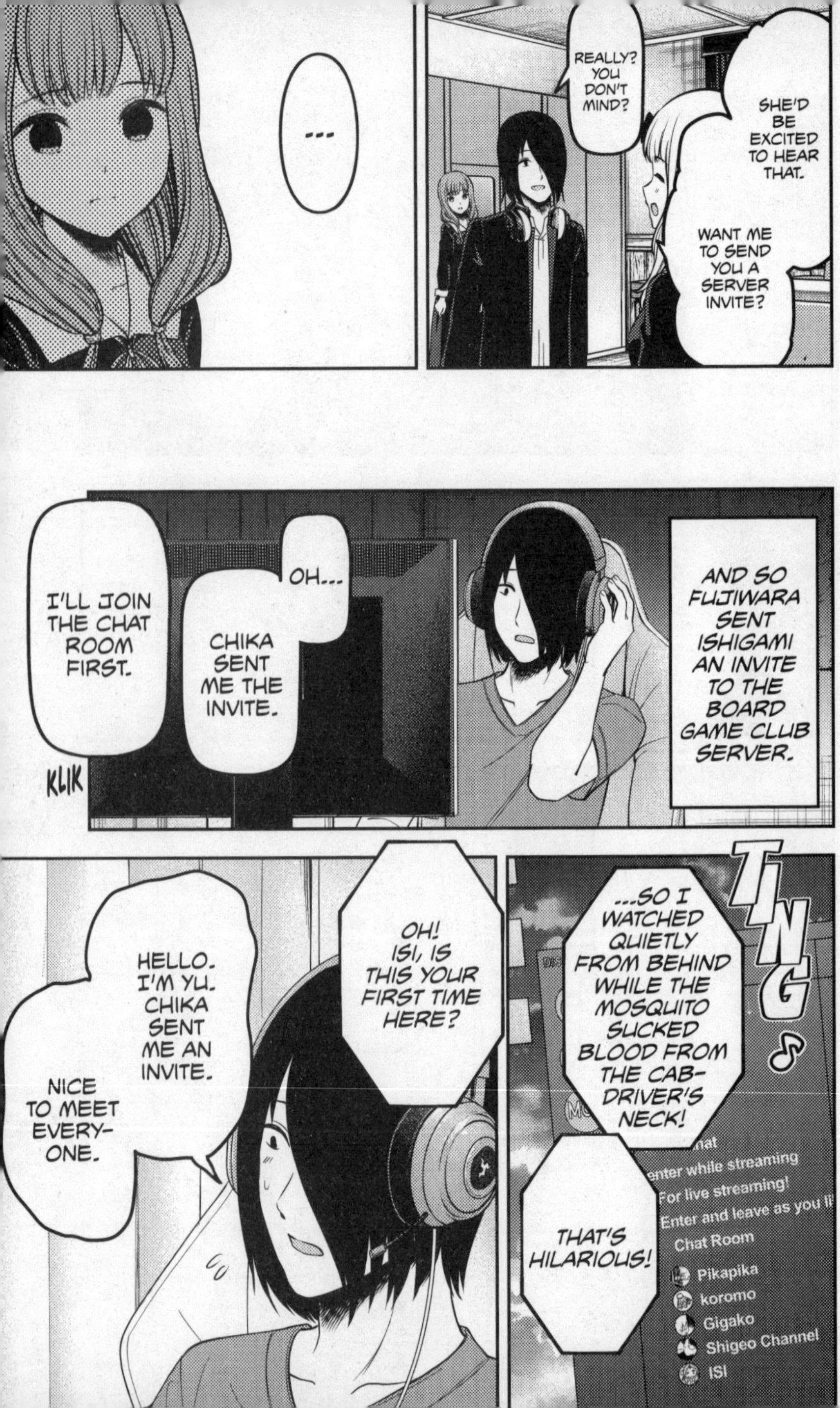
SHE'D BE EXCITED TO HEAR THAT.
WANT ME TO SEND YOU A SERVER INVITE?
REALLY? YOU DON'T MIND?
...
AND SO FUJIWARA SENT ISHIGAMI AN INVITE TO THE BOARD GAME CLUB SERVER.
OH...
CHIKA SENT ME THE INVITE.
I'LL JOIN THE CHAT ROOM FIRST.
KLIK
TING
...SO I WATCHED QUIETLY FROM BEHIND WHILE THE MOSQUITO SUCKED BLOOD FROM THE CAB-DRIVER'S NECK!
THAT'S HILARIOUS!
enter while streaming
For live streaming!
Enter and leave as you li
Chat Room
Pikapika
koromo
Gigako
Shigeo Channel
ISI
OH! ISI, IS THIS YOUR FIRST TIME HERE?
HELLO. I'M YU. CHIKA SENT ME AN INVITE.
NICE TO MEET EVERY-ONE.

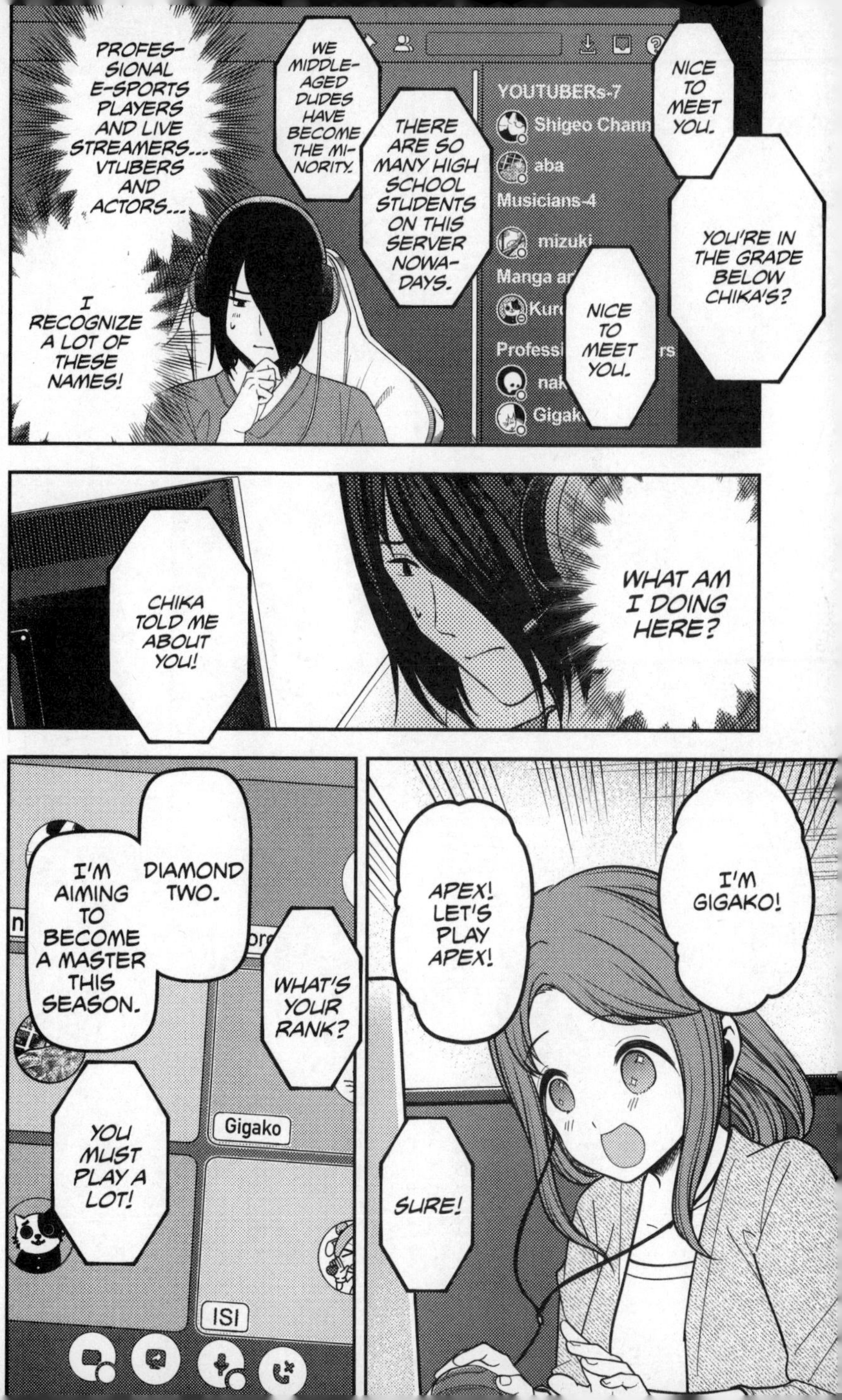
NICE TO MEET YOU.
YOUTUBERs-7
Shigeo Chann
aba
Musicians-4
mizuki
YOU'RE IN THE GRADE BELOW CHIKA'S?
NICE TO MEET YOU.
THERE ARE SO MANY HIGH SCHOOL STUDENTS ON THIS SERVER NOWADAYS.
WE MIDDLE-AGED DUDES HAVE BECOME THE MINORITY.
PROFESSIONAL E-SPORTS PLAYERS AND LIVE STREAMERS... VTUBERS AND ACTORS...
I RECOGNIZE A LOT OF THESE NAMES!
WHAT AM I DOING HERE?
CHIKA TOLD ME ABOUT YOU!
I'M GIGAKO!
APEX! LET'S PLAY APEX!
SURE!
DIAMOND TWO.
I'M AIMING TO BECOME A MASTER THIS SEASON.
WHAT'S YOUR RANK?
Gigako
YOU MUST PLAY A LOT!
ISI

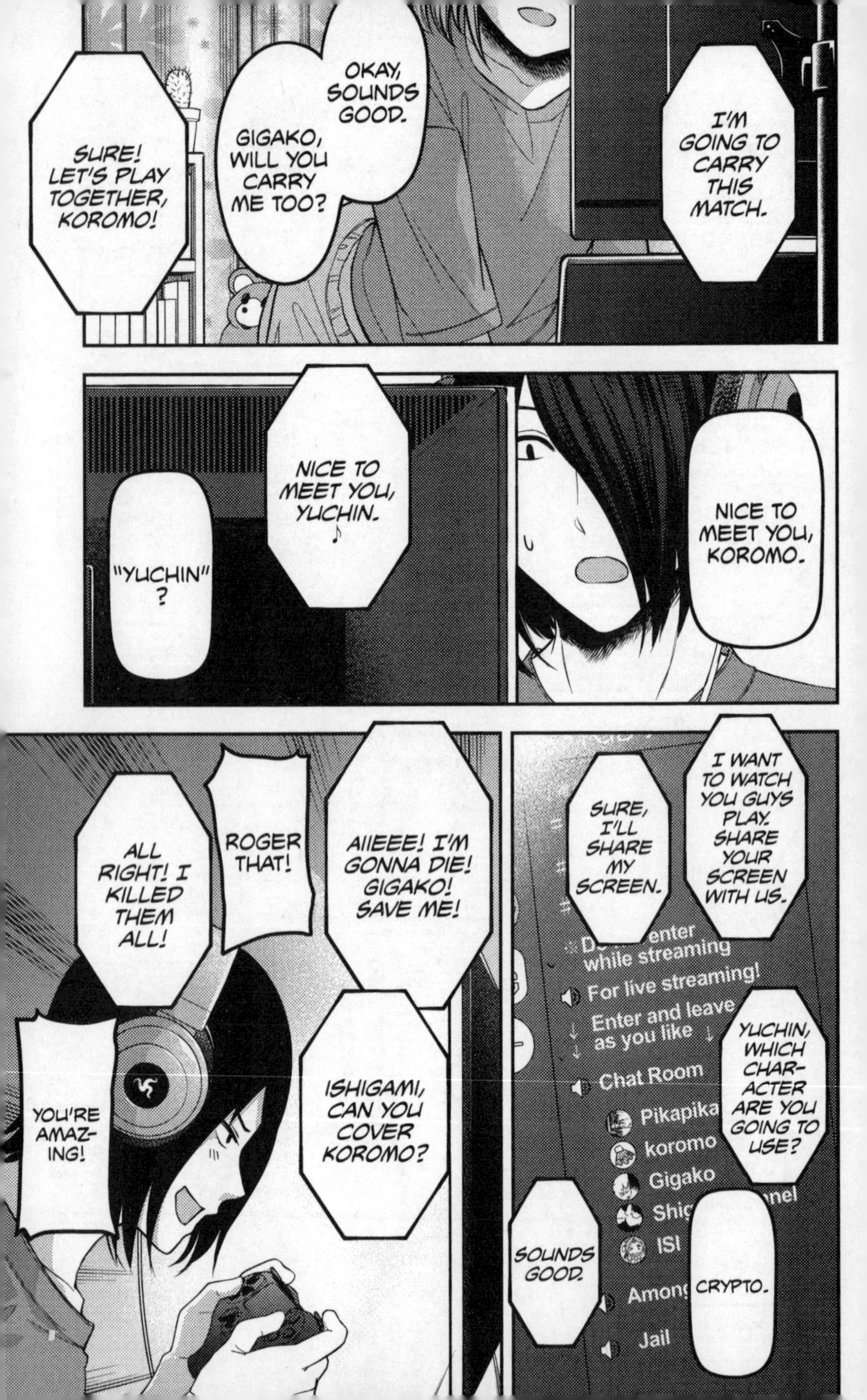
I'M GOING TO CARRY THIS MATCH.
OKAY, SOUNDS GOOD.
GIGAKO, WILL YOU CARRY ME TOO?
SURE! LET'S PLAY TOGETHER, KOROMO!
NICE TO MEET YOU, KOROMO.
NICE TO MEET YOU, YUCHIN. ♪
"YUCHIN"?
I WANT TO WATCH YOU GUYS PLAY. SHARE YOUR SCREEN WITH US.
SURE, I'LL SHARE MY SCREEN.
while streaming
For live streaming!
Enter and leave as you like
Chat Room
Pikapika
koromo
Gigako
ISI
Jail
YUCHIN, WHICH CHARACTER ARE YOU GOING TO USE?
CRYPTO.
SOUNDS GOOD.
AIIEEE! I'M GONNA DIE! GIGAKO! SAVE ME!
ROGER THAT!
ALL RIGHT! I KILLED THEM ALL!
ISHIGAMI, CAN YOU COVER KOROMO?
YOU'RE AMAZING!

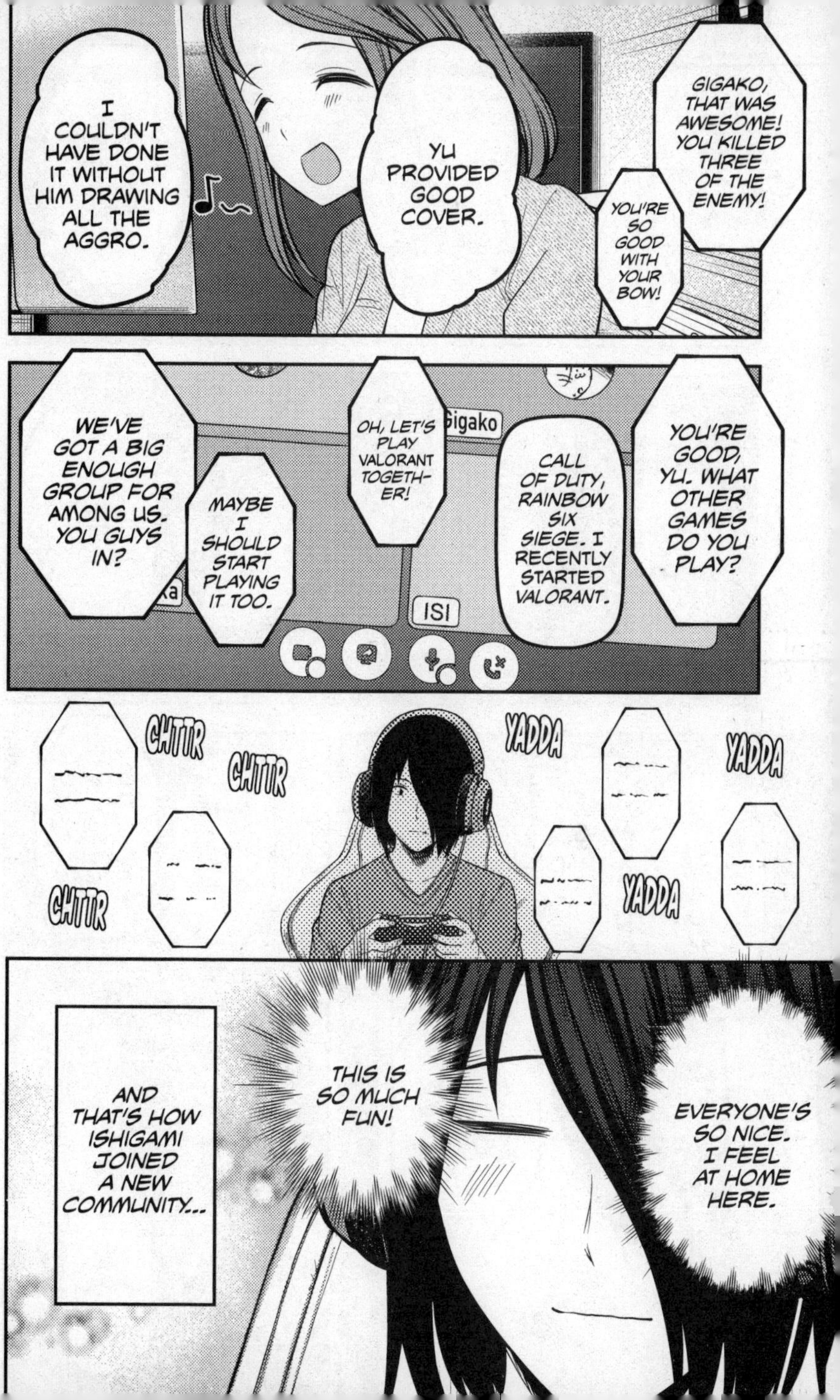
GIGAKO, THAT WAS AWESOME! YOU KILLED THREE OF THE ENEMY!
YOU'RE SO GOOD WITH YOUR BOW!
YU PROVIDED GOOD COVER.
I COULDN'T HAVE DONE IT WITHOUT HIM DRAWING ALL THE AGGRO.
YOU'RE GOOD, YU. WHAT OTHER GAMES DO YOU PLAY?
CALL OF DUTY, RAINBOW SIX SIEGE. I RECENTLY STARTED VALORANT.
Gigako
OH, LET'S PLAY VALORANT TOGETH-ER!
ISI
MAYBE I SHOULD START PLAYING IT TOO.
WE'VE GOT A BIG ENOUGH GROUP FOR AMONG US. YOU GUYS IN?
YADDA
YADDA
YADDA
CHTTR
CHTTR
CHTTR
EVERYONE'S SO NICE. I FEEL AT HOME HERE.
THIS IS SO MUCH FUN!
AND THAT'S HOW ISHIGAMI JOINED A NEW COMMUNITY...

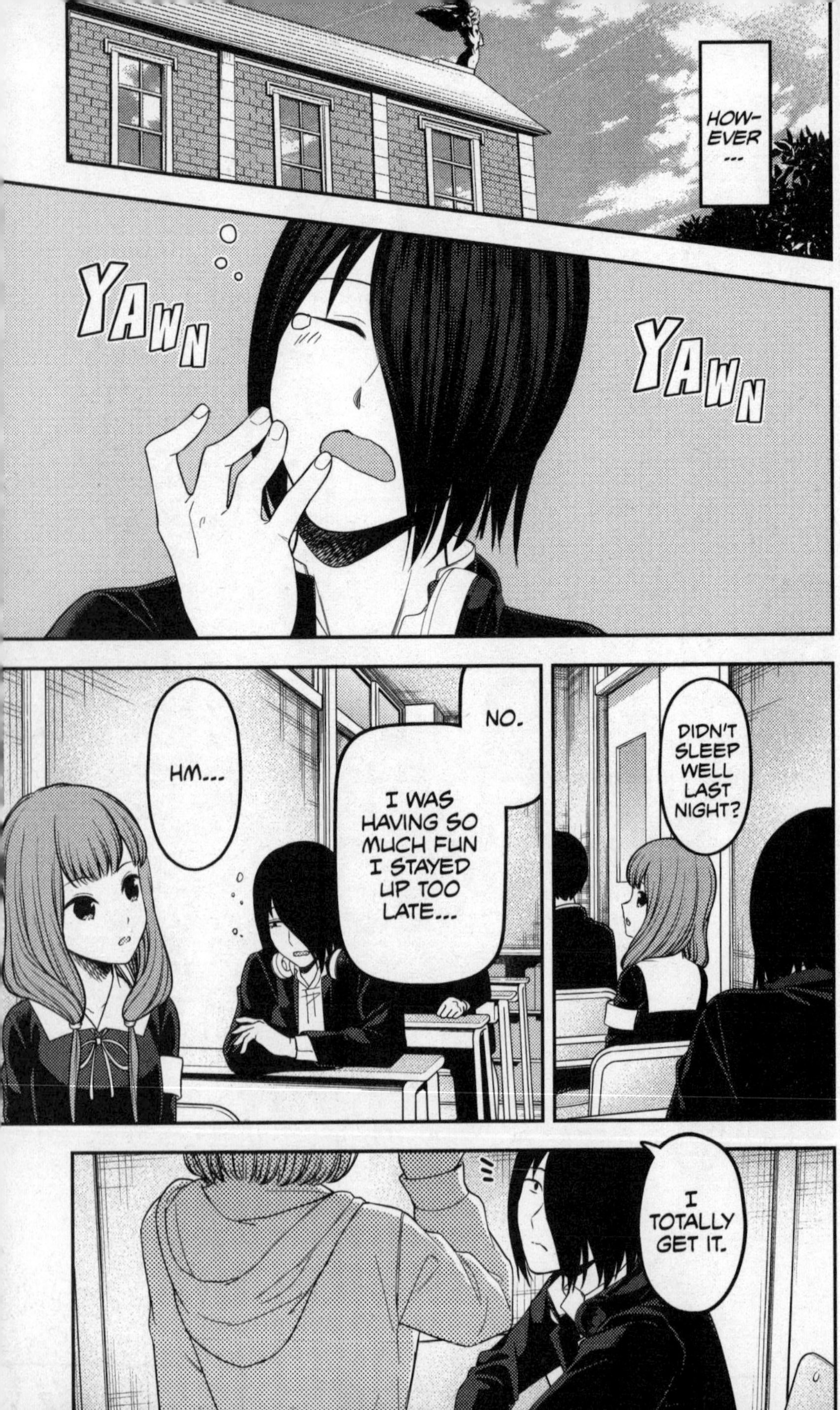
HOW-EVER---
YAWN
YAWN
DIDN'T SLEEP WELL LAST NIGHT?
NO.
I WAS HAVING SO MUCH FUN I STAYED UP TOO LATE...
HM...
I TOTALLY GET IT.

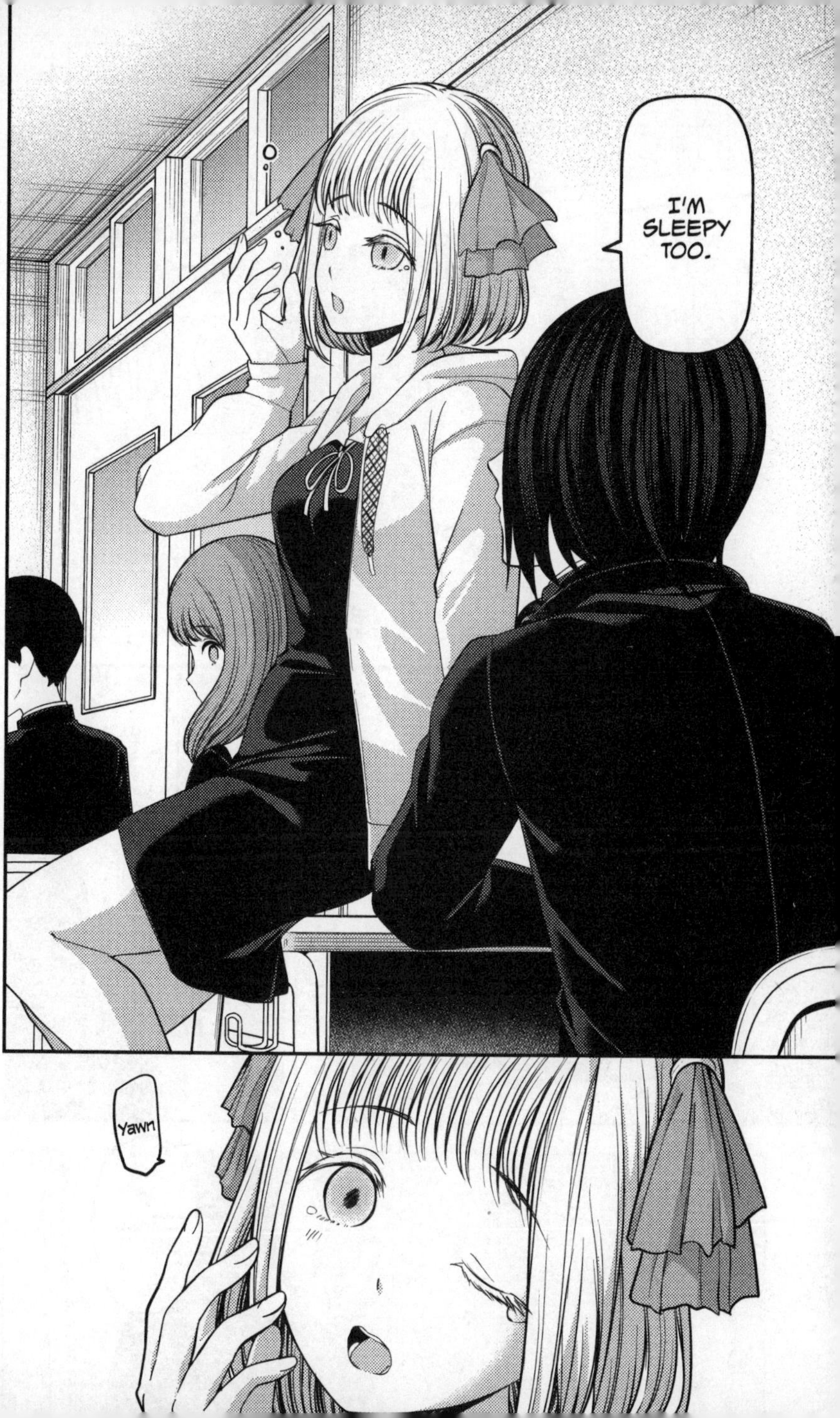
I'M SLEEPY TOO.
Yawn

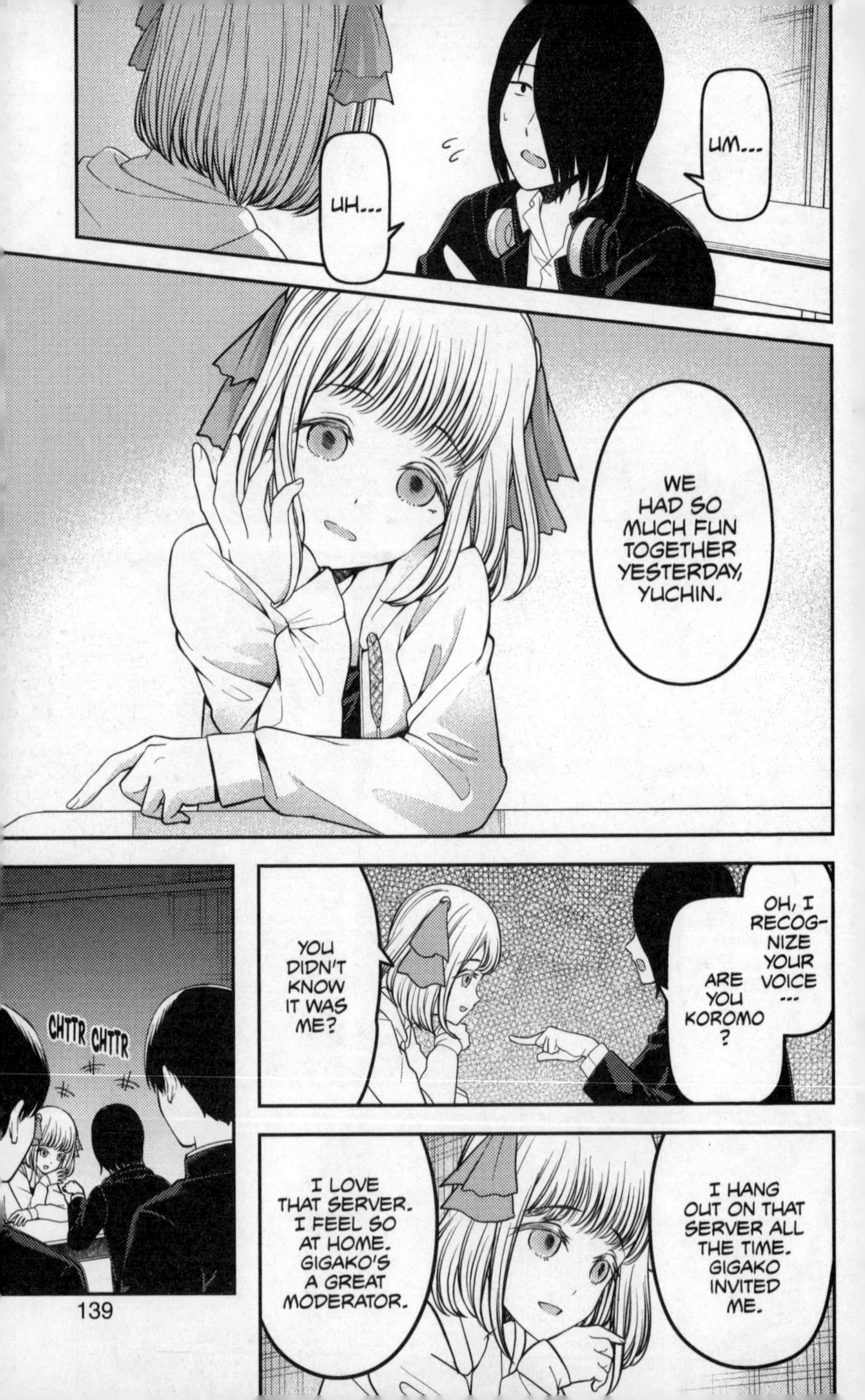
UM...
UH...
WE HAD SO MUCH FUN TOGETHER YESTERDAY, YUCHIN.
OH, I RECOGNIZE YOUR VOICE... ARE YOU KOROMO?
YOU DIDN'T KNOW IT WAS ME?
I HANG OUT ON THAT SERVER ALL THE TIME. GIGAKO INVITED ME.
I LOVE THAT SERVER. I FEEL SO AT HOME. GIGAKO'S A GREAT MODERATOR.
CHTTR CHTTR

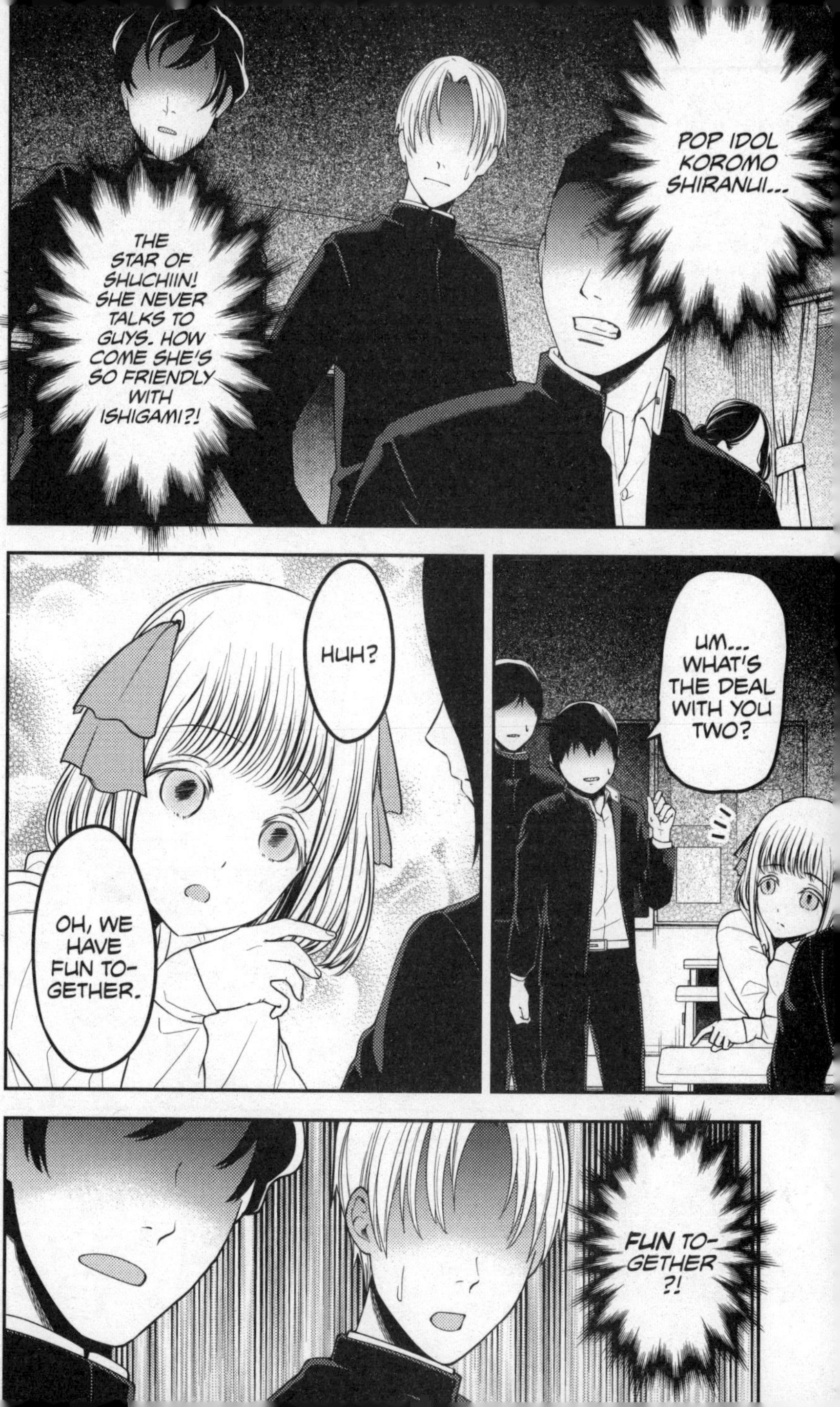
POP IDOL KOROMO SHIRANUI...
THE STAR OF SHUCHIIN! SHE NEVER TALKS TO GUYS. HOW COME SHE'S SO FRIENDLY WITH ISHIGAMI?!
UM... WHAT'S THE DEAL WITH YOU TWO?
HUH?
OH, WE HAVE FUN TO-GETHER.
FUN TO-GETHER?!

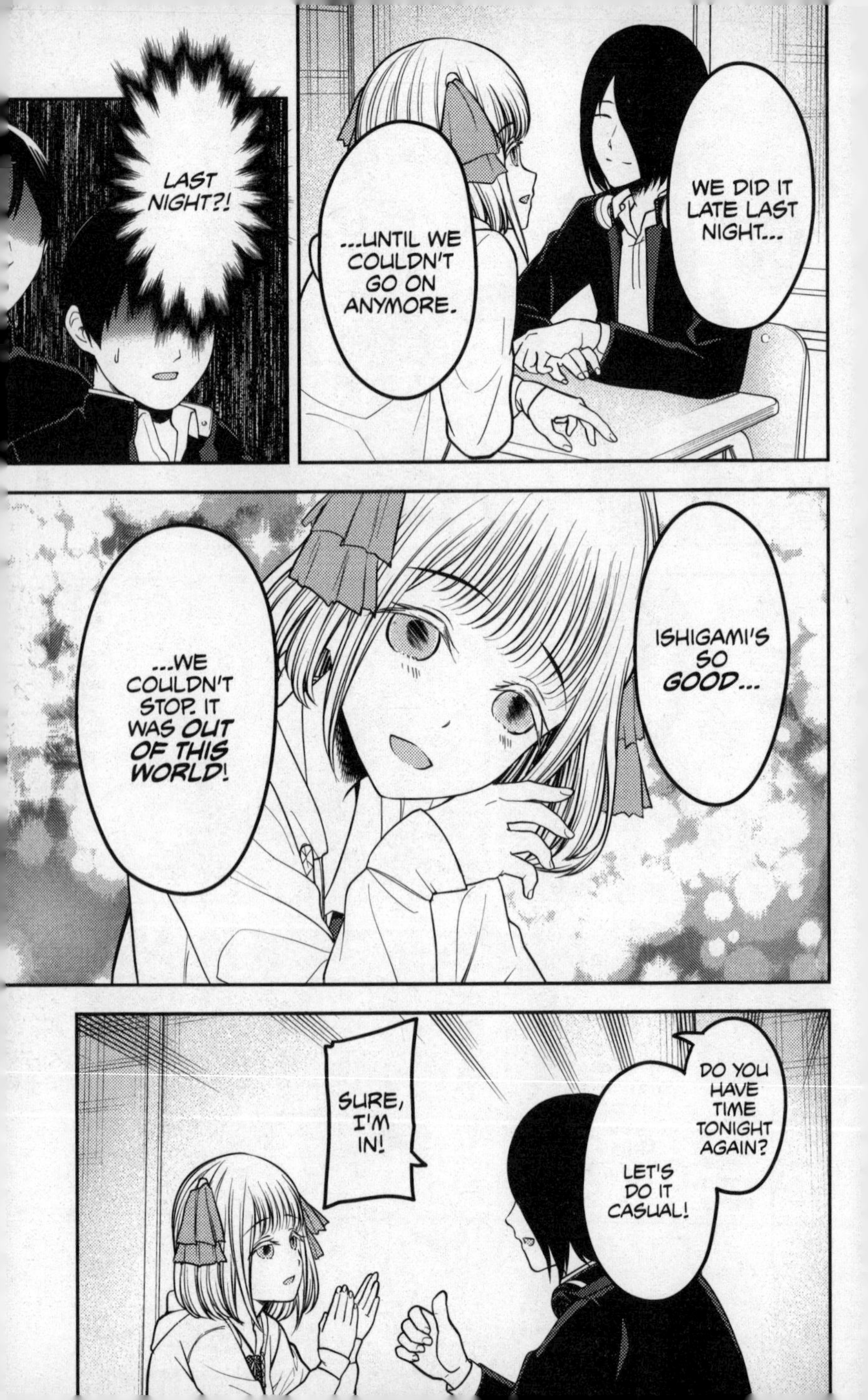
WE DID IT LATE LAST NIGHT...
...UNTIL WE COULDN'T GO ON ANYMORE.
LAST NIGHT?!
ISHIGAMI'S SO GOOD...
...WE COULDN'T STOP. IT WAS OUT OF THIS WORLD!
DO YOU HAVE TIME TONIGHT AGAIN?
LET'S DO IT CASUAL!
SURE, I'M IN!

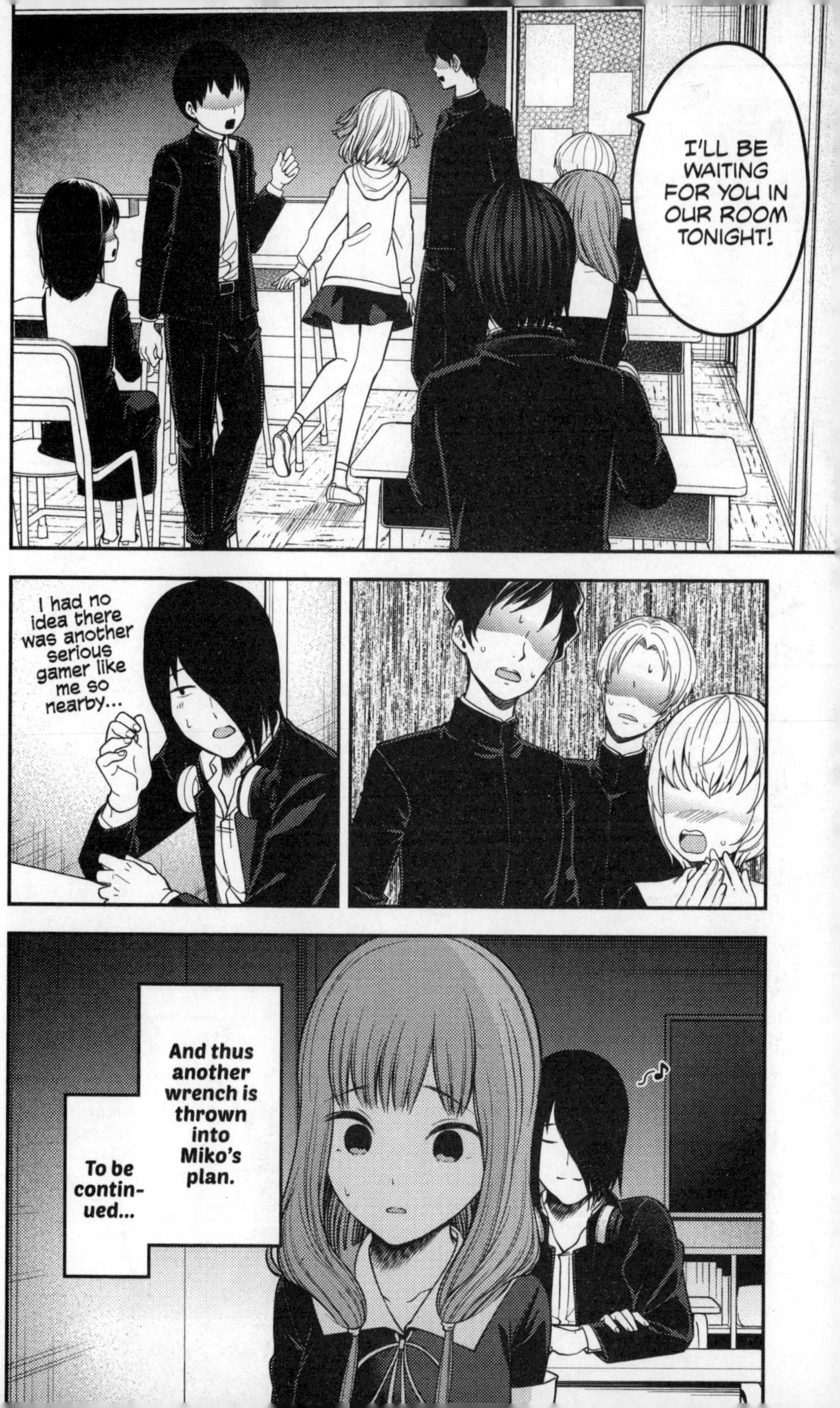
I'LL BE WAITING FOR YOU IN OUR ROOM TONIGHT!
I had no idea there was another serious gamer like me so nearby...
And thus another wrench is thrown into Miko's plan.
To be contin-ued...

Glossary (2)

· **Leaving someone on read**
Lazy people do this. They don't feel compelled to reply promptly after reading a message. Others can't accept the fact that some people don't like texting.

· **Pairs/Tinder**
Dating apps. The stigma is gone from modern dating apps. People view them as a normal way to meet potential partners.

· **FPS**
Short for "first-person shooter." FPS games have long been popular in the U.S. and Europe, and in recent years they've become popular in Japan too.

· **Aggro**
The amount of focus you draw from your enemies. The more aggro you have, the more your enemies will attack you. Thus you can act as a decoy, providing cover for your allies.

· *Apex Legends / Call of Duty / Rainbow Six Siege / VALORANT / Among Us*
Popular video games.

· **"Ishigami's so good we couldn't stop."**
Killing enemies is fun.

· **Casual**
Most PvP (player versus player) games have ranked matches and casual matches. In ranked matches, your score affects your ranking. The results of casual matches don't affect your rank.

· **"I'll be waiting for you in our room tonight!"**
Voice channels on Discord servers are called rooms. You meet online, not in an actual room in someone's home.

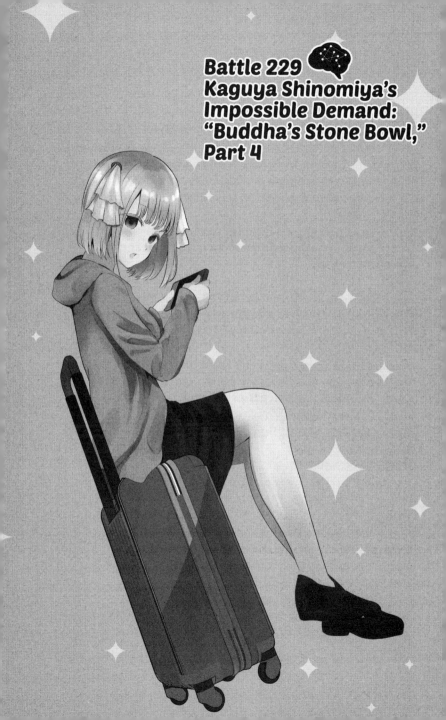

Battle 229 Kaguya Shinomiya's Impossible Demand: "Buddha's Stone Bowl," Part 4

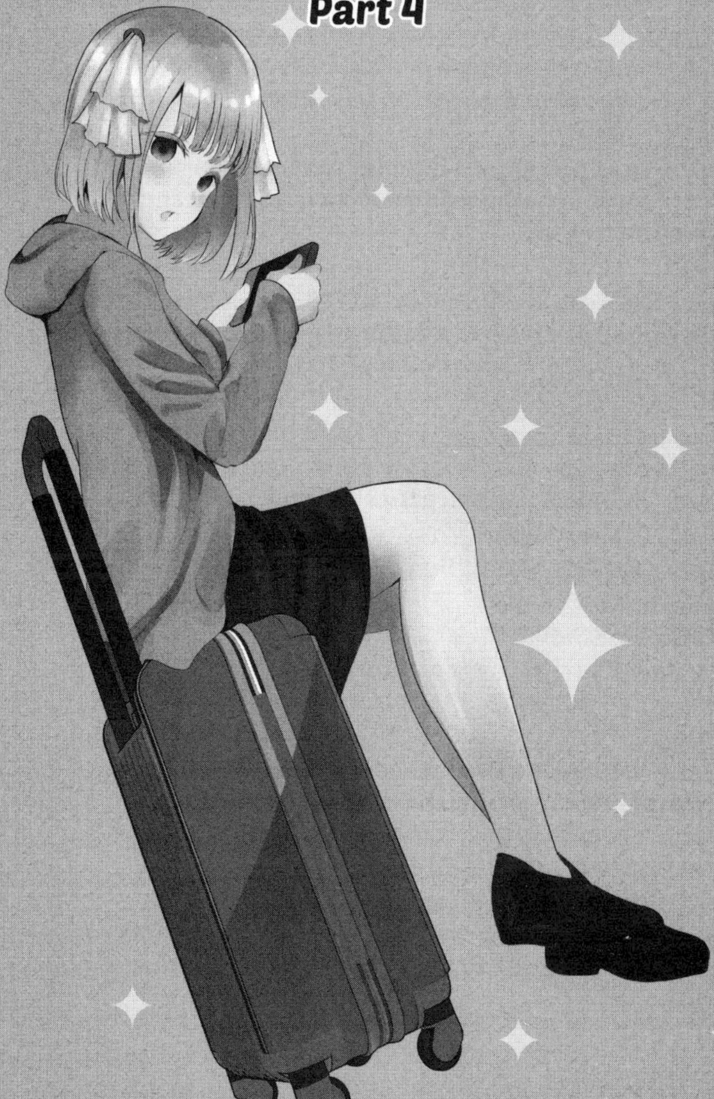

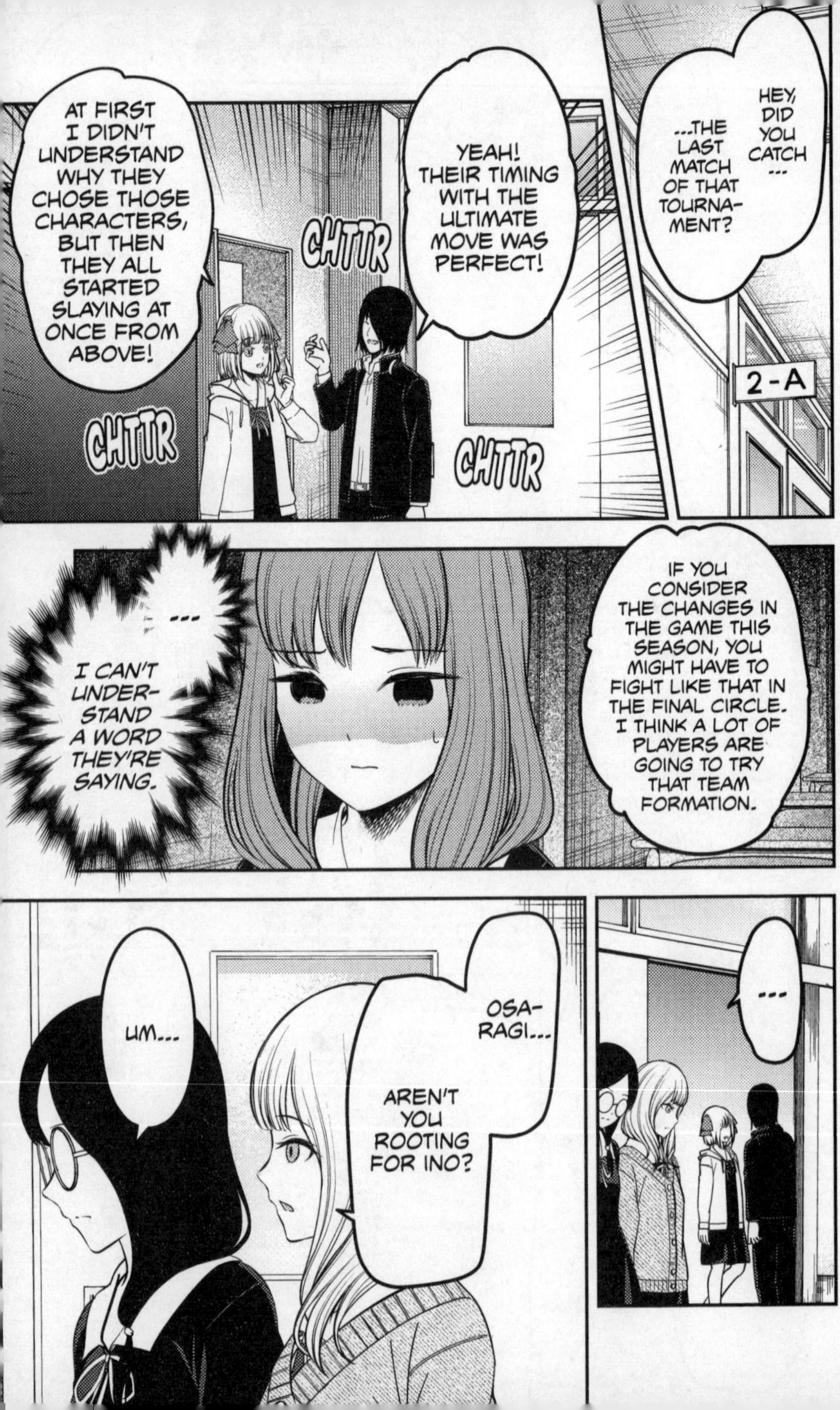
HEY, DID YOU CATCH ...
...THE LAST MATCH OF THAT TOURNAMENT?
YEAH! THEIR TIMING WITH THE ULTIMATE MOVE WAS PERFECT!
CHTTR
AT FIRST I DIDN'T UNDERSTAND WHY THEY CHOSE THOSE CHARACTERS, BUT THEN THEY ALL STARTED SLAYING AT ONCE FROM ABOVE!
CHTTR
CHTTR
IF YOU CONSIDER THE CHANGES IN THE GAME THIS SEASON, YOU MIGHT HAVE TO FIGHT LIKE THAT IN THE FINAL CIRCLE. I THINK A LOT OF PLAYERS ARE GOING TO TRY THAT TEAM FORMATION.
...
I CAN'T UNDERSTAND A WORD THEY'RE SAYING.
...
OSARAGI...
AREN'T YOU ROOTING FOR INO?
UM...

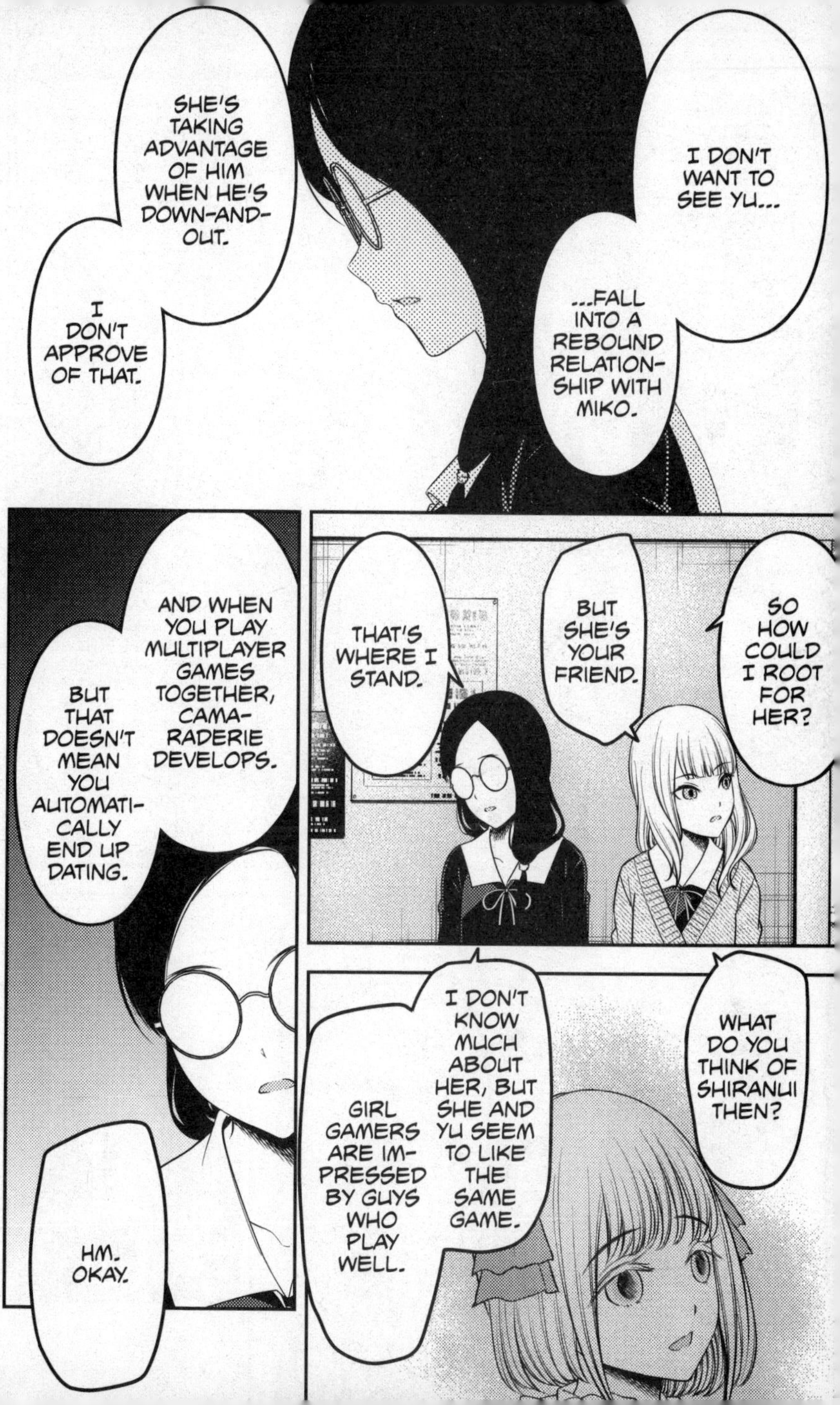
I DON'T WANT TO SEE YU...
...FALL INTO A REBOUND RELATIONSHIP WITH MIKO.
SHE'S TAKING ADVANTAGE OF HIM WHEN HE'S DOWN-AND-OUT.
I DON'T APPROVE OF THAT.
SO HOW COULD I ROOT FOR HER?
BUT SHE'S YOUR FRIEND.
THAT'S WHERE I STAND.
WHAT DO YOU THINK OF SHIRANUI THEN?
I DON'T KNOW MUCH ABOUT HER, BUT SHE AND YU SEEM TO LIKE THE SAME GAME.
GIRL GAMERS ARE IMPRESSED BY GUYS WHO PLAY WELL.
AND WHEN YOU PLAY MULTIPLAYER GAMES TOGETHER, CAMARADERIE DEVELOPS.
BUT THAT DOESN'T MEAN YOU AUTOMATICALLY END UP DATING.
HM. OKAY.

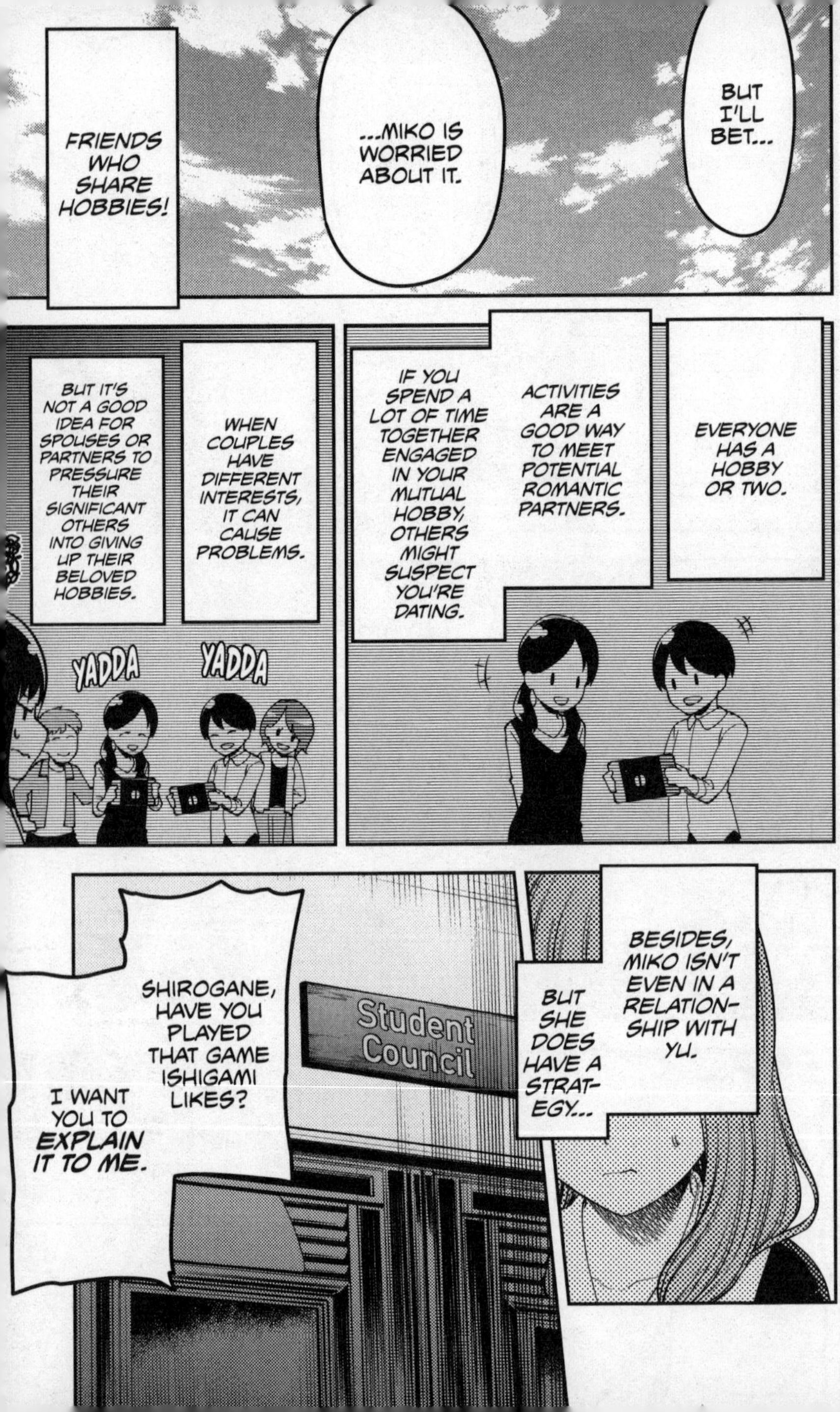
BUT I'LL BET...
...MIKO IS WORRIED ABOUT IT.
FRIENDS WHO SHARE HOBBIES!
EVERYONE HAS A HOBBY OR TWO.
ACTIVITIES ARE A GOOD WAY TO MEET POTENTIAL ROMANTIC PARTNERS.
IF YOU SPEND A LOT OF TIME TOGETHER ENGAGED IN YOUR MUTUAL HOBBY, OTHERS MIGHT SUSPECT YOU'RE DATING.
WHEN COUPLES HAVE DIFFERENT INTERESTS, IT CAN CAUSE PROBLEMS.
BUT IT'S NOT A GOOD IDEA FOR SPOUSES OR PARTNERS TO PRESSURE THEIR SIGNIFICANT OTHERS INTO GIVING UP THEIR BELOVED HOBBIES.
YADDA
YADDA
BESIDES, MIKO ISN'T EVEN IN A RELATIONSHIP WITH YU.
BUT SHE DOES HAVE A STRATEGY...
Student Council
SHIROGANE, HAVE YOU PLAYED THAT GAME ISHIGAMI LIKES?
I WANT YOU TO *EXPLAIN* IT TO ME.

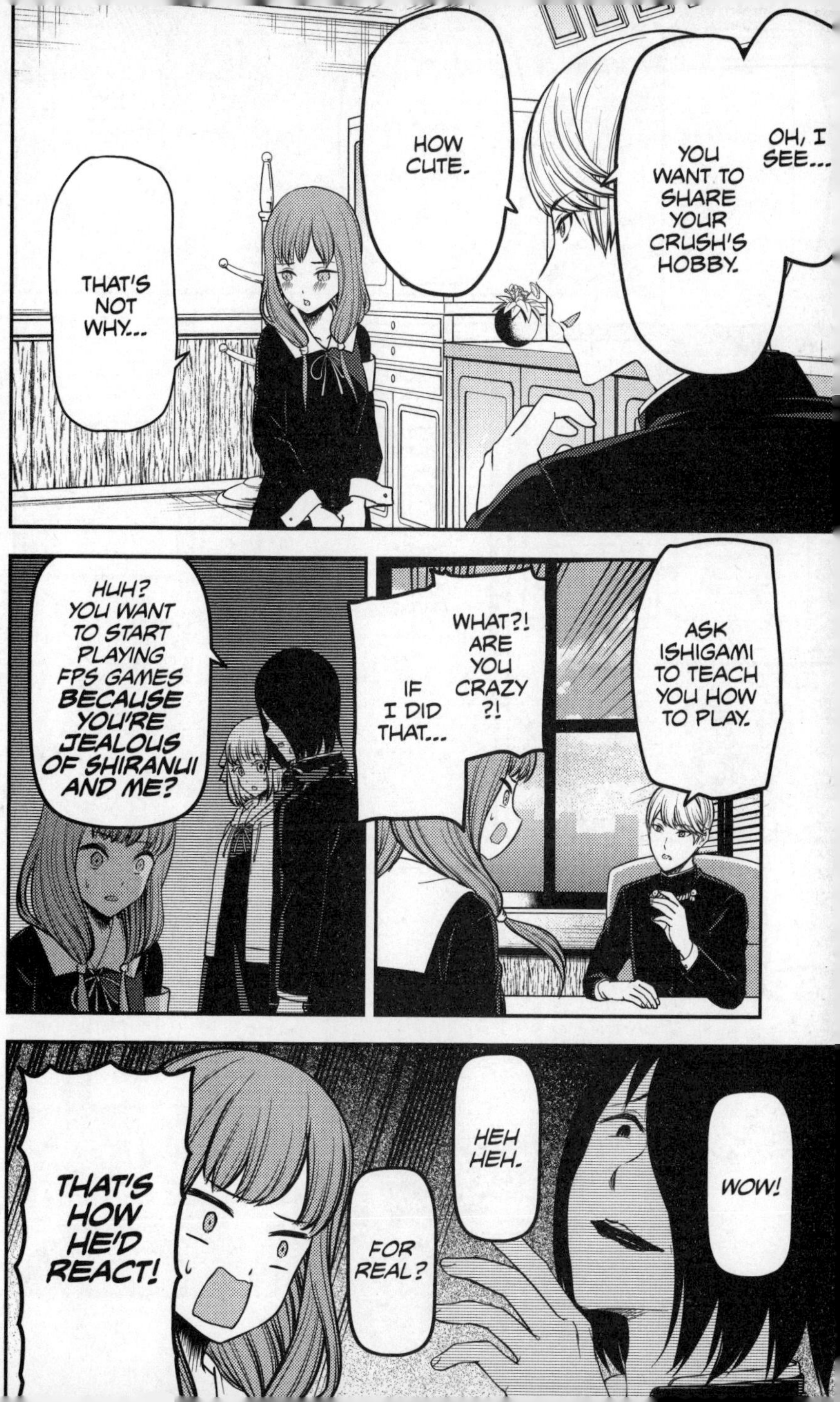
OH, I SEE...
YOU WANT TO SHARE YOUR CRUSH'S HOBBY.
HOW CUTE.
THAT'S NOT WHY...
ASK ISHIGAMI TO TEACH YOU HOW TO PLAY.
WHAT?! ARE YOU CRAZY?!
IF I DID THAT...
HUH? YOU WANT TO START PLAYING FPS GAMES BECAUSE YOU'RE JEALOUS OF SHIRANUI AND ME?
WOW!
HEH HEH.
FOR REAL?
THAT'S HOW HE'D REACT!

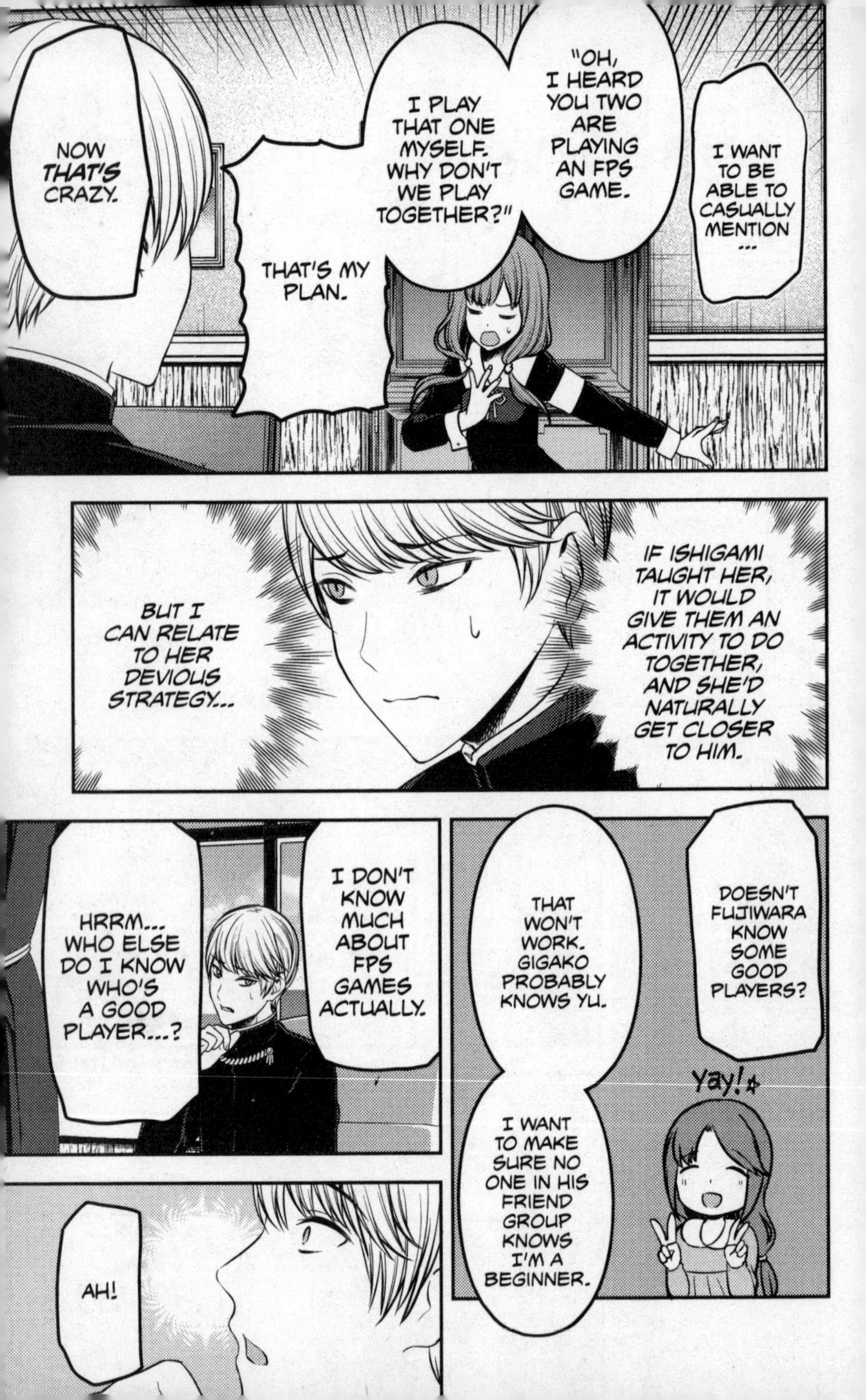
I WANT TO BE ABLE TO CASUALLY MENTION...
"OH, I HEARD YOU TWO ARE PLAYING AN FPS GAME.
I PLAY THAT ONE MYSELF. WHY DON'T WE PLAY TOGETHER?"
THAT'S MY PLAN.
NOW *THAT'S* CRAZY.
IF ISHIGAMI TAUGHT HER, IT WOULD GIVE THEM AN ACTIVITY TO DO TOGETHER, AND SHE'D NATURALLY GET CLOSER TO HIM.
BUT I CAN RELATE TO HER DEVIOUS STRATEGY...
DOESN'T FUJIWARA KNOW SOME GOOD PLAYERS?
THAT WON'T WORK. GIGAKO PROBABLY KNOWS YU.
I WANT TO MAKE SURE NO ONE IN HIS FRIEND GROUP KNOWS I'M A BEGINNER.
Yay!☆
I DON'T KNOW MUCH ABOUT FPS GAMES ACTUALLY.
HRRM... WHO ELSE DO I KNOW WHO'S A GOOD PLAYER...?
AH!

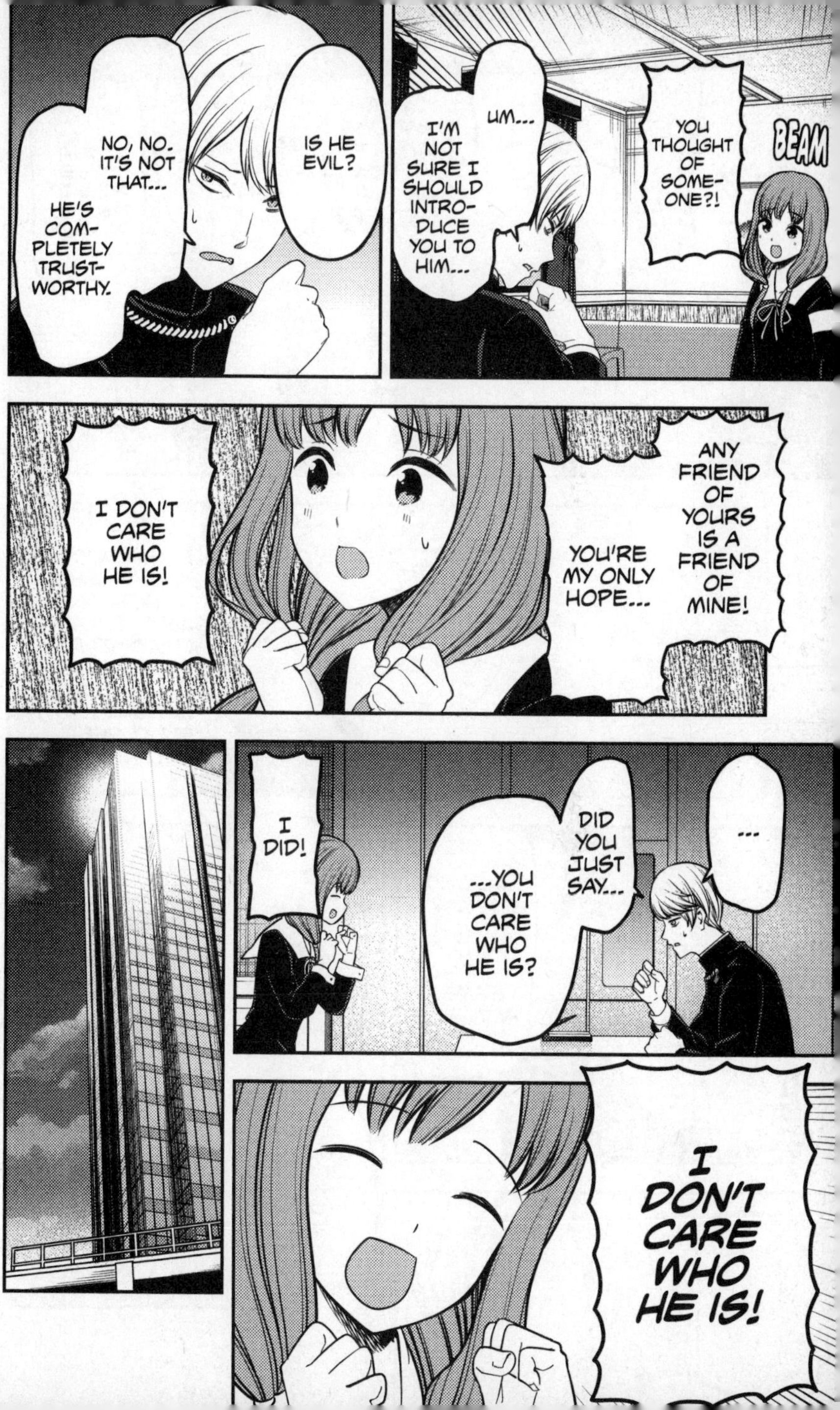
BEAM
YOU THOUGHT OF SOMEONE?!
UM...
I'M NOT SURE I SHOULD INTRODUCE YOU TO HIM...
IS HE EVIL?
NO, NO. IT'S NOT THAT...
HE'S COMPLETELY TRUSTWORTHY.
ANY FRIEND OF YOURS IS A FRIEND OF MINE!
YOU'RE MY ONLY HOPE...
I DON'T CARE WHO HE IS!
...
DID YOU JUST SAY...
...YOU DON'T CARE WHO HE IS?
I DID!
I DON'T CARE WHO HE IS!

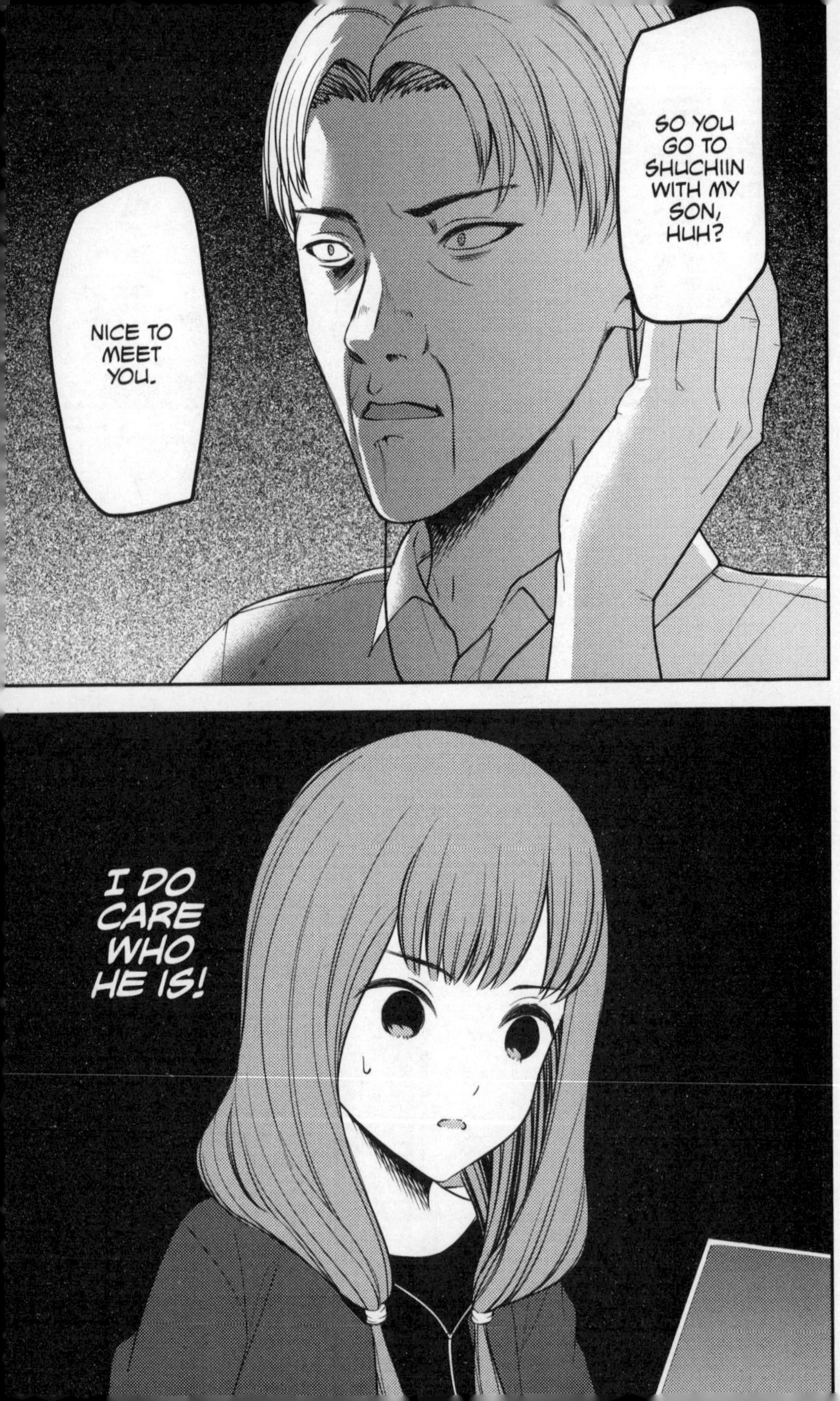
SO YOU GO TO SHUCHIIN WITH MY SON, HUH?
NICE TO MEET YOU.
I DO CARE WHO HE IS!

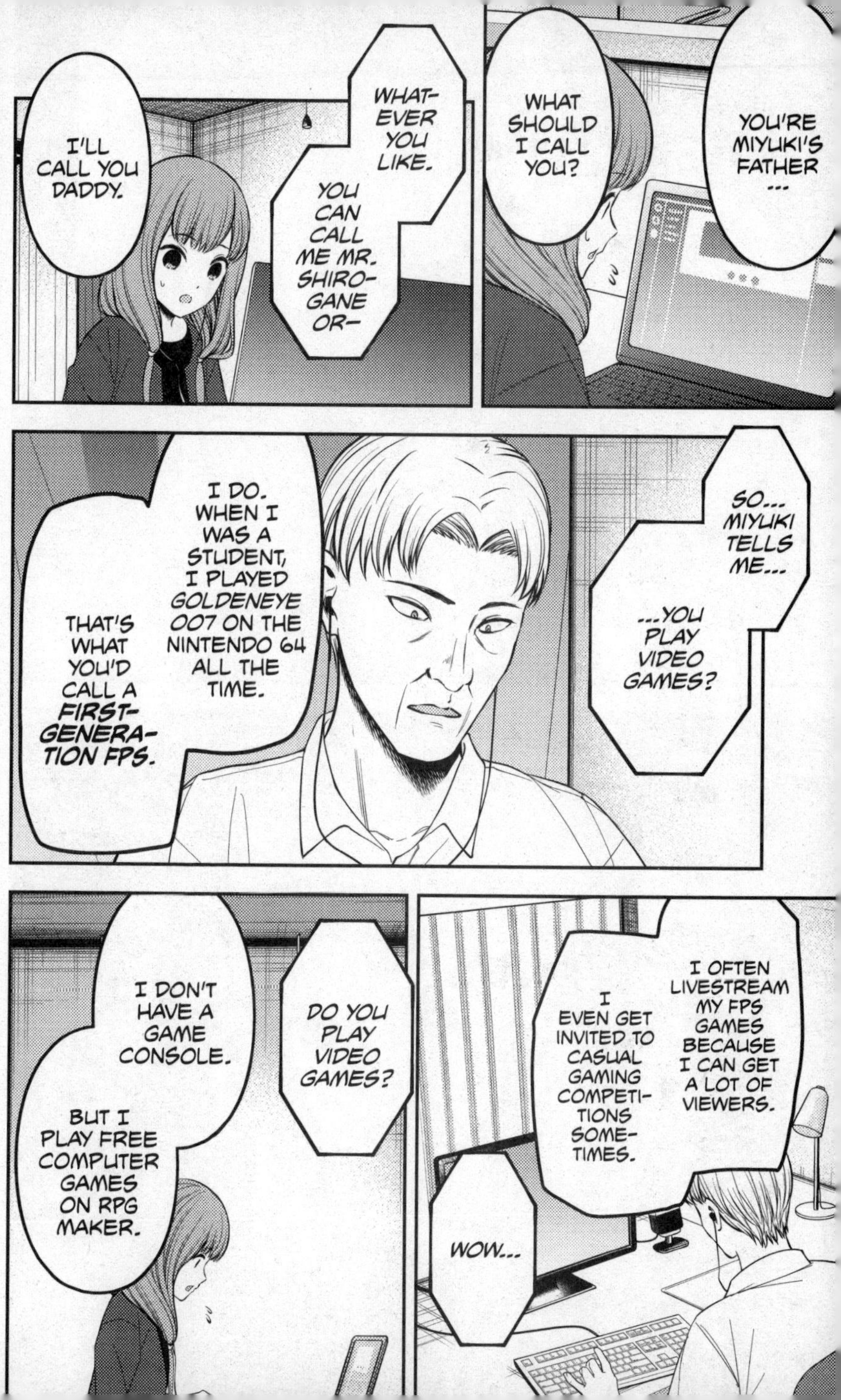
YOU'RE MIYUKI'S FATHER...
WHAT SHOULD I CALL YOU?
WHATEVER YOU LIKE.
YOU CAN CALL ME MR. SHIROGANE OR—
I'LL CALL YOU DADDY.
SO... MIYUKI TELLS ME...
...YOU PLAY VIDEO GAMES?
I DO. WHEN I WAS A STUDENT, I PLAYED GOLDENEYE 007 ON THE NINTENDO 64 ALL THE TIME.
THAT'S WHAT YOU'D CALL A FIRST-GENERATION FPS.
I OFTEN LIVESTREAM MY FPS GAMES BECAUSE I CAN GET A LOT OF VIEWERS.
I EVEN GET INVITED TO CASUAL GAMING COMPETITIONS SOMETIMES.
WOW...
DO YOU PLAY VIDEO GAMES?
I DON'T HAVE A GAME CONSOLE.
BUT I PLAY FREE COMPUTER GAMES ON RPG MAKER.

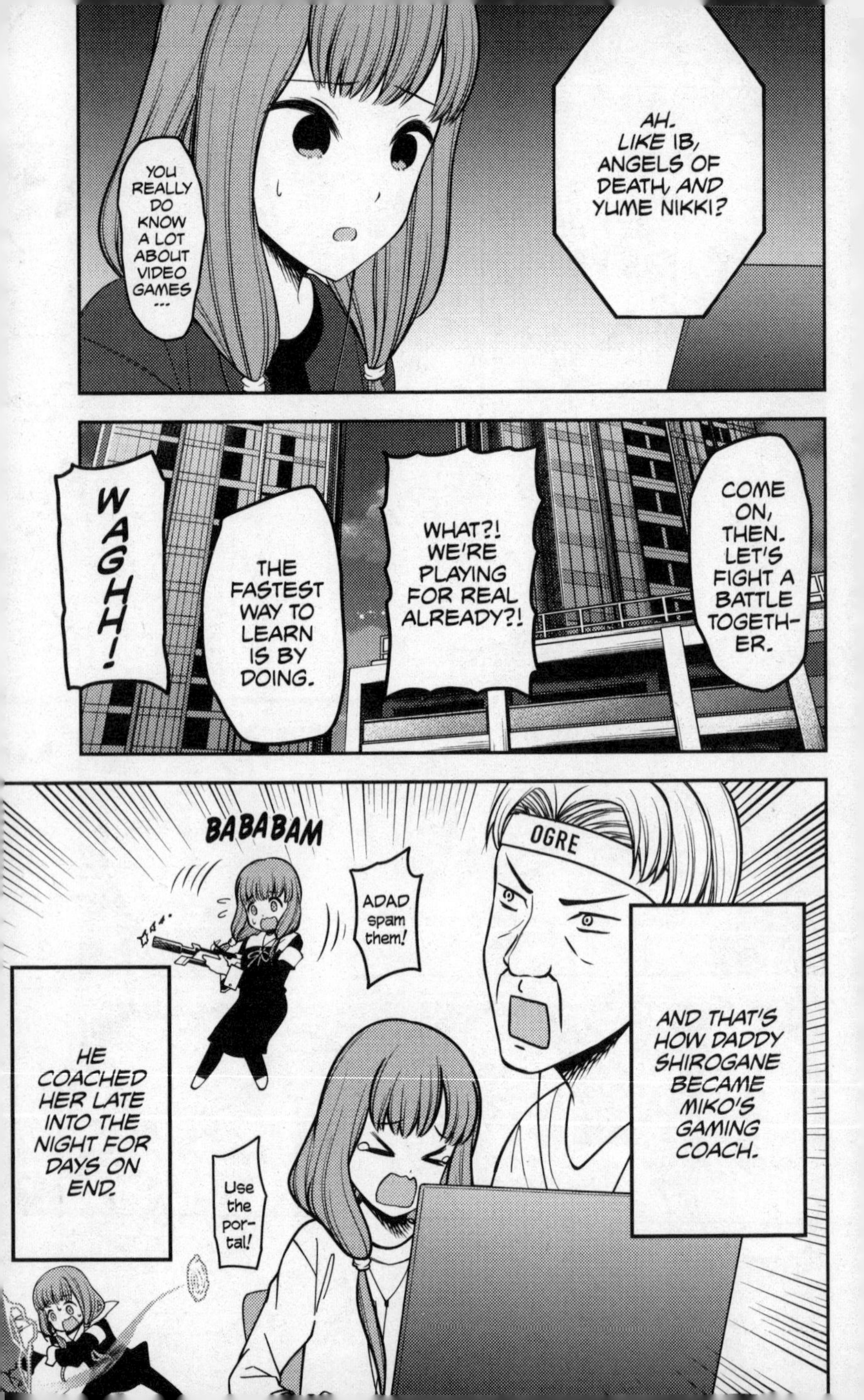
AH. LIKE IB, ANGELS OF DEATH, AND YUME NIKKI?
YOU REALLY DO KNOW A LOT ABOUT VIDEO GAMES...
COME ON, THEN. LET'S FIGHT A BATTLE TOGETH-ER.
WHAT?! WE'RE PLAYING FOR REAL ALREADY?!
THE FASTEST WAY TO LEARN IS BY DOING.
WAGHH!
OGRE
AND THAT'S HOW DADDY SHIROGANE BECAME MIKO'S GAMING COACH.
BABABAM
ADAD spam them!
HE COACHED HER LATE INTO THE NIGHT FOR DAYS ON END.
Use the por-tal!

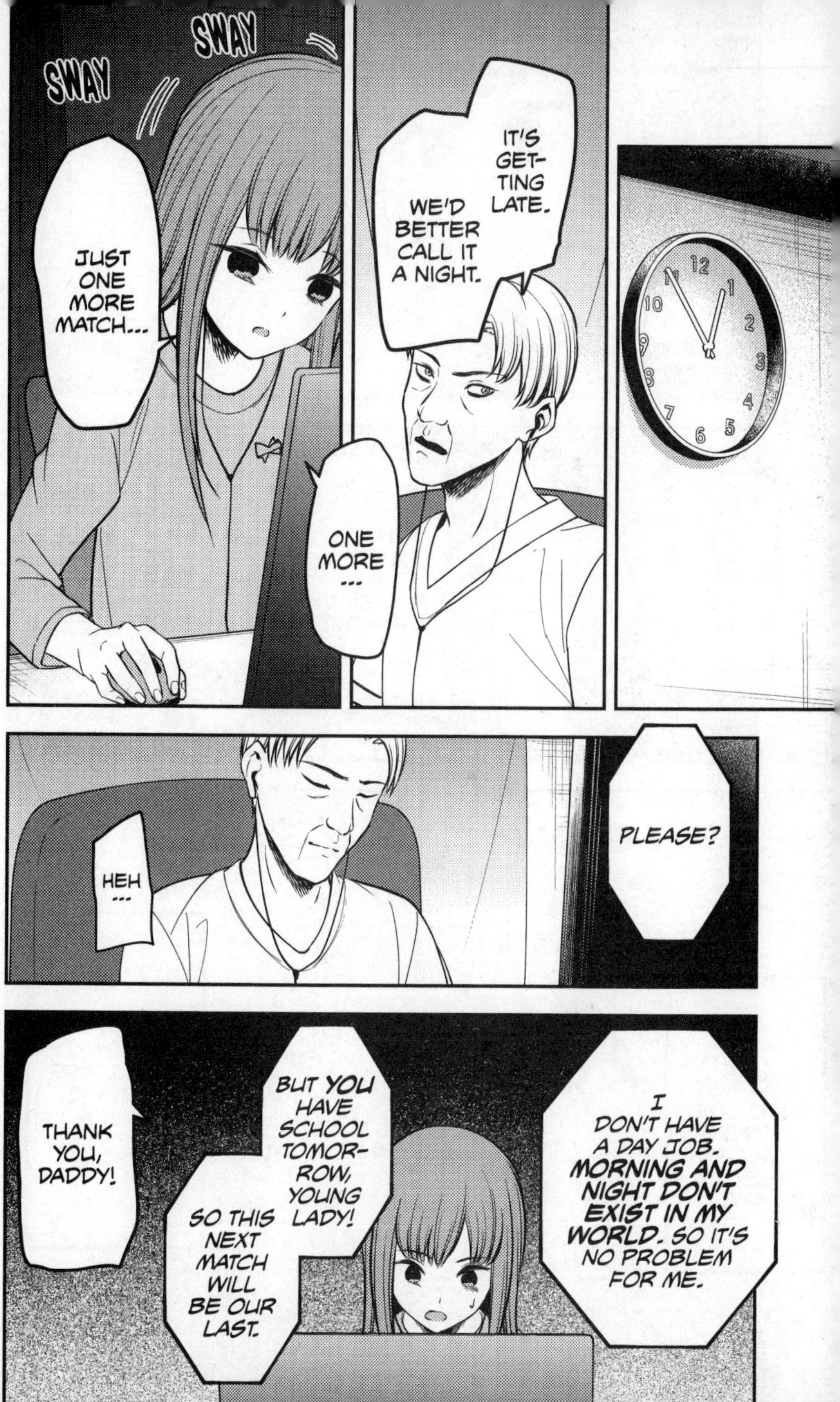

IT'S GETTING LATE.
WE'D BETTER CALL IT A NIGHT.
ONE MORE...
SWAY
SWAY
JUST ONE MORE MATCH...
PLEASE?
HEH...
I DON'T HAVE A DAY JOB. MORNING AND NIGHT DON'T EXIST IN MY WORLD. SO IT'S NO PROBLEM FOR ME.
BUT YOU HAVE SCHOOL TOMORROW, YOUNG LADY!
SO THIS NEXT MATCH WILL BE OUR LAST.
THANK YOU, DADDY!

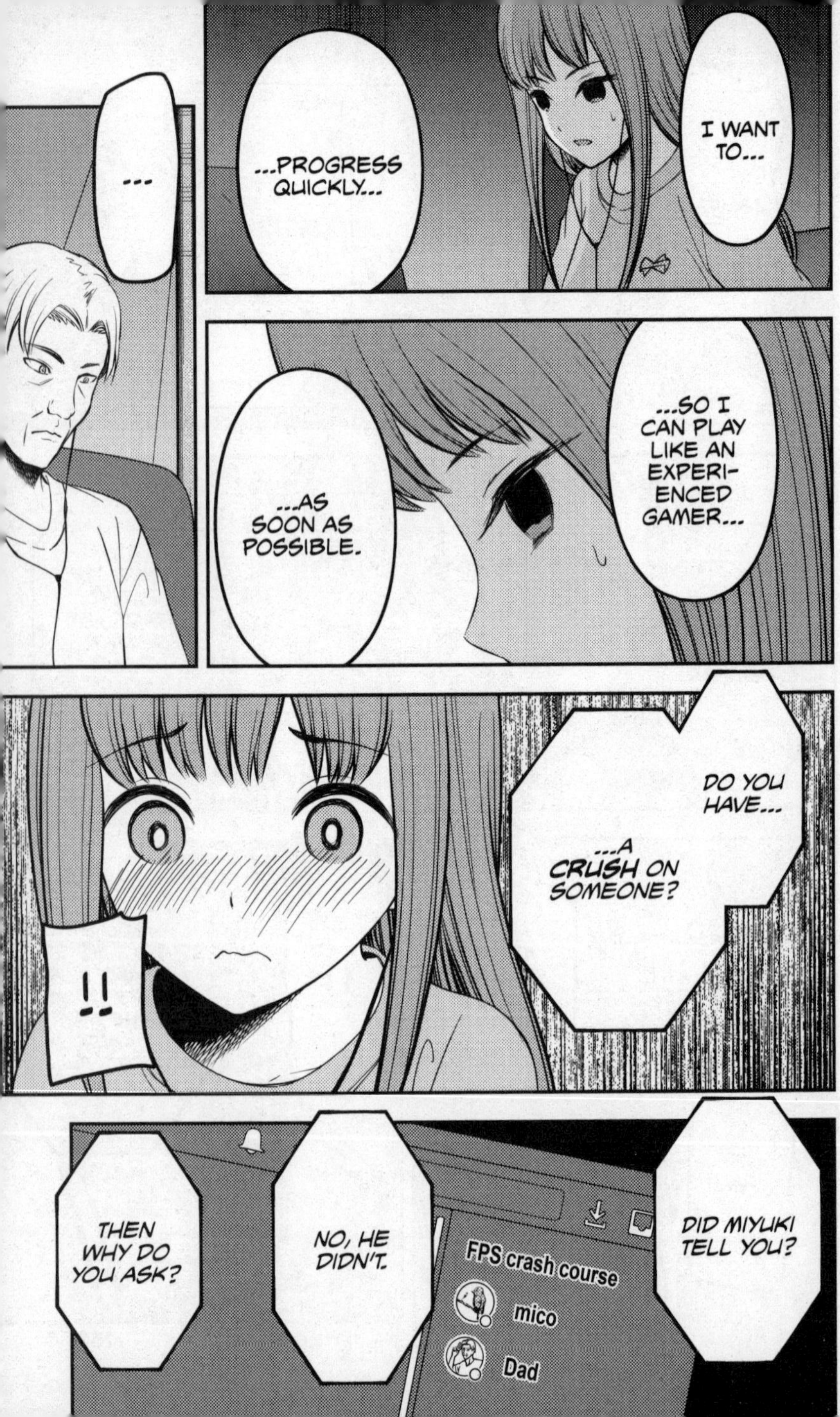
I WANT TO...
...PROGRESS QUICKLY...
...SO I CAN PLAY LIKE AN EXPERIENCED GAMER...
...AS SOON AS POSSIBLE.
...
DO YOU HAVE...
...A CRUSH ON SOMEONE?
!!
DID MIYUKI TELL YOU?
FPS crash course
mico
Dad
NO, HE DIDN'T.
THEN WHY DO YOU ASK?

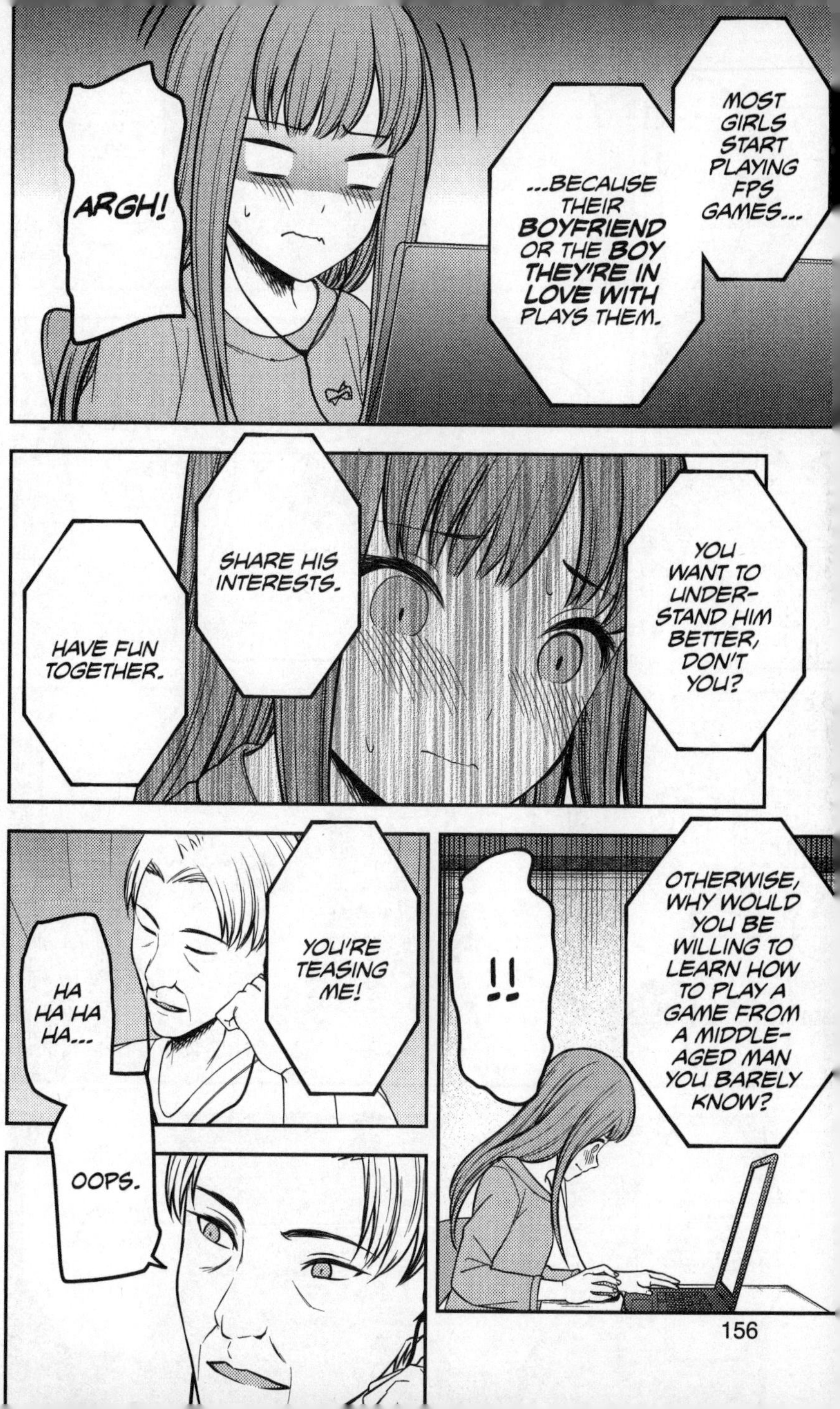
MOST GIRLS START PLAYING FPS GAMES...
...BECAUSE THEIR BOYFRIEND OR THE BOY THEY'RE IN LOVE WITH PLAYS THEM.
ARGH!
YOU WANT TO UNDER-STAND HIM BETTER, DON'T YOU?
SHARE HIS INTERESTS.
HAVE FUN TOGETHER.
OTHERWISE, WHY WOULD YOU BE WILLING TO LEARN HOW TO PLAY A GAME FROM A MIDDLE-AGED MAN YOU BARELY KNOW?
!!
YOU'RE TEASING ME!
HA HA HA HA...
OOPS.

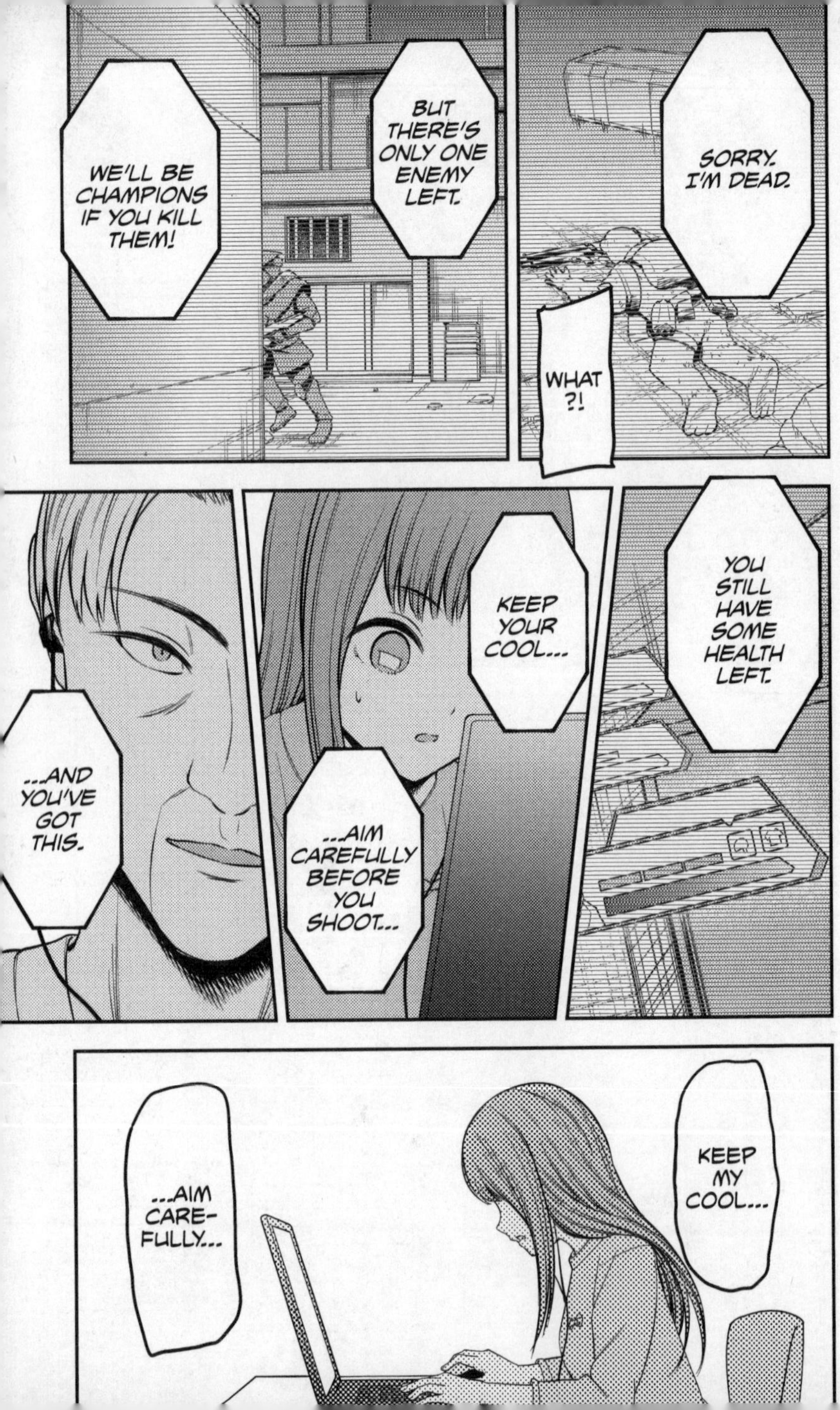
SORRY. I'M DEAD.
WHAT?!
BUT THERE'S ONLY ONE ENEMY LEFT.
WE'LL BE CHAMPIONS IF YOU KILL THEM!
YOU STILL HAVE SOME HEALTH LEFT.
KEEP YOUR COOL...
...AIM CAREFULLY BEFORE YOU SHOOT...
...AND YOU'VE GOT THIS.
KEEP MY COOL...
...AIM CARE-FULLY...

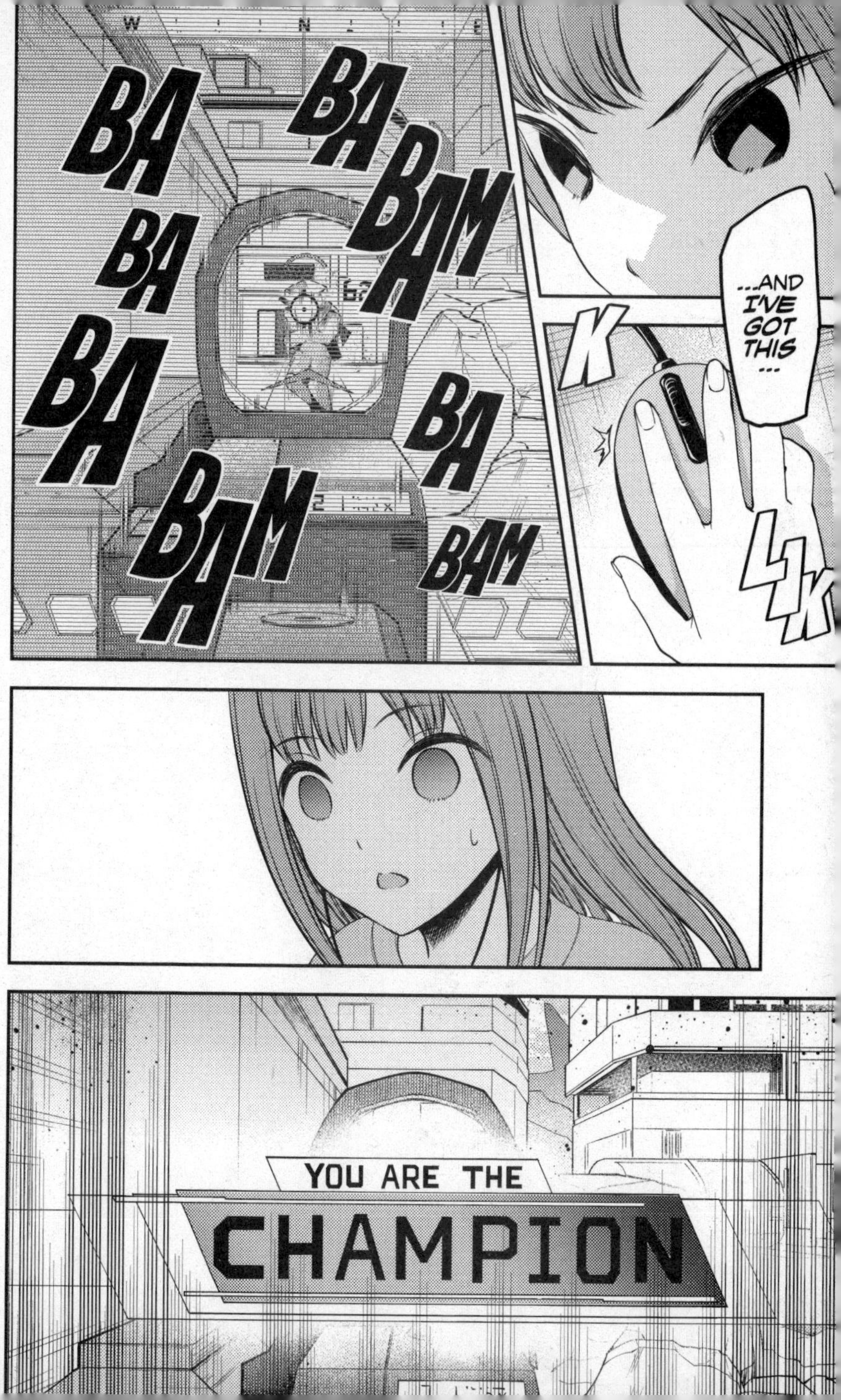
...AND I'VE GOT THIS ---
K
LIK
BABABAM
BA
BA
BA
BA
BABAM
BA
BA
BAM
YOU ARE THE
CHAMPION

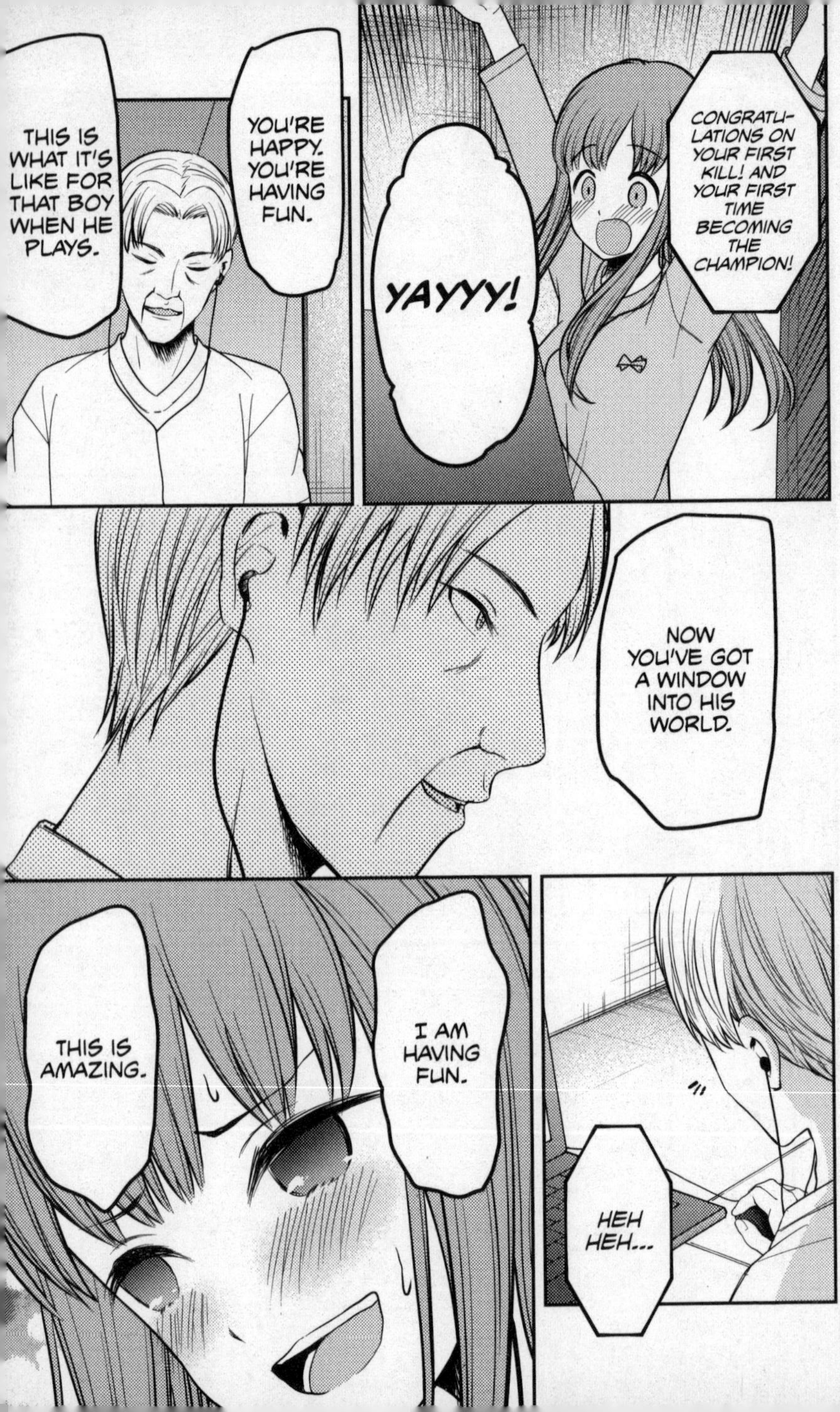
CONGRATULATIONS ON YOUR FIRST KILL! AND YOUR FIRST TIME BECOMING THE CHAMPION!
YAYYY!
YOU'RE HAPPY. YOU'RE HAVING FUN.
THIS IS WHAT IT'S LIKE FOR THAT BOY WHEN HE PLAYS.
NOW YOU'VE GOT A WINDOW INTO HIS WORLD.
HEH HEH...
I AM HAVING FUN.
THIS IS AMAZING.

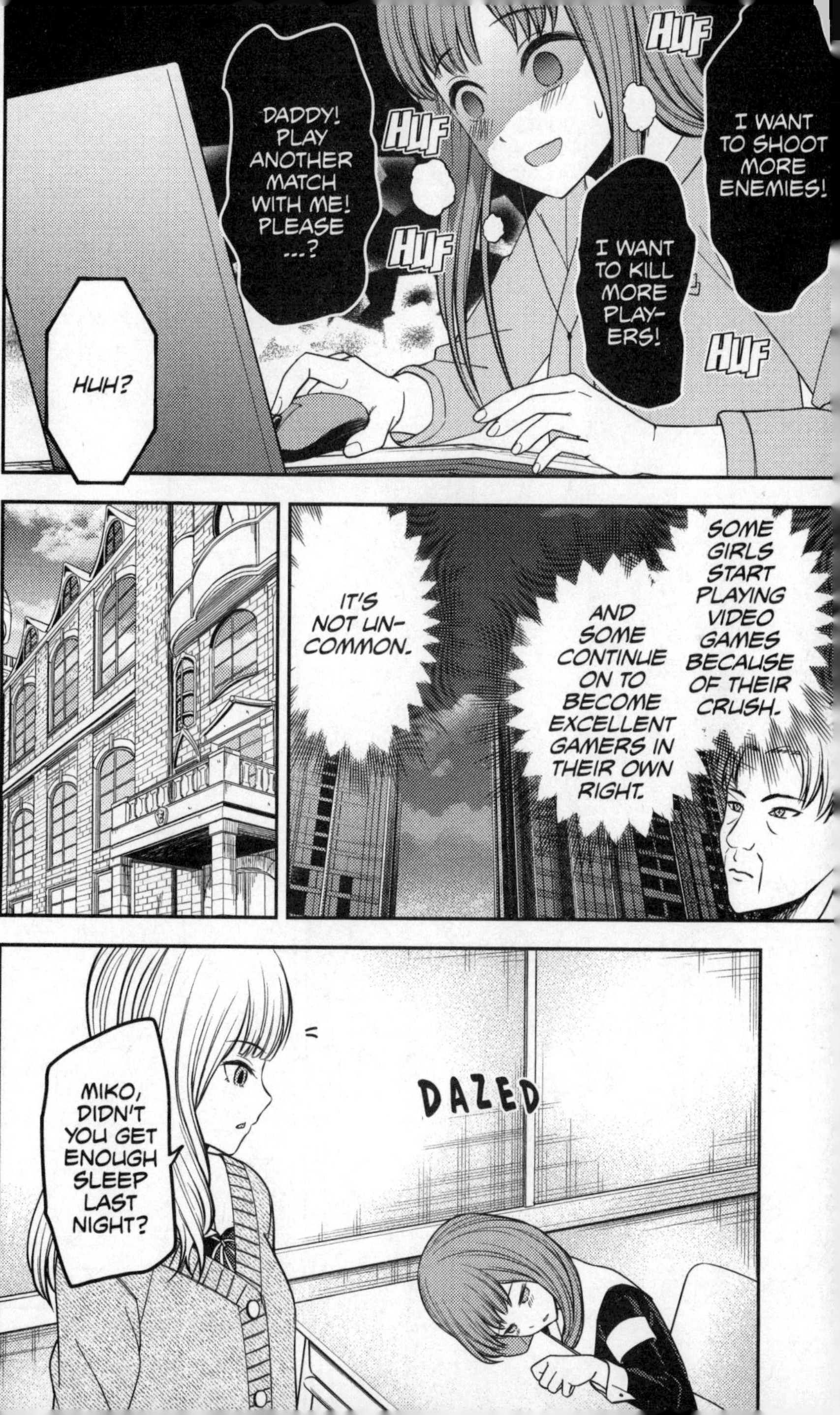
HUF
I WANT TO SHOOT MORE ENEMIES!
I WANT TO KILL MORE PLAY-ERS!
HUF
DADDY! PLAY ANOTHER MATCH WITH ME! PLEASE ...?
HUF
HUF
HUH?
SOME GIRLS START PLAYING VIDEO GAMES BECAUSE OF THEIR CRUSH.
AND SOME CONTINUE ON TO BECOME EXCELLENT GAMERS IN THEIR OWN RIGHT.
IT'S NOT UN-COMMON.
DAZED
MIKO, DIDN'T YOU GET ENOUGH SLEEP LAST NIGHT?

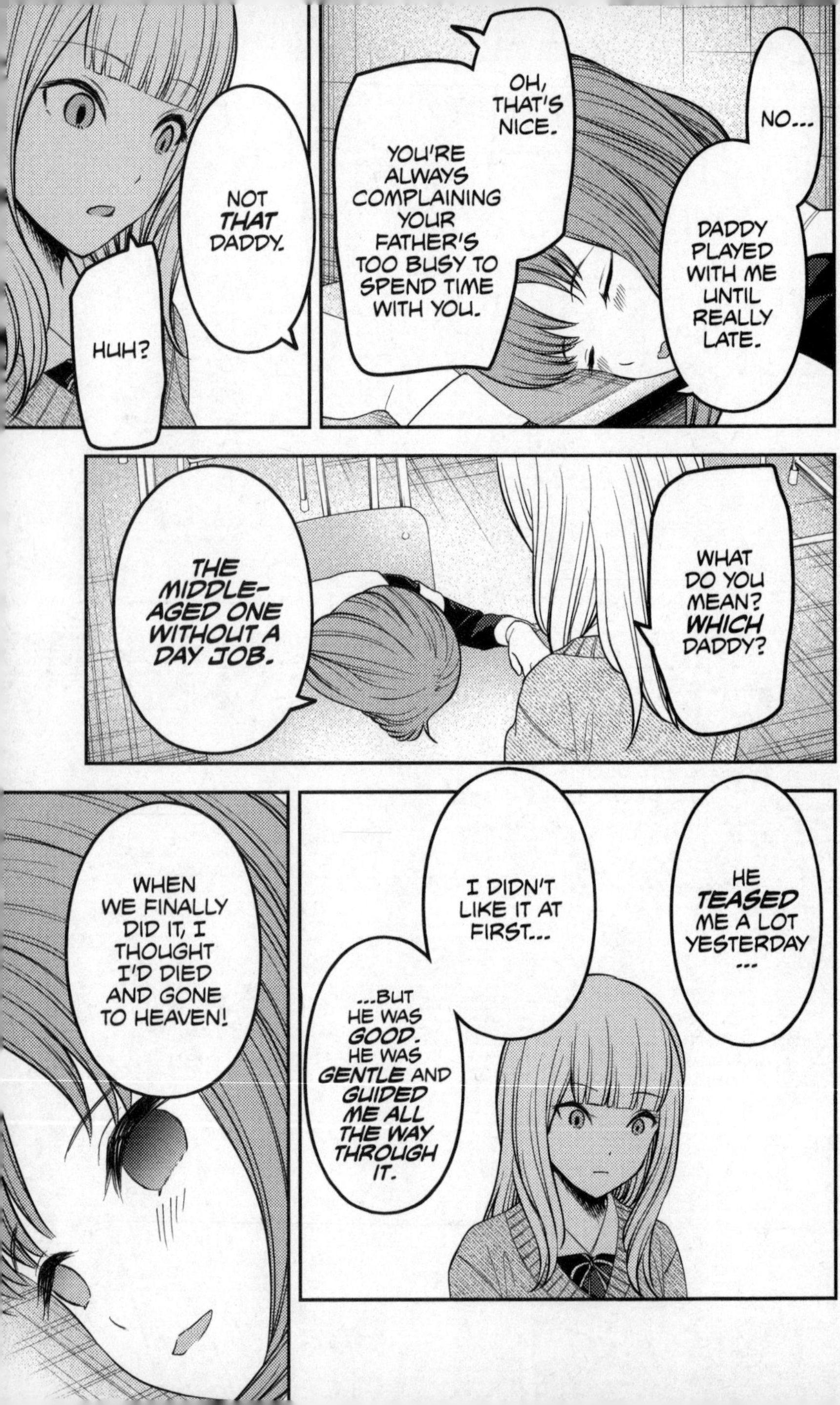
NO...
DADDY PLAYED WITH ME UNTIL REALLY LATE.
OH, THAT'S NICE.
YOU'RE ALWAYS COMPLAINING YOUR FATHER'S TOO BUSY TO SPEND TIME WITH YOU.
NOT *THAT* DADDY.
HUH?
WHAT DO YOU MEAN? *WHICH* DADDY?
THE MIDDLE-AGED ONE WITHOUT A DAY JOB.
HE *TEASED* ME A LOT YESTERDAY ...
I DIDN'T LIKE IT AT FIRST...
...BUT HE WAS *GOOD*. HE WAS *GENTLE* AND *GUIDED ME ALL THE WAY THROUGH* IT.
WHEN WE FINALLY DID IT, I THOUGHT I'D DIED AND GONE TO HEAVEN!

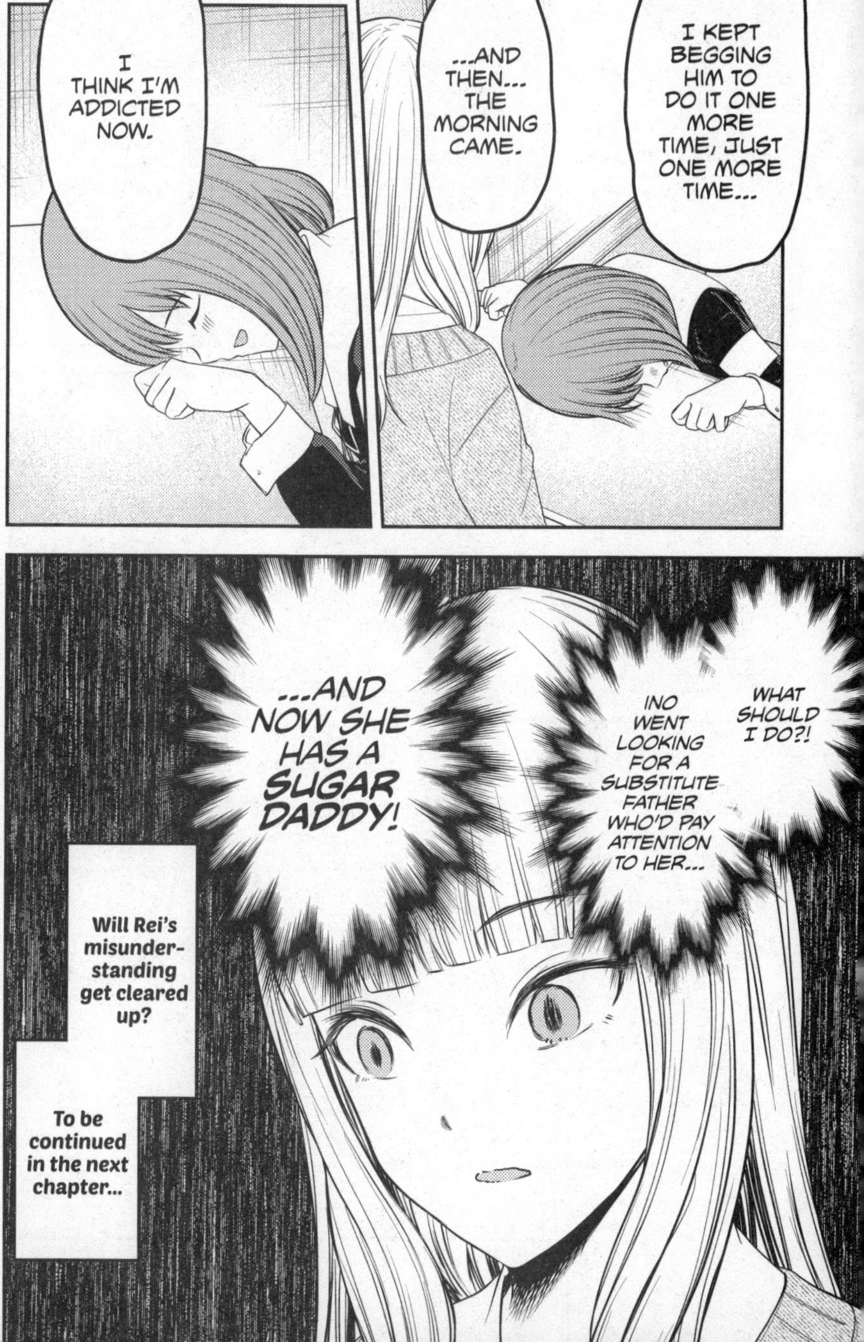
I KEPT BEGGING HIM TO DO IT ONE MORE TIME, JUST ONE MORE TIME...
...AND THEN... THE MORNING CAME.
I THINK I'M ADDICTED NOW.
WHAT SHOULD I DO?!
INO WENT LOOKING FOR A SUBSTITUTE FATHER WHO'D PAY ATTENTION TO HER...
...AND NOW SHE HAS A SUGAR DADDY!
Will Rei's misunder-standing get cleared up?
To be continued in the next chapter...

← Chika's home is this way.

FLTTR

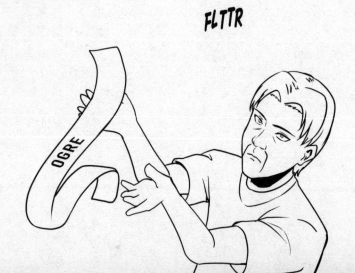

KAGUYA-SAMA
LOVE IS WAR

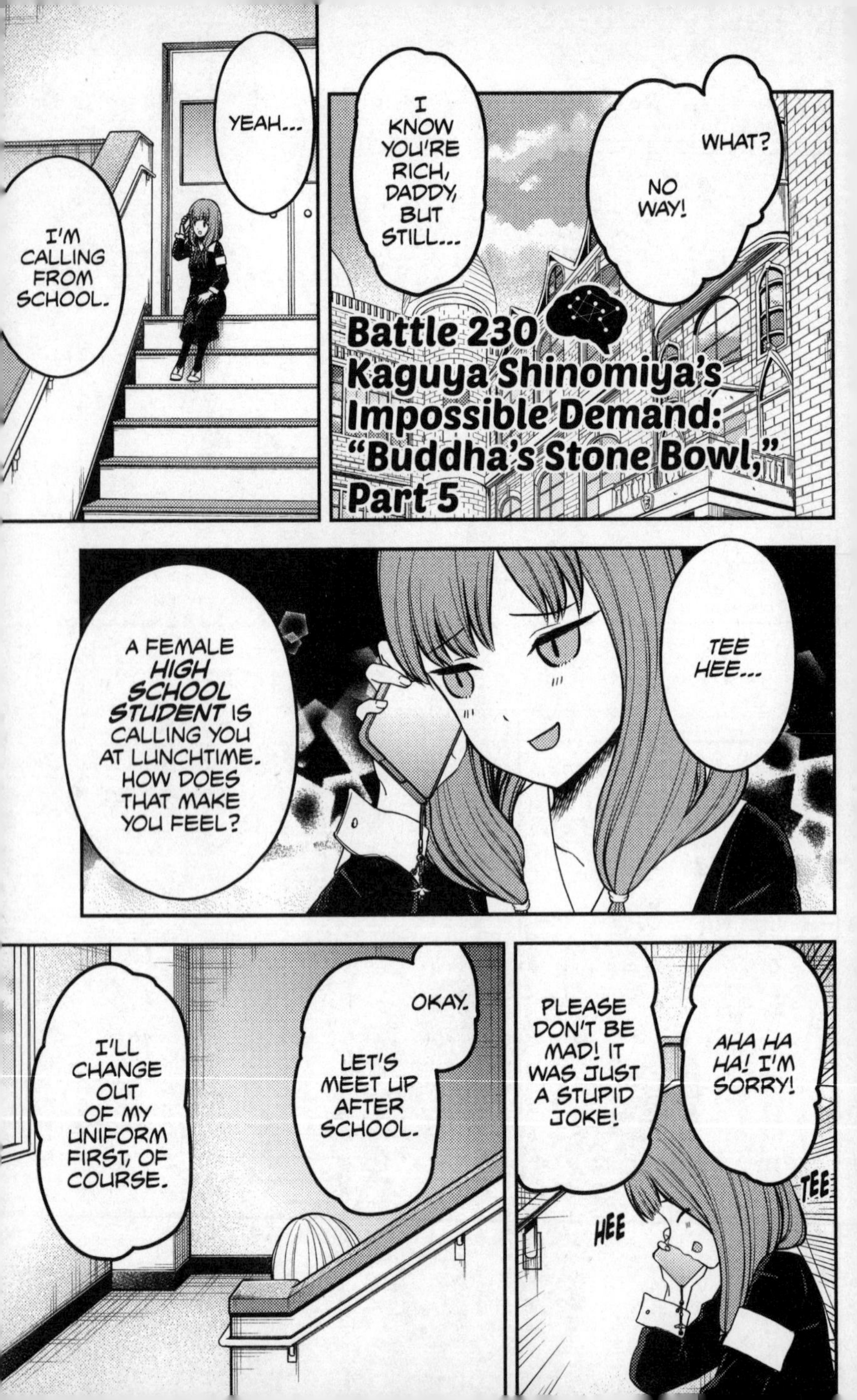
WHAT?
NO WAY!
I KNOW YOU'RE RICH, DADDY, BUT STILL...
Battle 230 Kaguya Shinomiya's Impossible Demand: "Buddha's Stone Bowl," Part 5
YEAH...
I'M CALLING FROM SCHOOL.
TEE HEE...
A FEMALE HIGH SCHOOL STUDENT IS CALLING YOU AT LUNCHTIME. HOW DOES THAT MAKE YOU FEEL?
AHA HA HA! I'M SORRY!
PLEASE DON'T BE MAD! IT WAS JUST A STUPID JOKE!
TEE
HEE
OKAY.
LET'S MEET UP AFTER SCHOOL.
I'LL CHANGE OUT OF MY UNIFORM FIRST, OF COURSE.

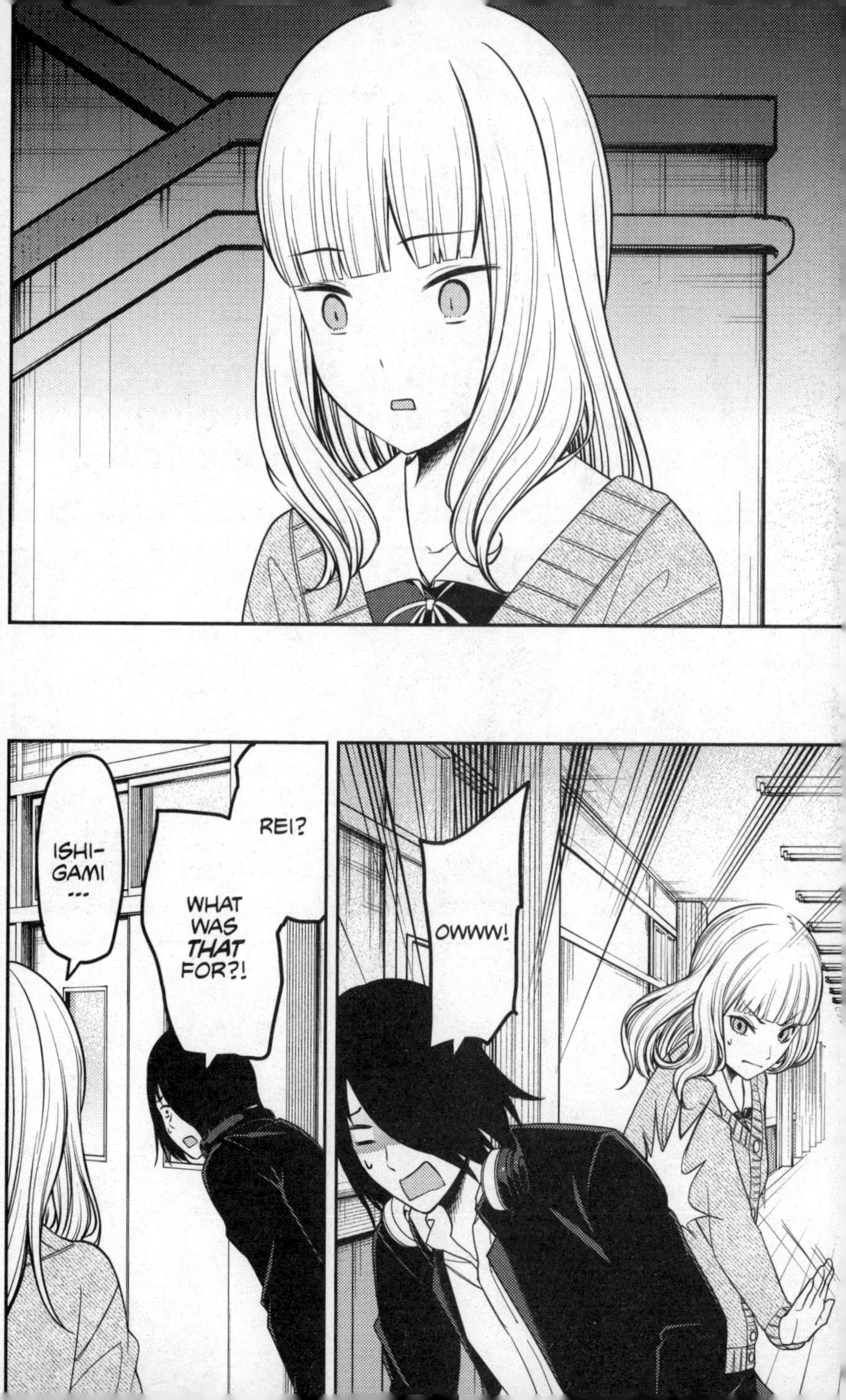
OWWW!
REI?
WHAT WAS THAT FOR?!
ISHI-GAMI---

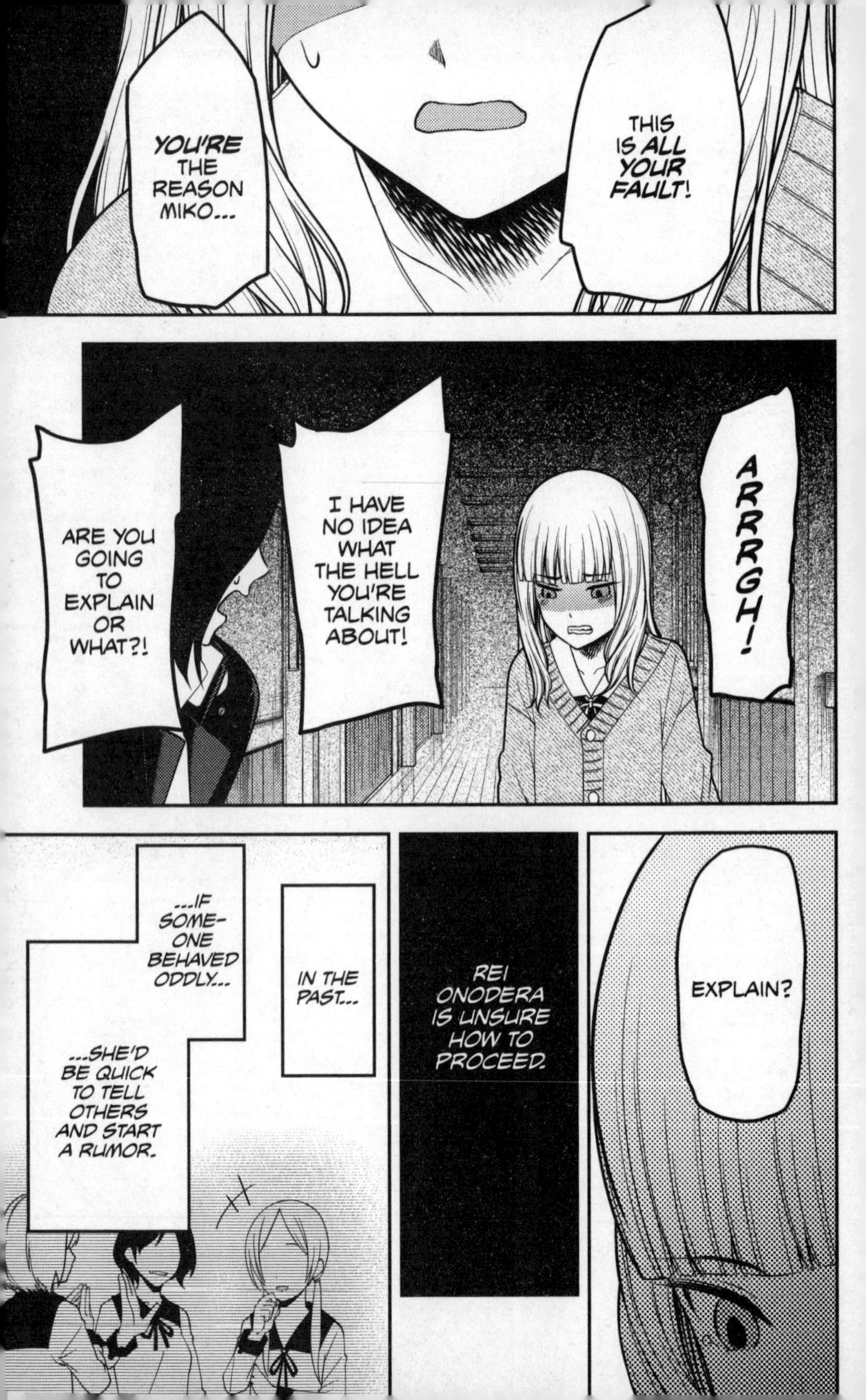
THIS IS ALL YOUR FAULT!
YOU'RE THE REASON MIKO...
ARRRGH!
I HAVE NO IDEA WHAT THE HELL YOU'RE TALKING ABOUT!
ARE YOU GOING TO EXPLAIN OR WHAT?!
EXPLAIN?
REI ONODERA IS UNSURE HOW TO PROCEED.
IN THE PAST...
...IF SOMEONE BEHAVED ODDLY...
...SHE'D BE QUICK TO TELL OTHERS AND START A RUMOR.

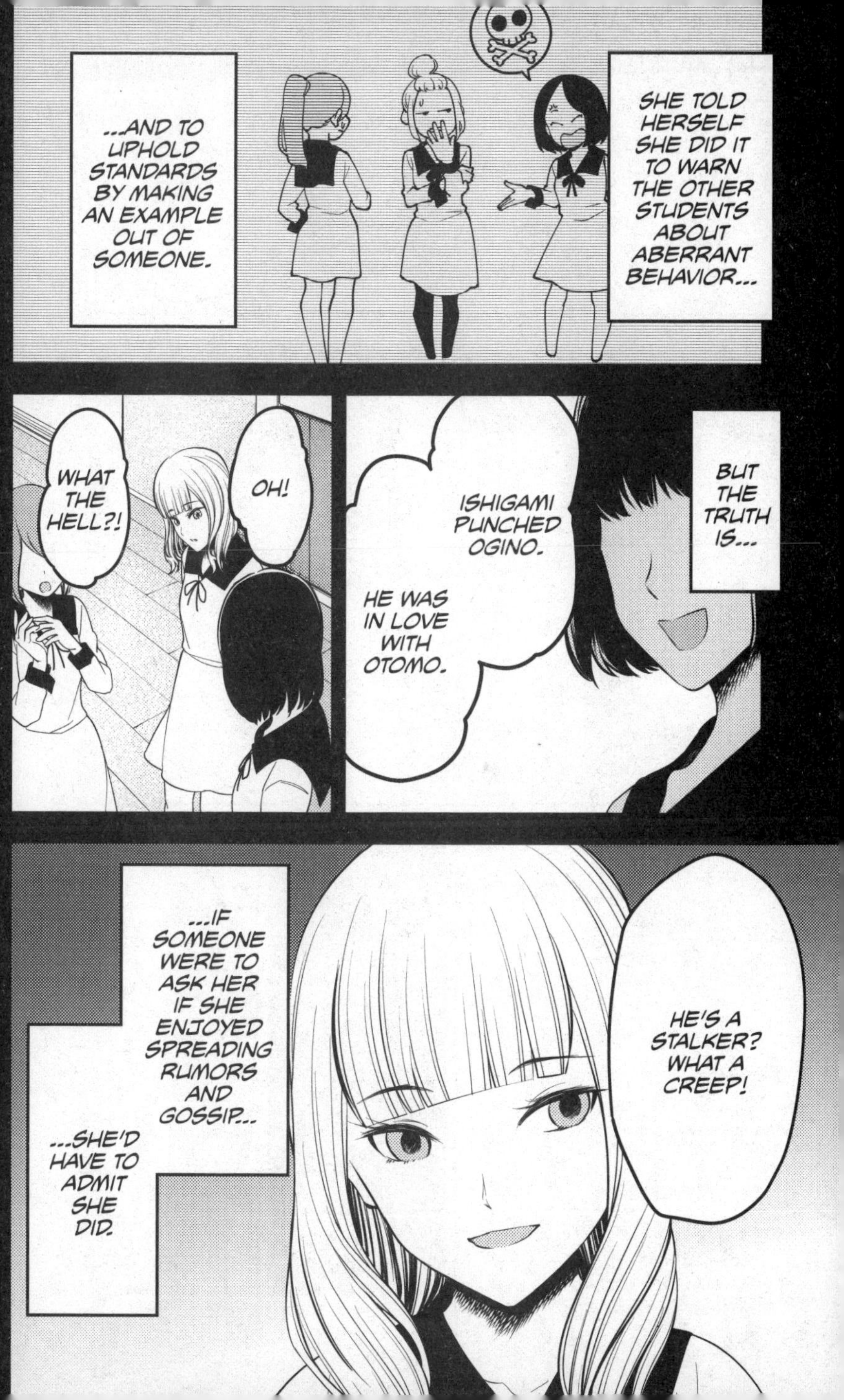
SHE TOLD HERSELF SHE DID IT TO WARN THE OTHER STUDENTS ABOUT ABERRANT BEHAVIOR...
...AND TO UPHOLD STANDARDS BY MAKING AN EXAMPLE OUT OF SOMEONE.
BUT THE TRUTH IS...
ISHIGAMI PUNCHED OGINO.
HE WAS IN LOVE WITH OTOMO.
OH!
WHAT THE HELL?!
HE'S A STALKER? WHAT A CREEP!
...IF SOMEONE WERE TO ASK HER IF SHE ENJOYED SPREADING RUMORS AND GOSSIP...
...SHE'D HAVE TO ADMIT SHE DID.

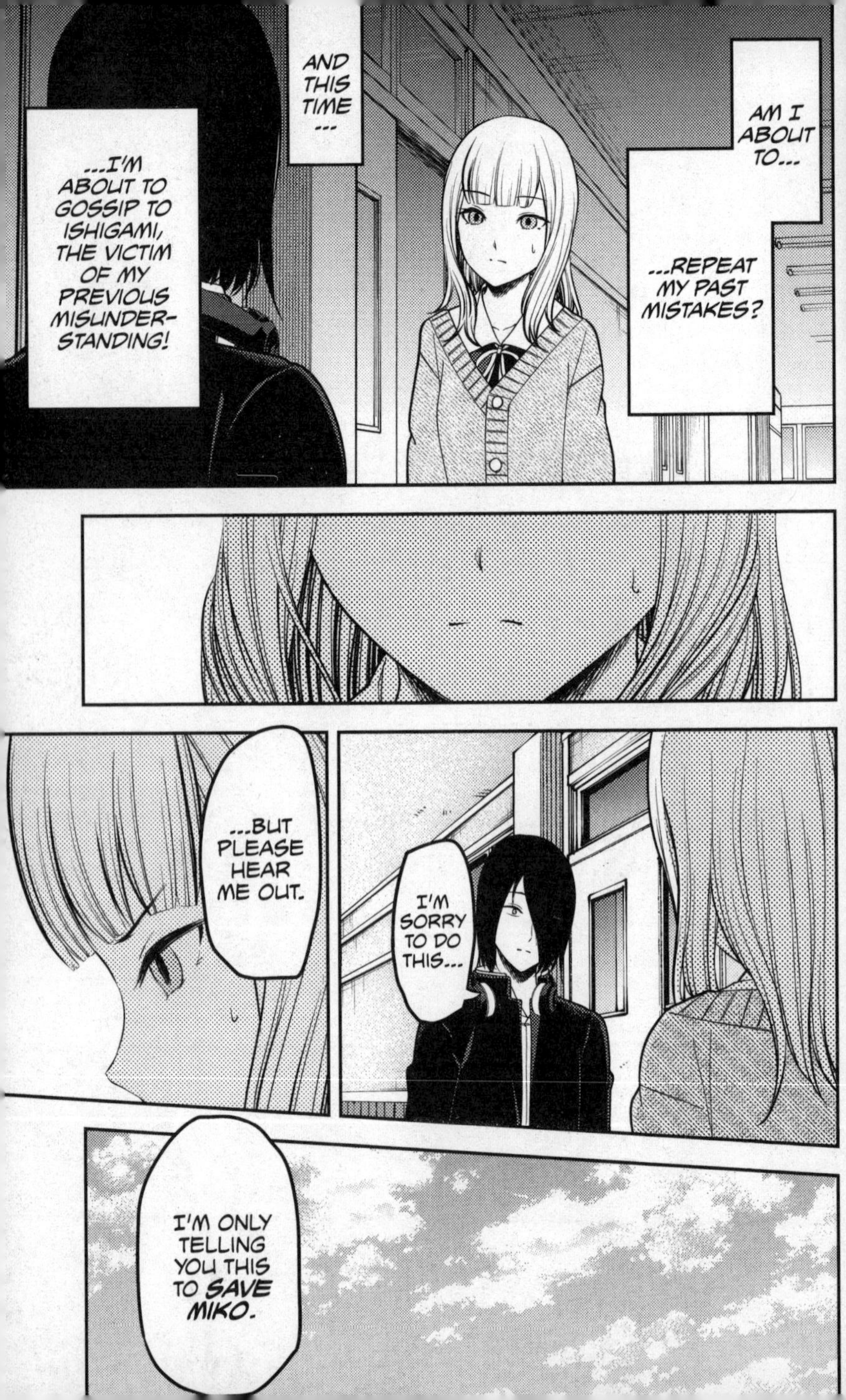
AM I ABOUT TO...
...REPEAT MY PAST MISTAKES?
AND THIS TIME ---
...I'M ABOUT TO GOSSIP TO ISHIGAMI, THE VICTIM OF MY PREVIOUS MISUNDER-STANDING!
I'M SORRY TO DO THIS...
...BUT PLEASE HEAR ME OUT.
I'M ONLY TELLING YOU THIS TO *SAVE* *MIKO*.

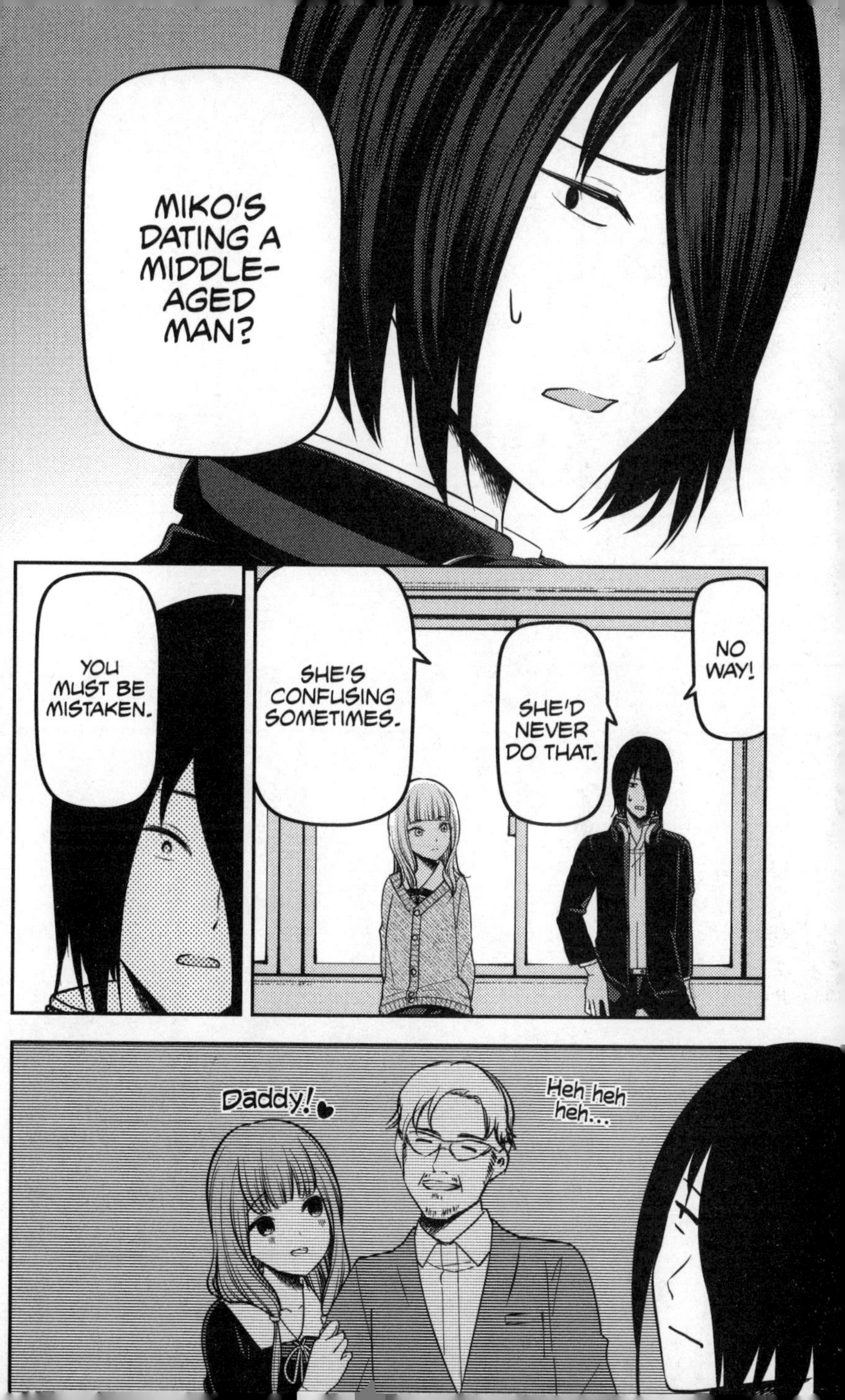
MIKO'S DATING A MIDDLE-AGED MAN?
NO WAY!
SHE'D NEVER DO THAT.
SHE'S CONFUSING SOMETIMES.
YOU MUST BE MISTAKEN.
Heh heh heh...
Daddy!

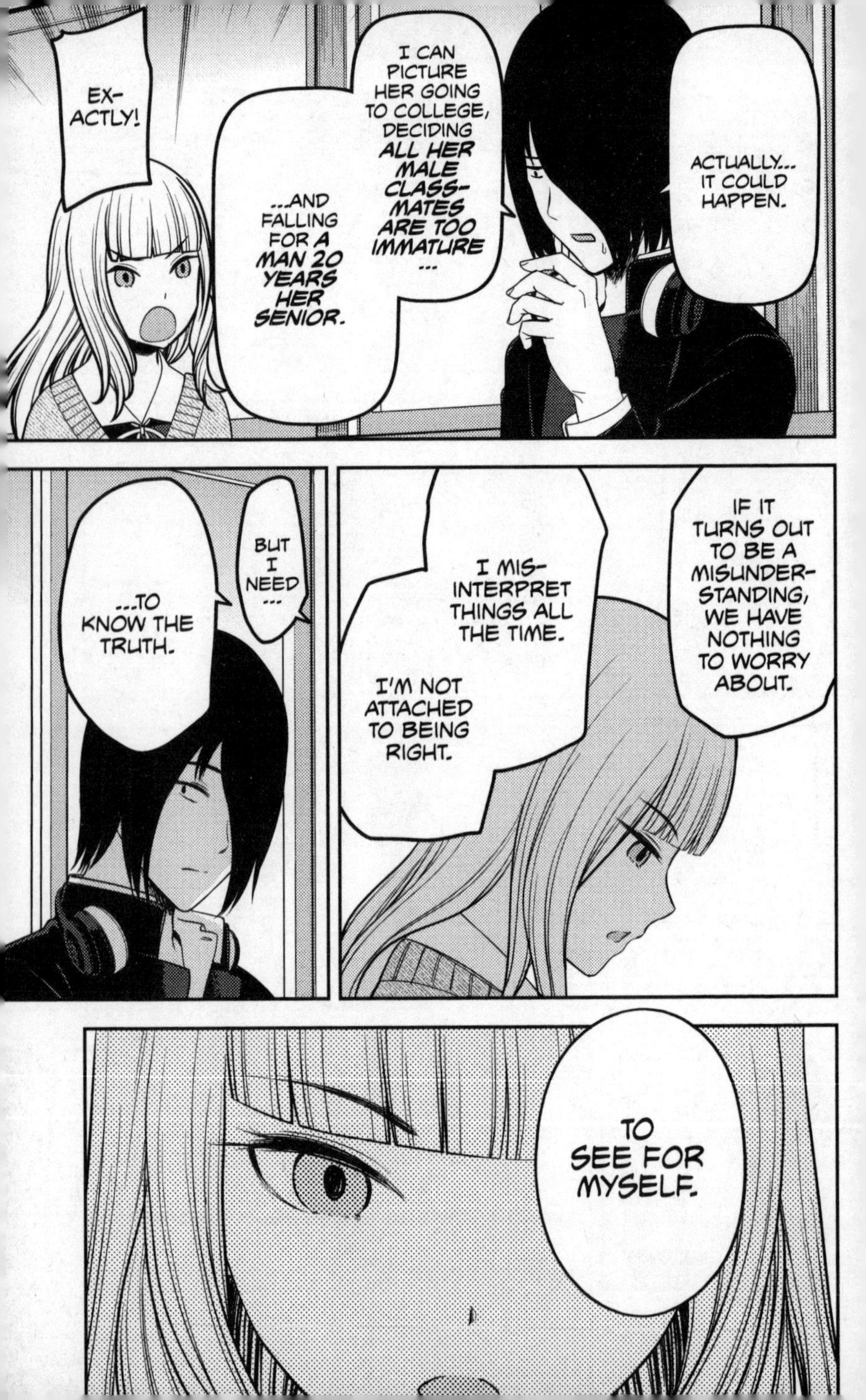
ACTUALLY... IT COULD HAPPEN.
I CAN PICTURE HER GOING TO COLLEGE, DECIDING ALL HER MALE CLASS-MATES ARE TOO IMMATURE ...
...AND FALLING FOR A MAN 20 YEARS HER SENIOR.
EX-ACTLY!
IF IT TURNS OUT TO BE A MISUNDER-STANDING, WE HAVE NOTHING TO WORRY ABOUT.
I MIS-INTERPRET THINGS ALL THE TIME.
I'M NOT ATTACHED TO BEING RIGHT.
BUT I NEED ...
...TO KNOW THE TRUTH.
TO SEE FOR MYSELF.

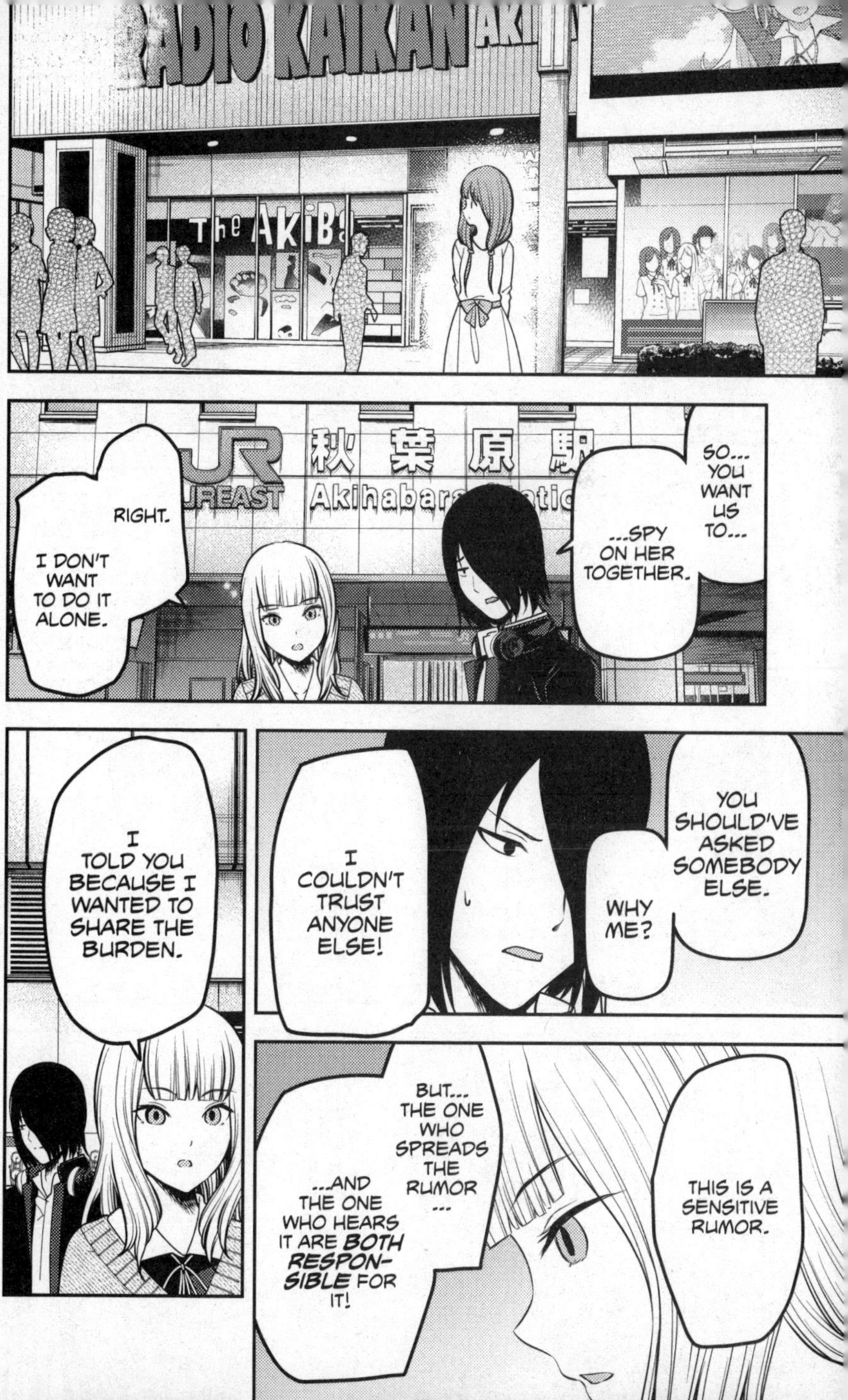
ADIO KAIKAN
SO... YOU WANT US TO...
...SPY ON HER TOGETHER.
RIGHT.
I DON'T WANT TO DO IT ALONE.
YOU SHOULD'VE ASKED SOMEBODY ELSE.
WHY ME?
I COULDN'T TRUST ANYONE ELSE!
THIS IS A SENSITIVE RUMOR.
BUT... THE ONE WHO SPREADS THE RUMOR...
...AND THE ONE WHO HEARS IT ARE *BOTH RESPONSIBLE* FOR IT!
I TOLD YOU BECAUSE I WANTED TO SHARE THE BURDEN.

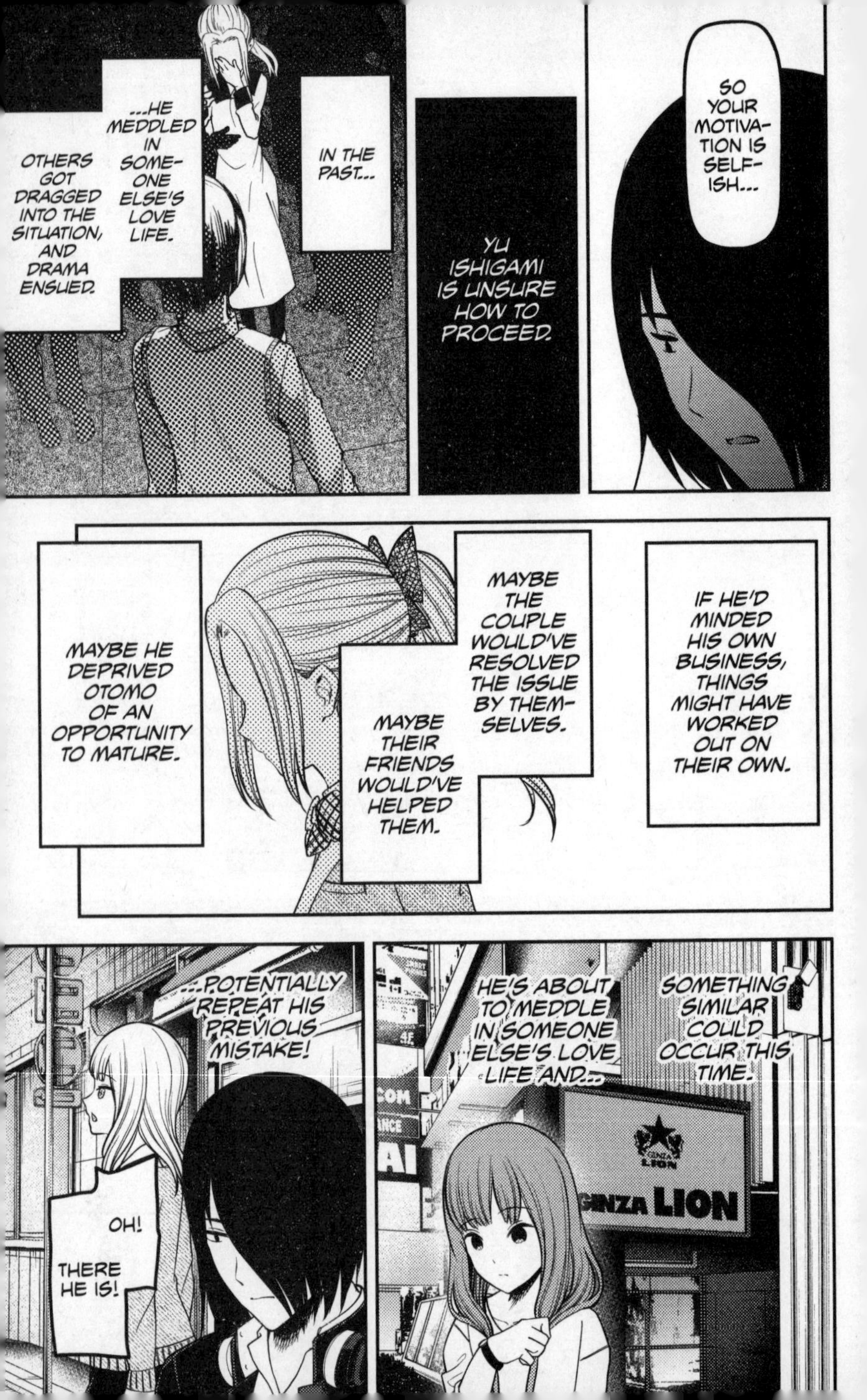
SO YOUR MOTIVATION IS SELFISH...
YU ISHIGAMI IS UNSURE HOW TO PROCEED.
IN THE PAST...
...HE MEDDLED IN SOMEONE ELSE'S LOVE LIFE.
OTHERS GOT DRAGGED INTO THE SITUATION, AND DRAMA ENSUED.
IF HE'D MINDED HIS OWN BUSINESS, THINGS MIGHT HAVE WORKED OUT ON THEIR OWN.
MAYBE THE COUPLE WOULD'VE RESOLVED THE ISSUE BY THEMSELVES.
MAYBE THEIR FRIENDS WOULD'VE HELPED THEM.
MAYBE HE DEPRIVED OTOMO OF AN OPPORTUNITY TO MATURE.
SOMETHING SIMILAR COULD OCCUR THIS TIME.
HE'S ABOUT TO MEDDLE IN SOMEONE ELSE'S LOVE LIFE AND...
...POTENTIALLY REPEAT HIS PREVIOUS MISTAKE!
OH!
THERE HE IS!

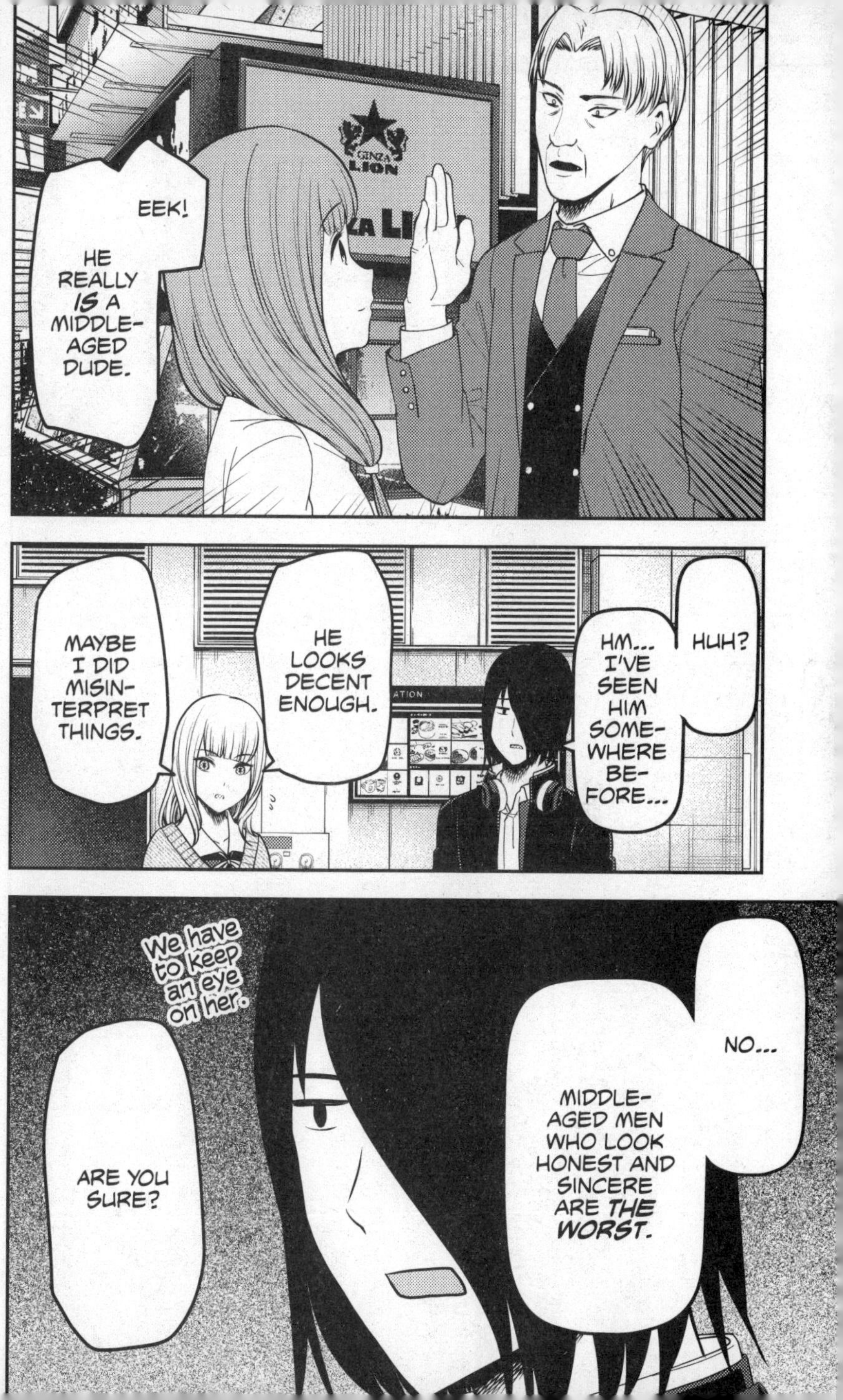
GINZA LION
EEK!
HE REALLY IS A MIDDLE-AGED DUDE.
HUH?
HM... I'VE SEEN HIM SOMEWHERE BEFORE...
HE LOOKS DECENT ENOUGH.
MAYBE I DID MISINTERPRET THINGS.
NO...
MIDDLE-AGED MEN WHO LOOK HONEST AND SINCERE ARE THE WORST.
We have to keep an eye on her.
ARE YOU SURE?

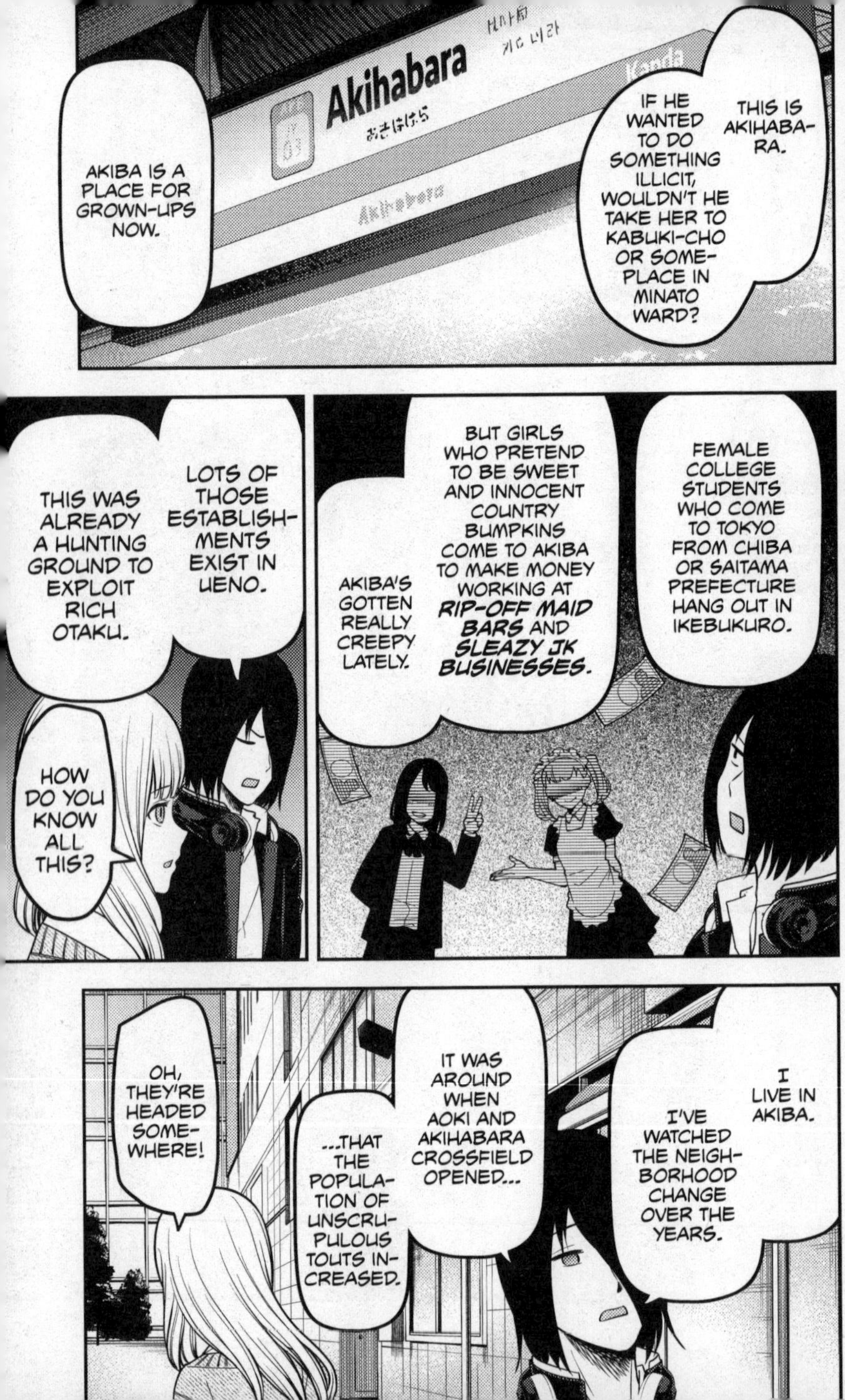

Akihabara
あきはばら
Kanda
THIS IS AKIHABARA.
IF HE WANTED TO DO SOMETHING ILLICIT, WOULDN'T HE TAKE HER TO KABUKI-CHO OR SOMEPLACE IN MINATO WARD?
AKIBA IS A PLACE FOR GROWN-UPS NOW.
FEMALE COLLEGE STUDENTS WHO COME TO TOKYO FROM CHIBA OR SAITAMA PREFECTURE HANG OUT IN IKEBUKURO.
BUT GIRLS WHO PRETEND TO BE SWEET AND INNOCENT COUNTRY BUMPKINS COME TO AKIBA TO MAKE MONEY WORKING AT RIP-OFF MAID BARS AND SLEAZY JK BUSINESSES.
AKIBA'S GOTTEN REALLY CREEPY LATELY.
LOTS OF THOSE ESTABLISHMENTS EXIST IN UENO.
THIS WAS ALREADY A HUNTING GROUND TO EXPLOIT RICH OTAKU.
HOW DO YOU KNOW ALL THIS?
I LIVE IN AKIBA.
I'VE WATCHED THE NEIGHBORHOOD CHANGE OVER THE YEARS.
IT WAS AROUND WHEN AOKI AND AKIHABARA CROSSFIELD OPENED...
...THAT THE POPULATION OF UNSCRUPULOUS TOUTS INCREASED.
OH, THEY'RE HEADED SOMEWHERE!

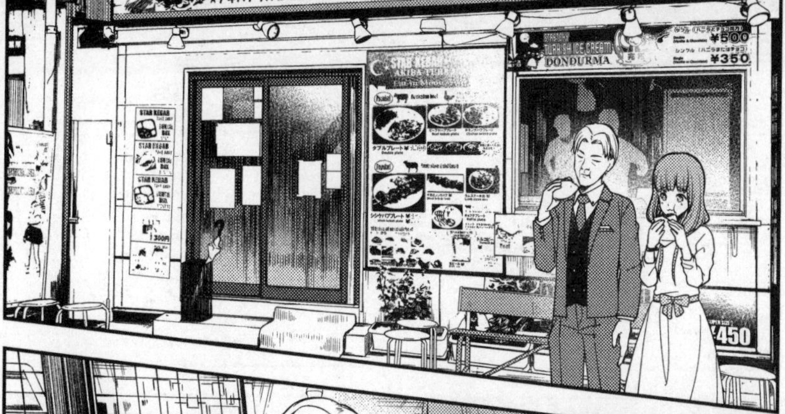
STAR KEBAB
STRETCHY TURKISH ICE CREAM
DONDURMA
¥500
¥350
¥450
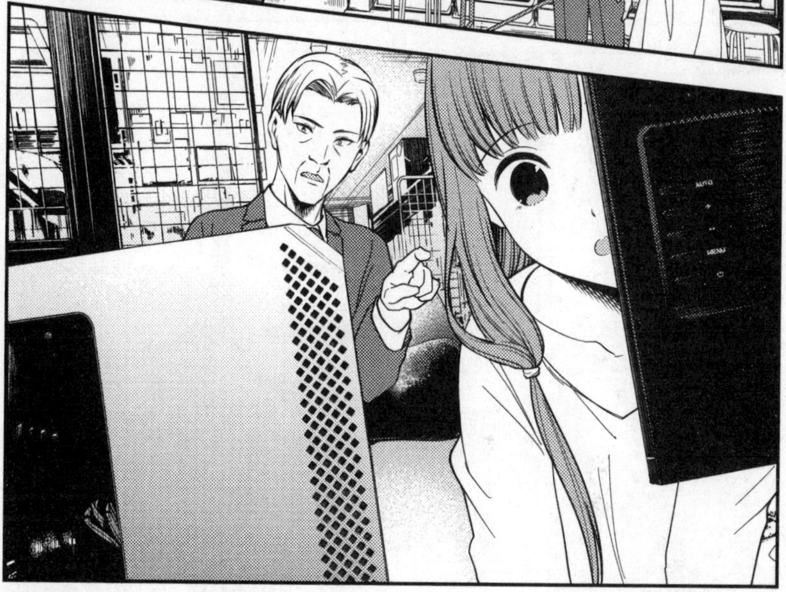
AUTO
MENU
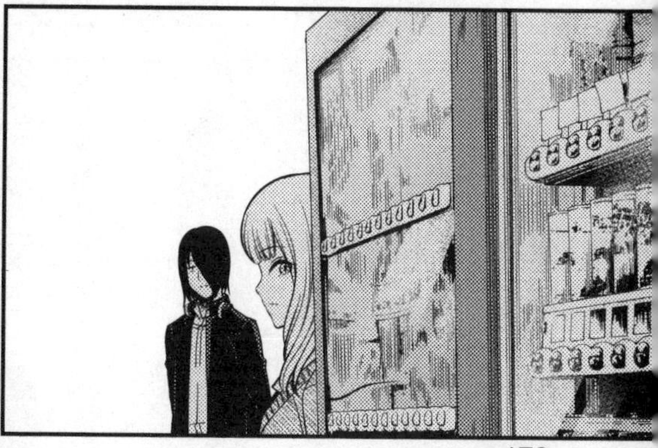
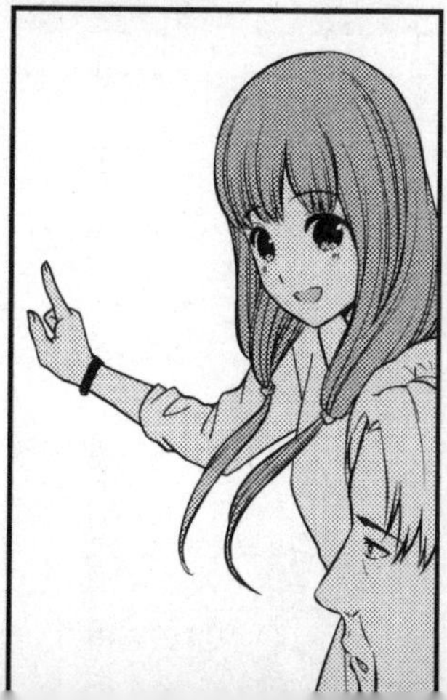

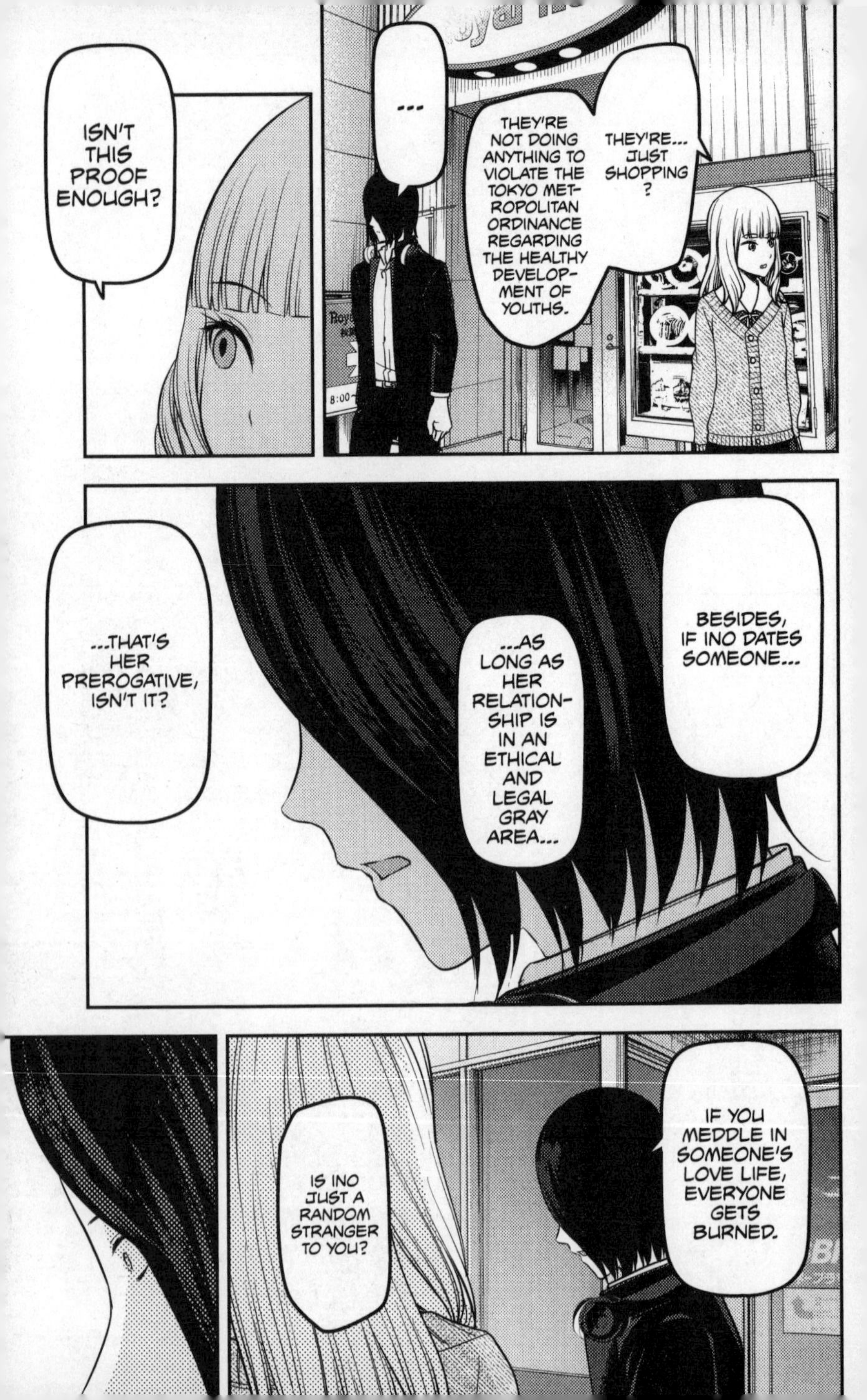
THEY'RE... JUST SHOPPING?
THEY'RE NOT DOING ANYTHING TO VIOLATE THE TOKYO METROPOLITAN ORDINANCE REGARDING THE HEALTHY DEVELOPMENT OF YOUTHS.
...
ISN'T THIS PROOF ENOUGH?
BESIDES, IF INO DATES SOMEONE...
...AS LONG AS HER RELATIONSHIP IS IN AN ETHICAL AND LEGAL GRAY AREA...
...THAT'S HER PREROGATIVE, ISN'T IT?
IF YOU MEDDLE IN SOMEONE'S LOVE LIFE, EVERYONE GETS BURNED.
IS INO JUST A RANDOM STRANGER TO YOU?

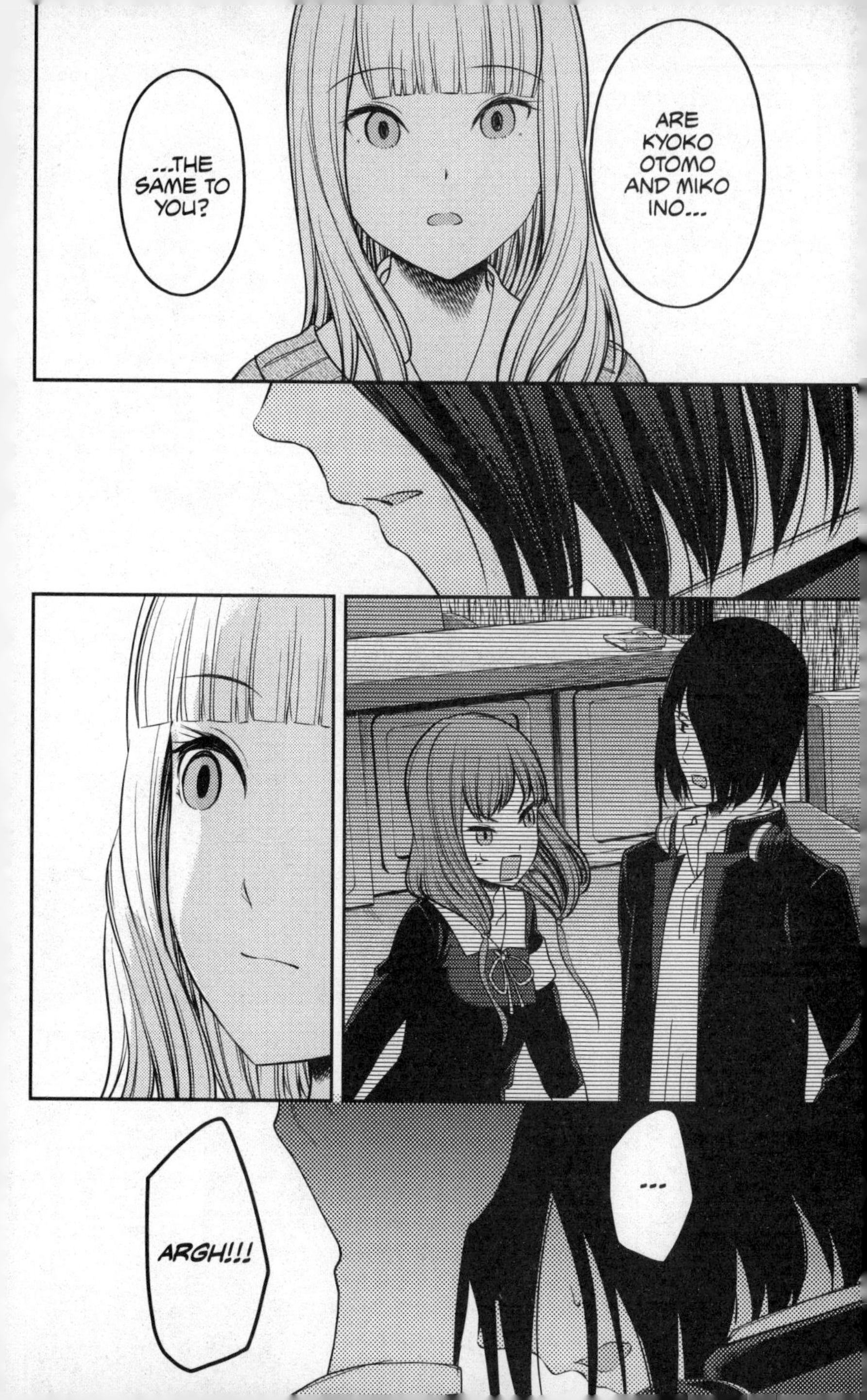
ARE KYOKO OTOMO AND MIKO INO...
...THE SAME TO YOU?
...
ARGH!!!

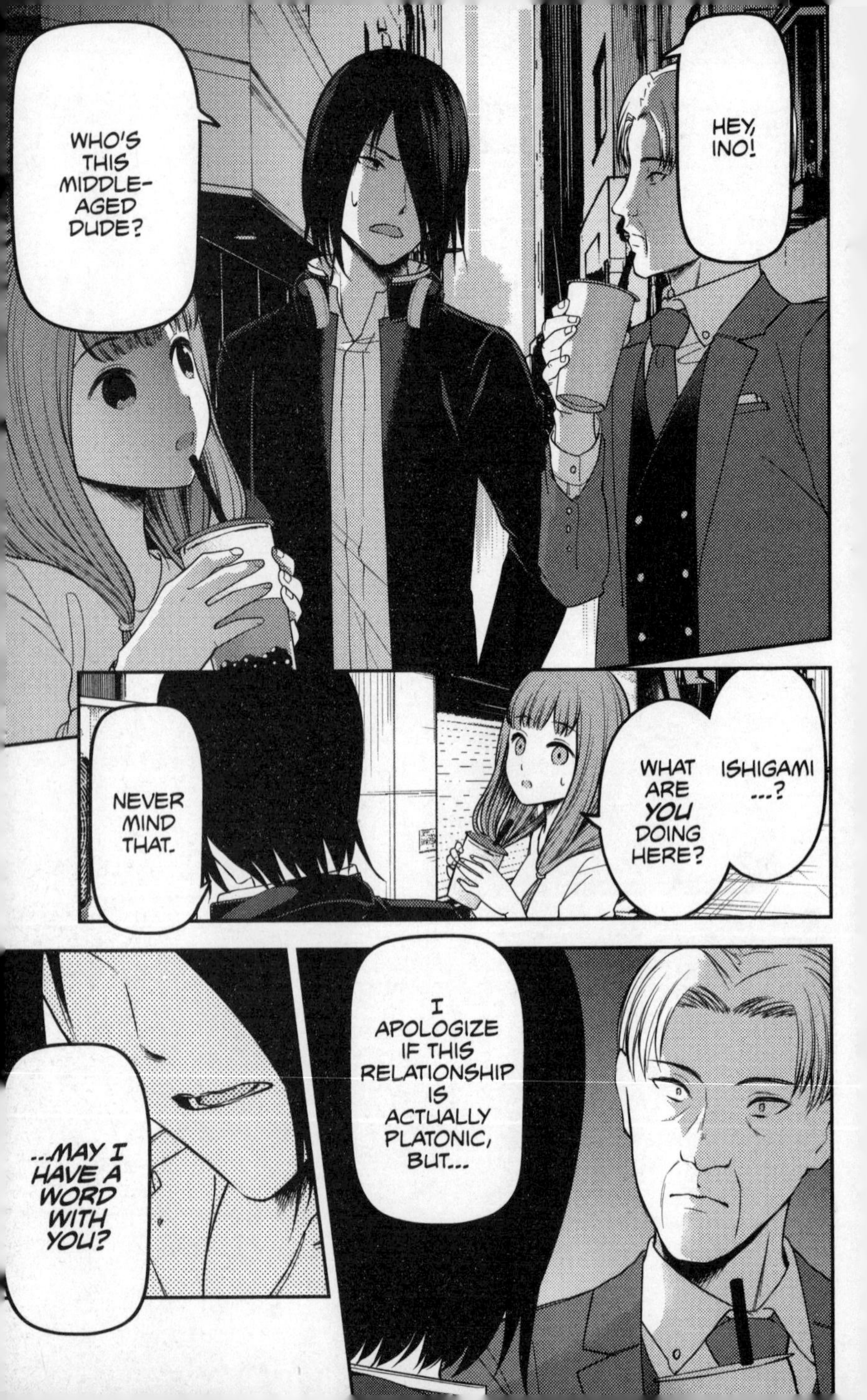
HEY, INO!
WHO'S THIS MIDDLE-AGED DUDE?
ISHIGAMI ...?
WHAT ARE YOU DOING HERE?
NEVER MIND THAT.
I APOLOGIZE IF THIS RELATIONSHIP IS ACTUALLY PLATONIC, BUT...
...MAY I HAVE A WORD WITH YOU?

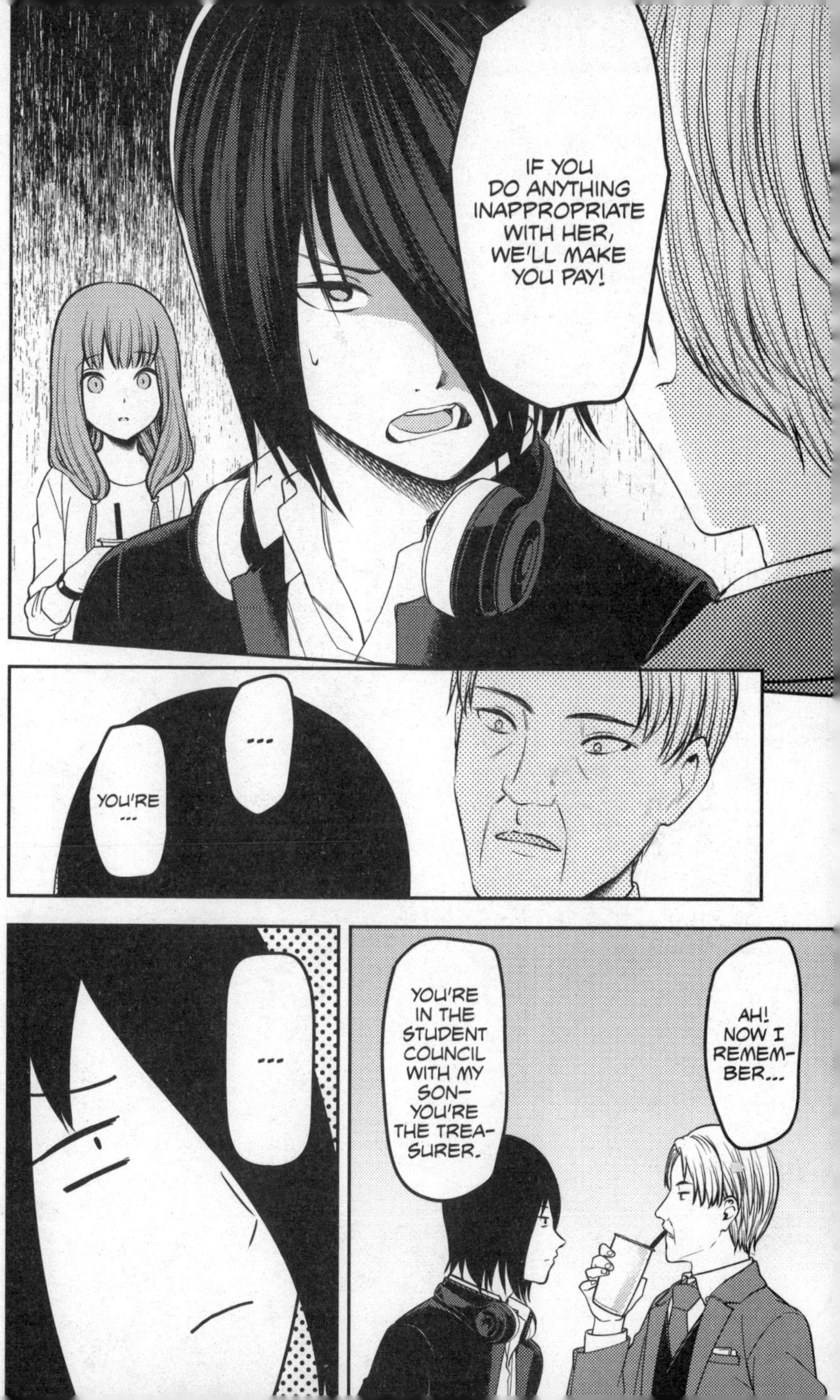
IF YOU DO ANYTHING INAPPROPRIATE WITH HER, WE'LL MAKE YOU PAY!
...
YOU'RE ...
AH! NOW I REMEMBER...
YOU'RE IN THE STUDENT COUNCIL WITH MY SON— YOU'RE THE TREASURER.
...

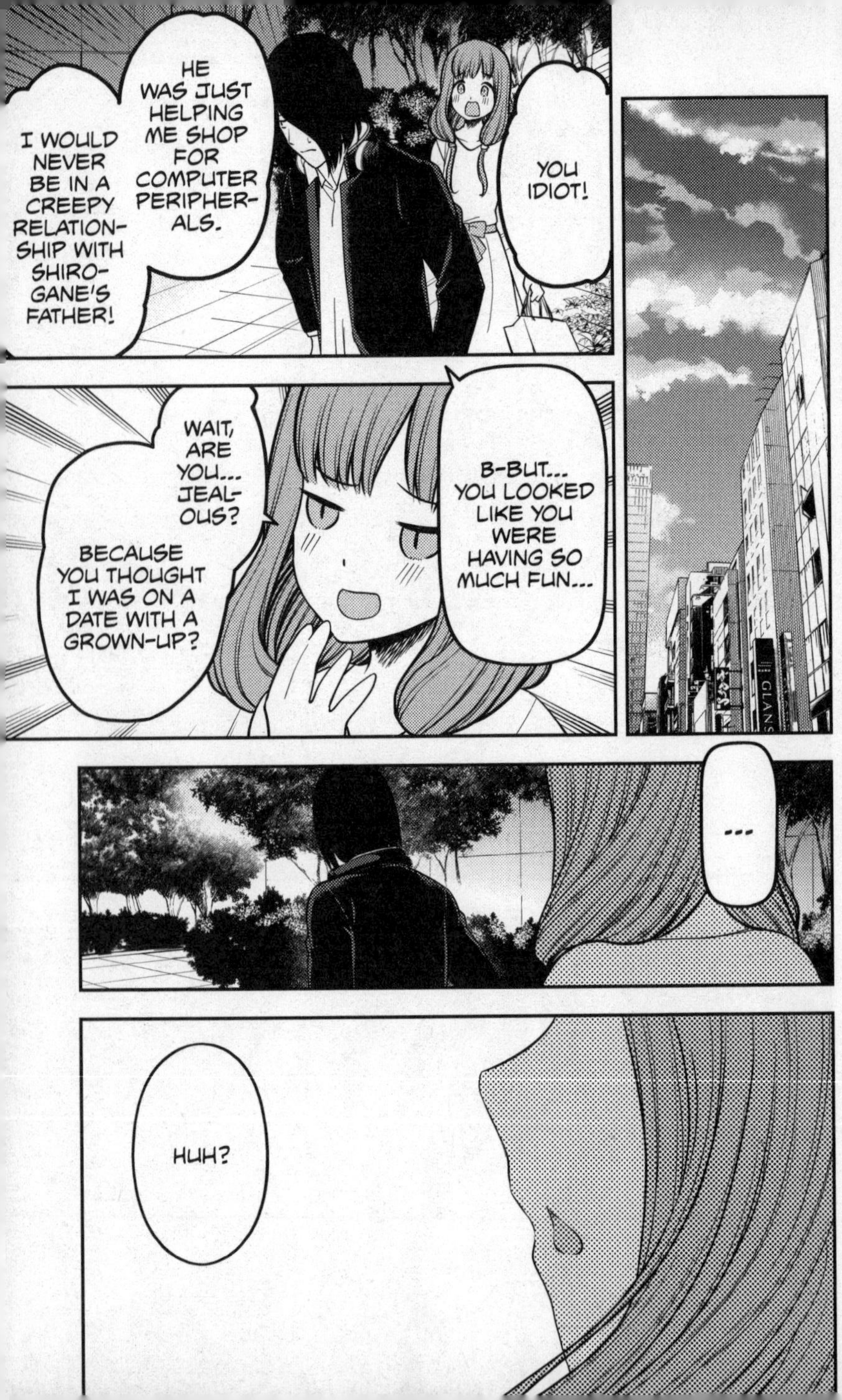
YOU IDIOT!
HE WAS JUST HELPING ME SHOP FOR COMPUTER PERIPHERALS.
I WOULD NEVER BE IN A CREEPY RELATIONSHIP WITH SHIROGANE'S FATHER!
B-BUT... YOU LOOKED LIKE YOU WERE HAVING SO MUCH FUN...
WAIT, ARE YOU... JEALOUS?
BECAUSE YOU THOUGHT I WAS ON A DATE WITH A GROWN-UP?
...
HUH?

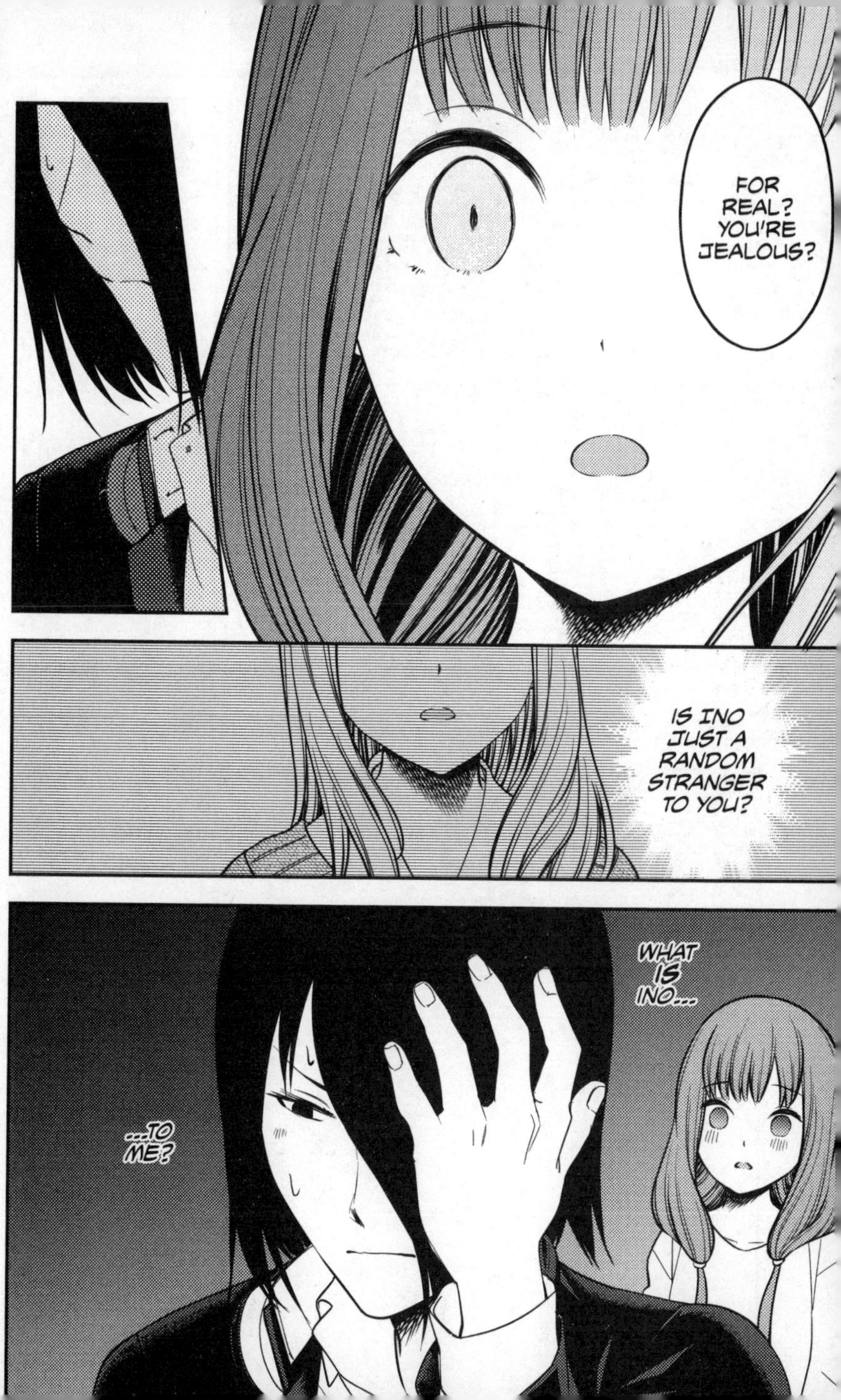
FOR REAL? YOU'RE JEALOUS?
IS INO JUST A RANDOM STRANGER TO YOU?
WHAT IS INO...
...TO ME?

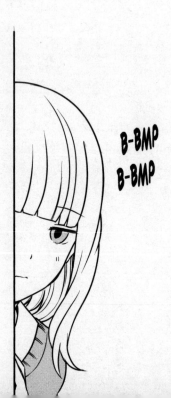

B-BMP
B-BMP

KAGUYA-SAMA
LOVE IS WAR

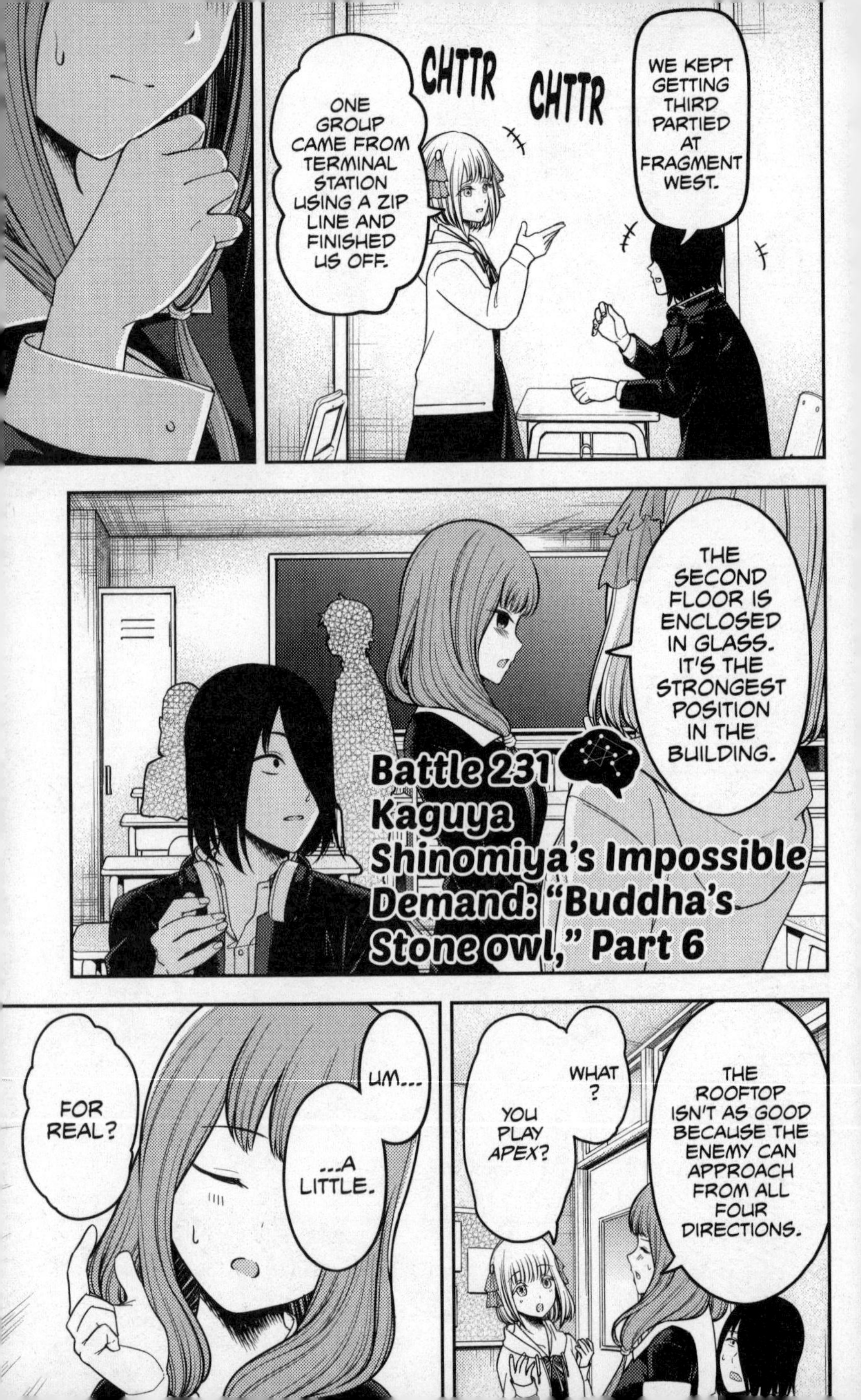
WE KEPT GETTING THIRD PARTIED AT FRAGMENT WEST.
CHTTR
CHTTR
ONE GROUP CAME FROM TERMINAL STATION USING A ZIP LINE AND FINISHED US OFF.
THE SECOND FLOOR IS ENCLOSED IN GLASS. IT'S THE STRONGEST POSITION IN THE BUILDING.
Battle 231 Kaguya Shinomiya's Impossible Demand: "Buddha's Stone owl," Part 6
THE ROOFTOP ISN'T AS GOOD BECAUSE THE ENEMY CAN APPROACH FROM ALL FOUR DIRECTIONS.
WHAT?
YOU PLAY APEX?
UM...
...A LITTLE.
FOR REAL?

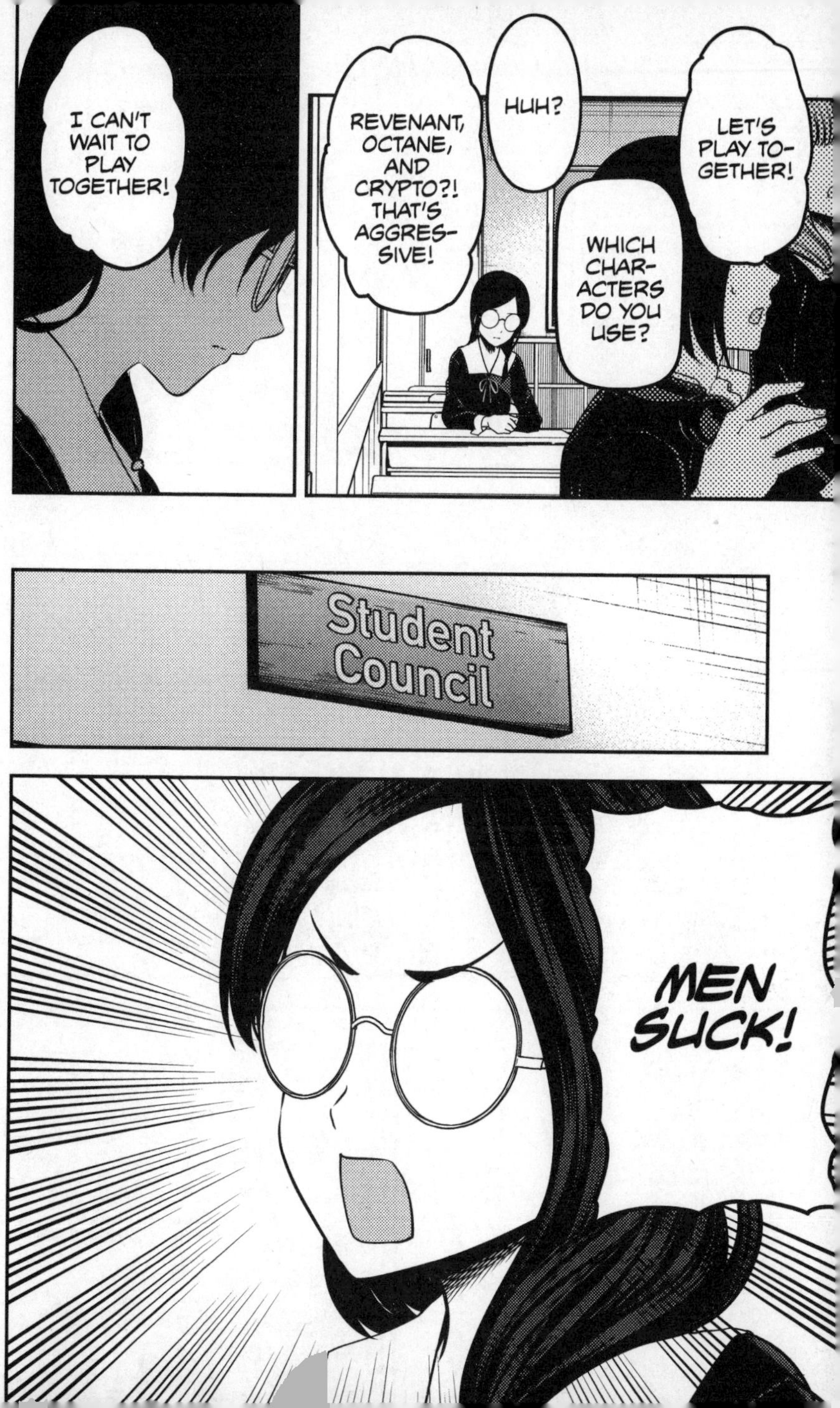
LET'S PLAY TO-GETHER!
WHICH CHAR-ACTERS DO YOU USE?
HUH?
REVENANT, OCTANE, AND CRYPTO?! THAT'S AGGRES-SIVE!
I CAN'T WAIT TO PLAY TOGETHER!
Student Council
MEN SUCK!

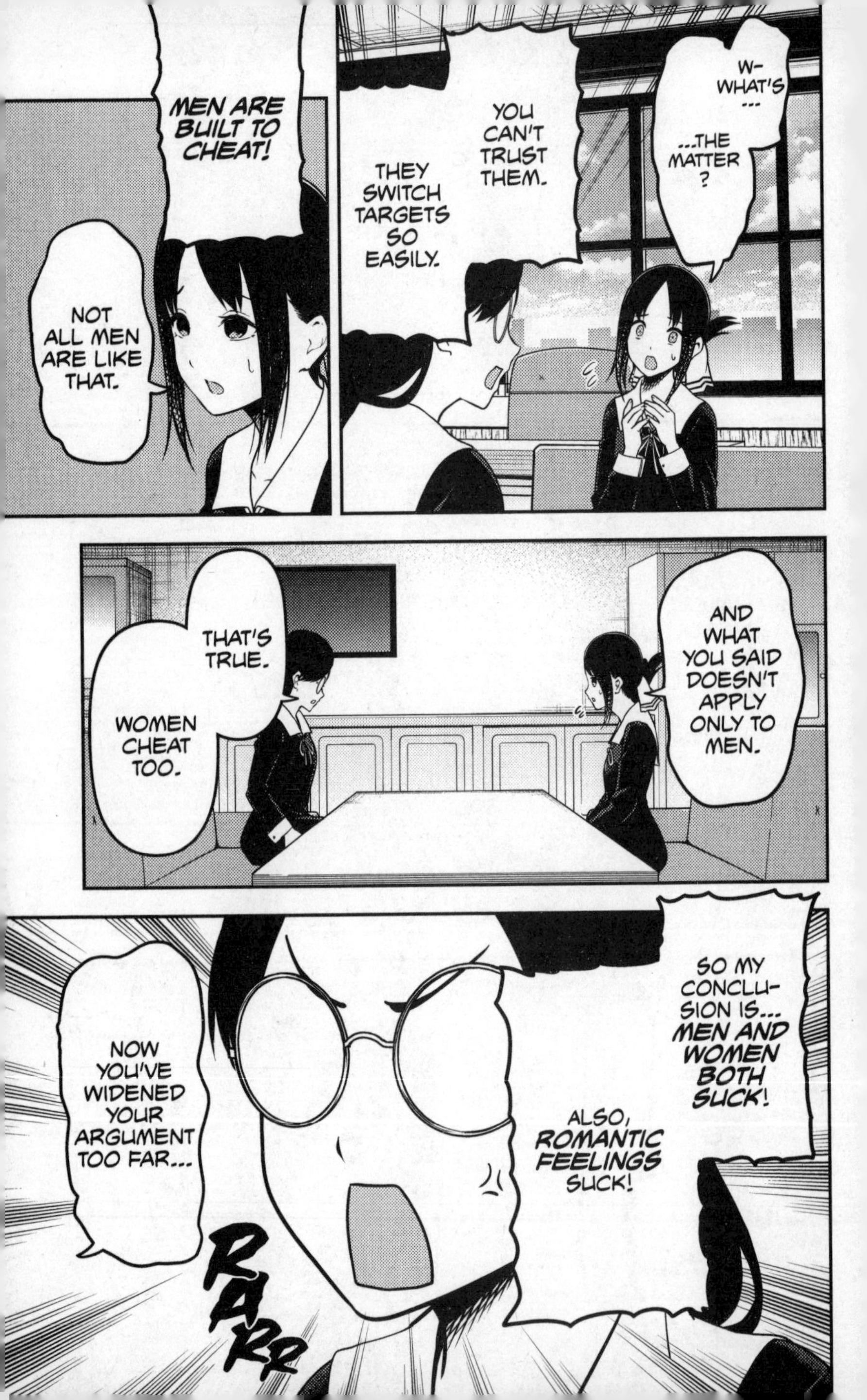
W-WHAT'S... ...THE MATTER?
YOU CAN'T TRUST THEM.
THEY SWITCH TARGETS SO EASILY.
MEN ARE BUILT TO CHEAT!
NOT ALL MEN ARE LIKE THAT.
AND WHAT YOU SAID DOESN'T APPLY ONLY TO MEN.
THAT'S TRUE.
WOMEN CHEAT TOO.
SO MY CONCLUSION IS... MEN AND WOMEN BOTH SUCK!
ALSO, ROMANTIC FEELINGS SUCK!
NOW YOU'VE WIDENED YOUR ARGUMENT TOO FAR...
RARR

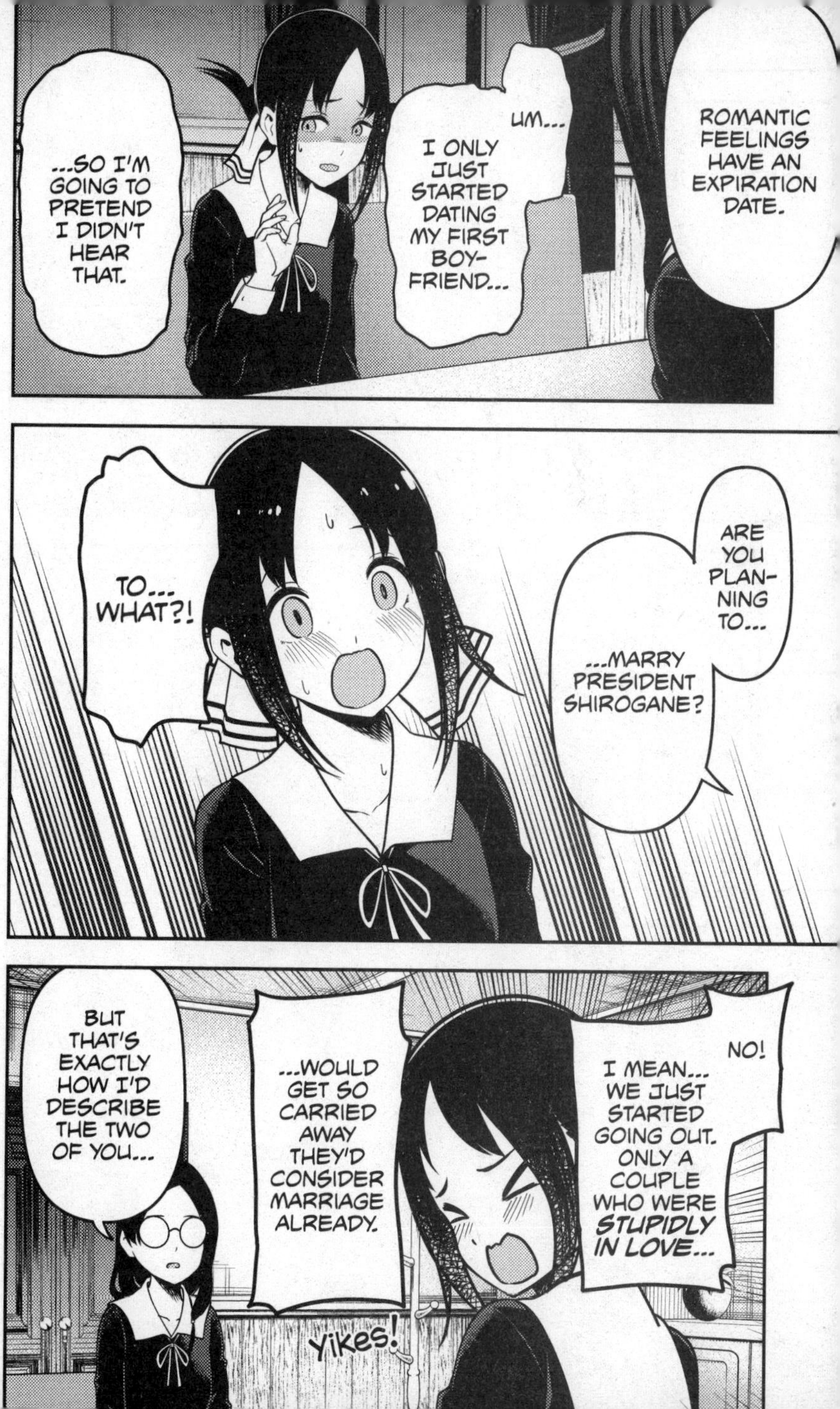
ROMANTIC FEELINGS HAVE AN EXPIRATION DATE.
UM...
I ONLY JUST STARTED DATING MY FIRST BOY-FRIEND...
...SO I'M GOING TO PRETEND I DIDN'T HEAR THAT.
ARE YOU PLANNING TO...
...MARRY PRESIDENT SHIROGANE?
TO... WHAT?!
NO!
I MEAN... WE JUST STARTED GOING OUT. ONLY A COUPLE WHO WERE *STUPIDLY IN LOVE*...
...WOULD GET SO CARRIED AWAY THEY'D CONSIDER MARRIAGE ALREADY.
Yikes!
BUT THAT'S EXACTLY HOW I'D DESCRIBE THE TWO OF YOU...

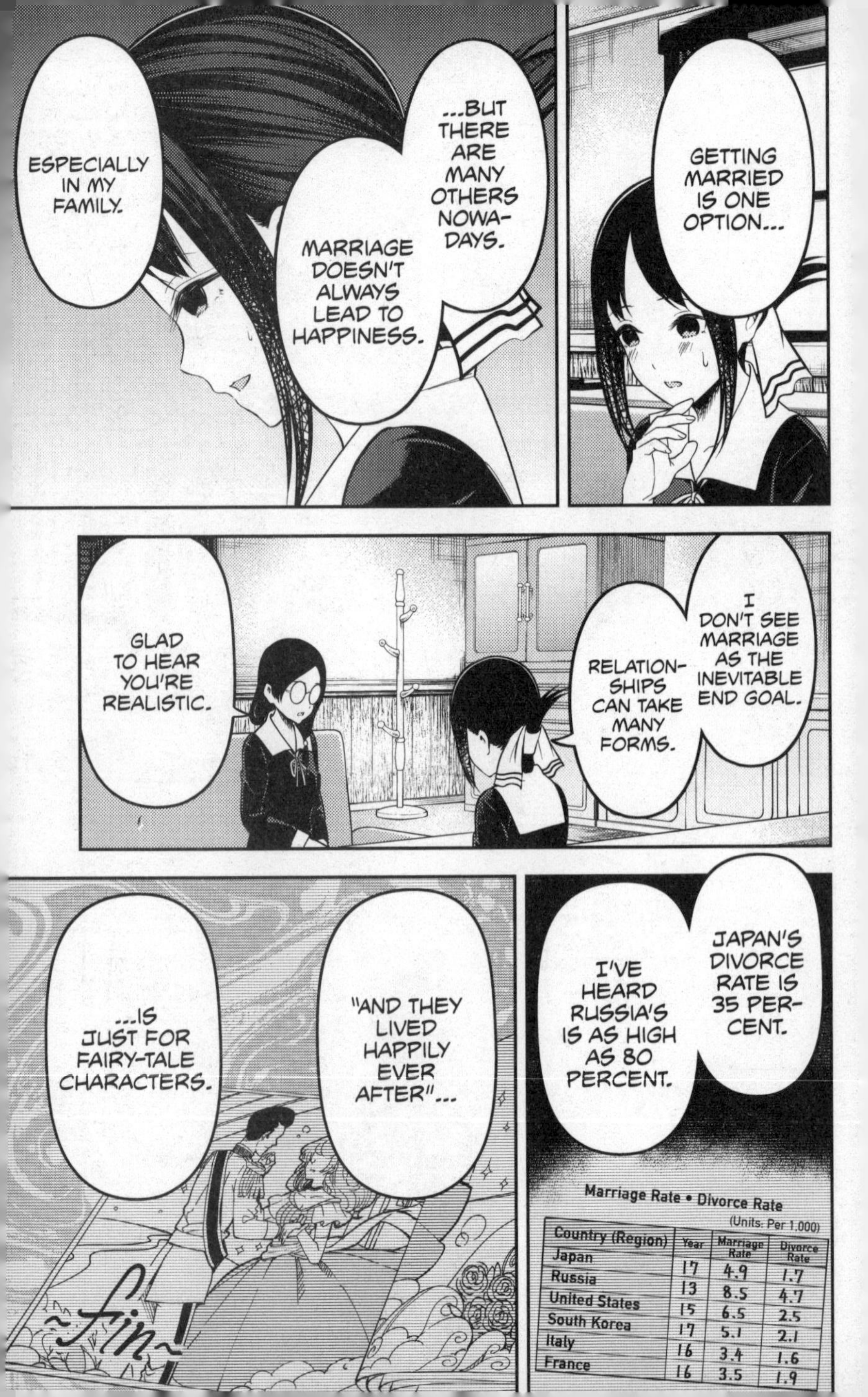
GETTING MARRIED IS ONE OPTION...
...BUT THERE ARE MANY OTHERS NOWADAYS.
MARRIAGE DOESN'T ALWAYS LEAD TO HAPPINESS.
ESPECIALLY IN MY FAMILY.
I DON'T SEE MARRIAGE AS THE INEVITABLE END GOAL.
RELATIONSHIPS CAN TAKE MANY FORMS.
GLAD TO HEAR YOU'RE REALISTIC.
JAPAN'S DIVORCE RATE IS 35 PERCENT.
I'VE HEARD RUSSIA'S IS AS HIGH AS 80 PERCENT.
Marriage Rate • Divorce Rate
(Units: Per 1,000)

Country (Region)	Year	Marriage Rate	Divorce Rate
Japan	17	4.9	1.7
Russia	13	8.5	4.7
United States	15	6.5	2.5
South Korea	17	5.1	2.1
Italy	16	3.4	1.6
France	16	3.5	1.9

"AND THEY LIVED HAPPILY EVER AFTER"...
...IS JUST FOR FAIRY-TALE CHARACTERS.
~fin~

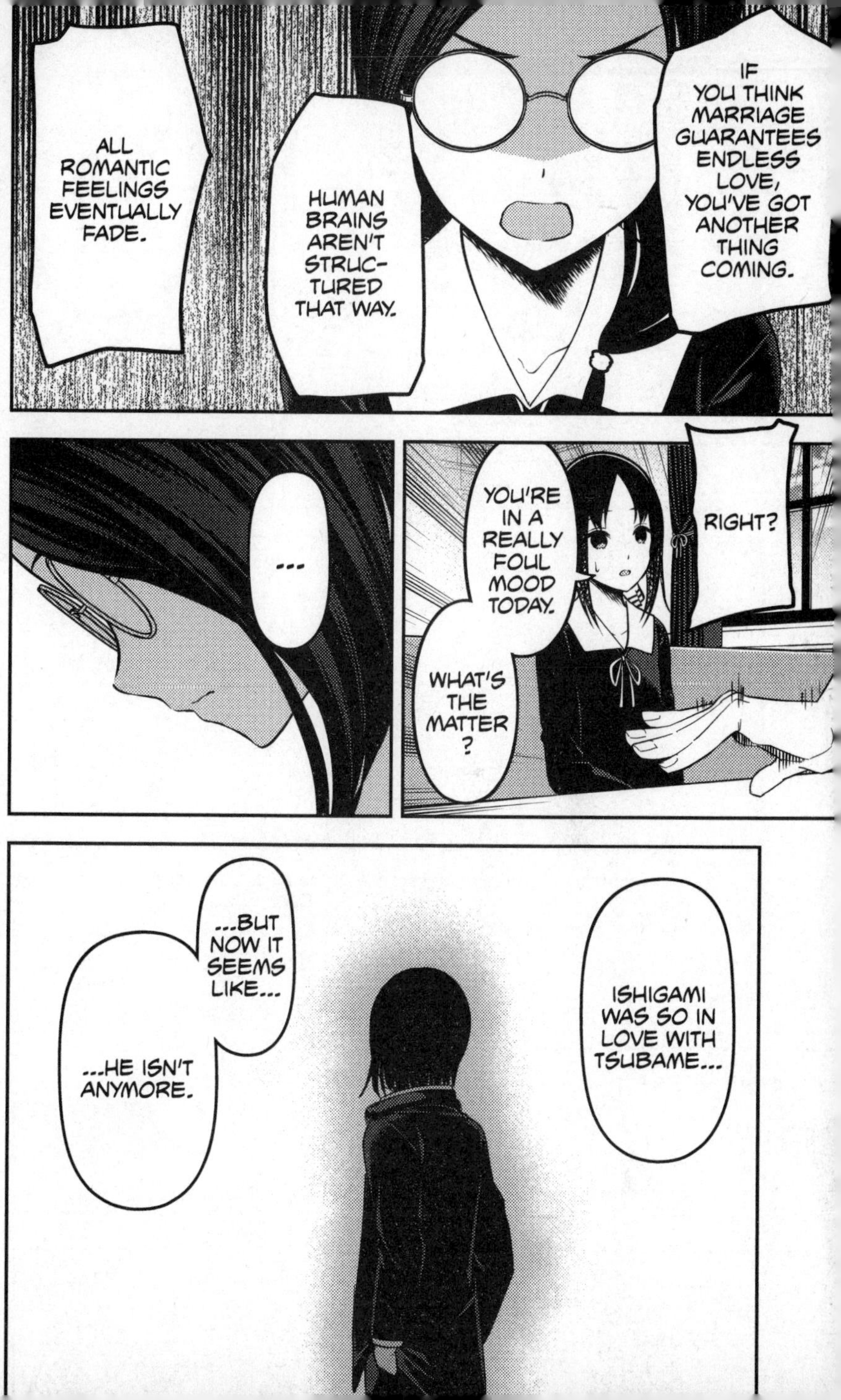
IF YOU THINK MARRIAGE GUARANTEES ENDLESS LOVE, YOU'VE GOT ANOTHER THING COMING.
HUMAN BRAINS AREN'T STRUC-TURED THAT WAY.
ALL ROMANTIC FEELINGS EVENTUALLY FADE.
RIGHT?
YOU'RE IN A REALLY FOUL MOOD TODAY.
WHAT'S THE MATTER?
...
ISHIGAMI WAS SO IN LOVE WITH TSUBAME...
...BUT NOW IT SEEMS LIKE...
...HE ISN'T ANYMORE.

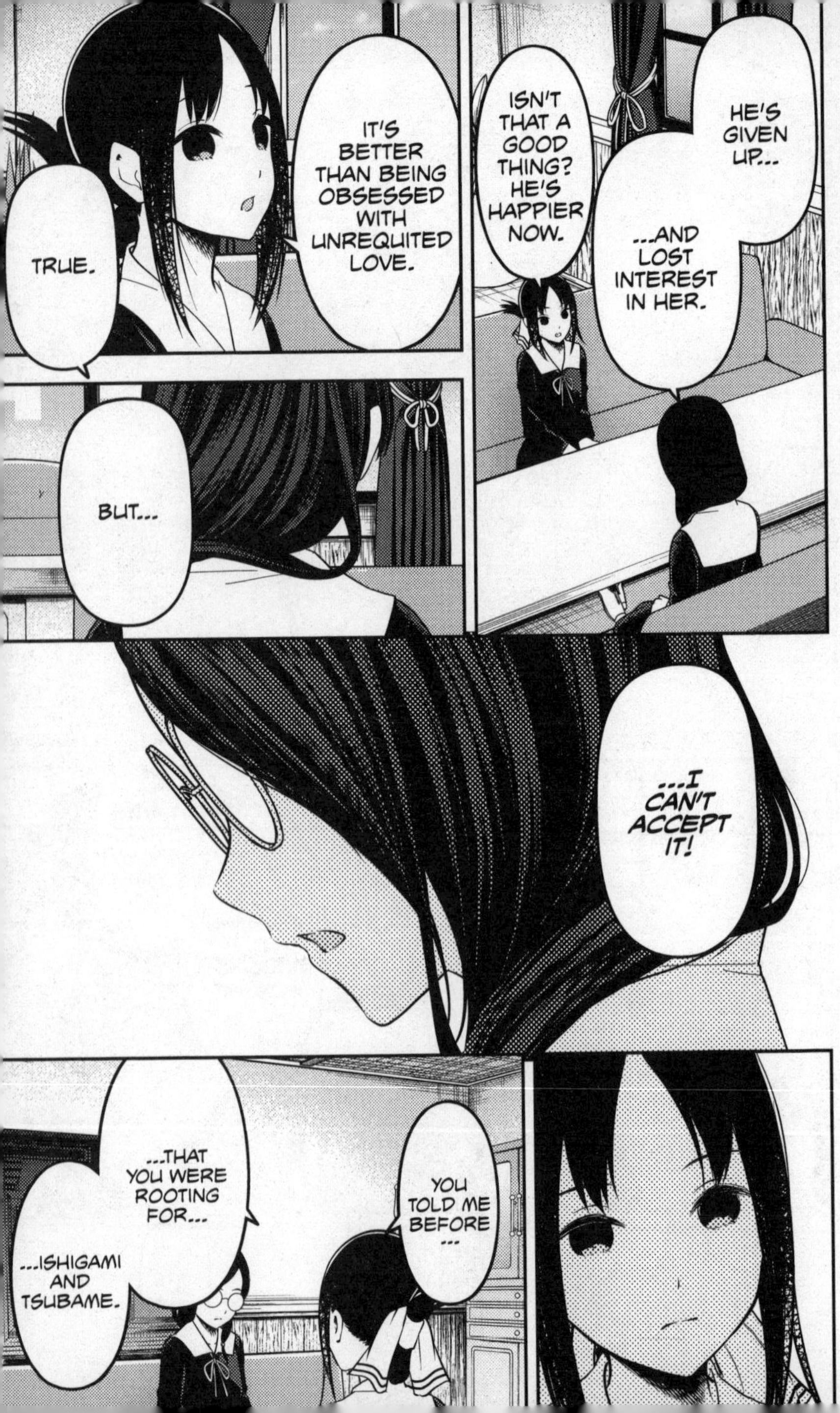
HE'S GIVEN UP...
...AND LOST INTEREST IN HER.
ISN'T THAT A GOOD THING? HE'S HAPPIER NOW.
IT'S BETTER THAN BEING OBSESSED WITH UNREQUITED LOVE.
TRUE.
BUT...
...I CAN'T ACCEPT IT!
YOU TOLD ME BEFORE...
...THAT YOU WERE ROOTING FOR...
...ISHIGAMI AND TSUBAME.

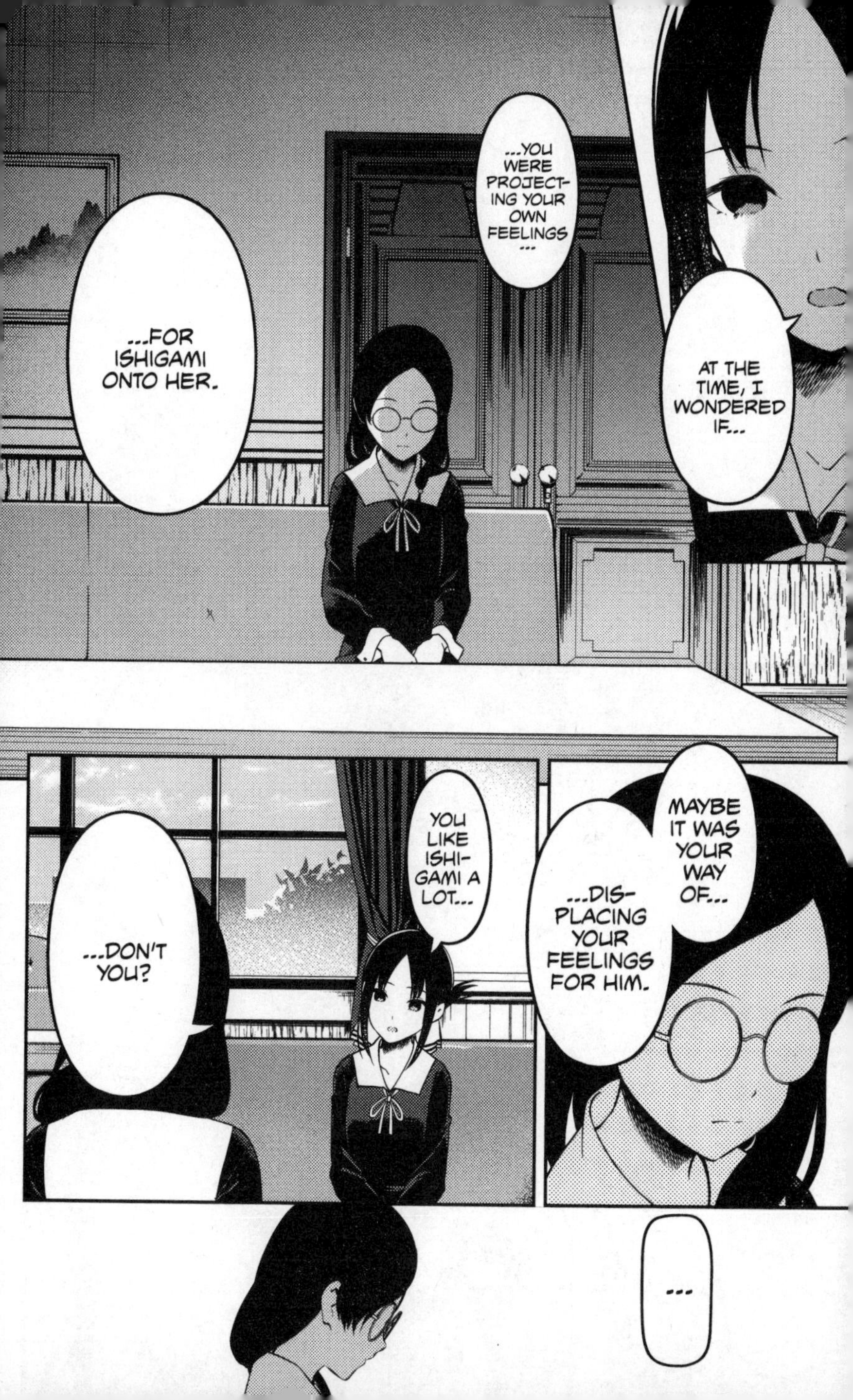
AT THE TIME, I WONDERED IF...
...YOU WERE PROJECT-ING YOUR OWN FEELINGS...
...FOR ISHIGAMI ONTO HER.
MAYBE IT WAS YOUR WAY OF...
...DIS-PLACING YOUR FEELINGS FOR HIM.
YOU LIKE ISHI-GAMI A LOT...
...DON'T YOU?
...

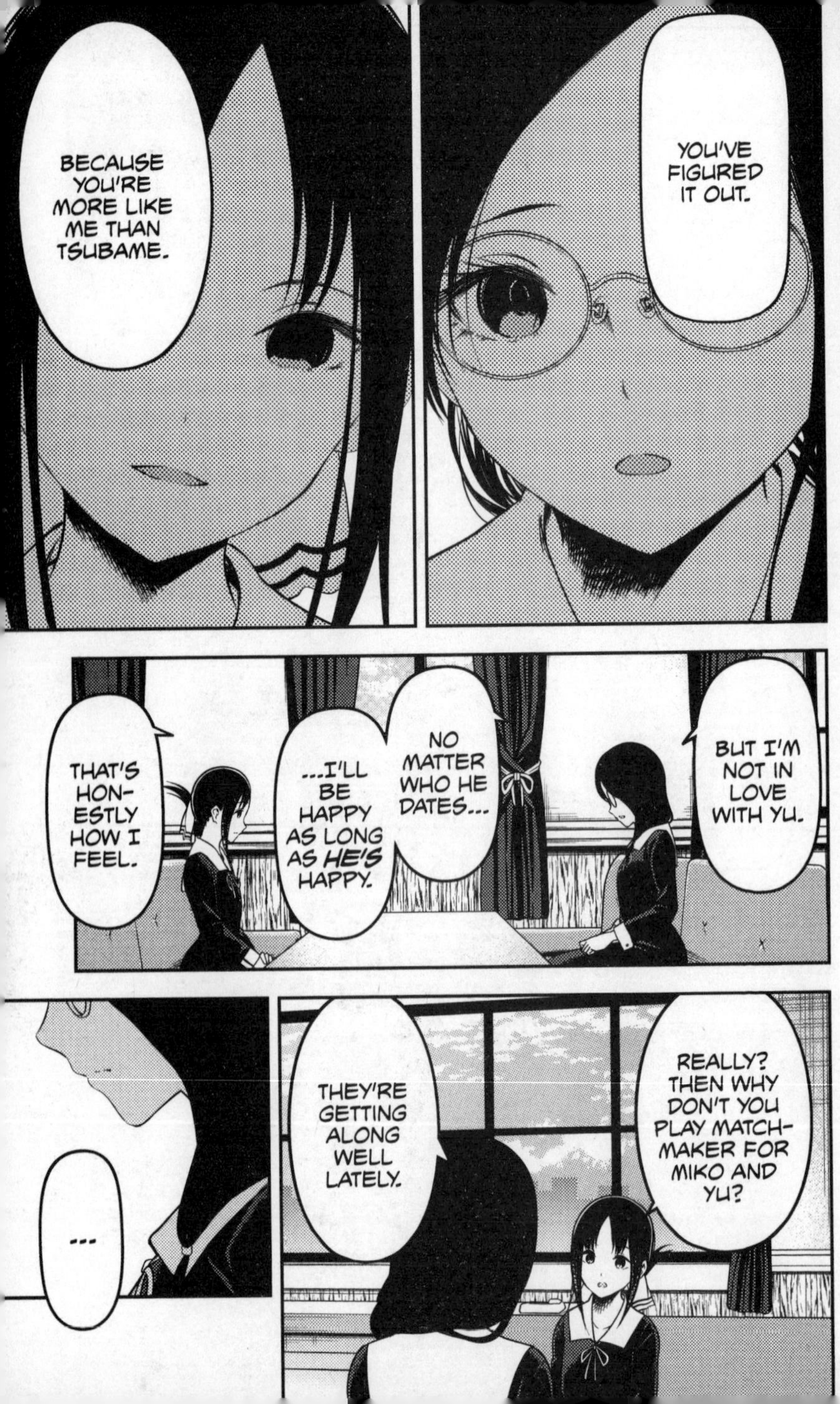
YOU'VE FIGURED IT OUT.
BECAUSE YOU'RE MORE LIKE ME THAN TSUBAME.
BUT I'M NOT IN LOVE WITH YU.
NO MATTER WHO HE DATES...
...I'LL BE HAPPY AS LONG AS *HE'S* HAPPY.
THAT'S HON-ESTLY HOW I FEEL.
REALLY? THEN WHY DON'T YOU PLAY MATCH-MAKER FOR MIKO AND YU?
THEY'RE GETTING ALONG WELL LATELY.
...

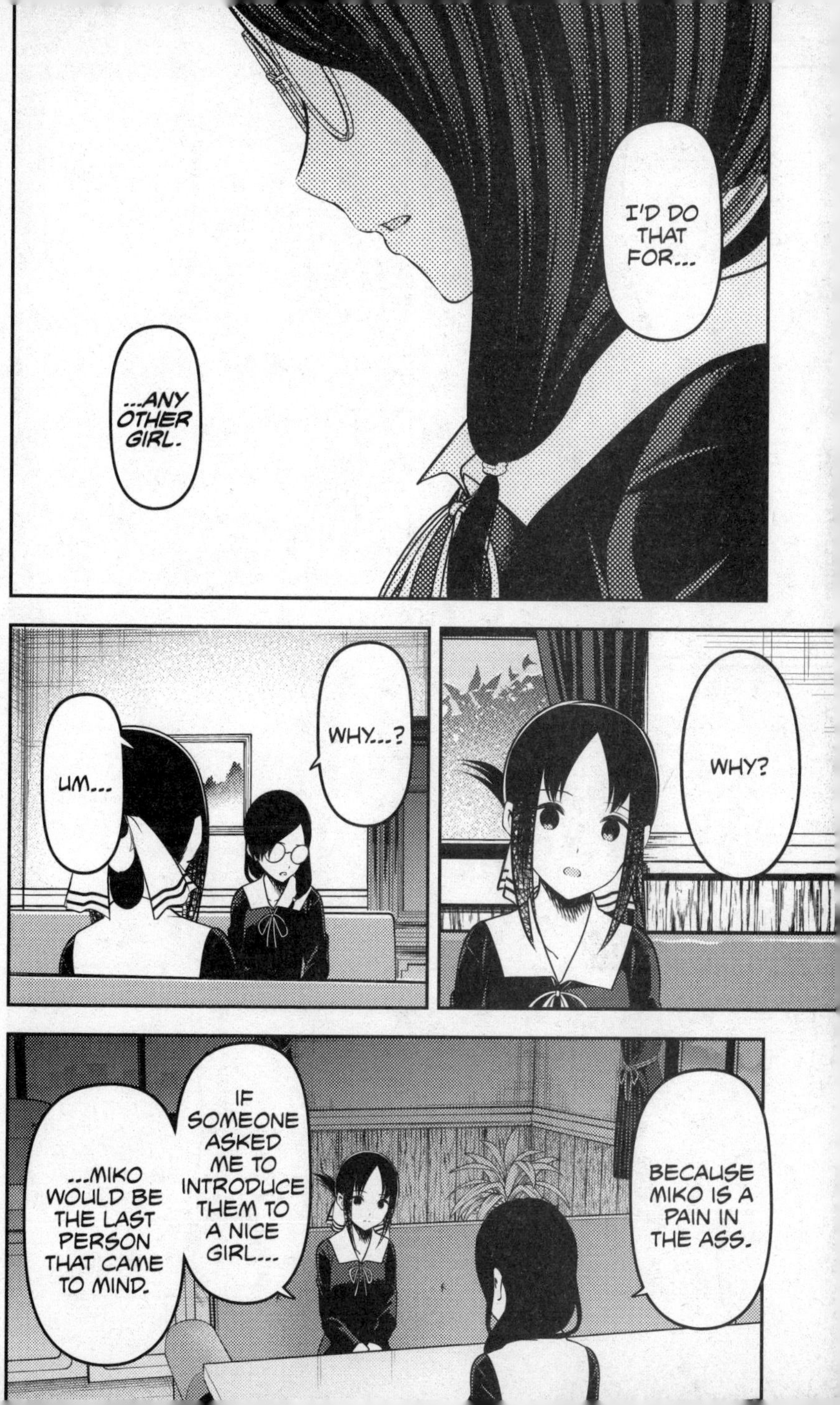
I'D DO THAT FOR...
...ANY OTHER GIRL.
WHY?
WHY...?
UM...
BECAUSE MIKO IS A PAIN IN THE ASS.
IF SOMEONE ASKED ME TO INTRODUCE THEM TO A NICE GIRL...
...MIKO WOULD BE THE LAST PERSON THAT CAME TO MIND.

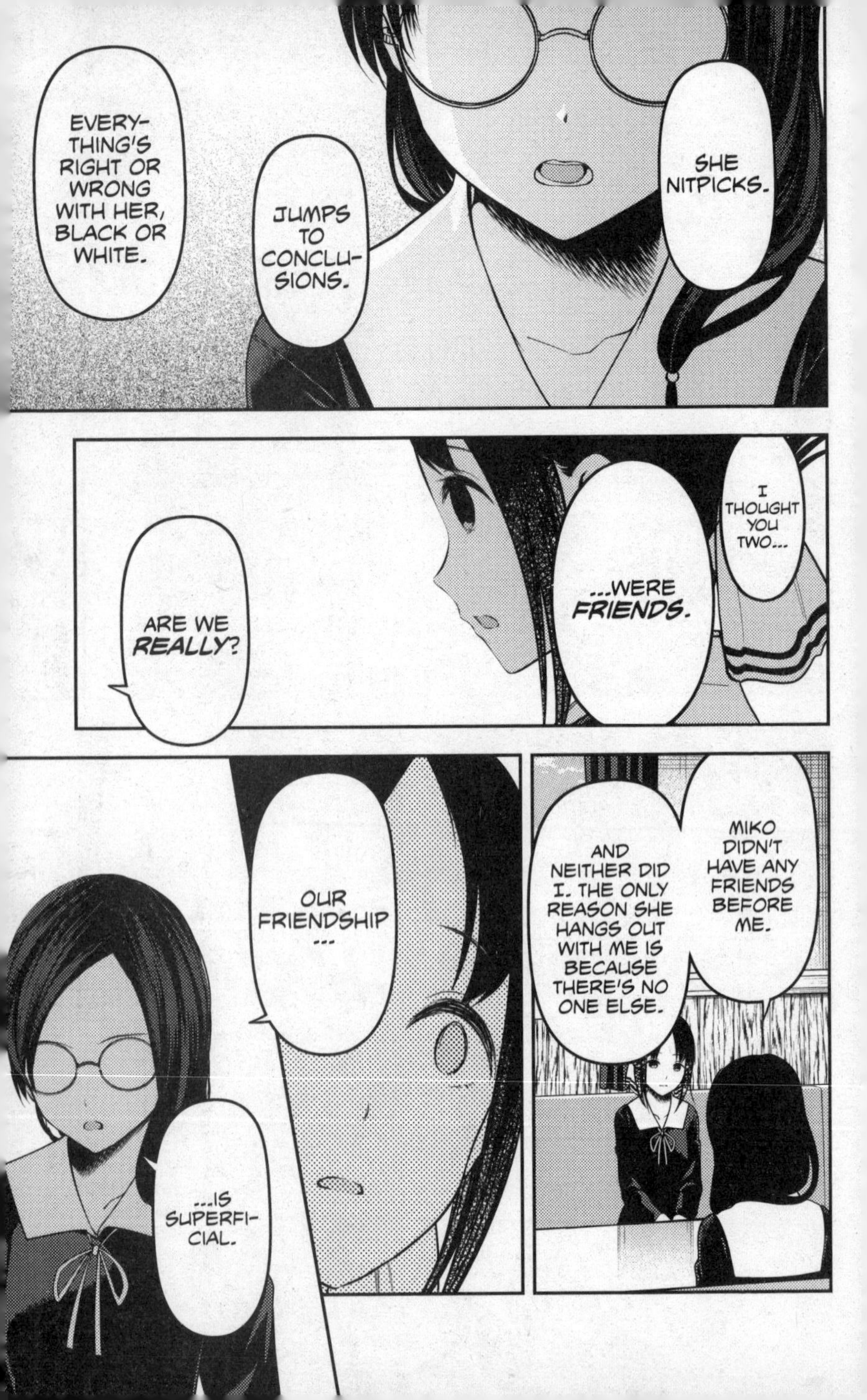
SHE NITPICKS.
JUMPS TO CONCLUSIONS.
EVERYTHING'S RIGHT OR WRONG WITH HER, BLACK OR WHITE.
I THOUGHT YOU TWO...
...WERE *FRIENDS*.
ARE WE *REALLY*?
MIKO DIDN'T HAVE ANY FRIENDS BEFORE ME.
AND NEITHER DID I. THE ONLY REASON SHE HANGS OUT WITH ME IS BECAUSE THERE'S NO ONE ELSE.
OUR FRIENDSHIP...
...IS SUPERFICIAL.

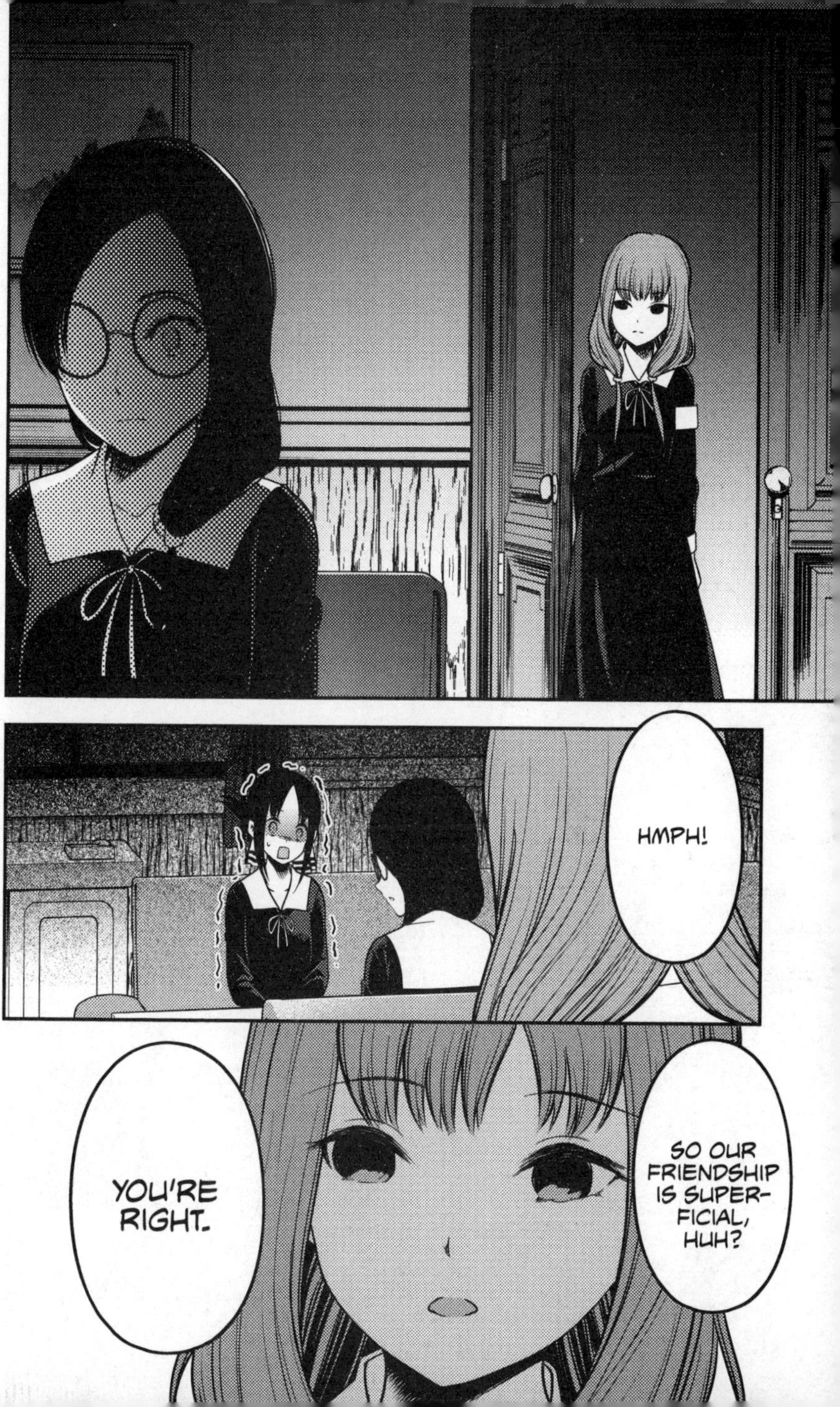
HMPH!
SO OUR FRIENDSHIP IS SUPER-FICIAL, HUH?
YOU'RE RIGHT.

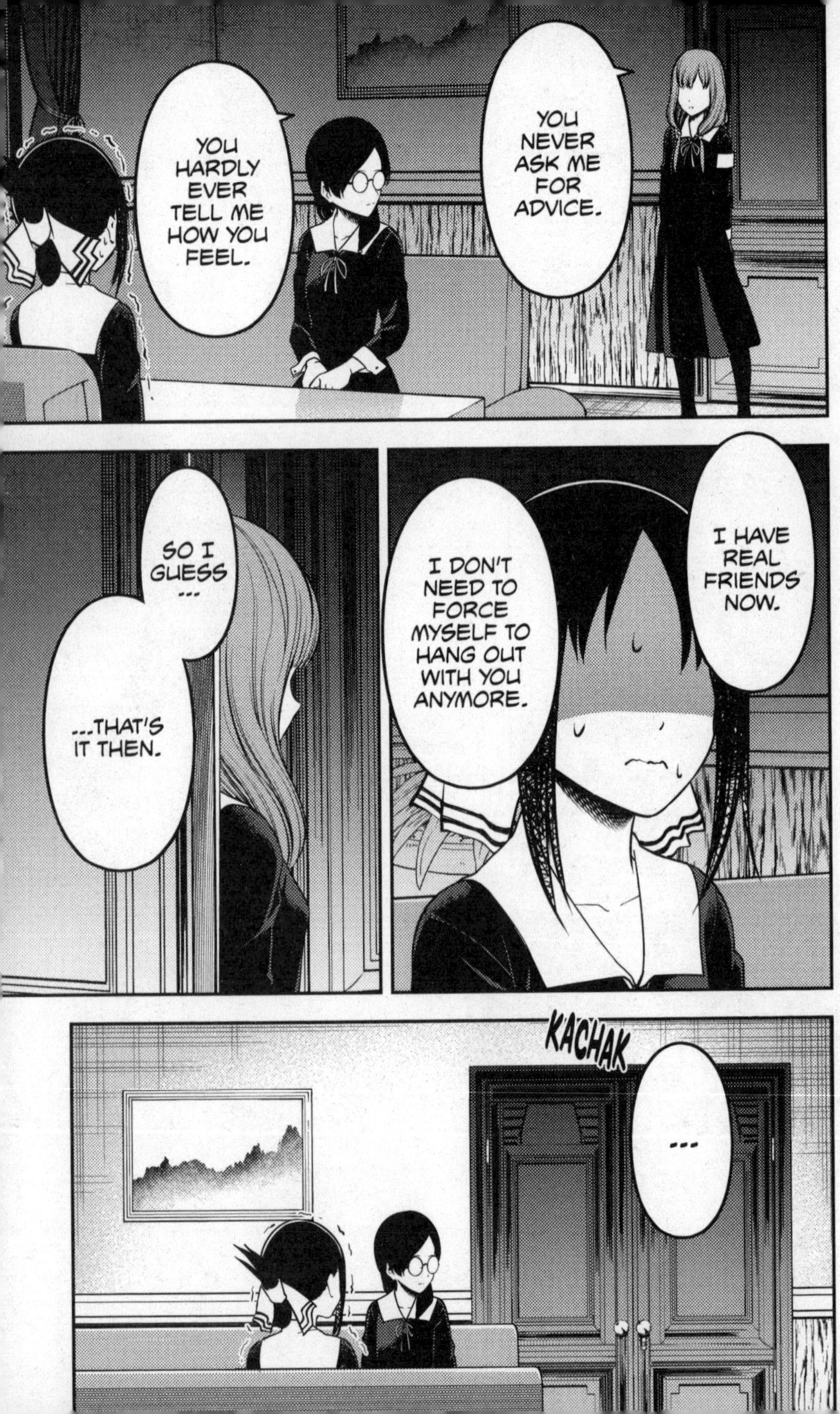
YOU NEVER ASK ME FOR ADVICE.
YOU HARDLY EVER TELL ME HOW YOU FEEL.
I HAVE REAL FRIENDS NOW.
I DON'T NEED TO FORCE MYSELF TO HANG OUT WITH YOU ANYMORE.
SO I GUESS...
...THAT'S IT THEN.
KACHAK
...

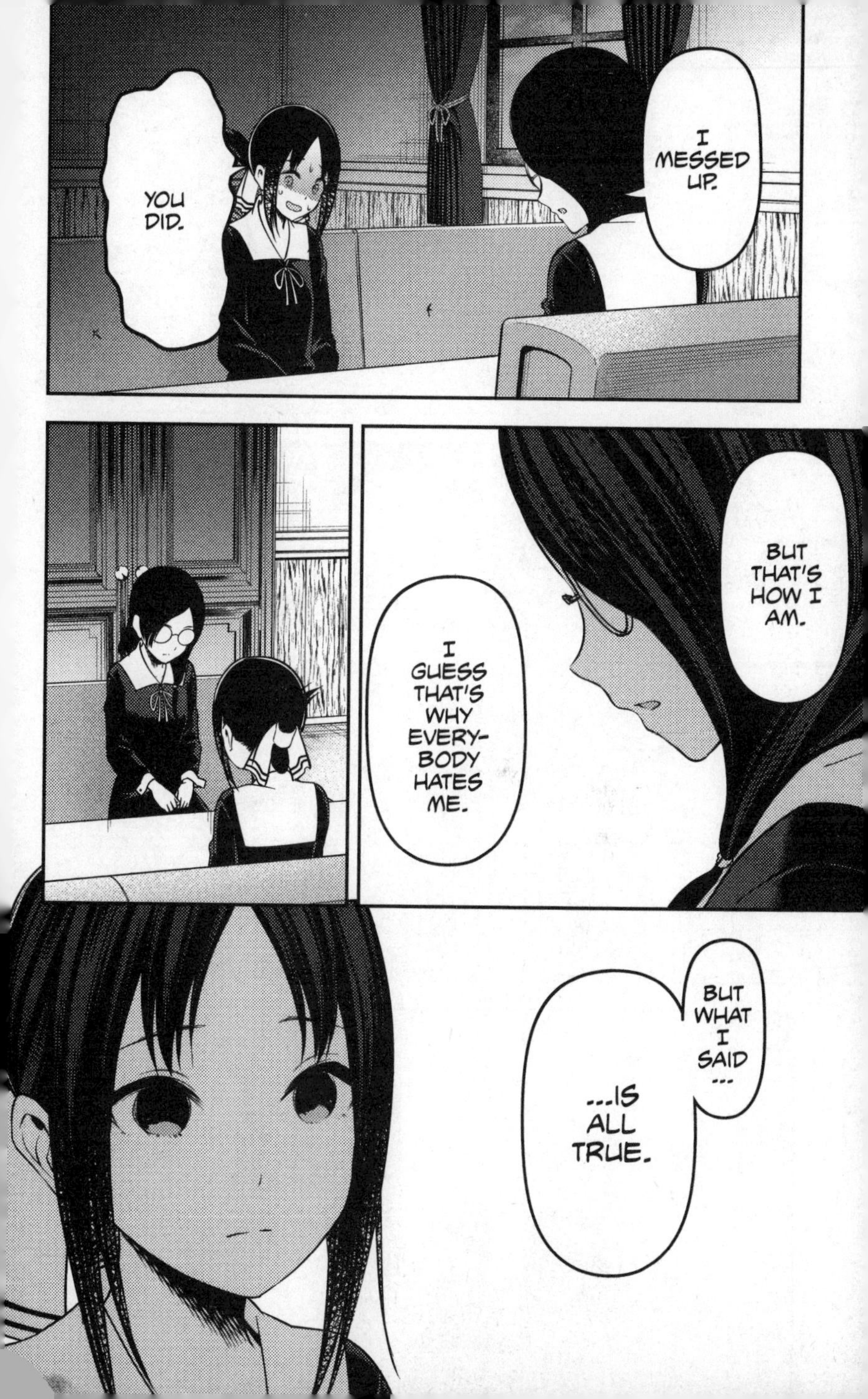
I MESSED UP.
YOU DID.
BUT THAT'S HOW I AM.
I GUESS THAT'S WHY EVERY-BODY HATES ME.
BUT WHAT I SAID...
...IS ALL TRUE.

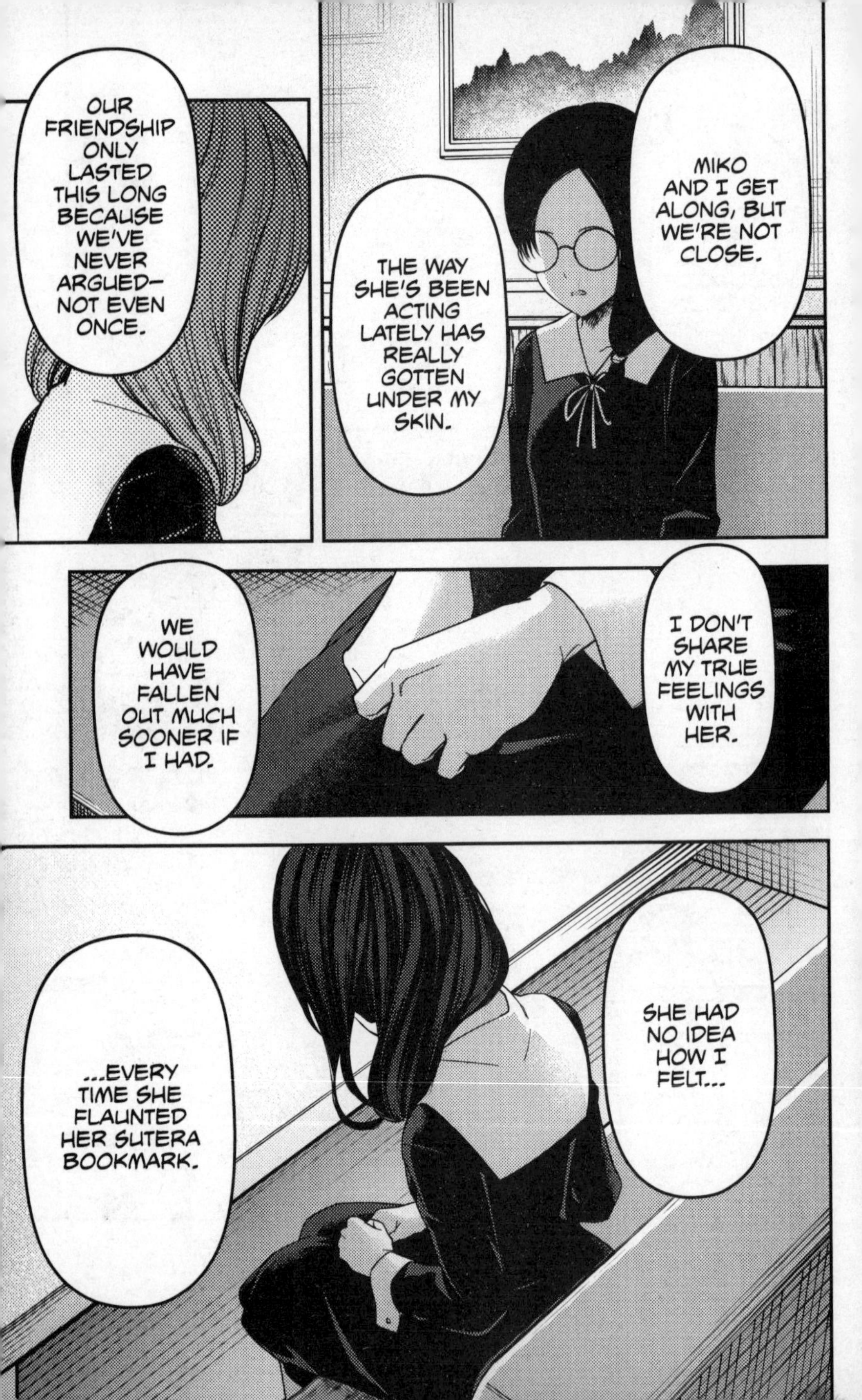
MIKO AND I GET ALONG, BUT WE'RE NOT CLOSE.
THE WAY SHE'S BEEN ACTING LATELY HAS REALLY GOTTEN UNDER MY SKIN.
OUR FRIENDSHIP ONLY LASTED THIS LONG BECAUSE WE'VE NEVER ARGUED—NOT EVEN ONCE.
I DON'T SHARE MY TRUE FEELINGS WITH HER.
WE WOULD HAVE FALLEN OUT MUCH SOONER IF I HAD.
SHE HAD NO IDEA HOW I FELT...
...EVERY TIME SHE FLAUNTED HER SUTERA BOOKMARK.

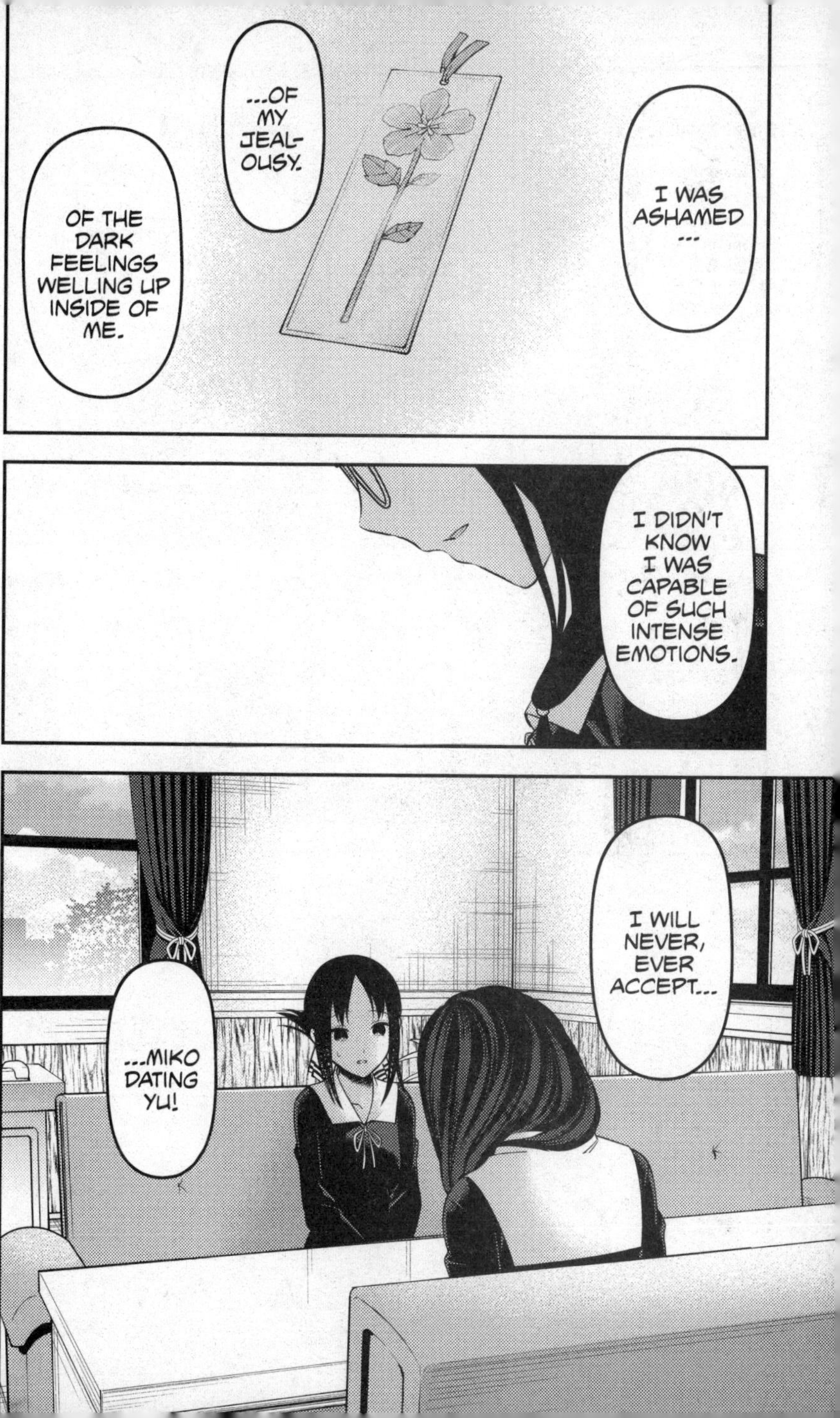
I WAS ASHAMED ...
...OF MY JEAL-OUSY.
OF THE DARK FEELINGS WELLING UP INSIDE OF ME.
I DIDN'T KNOW I WAS CAPABLE OF SUCH INTENSE EMOTIONS.
I WILL NEVER, EVER ACCEPT...
...MIKO DATING YU!

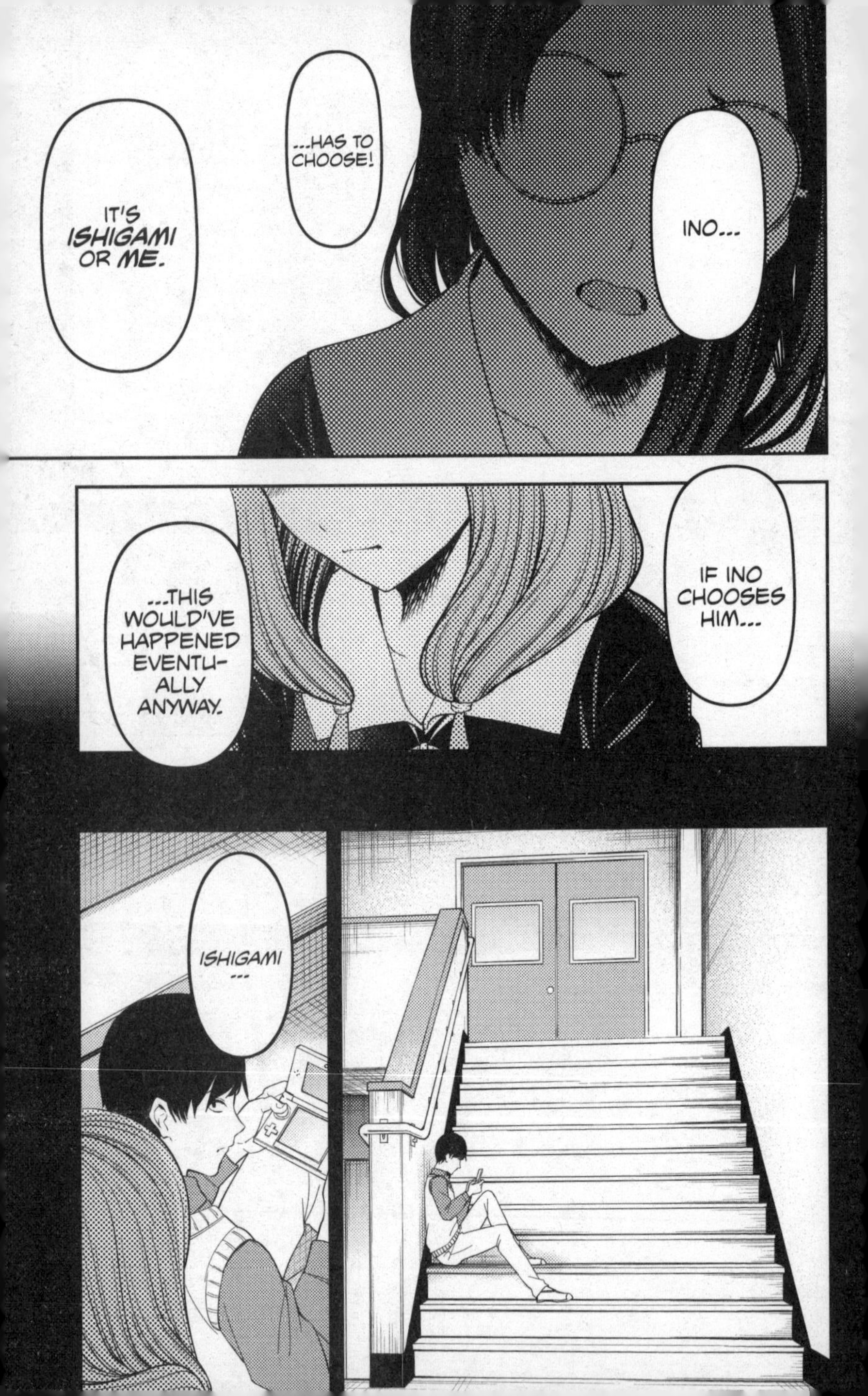
INO...
...HAS TO CHOOSE!
IT'S ISHIGAMI OR ME.
IF INO CHOOSES HIM...
...THIS WOULD'VE HAPPENED EVENTU-ALLY ANYWAY.
ISHIGAMI ...

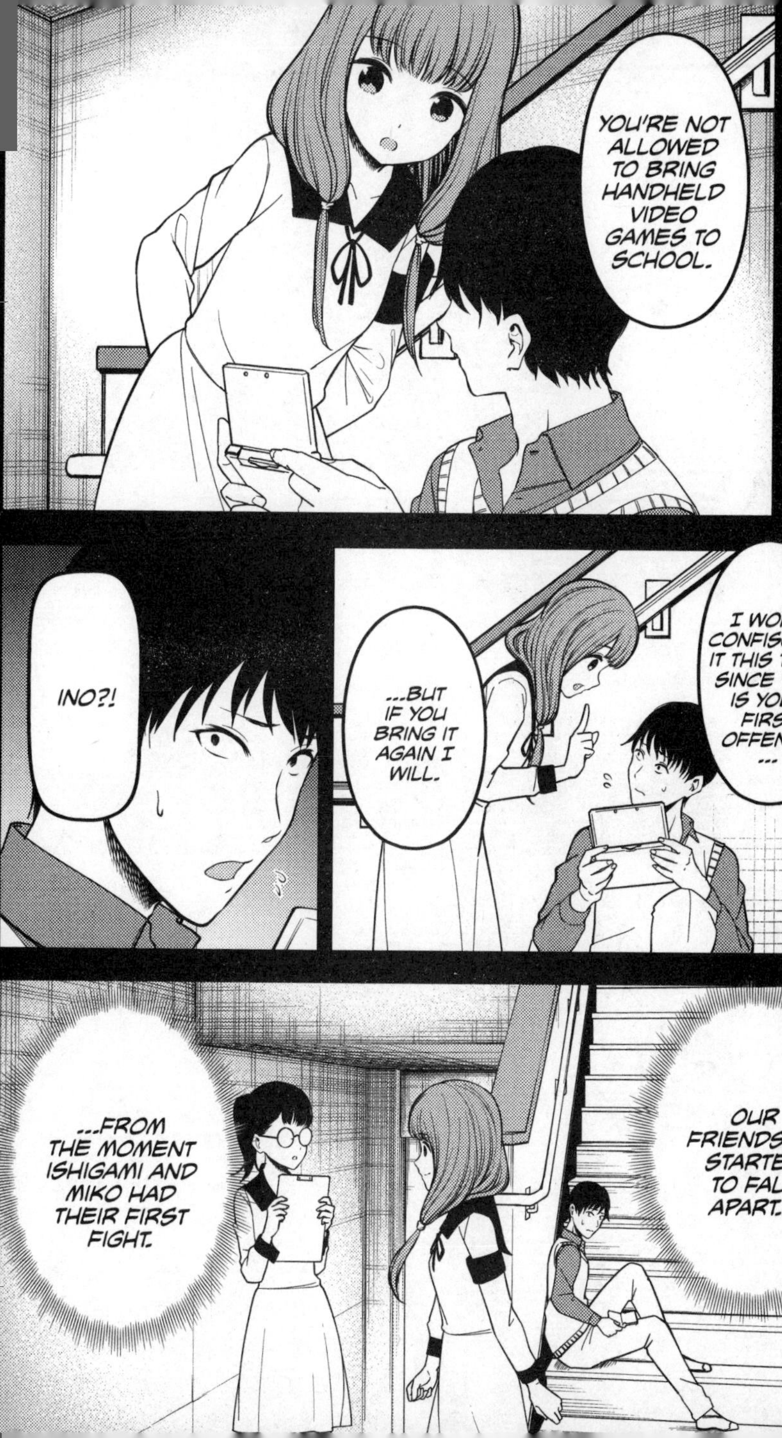
YOU'RE NOT ALLOWED TO BRING HANDHELD VIDEO GAMES TO SCHOOL.
I WON'T CONFISCATE IT THIS TIME, SINCE THIS IS YOUR FIRST OFFENSE...
...BUT IF YOU BRING IT AGAIN I WILL.
INO?!
OUR FRIENDSHIP STARTED TO FALL APART...
...FROM THE MOMENT ISHIGAMI AND MIKO HAD THEIR FIRST FIGHT.

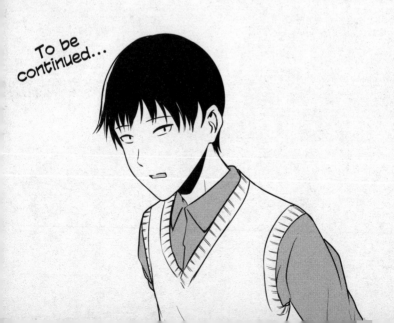

To be continued...

PEOPLE ARE MIRRORS FOR EACH OTHER. AND THOSE MIRRORS ARE ALWAYS FLAWED.

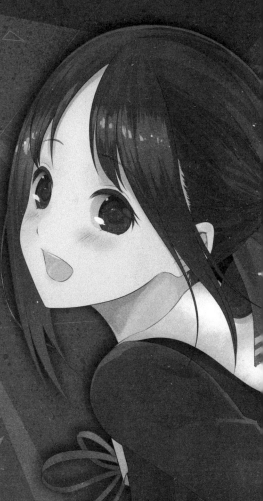

AKA AKASAKA

Aka Akasaka got his start as an assistant to Jinsei Kataoka and Kazuma Kondou, the creators of *Deadman Wonderland*. His first serialized manga was an adaptation of the light novel series *Sayonara Piano Sonata*, published by Kadokawa in 2011. *Kaguya-sama: Love Is War* began serialization in *Miracle Jump* in 2015 but was later moved to *Weekly Young Jump* in 2016 due to its popularity.

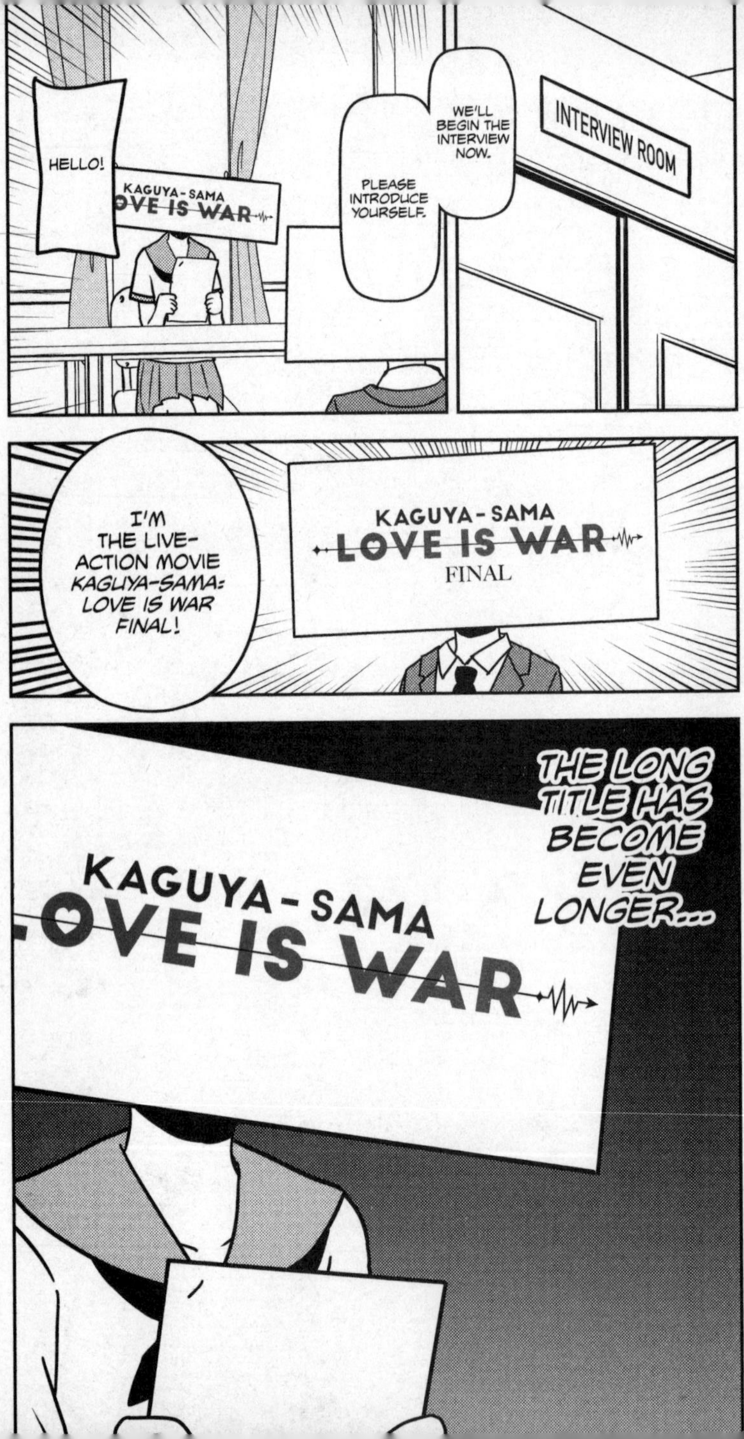
INTERVIEW ROOM
WE'LL BEGIN THE INTERVIEW NOW.
PLEASE INTRODUCE YOURSELF.
KAGUYA-SAMA LOVE IS WAR
HELLO!
KAGUYA-SAMA LOVE IS WAR FINAL
I'M THE LIVE-ACTION MOVIE KAGUYA-SAMA: LOVE IS WAR FINAL!
THE LONG TITLE HAS BECOME EVEN LONGER...
KAGUYA-SAMA LOVE IS WAR

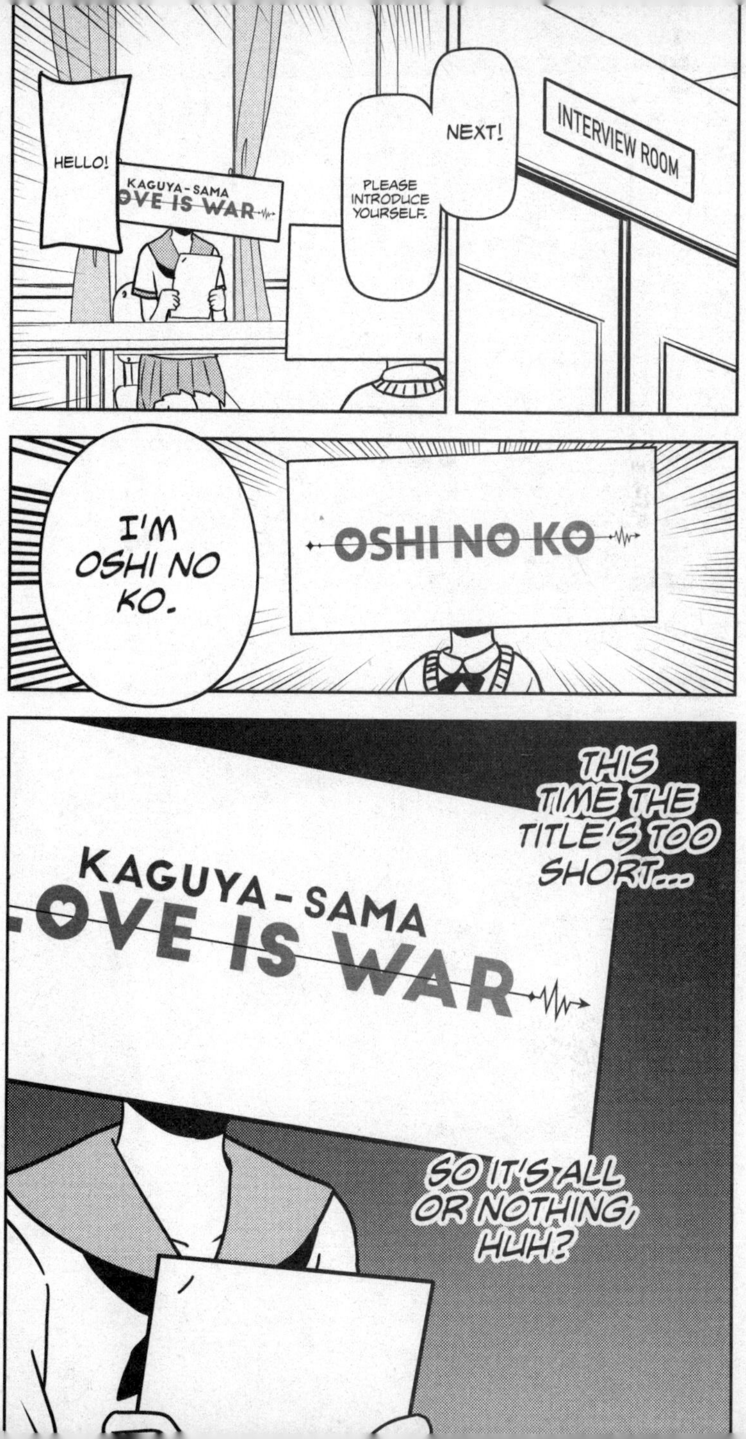
INTERVIEW ROOM
NEXT!
PLEASE INTRODUCE YOURSELF.
KAGUYA-SAMA
OVE IS WAR
HELLO!
OSHI NO KO
I'M OSHI NO KO.
THIS TIME THE TITLE'S TOO SHORT...
KAGUYA-SAMA
OVE IS WAR
SO IT'S ALL OR NOTHING, HUH?

KAGUYA-SAMA
LOVE IS WAR

SHONEN JUMP EDITION

23

STORY AND ART BY
AKA AKASAKA

Translation/Tomo Kimura
English Adaptation/Annette Roman
Touch-Up Art & Lettering/Steve Dutro
Cover & Interior Design/Alice Lewis
Editor/Annette Roman

KAGUYA-SAMA WA KOKURASETAI~TENSAITACHI NO REN'AI ZUNO SEN~
© 2015 by Aka Akasaka
All rights reserved.
First published in Japan in 2015 by SHUEISHA Inc., Tokyo.
English translation rights arranged by SHUEISHA Inc.

Printed in the U.S.A.

Published by VIZ Media, LLC
P.O. Box 77010
San Francisco, CA 94107

10 9 8 7 6 5 4 3 2 1
First printing, August 2022

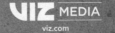

viz.com

COMING NEXT VOLUME

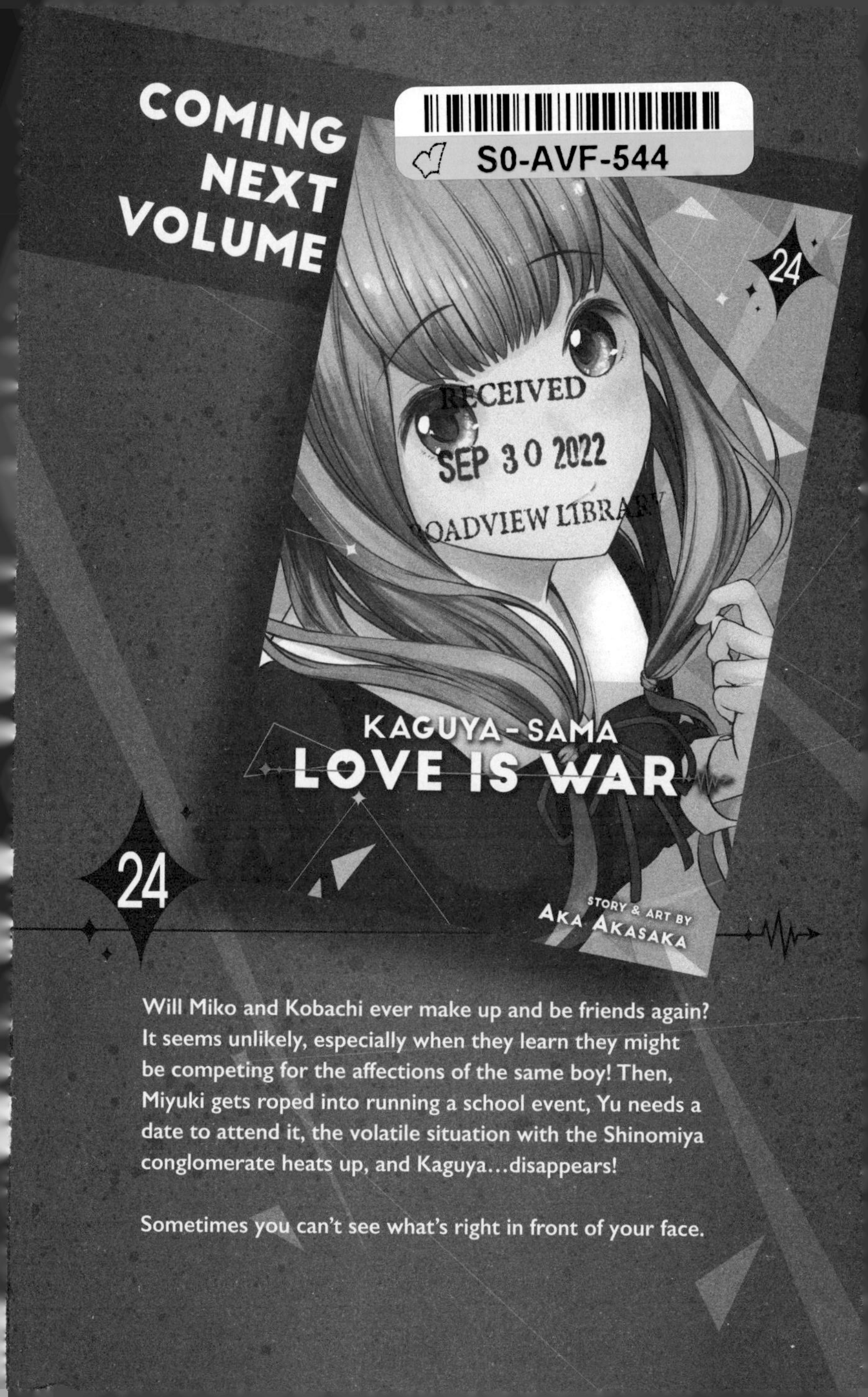
24
KAGUYA-SAMA
LOVE IS WAR
STORY & ART BY
AKA AKASAKA

24

Will Miko and Kobachi ever make up and be friends again? It seems unlikely, especially when they learn they might be competing for the affections of the same boy! Then, Miyuki gets roped into running a school event, Yu needs a date to attend it, the volatile situation with the Shinomiya conglomerate heats up, and Kaguya…disappears!

Sometimes you can't see what's right in front of your face.